Ge... Augsburg College
Minn...

PARTIES, OPPOSITION AND SOCIETY IN WEST GERMANY

PARTIES, OPPOSITION AND SOCIETY IN WEST GERMANY

Eva Kolinsky

ST MARTIN'S PRESS
New York

All rights reserved. For information, write:
St. Martin's Press, Inc., 175 Fifth Avenue, New York, NY 10010
First published in the United States of America in 1984

Library of Congress Cataloging in Publication Data

Kolinsky, Eva.
   Parties, opposition, and society in West Germany.
   Bibliograpy:p.
   Includes index.
   1. Political parties—Germany (West) 2. Germany (West)
—Politics and government. 3. Germany (West)—Social
conditions. I. Title.
JN3971.A979K66   1984   324.243   83-40707

ISBN 0-312-59746-0

Printed and bound in Great Britain

CONTENTS

List of Tables
Acknowledgements
Introduction   1

PART ONE: PARTIES AND SOCIETY 17

1. Parties and Society (I) 17
2. Parties and Society (II): Changes in
   Party Support 54
3. The SPD in Transition 73
4. Problems of Party Stability: The FDP 101
5. The Christian Democrats: Party
   Organization and Membership
   Development 122

PART TWO: OPPOSITION AND SOCIETY 165

6. Youth and Politics 168
7. Opposition from the Left - Communism,
   Student Movement, Terrorism 205
8. Opposition from the Right - Neonazism
   in West German Society 253
9. The Green Party, a New Factor in the West
   German Political Landscape 292

CONCLUSION: PARTIES, OPPOSITION, AND SOCIETY
             IN WEST GERMANY 339

TABLES

I.1	Elections to the Bundestag, 1949-1983	5
1.1	Party Representation in the Economic Council and in the Parliamentary Council 1947-1948	19
1.2	Public Funding of Political Parties 1960-1964	27
1.3	Party Income 1969-1978 in Deutschmark	31
1.4	Sources of Party Income 1969-1978 in %	32
1.5	Donations 1968-1977	34
1.6	Trade Union Members in the Bundestag, 1949-1983	42
1.7	Trade Unionists in the 8th Bundestag	42
1.8	The Occupational Structure of Parliamentary Representation, 1972-1980	45
2.1	The Social Composition of Party Support: Voters	58
2.2	Party Preferences by Occupation	59
2.3	Electoral Decisions by Occupation and Denomination	62-63
2.4	Electoral Preferences by Age and Sex......	67
2.5	Voting in the 1978-1979 Land Elections by Age	68
3.1	The Social Composition of Party Memberships	76
3.2	The Social Composition of the SPD, Members and Functionaries	77
3.3	The Occupational Structure of SPD Membership 1977 and 1981	78
3.4	The Educational Background of SPD Members and Functionaries	79
4.1	FDP Membership Gains and Losses 1969-1976	104
4.2	The Social Composition of FDP Membership	107
4.3	Income Levels of FDP Members and Voters ..	108
5.1	CSU Election Results 1946-1983	131
5.2	Changes of the CDU Membership: Occupational Structure	135

Tables

5.3	CDU Educational Profile	139
5.4	The Age Structure of CDU Membership	140
5.5	Membership Duration 1945-1977	141
5.6	CDU Office Holders and Duration of Party Membership	150
5.7	The Social Composition of the CDU Membership and Leadership	151
5.8	The Occupational Structure of CDU Members and Officer Holders	153
6.1	Democratic Attitudes Across the Generations	182
6.2	Self-Identification on a Left-Right Scale	182
6.3	Satisfaction with Democracy in the Federal Republic of Germany	184
6.4	Citizens and Political Influence	187
6.5	Discontent and Disinterest by Occupation	190
6.6	Dissent and Educational Achievement	191
6.7	Protest Potential by Age: attitudes towards squatting	195
6.8	Violence and Student Politics	196
8.1	The NPD in Local and District Assemblies	262
8.2	NPD Membership 1964-1982	263
8.3	NPD Voters 1965-1967, Occupational Structure	265
8.4	NPD Members 1966-1969, Occupational Structure	266
8.5	Neonazi Offenders by Occupation and by Age	282
9.1	The Green Party in Elections 1978-1983	294
9.2	Voting in Land Elections by Age	314
9.3	Attitudes towards the Greens by Social Characteristics	316
9.4	Environmental Issues in Established Parties	321
9.5	Opinions on the Stationing of Cruise Missiles	328

ACKNOWLEDGEMENTS

In planning and writing this book, I was fortunate
enough to receive much support, and would like to
express my thanks. The University of Aston funded
several research trips to West Germany between 1978
and 1983. A generous grant from the German Academic
Exchange Service in 1983 was partly used to collect
additional data for this study. I am most grateful
for the financial assistance, and for the confidence
in my work. I am also indebted to colleagues at
West German universities and research institutes, in
particular Dr. Richard Stöss at the Zentralinstitut
für politische Wissenschaft at the Free University
of Berlin, Dr. Klaus Troitzsch of the
Forschungsstelle Parteiendemokratie in Koblenz, to
Prof. Dr. Karl Dietrich Bracher for an invitation to
the Institut für politische Wissenschaft at the
University of Bonn, and to Dr. Birgit Meyer for
assisting with locating sources and making contacts.
Their interest in the problems under discussion, and
the exchange of ideas have helped to shape this book.
A good deal of archive work has been carried out.
Wherever I researched, I received tireless help,
valuable advise, and was granted excellent working
facilities. Particular thanks are due to Dr. Peter
Munkell from the SPD archives in Bonn, to Dr.
Pradier from the FDP archives, then in Bonn, to Dr.
Schwarz from the archives of the Konrad Adenauer
Foundation, to Herrn Schnarbach from the archives of
the Zentralinstitut für politische Wissenschaft and
to their staff who assisted me so well. I would
also like to thank members of staff at the various
party headquarters who helped with interviews,
materials and statistical data, especially Dr. Hans-
Jürgen Beyer (FDP), Frau Doris Biesenbaum (SPD) Dr.
Hans Esser (CDU), Dr. Andreas Hartwig (CDU) Frau
Gustine Johannsen (Grüne), Frau A. Niedermair (CSU),

Acknowledgements

Dr. Klaus Suchanek (SPD), Herrn Eberhard Walde (Grüne), Frau Helga Ziemann (SPD) and all their colleagues who did their best to make my research trips profitable and informative.

In the early stages of the research, Dr. Wolfgang Falke and Dr. Stephanie Hansen from the Social Science Research Institute of the Konrad Adenauer Foundation assisted with materials and valuable discussions. I would also like to thank colleagues and friends closer to home for their suggestions, comments and support throughout, in particular Prof. Dennis Ager, Dr. William E. Paterson, Dr. Gordon Smith and Mr. Christopher Upward. I also wish to thank Mrs. Jacqui Walker for producing the typescript at short notice. Special thanks are due to my students at the University of Aston whose eagerness to understand contemporary Germany has been an incentive to write this book.

Despite the broad academic and financial support I enjoyed in the preparation of <u>Parties, Opposition and Society</u>, little would have been achieved without the patience and consideration of my family. In many ways, this is really their book: I would like to dedicate it to Martin, Harry, and Daniel.

INTRODUCTION

The interface of parties, opposition and society has changed considerably from those days, over one hundred years ago, when government began to be based on an elected parliament to parliamentary democracy of the eighties in the Federal Republic. In Imperial Germany, parliament was elected by all male adults and seemed to be the closest approximation to a voice of society. Yet it lacked the powers to choose and to control government, and to bring party majorities to bear on the composition and the course of the state leadership.[1] Parties and parliament were basically in opposition to the state. Without responsibilities of government, and without the need to contribute to agreed policies, parties pursued partisan interests and developed into mouthpieces of rival ideologies or social segments. Indeed, their claims to political legitimacy seemed to be based on their ability to voice sectional and partisan concerns in a forceful and audible manner.[2] Splintering and the polarization between parties and also between parties and state continued even after the Weimar constitution had granted parliament full powers. After 1919, party majorities in parliament combined to choose and to legitimize governments and in principle parties could develop responsible party government. Despite these constitutional possibilities, most parties of the Weimar era retained their opposition to the state. They also retained their partisan allegiances and their inability to formulate political compromise.[3] Opposition was now directed against the democratic form of government and challenged the legitimate role of the very parliament to which the parties were elected. The abolition of parliamentary control through Presidential Decree at the end of the Weimar Republic and finally through the Enabling Act in March 1933 was thus readily

1

Introduction

endorsed by most of the parties and their voters.[4] The eruption of extra-parliamentary conflicts, the street fighting, mass demonstrations and rallies which dominated the late twenties and the early thirties underline the erosion of parliamentary politics in parties and society. At that time, political impact was sought not through parliamentary democracy and its institutions but outside and against them.

One of the major challenges for post-war Germany was to develop a new interface between parties, opposition and society which would not be trapped by the pitfalls of Weimar and which would free the path towards responsible party government. A voice of society through political parties and parliament in government and state leadership had to emerge.

When the Allies and their military governments in Germany considered reeducating the country towards political democracy, they found the population not altogether ready to move in this direction. An estimated one third of the conquered Germans held firm antidemocratic views according to screenings and surveys at the time.[5] Initial attempts at weeding out formerly active Nazis and exchange administrative elites through denazification made a temporary impact only. They were soon abandoned.[6] The substantive changes towards democracy occurred at a slower pace. In 1951, 94% of West Germans felt they had been better off in the past.[7] By 1973, about three in four stressed they were better off in the present than at any time before. Similar transitions took place on all levels of post-war political realities. For example, when the Basic Law was proclaimed in 1949, 40% of the population remained indifferent to it, 33% were moderately interested, 21% very interested in the new constitution.[8] This lack of enthusiasm had already struck contemporaries. It reflected a hesitation to launch into a state while so many matters, not least the existence of a united Germany remained unsettled. It may also have reflected a reluctance about democracy as a system of government and a framework for society. While half the population in 1949 were in favour of creating a state from the three Western zones of occupation, 26% remained indifferent, 23% opposed.

Such reservations gradually subsided and West Germans not only accepted their state but developed a national consciousness and national pride aimed at that state, the Federal Republic.[9]

A similar trend can be observed for all major political institutions. In 1951, 7% of the adult population thought the Bundestag was an excellent

Introduction

thing, a further 28% expressed some support, the remainder was doubtful or negative. Fifteen years later, 5% were enthusiastic parliamentarians, pragmatic acceptance of the Bundestag had risen to 53%.[10] In the early days of the Federal Republic, about one quarter of the population thought the Bundestag represented the interests of the people, by the late sixties, twice as many did so. Acceptance of the party system also took some time. In 1952, 21% of the population preferred a one party state, in 1972, 8% did so. Competition between several political parties was favoured by 90% of West German adults in 1977, compared with 67% five years earlier.[11] More examples could be cited to show how West Germans have gradually settled into their democracy and developed political attitudes conducive to parliamentary government.

The acceptance of democratic institutions was greatly helped by the economic successes of the fifties and the increased political importance of the Federal Republic on an international scale. When Almond and Verba conducted their study of five political cultures, they found that only 7% of West Germans expressed pride in their political institutions compared with 85% Americans and 46% Britons.[12] In Germany, pride tended to be aroused by the economic system (33%) and the national character (36%). A 1978 survey put the same questions. The results were interestingly different and similar. As before, the economy scored highest (40%), followed by the political system (31%) and by national character (25%).[13] Among young people, pride in the political system outstripped pride in the economy. The role of midwife to a widespread acceptance of democratic principles and political realities in West German society may have been played by the economic miracle of the first hour, by the upsurge of prosperity on all levels of German society. It has also been suggested that the acceptance of democratic principles was an acceptance of the principles of government adopted by the state and thus perhaps just a remnant of unquestioning endorsement of the state of a more authoritarian vintage. Even if such traces could be found, the outcome seems more important, the gradual endorsement of democratic institutions and principles in the Federal Republic. And this distinguishes contemporary West Germany from Weimar where things went the opposite way.[14]

The interrelation of parties, opposition and society has overcome much of its pre-1945 legacy. Electoral turnout indicates that West Germans are in

Introduction

basic agreement with their parties.[15] In international comparison, turnout is high averaging over 85%. Yet, it was also high in Weimar Germany and before and may not be an effective test of democratic loyalties. The commitment of the political parties to subscribe to the democratic principles laid down in the Basic Law seems a more accurate measure. Article 21 and the special party legislation of 1967 make it a requirement for all political parties in West Germany to abide by democratic principles and to organize along democratic lines. Among the powers of the Constitutional Court are those to ban undemocratic parties, a prerogative which has been activated against the right extremist <u>Sozialistische Reichspartei</u> in 1952 and against the Communist Party in 1956.[16] Although it could be argued that this constitutional requirement limits the scope of opposition and may well prohibit policies which aim at an alternative political system, the overall stability of West German politics and the consolidation of political democracy have been greatly aided by the democracy clause.

Splintering and partisan politics also belong to the past. Electoral support in the Federal Republic has increasingly moved toward the larger political parties (Table I.1). While eleven parties held seats in the first Bundestag, the number of parties was down to three between 1961 and 1983.[17] In March 1983, the Green Party entered the Bundestag; for the first time in over twenty years, the established three have a newcomer-partner. In 1949, these three, CDU/CSU, SPD and FDP won 72.1% of the popular vote, in 1980, 98%. Party political concentration displaced political splintering. The vast majority of West German voters endorse those political parties which have been their voice in parliament and acted in government or in parliamentary opposition during the lifetime of the Federal Republic. Party concentration was aided by initial Allied licencing prerogatives. These limited the number of parties and monitored democratic commitment. The electoral legislation of the Federal Republic might also have had some effect.[18] A five percent hurdle was introduced to keep small parties out of parliament. This hurdle applied to regions in 1949, to the Federal Republic as a whole in subsequent elections. A second hurdle pertained to directly won seats: at first one, later three were required to admit a party to the Bundestag. The most effective measure to streamline the party system may have been the decision to introduce a combined system of proportional representation and first-past-the-post voting.

Introduction

Table I.1: Elections to the Bundestag, 1949-1983

Distribution of votes and party political concentration

Year	Political Parties				Aggregates of Votes		
	CDU/CSU	SPD	FDP	Others	CDU/CSU SPD	CDU/CSU SPD,FDP	Number of parties in BT
1948	31	29.2	11.9	27.9	60.2	72.1	11
1953	45.2	28.8	9.5	16.5	74.2	83.5	6
1957	50.2	31.8	7.7	10.3	82.0	89.7	4+
1961	45.3	36.2	12.8	5.7	81.5	94.3	3
1965	47.6	39.3	9.5	3.6	86.9	96.4	3
1969	46.1	42.7	5.8	5.4 NPD= 4.3	88.8	94.6	3
1972	44.9	45.8	8.4	0.9	90.7	99.1	3
1976	48.6	42.6	7.9	0.9	91.2	99.1	3
1980	44.5	42.9	10.6	2.0 Greens = 1.5	87.4	98.0	3
1983	48.8	38.3	6.9	6.0 Greens = 5.6	87.2	94.0	4

+ The <u>Deutsche Partei</u> passed the 5% hurdle only because it entered an electoral agreement with the CDU.

Sources: Peter Schindler, Parlaments- und Wahlstatistik, Zeitschrift für Parlamentsfragen 1, April 1981 p. 6; SZ Sonderausgabe BTW 83, 8.3.1983

In the fifties, the CDU absorbed the conservative opposition, not least its coalition partners. The CDU integrated most of the political right into mainstream politics. Between 1949 and 1953, it gained 14% and experienced a so called electoral miracle. In 1957, it won an absolute majority. The SPD, by comparison, made slower advances but increased from election to election between 1953 to 1972 (Table I.1). The FDP, the only surviving smaller party, made no electoral headway and remained wedged between a maximum of 12.8% in 1961 and its minimum to date of 5.8% in 1969. Its place in West German politics seems defined by the challenge to survive the electoral hurdles. By contrast, the two large

Introduction

parties have extended their support in society: in 1949, both commanded about one third of the popular vote, by 1980, their respective share was near the mid-forty mark. Their combined vote grew from just over 60% to over 87%. This process of broad popular endorsement of the two large parties or party blocks has been analysed as the success of a non-partisan concept of party organization which claims to reflect the breadth of society and social groups: the Volkspartei.[20] "The Volkspartei represents one way of ensuring mass attachment to the political system, of securing democratic integration."[21] Regarding the interrelation of parties, opposition and society, the emergence of the Volkspartei means parties enjoy the support of most voters. It also means each Volkspartei claims to have overcome partisan interest affiliations. Theoretically such a party embraces the whole spectrum of social support. CDU/CSU and SPD have moved closer together in their social bases and in their political positions. We shall evaluate later remaining differences in the social composition of electorates and party memberships. For the SPD, the change towards a Volkspartei was marked by the Godesberg Programme which explicitly abandoned Marxist principles of social and political reconstruction and accepted the realities which had evolved in the Federal Republic. The CDU started out as a catch-all party, a Volkspartei.[22]

The new social and political proximity of West German political parties has been called a 'party cartel'; parties, at least those with parliamentary representation, seemed to have become virtually indistinguishable from one another. Under the guise of electoral competition and plurality, something like a one party state allegedly emerged.[23] Others evaluated the proximity of political programmes and aims more charitably as a breakthrough towards consensus politics and coalition governments with stable majorities.[24] Here, consensus and an ability to arrive at compromise are seen as preconditions of succcessful parliamentary democracy. Beyond these polarized views, this study examines the proximity and the differences between parties by scrutinizing which segments of society are reflected in the major parties and in those on the fringes of West German politics.

In the German context, the practice of parliamentary work and the scope of political opposition tend to strengthen the politics of workable compromise and consensus. The Bundestag and the land parliaments are organized as so called working parliaments with a number of specialist committees

Introduction

which prepare legislation and conduct the bulk of parliamentary reasoning. Plenary sessions give government and opposition the chance to voice their broad political positions.[25] All parliamentary parties cooperate in committees in accordance with the number of seats they hold. Chairmanships of committees are also allocated in accordance to party strength. In other words, all parties, whether in government or in opposition, are actively involved in the legislative process. The integration of opposition is perhaps the most astounding feature of German politics. In the British model of democracy which has frequently been used to formulate how parliamentary democracy should work, the Leader of the Opposition holds an official, paid post but the opposition party is not involved in legislative deliberations beyond contributions in the House of Commons.[26] The task of such opposition is to formulate political alternatives, to develop alternative policies. The city state of Hamburg inserted a clause into its constitution which makes it the duty of opposition to formulate such alternative policies, "The opposition is an essential component of democracy. It has the permanent task to voice publicly its criticism of the government programme in principle and in detail. It is the political alternative to the governing majority."[27] De facto, such distance between government and opposition is difficult to achieve in West Germany. There is the political and social similarity of the Volksparteien which do not invite intransigent political alternatives. There is the experience of the SPD in the fifties of opposition as a stigma. When it challenged the government on major areas such as West Integration and rearmament, it reaped public mistrust. Only after the party began publishing its voting record in the Bundestag to prove that in fact it supported most bills which came before parliament and after it gradually abandoned its intentions towards political alternatives for Germany could it calm the suspicions it had encountered.[28]

Statistics of parliamentary voting have shown that most legislative measures in the Bundestag and in the land parliaments enjoy the support of all political parties. The dimension of conflict and alternatives between government and opposition has already been ironed out in the committee stage, i.e. behind closed doors. When parties come to vote on legislation, consensus has been established. Opposition in the German parliamentary system has become part of the governing process, it is integrated. This matches public expectation about the

Introduction

scope of opposition. Most West Germans are agreed that opposition is part of democratic government. Nearly 90% endorsed it in the seventies, 57% stressed it was very important.[29] This endorsement of opposition cannot be taken for an endorsement of conflict with the government of the day.[30] In 1971, 68% of West German adults stressed "it is not the task of the opposition to criticize the government but to support its work."[31] Young people (61%) and students (28%) were less likely to regard cooperation as the most important facet of opposition. A survey among pupils in a Secondary Modern School (Hauptschule) came to similar findings. The young people were asked: "Do you think that the criticism of the government by an opposition should have its limits?". 65% felt opposition should be limited, 17% disagreed.[32] Edinger noted in the sixties a discrepancy between accepting democratic norms and a political behaviour which would relate to these norms.[33] In his evaluation, West Germans were democrats of principles, not so much of practice.

The endorsement of the principle of opposition and the reluctance to face up to an articulation of conflict does not seem adequately explained as a flaw in the democratic political culture. Far from being out of step, it seems to reflect the specific format of West German party government which rests on an integrated opposition, on compromise and consensus. Conflict and demands for fundamental alternatives are shunned or even forbidden as disruptions of the democratic fabric of society. They are not valued as enrichments. One could also expect the scope of opposition to be enhanced by the federal structure of West Germany. A party of coalition which might form the government in Bonn does not constitute the government in each of the lander. Lander might be governed by the opposition or a coalition arrangement different from that established on the national level.[34] In theory, the federal structure provides the chance for opposition parties to set up some kind of model government in their lander and show the electorate the realities and advantages of their policies. The lander, however, do not have enough independence to allow for this kind of political diversity. Since 1949, the legislative scope of land parliaments has narrowed with more and more jurisdiction transferred to the Bundestag. The expanded scope of central government curtails the leeway of the lander and of opposition parties to model institutions and policies. At the same time, the political representation of the

Introduction

lander in central government, the Bundesrat has become more important since about three quarters of all Bundestag legislation concerns the lander and therefore permits their scrutiny and right of veto.[35] The Bundesrat is the voice of lander governments who delegate members to West Germany's second chamber. Delegates of one land cast their votes en block to articulate regional interests. De facto, the Bundesrat functions along party-political dividing lines. Governments of the same colour have tended to pool their votes obliterating regional concerns.

While national governments and Bundesrat majorities belonged to the same party, the potential of the Bundesrat as an instrument of opposition remained obscured. In the early seventies, the SPD/FDP government in Bonn had to face considerable regional gains by the CDU/CSU and a party polarization between Bundestag and Bundesrat majorities. This resulted in a virtual stalemate of legislation. Government encountered opposition not so much in the Bundestag and during the committee stage, but in the Bundesrat which could refer most drafts back to the Bundestag for further consideration or force the mediating panel to hammer out an acceptable compromise. Political evaluations of opposition through the lander representation have been controversial. Some fear a deadlock of government,[36] others an erosion of parliamentary politics.[37] Some argue full use should be made of the Bundesrat in national government, others claim the regional focus has been distorted, even betrayed by party politics.

In this context, we shall not attempt to join the combatants. The controversy itself indicates that the notion of agreed and settled consensus in politics might not be altogether accurate when describing West Germany. Behind the apparently unison party pronouncements, conflicting political positions have survived or surfaced. The integrative force of the Volkspartei has not evened out all political and social divisions. The new format of broadly based politics has blunted the piercing edges and created a climate of political cooperation. It also created a climate of parties competing to some extent for the same social support. Less apparent are the partisan interests which are articulated in and through political parties. One might speak of an incomplete transition to Volksparteien, of a dual reality of catch-all and interest parties in West Germany. One might also speak of an ambivalence of opposition, an

9

Introduction

ambivalence strongly indebted to traditions of anti-system opposition. An analysis of the social composition of parties inside and outside parliaments can link these overall trends of political culture and practice to West German society today, its occupational structure, its status levels, its generation. This, in short, is the aim of this book.

The first part examines the place of the three established parties in society. Chapter 1 looks at interest affiliation. Rather than taking programmes and pronouncements which have all been tuned to the catch-all pitch and include something for all social groups, interest affiliation is discussed in relation to party finance and parliamentary representation. Two tendencies emerge: the established parties have retained interest affiliations with trade unions or industry and business respectively. They also attempted to gain recognition as semi-official organs of the state. Parties and state administration have moved close together for all three established parties, not least due to the growing involvement of civil servants in parties and their political representation.

Chapter 2 compares the electoral support of SPD, FDP and CDU/CSU to further clarify the position of parties in society. Social differences between parties emerge along social status lines and along a denominational divide. Religion, which had declined as a factor in politics since the fifties, reasserted itself in electoral choices during the seventies.

The electorates of SPD, FDP and CDU/CSU are socially clearly different. Party memberships and in particular party leaderships are not. For all three they increasingly draw on a narrow segment of better educated white collar professions, notably on civil servants (chapters 3-5). For each of the parties, the seventies brought distinctive pressures of adjustment and change. In the SPD, the membership has remained largely passive and a small body of functionaries who no longer fit into the working class traditions have begun to shape the party. The CDU had to meet the influx of new members and the onset of opposition with building up an effective party machinery and a reservoir of posts for its position-oriented membership. The CSU had already been transformed into a party apparatus with a fast growing membership and experienced the least upheaval in the seventies. The FDP, by contrast, has been marred throughout by organizational weakness and membership fluctuations which all but endangered

Introduction

the party's political survival.

The social and educational divide which separates party memberships from party electorates has shaped the scope of opposition outside the established parties. Although electorates are broadly based, party organizations are not. In their function to recruit potential leaders and political elites from the whole of society, the three political parties which have been represented in the Bundestag since 1949 have not succeeded. Their grip on society is narrow, narrowing despite a numerical increase in party membership overall during the seventies. Part Two, Opposition and Society explores some groups and parties outside the established framework of political representation to determine their political intentions and the depth of their social support. If parties as quasi official organs of the state, as machineries who no longer reflect the social breadth of their electorates in their leaderships or their policies can be charged with having distanced themselves from society, have opposition groups and voices in West Germany stepped in to provide the vital link between politics and people? We shall try to answer this question by looking at various political alternatives of the left, of the right and of the ecology movement. Chapter 6 prepares the ground for this discussion by analysing whether young people in West Germany have cancelled the consensus with their state, with the political parties and the institutions, as has been suggested in a great number of recent publications. A social divide emerges, with the lower educated inclined towards the political right or towards political apathy and the higher educated towards the left or towards political protest. The majority of young West Germans, however, remain integrated into the existing electoral choices and parties. Chapters 7 and 8 examine the political extremes right and left and the reasons for their stagnation. Chapter 9 looks at the ecology party, its political profile, social support and electoral prospects and its contribution to the profile of opposition in parliament.

Despite considerable differences in political orientation and social backing between these groups, they share a tendency towards anti-system opposition. Even the ecology party The Greens which has elected delegates, has yet to develop a concept of parliamentary opposition. While opposition within parliaments tends to be integrated with perhaps overmuch consensus, opposition outside still seems to run into the cul-de-sac of antidemocratic

Introduction

politics and mistake political alternatives for fundamentalist dissent. This tendency towards all-out opposition has also been borne out by the propensity of opposition on the left, on the right and in the field of anti-nuclear protest to endorse and even advocate the use of violence as a means of political action. Repeatedly during the seventies and eighties, the working consensus of West German society seemed to come under pressure from anti-democratic challengers. Some challenges from outside parliaments and established parties called for society to have a bigger voice and a more manifold voice in political affairs. To that extent, parties, opposition and society are under review to enhance the realities of political democracy in West Germany.

FOOTNOTES

1. A good discussion in Ralf Dahrendorf, Society and Democracy in Germany, Weidenfels and Nicolson 1967, also Heino Kaack, Geschichte und Struktur der politischen Parteien, Opladen (Westdt. Verlag) 1971.
2. Good overview in Gordon Smith, Democracy in Western Germany, Heinemann 1979 pp. 9-16.
3. Useful survey of election results and successive governments in Falk Esche (ed.) Parteiendemokratie. Wahlen und Parteien in der Bundesrepublik, Hamburg (Hoffmann und Campe) 1978 pp. 206-207, Karl Dietrich Bracher, Die Auflösung der Weimarer Republik, Villigen (Ring Verlag) 1971, Erich Matthias and Rudolf Morsey (eds.), Das Ende der Parteien, Düsseldorf (Droste) 1960, Hans Mommsen et. al. (eds.) Industrielles System und politische Entwicklung in der Weimarer Republik, Düsseldorf (Droste) 1974 esp. chs. 5 and 6.
4. e.g. Gordon Craig, Germany 1866-1945, Clarendon Press 1978 chs. 11-15. Volker Berghahn, Modern Germany, Cambridge University Press 1982, ch. 2.
5. Some of the findings were published in the Allied Bombing survey, see also Huster, Kraiker et. al. Determinanten der westdeutschen Restauration 1945-1949, Frankfurt (Suhrkamp) 1976 chs. 2 and 3.
6. Lutz Niethammer, Die Mitläuferfabrik, Bonn (Dietz) 1982.
7. The figures for 1951 from Alfred Grosser, Die Bonner Demokratie. Deutschland von aussen gesehen, Düsseldorf (Droste) 1960 p. 22. The question "When were you personally best off?"

brought the following replies:
   Imperial Germany   45%
   Between 1920 and 1933:   7%
   Between 1933 and 1938:   40%
   after 1945:   2%
Data for 1973 from Gebhard Schweigler, National Consciousness in Divided Germany, Sage 1975, p. 187.
   8. See David P. Conradt, The German Polity, Longmans 1978 p. 17.
   9. Schweigler ibid. and Helge Pross, Was ist heute deutsch? Reinbek (Rowohlt) 1982.
   10. Schweigler ibid. p. 198.
   11. Data from Martin and Sylvia Greiffenhagen, Ein schwieriges Vaterland, Munich (List) 1979 p. 355.
   12. Gabriel Almond and Sydney Verba, The Civic Culture, Little, Brown and Co, 1965 p. 64, also dto. The Civic Culture Revisited, ibid. 1980 with an assessment by David Conradt of the transformations in Germany.
   13. Greiffenhagen ibid. p. 359.
   14. e.g. Hans Heigert et. al. International Conference "Nationalsozialismus und Machtergreifung", Berlin January 1983, see Das Parlament 29.1.1983 p. 24. Also: Richard Löwenthal, "Bonn und Weimar: zwei deutsche Demokratien" in Nach dreissig Jahren. Die Bundesrepublik Deutschland - Vergangenheit - Gegenwart - Zukunft, ed. Walter Scheel, Stuttgart (Klett:Cotta) 1979 p. 69 ff.
   15. Rainer M. Lepsius, "Institutional Structures and Political Culture" in Herbert Döring and Gordon Smith (eds.), Party Government and Political Culture in Western Germany, Macmillan 1982 pp. 119-120.
   16. Documentation in Horst Säcker, Das Bundesverfassungsgericht, Munich (Bayrische Landeszentrale für politische Bildung) 1977 pp. 68-70.
   17. Peter Schindler, "Parlaments - und Wahlstatistik" in Z Parl 1, April 1981 p. 6. Also: Werner Kaltefleiter, "Wandlungen des deutschen Parteiensystems" in Aus Politik und Zeitgeschichte B 14, 1975 pp. 3-10. Eva Kolinsky, "Das Parteiensystem der Bundesrepublik Deutschland" in Bundesrepublik Deutschland. Ein Studienbuch, Bath University Press 1982 pp. 28-49.
   18. Good summary in Eckhart Jesse, Die Demokratie in der Bundesrepublik, Berlin (Colloquium) 1977 pp. 53-56.
   19. Manfred Rowold, Im Schatten der Macht. Zur Oppositionsrolle der nicht-etablierten Parteien, Düsseldorf (Droste) 1974 p. 81 ff.

Introduction

20. Gordon Smith, "The German Volkspartei and the Career of the Catch-all Concept" in Döring and Smith, ibid. p. 59-76.
21. Ibid. p. 59.
22. Otto Kirchheimer "Wandlungen der politischen Opposition" in Kirchheimer, Politik und Verfassung, Frankfurt (Suhrkamp) 1964 pp. 123-150.
23. Dietrich Staritz, Das Parteiensystem in der Bundesrepublik, Opladen (Westdeutscher Verlag) 1980. Wolf Dieter Narr (ed.) Auf dem Wege zum Einparteienstaat, Opladen (Westdt. Verlag) 1977.
24. e.g. The West German Model: Perspectives on a Stable State ed. William E. Paterson and Gordon Smith, WEP (Special Issue) May 1981.
25. A good analysis of the institutional framework in Frank Pilz, Einführung in das politische System der Bundesrepublik Deutschland, Munich (Beck) 1977.
26. Hannah Vogt, Parlamentarische und ausserparlamentarische Opposition, Opladen (Leske) 1972 p. 47.
27. Ibid.
28. Douglas A. Chalmers, The Social Democratic Party of Germany. From Working Class Movement to Modern Political Party, Yale University Press 1974 p. 93, also Kurt Klotzbach, Der Weg zur Staatspartei. Programmatik, praktische Politik und Organisation der deutschen Sozialdemokratie 1945 bis 1965, Berlin:Bonn (Dietz) 1982.
29. A survey by Max Kaase quoted in Greiffenhagen ibid. p. 356.
30. This aspect is for instance overlooked in the discussion by David Conradt, The German Polity ibid. p. 53.
31. Greiffenhagen ibid. p. 376.
32. K. Wasmund, Politische Orientierungen Jugendlicher, Munich (Juventa) 1977 p. 290.
33. Lewis J. Edinger, Politics in Germany, Little, Brown and Co, 1968 p. 107.
34. Gerhard Lehmbruch, "Party and Federation in Germany: a Developmental Dilemma" in Government and Opposition, Summer 1978 pp. 160 ff.
35. Heidrun Abromeit, "Politisierung des Bundesrates" in Z Parl 4, 1982 p. 465.
36. Lehmbruch ibid. pp. 173 ff.
37. "Missbrauch des Bundesrates? Dokumentation einer aktuellen Auseinandersetzung" in Z Parl 2, 1974 pp. 157-166.

Introduction

SUGGESTED READINGS

David P. Conradt, The German Polity, Longmans 1978
Ralf Dahrendorf, Society and Democracy in Germany, Weidenfels and Nicholson 1967
Herbert Döring/Gordon Smith (eds.), Party Government and Political Culture in Western Germany, MacMillan 1982
Lewis J. Edinger, Politics in Germany, Little Brown and Co, 1968
Martin and Sylvia Greiffenhagen, Ein schwieriges Vaterland, Munich (List) 1979
Eckhart Jesse, Die Demokratie in der Bundesrepublik, Berlin (Colloquium) 1977
William E. Paterson/Gordon Smith, The West German Model: Perspectives on a Stable State, Cass 1981
Manfred Rowold, Im Schatten der Macht, Düsseldorf (Droste) 1974
Gordon Smith, Democracy in Western Germany. Parties and Politics in the Federal Republic, Heinemann 1979, 2nd ed. 1982
Dietrich Staritz, Das Parteiensystem in der Bundesrepublik, Opladen (Westdeutscher Verlag) 1980

PART ONE: PARTIES AND SOCIETY

Chapter One

PARTIES AND SOCIETY IN WEST GERMANY (I)

POST-WAR CONDITIONS FOR PARTIES AND SOCIETY

All political parties in West Germany bear the scars of Nationalsocialism. For the duration of the regime, parties other than the one in power were illegal. The Communist Party and the Social Democratic Party were banned in 1933, their members persecuted, imprisoned, driven into exile or forced to conceal their political inclinations behind a facade of conformity. The dispersal and the forcible destruction of the labour movement and its political parties has been obscured by the fact that both KPD and SPD re-emerged in 1945 seemingly intact. The Communist party had received a new sense of unity and direction in the Soviet exile and through a close association with the Soviet occupation forces and their political goals. The amalgamation with the SPD in the Soviet zone to form the SED, Socialist Unity Party, was one of the results of this new cohesion.[1] Another was the cooperation with a number of SPD politicians and members which initially seemed to broaden and possibly modify the communist thrust into German politics.

By comparison, the SPD which regrouped after 1945 and refused to amalgamate with the Communists in the Western zones, looked less innovative. The SPD had survived the war divided into a number of wings according to their place of exile or their incarceration in concentration camps.[2] The dispersed leaders and the dispersed members re-activated the old organizational network, re-adopted the 1925 party programme, and seemed set to continue their Weimar policies. The SPD policies of the day and the party goals overall were formulated by its first post-war chairman, Kurt Schumacher, one of the survivors of Nazi persecution.[3]

Other political parties were more visibly disrupted: the liberals had been virtually devastated by Nazi gains in the late twenties and had, like all political parties, been suspended for the duration of the "Third Reich". As the other parties of the centre and of the right, they had obeyed the order to disband voluntarily. In 1948, the liberals amalgamated the separate progressive - and national liberal parties into the Free Democratic Party. The FDP in its present shape is a post-war creation. It retained some of the shakiness of the political middle ground which had marred the Weimar years.[4]

CDU and CSU are also new parties of the post-war period. They drew on the former catholic parties, the Centre and the Bavarian People's Party, as well as on former liberals and conservatives. One of the intentions of post-war reorganization was to go beyond the catholic electorate and attract "Christian" support. In Weimar, the Centre Party could only mobilize about one third of German catholics. The party amalgamation crossed the denominational boundaries and some of the old party lines.[5] This broad concept at its inception together with the mobilizing power of economic success in the late forties and early fifties made the CDU and the CSU into <u>Volksparteien</u>, broadly based parties which could elicit broad electoral support. The division of Germany aided this process somewhat: about 80% of former Centre Party voters had been resident in the territories of the Western zones of occupation. By contrast, the SPD had lost an estimated 50% of its electorate who had come from the Eastern regions in Weimar Germany.[6]

Perhaps the most significant aspect of party realignment after 1945 was that ultra-conservative and right-wing parties did not reappear directly. Their social and political power bases had been destroyed through the Nazi regime, through the transformations within the military elites and the final demotion of these elites once the war was lost and with the secession of the Eastern territories to Poland and to the Soviet Union. The licencing prerogatives of the Allies made it initially also impossible for such parties to reorganize and resume their work.[7] Although a good many parties of the right tried to make their way into German politics once the Allies had relinquished their controls, they came too late to break the advances of the others, especially of the Christian Democrats. They also came without the backing of a cohesive interest or social group which had given them so much political muscle prior to 1933.[8] The centre of party politics in West Germany had gravitated towards a middle ground. The distribution of seats in the Economic Council shows an early concentration of party support. The allocation of seats here was based on party representation in the lander of the American and British zones of occupation. As Table 1.1 indicates, the centrality of the party system was even more pronounced in the Parliamentary Council which also included delegates from the French zone in line with regional party strength.

Table 1.1: Party Representation in the Economic Council and in the Parliamentary Council, 1947-1949

	Political Party						
	KPD	SPD	Centre	CDU/CSU	FDP[1]	NLP[2]	WAV
Economic Council	3	20	2	20	4	2	1
Parliamentary Council	2	27	2	27	5	2	-

Sources: Kaack, Geschichte p. 189, Merkl, The Origins of the Federal Republic p. 59.
1) Until 1948 under a variety of names e.g. DVP, Dem.P, FDP.
2) NLP (Niedersächsische Landespartei) later became Deutsche Partei, DP when it organized on a national level.

The social upheavals which Nationalsocialism and World War II brought over Germany created further challenges for political parties. The war had claimed an estimated four million German casualties, mostly men in combat. Post-war society had a surplus of women and at that time women were politically closer to conservativism than to any other political direction. The war and the bomb damages had demolished about 15% of the housing stock. In some large cities such as Frankfurt, Berlin, Cologne, Hamburg, Mannheim, destruction was between 70 and 90%.[9] The dislocation of people was aggravated by the influx of refugees and expellees from the Eastern territories since 1944. They had initially been ordered out by the Nationalsocialist leadership to leave only scorched earth for the advancing Red Army. Later, millions were expelled. By 1947, twelve million refugees had poured into Germany and were compulsorily resettled in the least destroyed rural areas.[10] The degree of mobility and social mixing in these areas was without precedence. In some, such as Schleswig Holstein and Lower Saxony, over one third of their post-war population consisted of refugees. One might add to a profile of enforced social mobility the 9.6 million so called "displaced persons" who were stranded in Germany in 1945, some survivors of concentration camps for whom no homes or homelands could be found, others survivors of the forced labour programmes which had formed the backbone of the Nazi economy.[11] A census conducted in 1946 in the Western zones showed that the population had increased by 12% compared with pre-war times. It continued to increase with more refugees coming in, from the East and also from the Soviet zone and later the GDR. This unprecedented upheaval of social fabrics and settlement patterns has been called a "mobilized society".[12]

The political parties seemed to benefit in several ways from this mobilization. The geographical and social mix losened social traditions and class ties. It may have helped to create a politically more flexible electorate which was less incarcerated in interest - and class-ridden party preferences. This would be an important precondition for the development of catch-all parties in post-war Germany. Until 1948, all political parties recorded rapid increases in membership. The SPD had some 850,000 members by June 1948.[13] Most newcomers had been won in rural areas, in particular those with a high concentration of refugees. There is no information to show whether or not these refugees had belonged to the party in their original places of residence, but it seems likely that a large number of the gains were new admissions.[14] The CDU/CSU did similarly well and had 460,000 members in 1948. There are no data for the liberals.

The parties made a quick and successful entry into post-war society. The large memberships gave them a solid social base, some organizational depth and funds for further party work. One may also conclude that parties at the time were endorsed because they were seen as relevant to the problems and concerns of the day. They seemed to have become an accepted and vital voice in post-war society well before the creation of the Federal Republic. Matters, however, are not as straightforward as the rapid membership growth seems to indicate. Membership dwindled after the currency reform of 1948.[15] The membership levels of the first hour were only reached and surpassed in the seventies. What had happened? The SPD blamed the drop in membership numbers on the currency reform and argued that prices had become so steep that their supporters could no longer afford the extra expense of paying their party dues. It is unlikely that this is a full explanation since all parties, to our knowledge, experienced similar developments regardless of the overall prosperity or otherwise of their members. It seems more probable that party membership brought several concrete advantages at the time: for those implicated or possibly implicated by a Nazi past, it signified visible democratic loyalty. For those who had to make their way in new surroundings and in the previously closely knit rural communities, party membership provided an accessible social context and also access to services and connections which might help in obtaining goods and provisions for everyday life and contacts for starting a new career. Parties could be seen as platforms of utility. Once the currency reform had halted the stockpiling of goods and the black market economy, the system of connections and contacts which the party could provide, was no longer necessary and could be abandoned.[16]

The freak growth had effects other than bringing membership contributions into party coffers. With so many members flocking in, none of the parties, whether the revived SPD or the newly amalgamated CDU had to consider the degree of social change which had occurred in Germany or its own special basis and place in society. Regrouping rather than restructuring seemed sufficient. Despite the social mobilization and the shake-up of regional, political and occupational boundaries for the majority of people, the parties began the post-war era along the old grooves. Adjustment for the CDU/CSU was less evidently needed since it could capitalize on the catch-all tradition of the Centre Party and its broad Christian appeal. It also gained standing as the senior partner in government during the fifties. It regrouped as a party of the bourgeois centre, the <u>Bürgerblock</u> and gradually became its major component.[17] The regrouping meant in the long run that the CDU increased its electorate by absorbing affiliated parties.[18]

Adjustment in the SPD came late. It took until 1959 to officially moderate the position as a workers' interest party.[19] After Godesberg, the party was equipped to respond to the social changes which had reshaped post-war Germany: the rapid transform-

21

ation of the employment structure and the transformation of the class- and status divisions in society. It could then compete for the support of the group which seems to swing electoral success in advanced industrial societies: the new middle class of white collar employees, of civil servants and tertiary occupations.

INTEREST AFFILIATION - THE CASE OF PARTY FINANCE

The transition in the Federal Republic from interest - to people's parties has remained incomplete despite the changes mentioned above. Public awareness reflects this and continues to locate parties in different, even opposing political camps. The SPD continues to be ranked as predominantly a party for the workers, CDU/CSU and FDP as parties for the better off.[20] Parties have also placed themselves into distinct camps and associated with pressure groups from the two sides of industry. They still are a narrower voice of society than the characterization as <u>Volksparteien</u> seems to imply.

The knowledge that financial support from German industry had aided the Nazi party and facilitated its seizure of power, made party finance into a post-war issue and into some kind of testcase whether parties followed democratic lines and could represent democratic society. The Parliamentary Council stipulated in the Basic Law that parties should have a democratic organizational structure. For party finance, the Basic Law demanded public and open accounts. It took nearly twenty years for the relevant legislation to be completed. Matters of party finance needed repeated interventions by the Federal Constitutional Court. The parties themselves seemed to perceive little urgency for this issue. The SPD had regrouped as a membership party with income from membership dues supplemented by revenues from party property and some trade union assistance. The parties in power, the CDU/CSU with their coalition partners FDP and DP had again aligned themselves with industrial and economic interest groups. There is considerable evidence for an interpenetration of economic and government affairs. The personal friendship between Adenauer and the Chairman of the Federation of German Industry, Fritz Berg, during the fifties generated economic and foreign policies which often excluded the relevant ministers.[21] The close and volatile relationship between the Farmers' Union (Bauernverband) and the CDU/CSU included bartering agricultural concessions for the en bloc vote of the farming community.22 There is also evidence for an alliance between the Free Democratic and farming interests.23 A study of attitudes among West German business leaders in the fifties showed that business concerns outweighed commitment to political democracy at the time.24 Overall, antidemocratic tendencies persisted into post-war society. The political parties were nevertheless unperturbed by possible dangers that interest affiliation could restrict their political independence. They took pride in their close affiliation with the state and did not see that it might curtail the political scope of parties, in particular of oppositions. The case of party finance can illuminate the place of West German parties between society, organized interests and state.

Stages of Party Finance Since 1949

Since 1949, party finance developed in three stages. The first was characterized by the re-emergence of party finance through industrial funds. It lasted until the Federal Constitutional Court ruling in 1958. The second stage consisted of a measure of state finance between 1959 and 1966. Again, the Constitutional Court intervened and effected change. The third stage commenced in 1967 when party legislation was passed. It is characterized by a combination of finance through donations, state finance and parties' own funding.

The first decade in the Federal Republic was one of retrenchment. The SPD re-established itself as a mass party, relying, as it had done before, on its own sources of income. The rapid influx of new members in the early years provided an unexpectedly secure basis for party work although the decline in membership had weakened the party early on. In the forties and fifties, the SPD derived 80% of its income from membership contributions.25 Membership was the major source of party income and the major backbone for party organization. The membership losses may have contributed to the attempts of the SPD to adjust to the pace of social change in the fifties. The Godesberg reorientation tends to be seen predominantly as a response to electoral stagnation. The financial basis of the SPD suggests that the party's viability also depended on an intensified mobilizing power. Although the distribution of party income on types of expendiure is not known, the importance of the membership factor for the SPD party organization is evident. During the fifties, it constituted the major source of revenue. By comparison, other sources of income during the first stage of party finance had little relevance: party holdings consisted of 26 newspaper publishing houses, 30 printing works, 5 publishing companies, several bookshops and similar firms in 1956.[26] Incomes amounted to about 5%, although the use of facilities and services also aided party expenditure. A further 10% of SPD income were contributions by parliamentary delegates. Donations from industrial or other sources were quite insignificant.[27]

For CDU, CSU and FDP, members appeared to be less relevant as the basis of party organization. According to a report compiled by Rudolf Wildenmann,[28] between 80% and 85% of CDU, CSU, FDP and DP funds were donations from industry or business. Political parties involved in the West German coalition governments until 1966 established a close financial link with the organized interest sectors of industry and trade. With the German tradition of strong and cohesive pressure groups and a membership quota in these pressure groups of more than 90%, the liaison between economic interest and the parties of government was close. Similar to practices adopted during the Weimar Republic, donations were shared out among the so called bourgeois parties according to their relative strength. In an interview with the weekly magazine Der Spiegel in 1959, the general secretary of the Federation of German Industry, Stein, revealed the key applicable at the time. The CDU received 50%, the FDP 35% and the small coalition partner DP 15% of the donations on a national level. In the lander, the proportions could vary according to representation in parliament and other factors. The common feature was not to give any money to the SPD which continued to be seen as a standard bearer of socialism.[29] An ad hoc scheme of collecting and distributing funds existed already for the first federal elections.[30] Braunthal even asserts that the wording of the CDU election programme Düsseldorfer Leitsätze was formulated by the Federation of German Industry.[31]

The focus on donations from industry and business reduced the importance of the membership. Until 1956, CDU party representation was based on numbers of voters per region alone. Only a backbench revolt forced the 1956 party congress to rewrite the statutes and find a formula by which the number of votes a regional party could win and its membership were taken into account when calculating the number of delegates to which it was entitled. As an overall trend it may be stated, that finance through industry makes a party organization rather aloof from the need to recruit members. Wildenmann found that membership dues for the CDU were not even sufficient to cover the cost of party administration in the early fifties, let alone to cope with the heavy expenses of campaigning. In 1954 tax concessions were introduced to increase industry's willingness to raise donations. In order to benefit fully from the relief in taxation and in order to channel the funds into the desired political directions, so called Support Associations, Fördergesellschaften, or Citizens' Associations, Staatsbürgerliche Vereinigungen were founded. These associations were organized on a land or national level. Membership was open to interest groups or to individual firms. On the land level, regional industries and business would supply the funds, on the national level, the umbrella organizations for branches of the economy or the Federation of Germany Industry would collect the donations. Uwe Schleth, in his study of party finance, argues that the prime concern of these associations was to secure a CDU government and to safeguard the principles of a free market economy. Examples of punitive action by the associations tend to concern the FDP as the one party who tried to retain some political independence by voicing occasional dissent and objections against CDU policies. When the FDP for example withdrew its support from the CDU led government in Northrhine Westfalia in 1956, the regular financial contributions from the Support Association ceased to flow. The same punitive action was applied when the FDP withdrew from the coalition government over the moves to introduce a 10% electoral hurdle, a so called "ditch-election" system.[32] Apart from discouraging party membership, party finance through donations and outside funds has a further important consequence on organization: Regional parties have their own sources of finance, the regional Support Associations, and can develop a high degree of independence and diversity from the central party leadership. Conversely, party headquarters depend little on the regions or the rank and file for their finance and by the same token regional party structures depend little on the central organizational level. The political and regional diversity which lay at the root of both Christian Democratic and liberal party foundations, was reinforced by the system of party finance. A tentative link between regional parties was created by the recurring election campaigns. The observation that the CDU in the fifties and early sixties was hardly more than a voting club for the Chancellor aims at the dominant position of Adenauer for the policy line of the party but also at this heterogeneity. The smokescreen of national electioneering only temporarily welded into a cohesive party the independent land organizations, who were politically and financially capable of standing on their own feet.

Party Finance 1958-1966
The first phase of party finance created a political cleavage in the Federal Republic between parties dependent on funds from industry and business with little need for mass memberships and the SPD who had no access to such funds and relied mainly on its membership and party property to finance organization and elections. The second phase brought the parties closer together and established a new and common link with the state. In 1958, the Federal Constitutional Court objected to the tax concessions for donations on the grounds that equal opportunites could not be ensured for all political parties. The court feared an alliance between the wealthier groups in society and the governing parties.[33]

The Bundestag translated the Federal Constitutional Court's ruling into a political practice which may not fully have caught the spirit of the deliberations. Parties now gained a semi-official status and were financially supported by the state. This response appears to be in line with that dimension of German political tradition which idealizes the state as an above party, neutral arbitrator and questions political parties as biased, distorting and quarrelsome. The establishment of political parties as agents of the state reduced the elements of conflict between them and emphasized their consensus and similarity in outlook and values. The system of state finance which was introduced, was initially called "contributions to political education" (Sonderbeiträge für politische Bildung). Whatever their name, state funds freed the parties to a large extent from the pressures to recruit members and to generate an active following in society. Since 1964, state finance was known as "special funds for the political parties". The sum allocated annually rose from five million Deutschmark

Parties and Society

in 1959 to 38 million in 1966.[34] Flechtheim estimated that the parties funded themselves with well over 156 million Deutschmark during the period of state finance. The monies were distributed among the parties who held seats in parliaments on the federal or land level. Parties who did not win seats were excluded from public funding.

The lump sum payments to the parties were in addition to financial assistance given to the work of parliamentary parties and in addition to renumerations for members of parliament. These two forms of public finance have existed since the beginnings of the Federal Republic. They were intended to allow parties to adequately fulfil their political tasks. Between 1949 and 1979, the annual budget for parliamentary parties soared from DM 348,000 to DM 41.6 million.[35] In 1970, parliamentary parties were entitled to DM 19,100 per delegate.[36]

Public funding became increasingly important for party budgets during the second phase of party finance. The abolition of tax incentives for donations had reduced the flow of funds from industry, business and other donors. Parties with little revenue from membership contributions derived a growing proportion of their income directly from state finance. The earlier tendency to favour the upper levels of party organization and reduce the relevance of grass root membership were reinforced by state finance. Funds were paid to party

Table 1.2: Public funding of political parties, 1960-1964 (in % of party incomes)

Year	CDU	CSU**	SPD	FDP
1960	19.7	--	--	9.6
1961	9.6	11.5	--	9.2
1962	38.7	63.4	32.6	32.2
1963	40.5	80.3	--	42.3
1964	50.7	84.7	39.6	52.9

* Wildenmann represents the data which were submitted by the political parties themselves to the Federal Constitutional Court in 1966.
** In the court hearings, the CSU disclaimed these figures and maintained that it had a similar distribution of income to the CDU.

Source: Wildenmann p.19.

headquarters, according to votes. Membership was disregarded as an essential factor of party organization. Small parties who failed to get parliamentary representation also failed to get funds. They did not play an acknowledged role in the political life of West German society. This practice accelerated the rise of the three major parties and hampered alternative and oppositional voices in politics.

The Party Legislation of 1967

The danger implicit in this system of state funding for parties to lose some of their political independence and their scope for a more fundamental opposition led the Federal Constitutional Court in 1966 to object to state financing of political parties. One year later, the party legislation which was envisaged in the Basic Law, was finally passed. The initiative to secure the independence of the parties between society, interest groups and state was prescribed in detail by the Constitutional Court. In the judgement supporting the ban on state finance, the court developed a combined system of public finance and finance by donations to boost the parties' own resources. Public funding was deemed permissible if it related to the key task of political parties, to participate in elections and to enter parliamentary candidates for elections. The Court found the formula of a reimbursement of campaign costs according to the electoral returns. When the Bundestag agreed on the concrete way of allocating such public funds, it arrived at a sum of DM 2.50 per voter for parties who could win at least 2.5% of the total vote. Contrary to the previous formula of state finance, small parties who did not gain parliamentary representation were included in the reimbursement programme. The concept that only the established parties made a valid contribution to political education or to the formulation of the political will in society was revoked. The relatively high hurdle of 2.5% however appears to have been an attempt by the Bundestag to find a new way of curtailing opposition parties and of securing the dominant position of the big three. Following a complaint by the right extremist NPD against that hurdle, the Federal Constitutional Court developed the format which is still valid today: those parties qualify for a reimbursement of campaign costs who poll at least 0.5% of the popular vote. Campaign costs may be paid in instalments towards forthcoming elections once a party has cleared the 0.5% minimum. The Lander passed similar legislation.[37] In 1974, the amount paid per voter was raised to DM 3.50. Reimbursement of campaign funds did not acquire the dominant place in party finance which direct state funding had in the early sixties. It tends to contribute between one third and one fifth of the total income of the major parties. For small parties these funds can be essential. When the NPD had some electoral successes and won 4.3% in the 1969 elections, 65% of its income consisted of reimbursed election expenses. In 1980, the Green Party failed to gain parliamentary seats. The 1.5% of the second vote however sufficed to receive DM 1.9 million. The earlier electoral successes in the lander had helped the party to fund its campaign despite a relatively small membership of about 16,000 and a virtual lack of donations.[38] Overall, the reimbursement of campaign costs has developed into a mainstay of party finance. In 1976, the total expenditure of all political parties was estimated at DM 354 million, their total income through reimbursements at DM 145 million.[39]

The party legislation of 1967 restrained the tendency of parties to turn themselves into state agencies. It also undertook to regulate the affiliation between organized interest and political parties by making the parties accountable in public for their incomes and the sources of large donations. Accounts have to be submitted annually to the President of the Bundestag and are subsequently published in the official Bulletin. Sources of income are more readily discernible than prior to this legislation (see Tables 1.3 and 1.4).

Some overall trends may be stated: membership is still the largest source of revenue for the SPD and contributes 46% of party income. About one third still comes from public funds, via reimbursement and payments to parliamentary parties. Despite several years in the senior government position and despite efforts by the SPD treasurer to win financial support from industry, such donations contribute little to party funds. The monetary assistance from the trade unions is somewhat more controversial. In 1969, the Research Institute of German Industry in Cologne found no evidence for "a hole in the trade union purse through which workers' pennies could have rolled into the SPD election fund".[40] In 1972, a CDU inspired survey of election expenses claimed that the SPD received 26 million in electoral aid from the German Trade Union Federation.[41]

The claims and counterclaims point to the controversial nature of the topic and to the size of election expenditure. Before looking at the impact of election expenses on the pattern of party finance, the places of CDU, CSU and FDP between state and interest sectors warrant some comments. After two decades as a party with members as an accessory rather than an essential element, the CDU in the seventies doubled its membership.[41a] Members now contribute over one third of party income (see Tables 1.3 and 1.4). Funding from industry has decreased. It amounted to 30% in 1969, to about 18% in 1978. As with the SPD, about one third of party funds are raised through public finance. Of the smaller parties, the CSU is the wealthiest. In 1978, it declared DM 43 million income and was twice as well endowed as the FDP. Although it is confined to one land, Bavaria, it has about 170,000 members, twice as many as the FDP which is organized throughout the Federal Republic. CSU members contribute only 15% of the party's income. At 34%, donations are high. But the level of credit reported, 25% or 11 million in 1978, suggests that the CSU has access to additional funds. Whether these are indeed mounting debts or donations disguised as credits is difficult to determine. The vague criteria of the 1967 party legislation make it impossible to probe into the origins of these funds and there is no obligation to disclose sources and terms of credits. For the FDP, an attempt to avoid mounting party debts is evident. In 1969, 44% of party income was raised through credits, in 1978 only 6%. The high level of credits may be due to the political limbo of the FDP when it changed coalition partners and aligned itself with the SPD. After several terms in office, party finances have normalized. Donations amount to one third, membership to one fifth of a generally modest party income. Among the small parties outside parliament, the DKP enjoys a conspicuously high level of donations which renders it quite independent from organizational or electoral successes. The Office for the Protection of the Constitution reported that those funds originate in the GDR.[42] The NPD in contrast has been unable to secure donations and had to rely on reimbursement funds. With the electoral demise, the party has become indebted to the state and appears financially and organizationally paralyzed.

Table 1.3: Party Income 1969-1978 (figures adjusted to the nearest million)

	Year	Membership dues	Funds via parliamentary candidates	Property	Party rallies and publications	Donations	Credits	Reimbursements of campaign funds	Others	TOTAL INCOME
S	1969	21	6	2	1	12	–	22	1	65
P	1974	44	9	4	1	8	–	29	1	96
D	1978	58	13	1	–	9	17	27	2	127
C	1969	8	4	1	1	15	5	16	–	50
D	1974	26	8	3	1	27	1	22	1	89
U	1978	45	13	2	1	22	13	25	1	122
C	1969	1	1	–	–	7	1	4	–	14
S	1974	3	1	0.5	0.5	8	2.5	11	–	26.5
U	1978	7	3	–	–	14	11	8	–	43
F	1969	1.5	0.5	–	–	4	7	1	2	16
D	1974	3	1	1	–	6	1	5	2	19
P	1978	4	1.5	0.5	–	7	1	4	3	21
D	1969	0.5	–	–	–	2	–	–	–	2.5
K	1974	2	–	–	2	7	–	–	–	11
P	1978	3.5	0.5	–	4	5.5	0.5	–	–	14
N	1969	0.5	0.5	–	–	1	0.5	4.5	–	7
P	1974	0.5	–	–	–	1	–	0.5	–	2
D	1978	0.3	–	–	–	0.5	–	–	–	0.8

Source: Rechenschaftsberichte for the relevant years. (Figures rounded to show major sources of party revenue).

Table 1.4: Sources of Party Income in %

	Year	Membership dues	Funds via parliamentary candidates	Property	Party rallies and publications	Donations	Credits	Reimbursements of campaign funds	Others
S	1969	32	9	4	2	18	–	33	2
P	1974	45	9	4	2	8	–	30	2
D	1978	46	10	1	–	7	13	21	2
C	1969	16	8	2	2	30	10	32	–
D	1974	30	9	3	1	30	1	25	1
U	1978	37	11	2	0.5	18	10	20	0.5
C	1969	7	7	–	–	50	7	29	–
S	1974	11	4	2.5	2.5	30	10	41	–
U	1978	15	6	0.5	0.5	34	25	19	–
F	1969	10	2	–	–	25	44	6	13
D	1974	16	5	5	–	32	5	26	11
P	1978	20	8	1	1	32	6	18	14
D	1969	20	–	–	–	80	–	–	–
K	1974	18	–	–	18	64	–	–	–
P	1978	27	4	–	24	42	2	–	1
N	1969	7	7	–	–	14	7	65	–
P	1974	25	–	–	–	50	–	25	–
D	1978	38	–	–	–	62	–	–	–

Source: Rechenschaftsberichte for the relevant years. Because of adjustments total may not add up to 100.

Party Finance and Political Control: Intentions and Failures

True to the spirit of the Basic Law, the 1967 party legislation attempted to go further than a mere publication of sources of income. It stipulated that parties should reveal the identity of donors. The Bundestag suggested originally that institutions which donated DM 200,000 or more and individuals who gave DM 20,000 or more should be named. The Federal Constitutional Court again intervened to tighten the law and abolish the distinction between institutions and individuals. It was agreed to name the sources for all donations over DM 20,000, to lay open all interest affiliations of political parties. Without penalty clauses attached to the legislation, the rule proved hard to enforce. Among CDU and CSU donors, anonymity was frequent. In 1972, the CDU for example received DM 2.5 million from 9 unnamed benefactors. In 1973, 25 anonymous donors contributed DM 5.8 million.[43] In 1976, the accounts still showed one such donor who gave DM 75,000.[44] As before, the largest donations were made by the Associations which were founded in the fifties. Their membership and economic affiliations do not have to be disclosed. Even when donations are named, such identification can be farcical. Weber quotes examples of large amounts being given to the SPD by a Mr. Mayer, to the CDU by a Mr. Düren. The suspicion that these names are intended to conceal the financial sources rather than reveal them cannot be easily dispelled.

Despite the efforts to make affiliations between parties and interest groups transparent, despite the financial aid from the state and the membership drives among the parties, donations have acquired a new significance in the functioning of the West German political parties which suggests a new dependence on such funds. Looking at the size of donation over the last decade or so, election years stand out as the pinnacles of fund raising. In 1957, the parties spent a total of 40 million Deutschmark on campaigning, in 1976 nearly nine times as much.[45] A documentation compiled by the SPD about the 1972 elections suggested that CDU/CSU expenses amounted to DM 55.6 million, compared with 13 million for the SPD.[46] The FDP admitted to 9.3 million expenditure.[47] The CDU survey which was mentioned earlier arrived at altogether more staggering figures and quoted 122 million mark public money spent during the election year 1972 through the information fund of the federal ministries.[48]

Table 1.5: Donations (in millions), 1968-1977

Year	SPD	CDU	FDP	CSU
1968	2.5	5.0	2.1	2.0
1970	6.3	13.4	4.0	5.6
1972	22.3	50.4	8.8	10.2
1974	7.5	26.4	5.5	8.1
1976	19.6	53.7	14.3	12.6
1977	6.2	24.9	6.8	6.7

Source: Die Zeit 17, 1979.

Whichever set of figures reflects the true state of affairs, elections costs have long outstripped the regular sources of income for all parties. Tables 1.3 and 1.4 showed already the need to borrow money and accumulate debts. All parties record deficits. Yet efforts to agree a code of practice and limit election expenditure have repeatedly failed. German electioneering is heavily based on advertising, printed information and posters.[49] The scramble for voters tends to overrule caution or thirftiness. Two weeks before the election date in 1976, for example, the SPD found that its slogan "continue to work for a model Germany" lacked sparkle. In a society which had to digest the shock of the oil crisis, which still suffered unemployment and was teeming with fears that the economy might slow down, the message about achievements and progress sounded somewhat hollow. Regardless of expenses, the SPD revised the campaign and switched to the catch-all slogan "security for all".[50] In 1980, CDU and CSU fought a duplicated campaign since the two party machineries and their electoral staff could not work out a joint formula of how to run the campaign and how to present their candidate, Franz Joseph Strauss.[51] The cost of the two-pronged onslaught may never be laid open.

In 1983, the CDU launched a dual campaign. The first part was designed to recommend the Chancellor as a competent leader; the second part to elicit hopes of economic recovery with the slogan "Vote the Upswing-CDU". Oblivious of expenses, all election materials and posters were replaced to include the new theme. Following the 1976 elections, the SPD was accused of drawing on official resources and government facilities for its election campaigns.[53] In 1980, Schmidt again launched his campaign from the

Chancellory rather than from the party headquarters. The 1980 elections were preceded by a financial scandal involving the CDU.[54] A post-box company in Liechtenstein had channeled funds into the party, avoiding the strictures of the party legislation and also income tax. When the plot was detected, the chairman of the Federation of German Industry, Fasolt, had to resign. The groping for money seems all the more surprising as West German political parties are well off in international comparison. They spend more than parties elsewhere, and they receive more contributions from public funds than their counterparts in Western democracies.[55] Yet, in their own perception, West German parties have been starved of funds. In the mid-sixties, so called Political Foundations were created to ease the burden of the parties and help with educational tasks. In 1981, these foundations received 79 million Deutschmark from public funds compared with 9 million in 1968.[56] Taking all levels of public funding of political parties and their foundations together, 713 million Deutschmark were paid out between 1977 and 1980, a total of 615 million in the first part of the seventies. This is considerably more than American or British political parties receive from the state. Nevertheless, West German established parties found that the available funding would not cover the expenses for their self-assigned social and political tasks and their election styles. Repeated attempts at restricting campaign costs have failed, not least because all parties have access to additional funding and clandestine donations. When the SPD' treasurer declared the only new source of finance which was discovered in recent years was stringent economy,[57] he was not altogether frank. A donation scandal involving the Flick concern and all Bundestag parties has come to light in 1981. Flick used direct hand-outs to individual politicians and party treasurers to enlist the help of the relevant ministers in a business deal, reinvesting profits from a sale of shares without paying taxes.[58] As we had seen earlier, irregularities about party finance had come to light before the Flick case blew up. In May 1983, 1700 proceedings had been opened on suspicion of tax fraud. They involved prominent politicians like Count Lambsdorff, the Economics Minister, Walther Leisler Kiep, the CDU treasurer, Alfred Nau, the former SPD treasurer. The CDU involvement in these irregularities is all the more surprising as the liaison between industry and party has been well established and if anything, intensified during the period in opposition. Falling profits and the lack of tax incentives for donors may render it more difficult to raise the huge amounts which seem to be required for party finance and election costs. Alongside the CDU, an economic pressure group was set up in 1972 to promote aims shared by industry and party, in particular the social market economy. The <u>Wirtschaftsrat der CDU e.V</u> counts some of the largest West German enterprises among its members and aligns them with the party.59 The CSU has a similar group to back up the party. Although the <u>Wirtschaftsrat</u> is not formally part of the CDU organization, its purpose is to assist the party financially or with supportive campaigns during elections. Prominent party members such as Leisler Kiep or Dregger belong to the executives of party and <u>Wirtschaftsrat</u> and act as link-men between party and industry.

On the SPD side, the link with the trade union sector lacks such definite contours. The concern of the party to influence the unions during the fifties has given way since the Great Coalition and the acceptance of the Emergency Legislation by the SPD to a concern of trade unionists that the party might slide too far to the centre and detach itself from trade union and working class interests.60 The means to remedy this situation, however, lack force. The working party for matters of employment, <u>Arbeitsgemeinschaft für Arbeitnehmerfragen</u>, within the SPD is intended to voice the trade union standpoint. Today it functions as one of the various groups within the party, alongside the subsection for women, that for the self employed or the Young Socialists. In terms of financial resources or political influence, the trade union foothold within the party lacks significance. It can hardly be compared with the <u>Wirtschaftsrat</u>. It rather resembles the Social Committees (<u>Sozialausschüsse</u>) within the CDU, the workers' wings which have been retained from a more radical past but which have lost much of their impact on CDU policies.

The problems encountered by the SPD to replenish its party funds from donations were apparent in the 1981 accounts. It reported 8.2 million Deutschmark in donations compared with 10.5 million for the FDP, 8.3 million for the CSU and 20.9 million for the CDU.61

Despite these discrepancies in party funding, all four joined forces in an attempt to revise the restrictions imposed by the 1967 party legislation on funding and tax concessions for donations. In

1979, a move to provide tax incentives for political donations was halted by the Constitutional Court. In 1982, an investigative commission on party finance was set up under the chairmanship of the Federal President to explore new avenues for party finance.[62] A report with detailed recommendations was published on April 18, 1983. For the first time since the foundation of the Federal Republic had proposals on party finance not originated from the Constitutional Court but from a body of social scientists and lawyers from all party camps. Although it is yet unclear whether the Bundestag will proceed to change the law on party finance in the light of the recommendations and whether the Constitutional Court would uphold such changes, the report received approval from all parties but the Greens. The dual demands of improved tax concessions and improved state funding have been incorporated together with some provisions to grant equal opportunities for all political parties. The per-capita quota for election expenses is to be raised to DM 5. Donations should be tax deductible up to 5% of the donor's income - for large corporations, this could amount to millions. Equality between parties, in particular those who are less closely aligned with affluent donors, is to be ensured in two ways: the President of the Bundestag is to distribute public funds to all parties who poll 0.5% or more. Parties who have little access to private funds are expected to receive more state funding than their richer rivals. The second device concerns the voters: it is proposed to introduce a third vote to give each member of the electorate the chance to indicate which party should benefit from "his" DM 5. This <u>Buergerbonus</u> will then be shared out by the President of the Bundestag in an equitable manner.

Detailed discussions on changes or party finance are still under way. The report by the Commission on Party Finance, however, incorporates some important principles which have come to dominate political thinking on party finance in West Germany. The report presumes that as a major source of finance parties should rely on membership and membership contributions.

It also accepts that West German political parties cannot perform their tasks without considerable support through donations and through state funding. Transfers of state funds from political foundations to parties or from parliamentary representatives to party offices shall no longer be permitted. Questions of too much dependence on state support or on industrial - or business interests were not even raised. They were blotted out by the unison search for more funds. This has become a major headache for all parties, in particular for the SPD. The path of scaling down the degree of party expenditure, the costliness of party organizations, the sumptuous style of electioneering has been abandoned in favour of more state funds, more donations and easier access to both, to secure the self-assigned place of political parties in West Germany society.

The issue of party finance touches upon a raw nerve in the party system. The established parties continue to devise means and legislation to secure their dominant position. Despite the all too effective 5% hurdle, despite the advantages incurred by state contributions to the parties, despite the virtually unrivalled place of CDU, CSU, FDP and SPD, the parties hustle to thwart competition. Initiatives for political diversity tend to come from the Constitutional Court. In a recent judgement, the court ruled that an independent candidate should also be entitled to a reimbursement of campaign costs, provided he polls 10% in his constituency. Against the tradition of party monopoly above the local level, the Bundestag had to pass corresponding legislation in 1979.[63] The current re-thinking of party finance will not challenge the party monopoly. It is geared to grant the status of political parties as state-funded semi-official bodies, yet with easier access to other funds.

The commitment of political parties to their members, to their social basis seems less relevant if the organizational and political survival of a party is assured in other ways. In terms of party finance, West German political parties are on their way to intensify interest affiliation and their affiliation to the state.

WHO SPEAKS FOR THE PEOPLE? PARTIES AND SOCIETY IN PARLIAMENT

Interest groups were created in Germany as informal and powerful channels of influence on administration and government when political channels through parties and parliament were uncertain. Remnants of this type of influence have survived from Imperial Germany to this day. Overall, interest groups have been accepted as legitimate voices of society and, more important still, their access to government offices and parliamentary representatives has increasingly been monitored.[64] Cooperation between legislators and organized interest has become the rule, coercion and clandestine persuasion the frowned-upon exception. The seventies saw a drawn out debate about Interest Group Legislation, intended to scrutinize the democratic commitment and the political affiliations of all interest groups. It still lacks an agreed solution.[65] Cooperation with interest groups in policy making, corporatism, has become a core element of contemporary government,[66] but the issue of interest group representation still has a political sting to it in the Federal Republic. The moves towards special legislation sparked off a controversy whether perhaps the sole purpose of such legislation was to control the political muscle of the trade unions.[67] The accusation of trade union infiltration or even dominance in politics and in particular in parliament has become a well-tried cliché.[68] While the political right warns about a trade-union state, the left compiles evidence about a stranglehold of the employers and their interest organizations on all areas of legislation and policy formulation in West Germany.[69]

Fears of too much interest group influence have permeated publications on the subject from the start.[70] Some legislative processes have been studied in detail to determine the interaction of government, administration, parties and interest groups.[71] Our objectives in this section are altogether more modest: to survey the composition of parliamentary parties and compare interest affiliations across the party lines. If such affiliations can be shown, they would reflect upon the overall position in society of those political parties which are represented in the Bundestag. The social support and breadth of the people's party will be further analysed. The question of political muscle of interest sectors, of their influence on legislation and policy making cannot be attempted in our context. Here, further research seems to be needed if interest affiliation were to be evaluated beyond the cross-fire of partisan views.

The complexity of legislative decisions, the need for specialist legal expertise and for administrative experience have, in any case, shifted the centre of legislation from parliament and its members to the civil service and to the permanent staff in the relevant ministries.[72] Elected party representatives help to formulate and monitor legislation, they are seldom perpetrators of it. Detailed scripting which defines the scope of any new law, or amendment has become the responsibility of civil servants in the appropriate departments. This process also modifies a possible influence of interest representation and points to a new political development: the inroads of the civil service into the policy making areas of the political parties.

Parliament and Interest Groups
The openings for interest groups through political parties into parliament rest on the dual electoral system. The combination of proportional representation and majority voting in West Germany allows each party to select half its prospective candidates for direct election and the other half for nomination through party lists. List places are shared out according to the percentage of the total vote obtained by each party. Places on these lists are numbered and chances of winning a seat via the party list decrease the lower down a candidate's name has been put. For candidates who come into party politics from the outside, from the interest sectors for instance, it has been virtually impossible to gain nomination as a party candidate for a direct seat. Here, years of dedicated party work have been the prerequisite.[73] The land lists have been more accessible for such candidates. The institution of land lists bestows significant powers upon party organizations in selecting the political elite. Within the parties, influence on the composition of party lists tend to come from the top. Recommendations from top level functionaries seem to be virtually binding, branch- and district organization have little say. The circle of people who are actively involved in selecting candidates for parliamentary office in the Federal Republic has been very small.[74] For 1969, Kaack calculated that about 3% of the estimated 1.2 million party members at the time had some say in the selection procedure, i.e. attended selection meetings. This means that 0.1% of the electorate determined who would stand for parliament.[75] The parties' own reports about membership involvement in the seventies suggest that the circle has remained as small as ten years earlier with 50,000 people or 0.1% of the electorate deciding who would stand for parliamentary office.

In theory, outsiders and interest spokesmen could be placed on a land list on the recommendation of the regional party leadership. This seems to have been standard practice for CDU and CSU in the

Parties and Society

fifties and sixties.[76] Spokesmen of interest groups or party affiliated business sectors could serve a spell in their party articulating their concerns in parliament and the relevant committees. Although the West German system of nominations allows for this to happen, it appears that demand had never been buoyant. In the fifties, the chairman of the Federation of German Industry appealed for volunteers from industry and business to stand for election. At that time, chances to enter the Bundestag via a CDU land list were relatively high. Even then, prospective candidates from the interest sectors were hard to find. In the meantime, the political map has become tighter. In the 1980 elections, only 19 of the 248 constituencies changed colour, the remainder kept their party affiliation.[77] Direct candidates are now normally guaranteed a place near the top of the land list. This list itself has become more dependent on party commitment than on other influences. In other words, outsider representation has become more difficult although the dual electoral system gives the regional parties some leeway in honouring interest affiliations.

The involvement of parliamentary delegates with trade union or business affiliations in the Bundestag makes the overlap of parties and interest sectors more concrete. Trade union penetration has been documented more widely and discussed more controversially than other interest areas, and we shall open our brief survey by looking at the trade union sector.

Contrary to Britain, the German Trade Union Federation DGB is party-politically neutral. In practical terms this means that it does not sponsor parliamentary candidates. While the British Labour Party retains a close link with the trade union movement and recruits about half its deputies through the unions, SPD delegates rise through the party organization. Nevertheless, membership in unions is impressive. Overall, West German trade unions organize 38% of the work force. In 1981, 7.9 millions were members of DGB affiliated unions, a further 1.2 millions belonged to the white collar or civil service organizations. In the Bundestag, the proportion of trade union membership has risen steadily from 28% in 1949 to 63% in 1976.

Unionisation is most frequent among SPD delegates. In 1977, 222 of the 224 members of parliament or 99.1% belonged to a trade union.[78] 96 of the 254 CDU delegates - or 37.8% - were members of a trade union. Union membership is least common within the

41

Table 1.6: Trade Union Members in the Bundestag, 1949-1983

	1949	1953	1957	1961	1965	1969	1972	1976	1980	1983
No. of deputies	420	506	519	521	518	518	518	518	519	520
Members of unions	115	194	202	223	242	286	318	328	322	311
%	28	38	39	43	47	52	61	63	62	60

Source: Gewerkschaftliche Monatshefte 7, 1983 p.450.

FDP where 22.5% or 9 of the forty parliamentarians belonged to a trade union. Before jumping to the conclusion that the unions exercise control in the West German parliament and in the SPD in particular, the somewhat amorphous quantity "unions" has to be scrutinized and the significance of membership evaluated.

In the statistical data on membership, the DGB unions, the employees union DAG, the professional organizations for civil servants DBB, and the Police union GDP, journalists (DJV) as well as the Christian unions (CGB) appear under the same heading. In terms of possible political influence and in terms of close affiliation with particular parliamentary parties, these groups are less evenly aligned.

Table 1.7: Trade Unionists in the 8th German Bundestag (date 10.5.1977)

Trade Union	CDU/CSU (254)	%	SPD (224)	%	FDP (40)	%	Total (518)	%
DGB	22	8.7	209	93.3	5	12.5	236	45.6
DAG	7	2.7	1	0.4	-	-	8	1.5
GdP	-	-	2	0.8	-	-	2	0.4
CGB	17	6.7	-	-	-	-	17	3.3
DBB	42	16.7	4	1.8	3	7.5	49	9.5
DJV	8	3.1	6	2.7	1	2.5	15	2.9
Total	96	37.8	222	99.1	9	22.5	327	63.1

Source: Z Parl 1977 p.186.

Since 1972, increases in union membership have been due to gains by the Christian unions and the Civil Service Union who are predominantly CDU/CSU affiliated. In 1949, membership in unions other than the DBG unions was 2% among parliamentary delegates; it has since risen to around 17%.[79]

The shift in trade union membership to the white collar and civil service sectors is also evident among the DGB membership itself. In 1977, 145 of the 236 DGB union members in parliament belonged to a union for civil service employees. The Union of Public Service, Transport and Traffic ÖTV is the largest DGB union in parliament, followed by the Union for Education and Science, GEW. Representation in the Bundestag bears no correlation to overall union membership. The largest DGB union, the metal workers union IG Metall had in 1977 over 2.5 million members and only 35 members in parliament, 6 of them in the CDU/CSU. The Union of Education and Science whose members tend to be civil servants in the West German educational system, had just over 130,000 members and also 35 representatives in the Bundestag, 32 of them in the SPD. Apart from the Leather Union, all DGB affiliated unions have some members as deputies in parliament. There is, however, no institutionalized link between trade union parliamentarians which could mould them into a pressure group for trade union concerns. To equate union membership with a predominance of union objectives over party objectives overstates its possible impact. For the SPD, union membership has become a hallmark of progressive political commitment and also a device to secure re-nomination within the party.[80] Membership alone signifies at best an orientation, not a policy priority. Jürgen Weber suggested to disregard membership and focus on those parliamentary delegates who acted as officials in their interestgroups or unions before they were elected. While overall membership in unions has been increasing, the number of functionaries in parliament has declined. The Bundestag which was elected in 1972 had the highest number of union members and the lowest number of union functionaries among them.[81]

Looking at former union officials as potential spokesmen for union interest in parliament, Weber arrives at 50, or 20.7% in the SPD parliamentary party 1972-1976.[82] Taking all union representation, 22% of the SPD parliamentary party of that period could be seen as union affiliated. Figures for the CDU were much lower. DGB affiliated unions accounted for 2.2%, other unions i.e. mainly white collar and civil service associations for 11.5%. Weber also included data for interest affiliation with industry and business. While these sectors were minute with 1.2% or 0.8% for the SPD, they contributed significantly to the CDU/CSU parliamentary party. Officials of industrial interest groups constituted 9%, of agricultural-, artisan-, or trade-associations 12.4% of the CDU/CSU parliamentary party.

The comparison with the SPD-union affiliation is revealing. In numerical terms, both parties were equally close to their specific interest sectors: 50 DGB unionists in the SPD corresponded with 50 industrialists and employers in the CDU/CSU. Because of the strong representation of the civil service unions in the CDU/CSU, its interest affiliation measured by the number of parliamentarian functionaries was higher than in the SPD, 35.9% (84) CDU/CSU delegates as compared with 25.2% (61) SPD delegates were officials of their professional associations in the 7th German Bundestag. For the FDP, matters were more one-sided. It had an interest penetration of 33.3% or 14 members of parliament, all of whom were affiliated to the industrial and business sectors. This underlines the impact of interest groups on the political role of the FDP.

Within parliament, the composition of the committees which formulate legislative proposals can show how interest spokesmen pursue the areas of their immediate concern. The Committee for Food, Agriculture and Forestry drew in 1976 44.6% of its members from agricultural interest groups.[83] Trade Unionists were represented in the Committee for Labour and Social Order. The Economic Committee was well balanced: twenty six per cent of its members were affiliated to employees organizations, 33% to industrial and business associations.

Civil Servants in Parliament

The incomplete transition of the West German parties to *Volksparteien* and their political place alongside interest groups is borne out by parliamentary representation. Weber's comparisons suggest that the links are very similar for the two major parties. Warnings against the "trade union state" appear unfounded. Trade union representation itself showed a transition towards the civil service and white collar sector. Parliamentary representation also points to the tendency among West German parties to become semi-official bodies of the state.

The civil service expanded rapidly into parlia-

Parties and Society

mentary representation, and into the political parties and their office holders. As Table 1.8 shows, the social structure of the population and the social composition of the federal parliament are far apart. In the Bundestag - and in the land parliaments - civil servants, the self-employed, lawyers, doctors, journalists, tend to dominate. Working people seem hardly represented.

Table 1.8: The Occupational Structure of the Bundestag, 1972-1980

Occupation	Working Population 1972 %	Parliamentary Representation 1972 %	Parliamentary Representation 1976 %	Parliamentary Representation 1980 %
Self-employed	15.0	19.3	11.0	21.6
Civil servants	7.7	37.5	44.0	30.2
White collar employees	32.0	26.3	25.5 [1]	54.4 [2]
Workers	45.3	1.4	2.0	1.0
Others	-	15.3 [3]	-	1.2

1. 13% employees of parties, trade unions and interest groups.
2. includes 26.2% "professional politicians" affiliated to parties; also 11.6% employees of trade unions and interest groups.
3. listed in parliamentary handbook for their original occupation which no longer characterises their position, e.g. Georg Leber - bricklayer.

Source: Parteiendemokratie, p.163; Thayssen, Z Parl., 1977 p.183. For 1980: Z Parl 2, 1981 p. 185 and 192.

There is little difference between the three parties regarding the influx of civil servants into parliament.

The "Verbeamtung" - the take over by civil servants[84] - has several possible reasons. The specialised nature of legislative work requires, it could be argued, a comparatively high level of education. Members of parliament are much better educated than the population as a whole. Twenty per cent as compared with 74% of West Germans in 1976 had

45

secondary modern school education only. Seventy per cent of the Bundestags delegates had completed Abitur, the German 'A' level equivalent, compared with 6% of the general population.[85]

Well over half the members of parliament had obtained university degrees (295 in 1979). Most degrees, about 50%, were in law.[86] The educational background of parliamentarians is only one possible reason why the number of civil servants in parliament increased. Perhaps most significant are the specific privileges which allow civil servants to become politically active.

The notion of an above party state had prevented civil servants from getting involved in political affairs. It may have served as a breeding ground of anti-democratic attitudes. The Federal Republic, acting upon a lesson taught by history, permitted its civil servants and public employees to join parties and engage in politics. A number of civil servant positions in government, in the educational system, in the broader field of administration on the federal and the land levels, are directly dependent on the 'party book'. Party membership for civil servants and party political activity has the tangible edge of appointments, advancements, and career interests. The party functionaries, who are instrumental in nominating parliamentary candidates, are often themselves recruited from the civil service. A certain reproduction of the weight of the civil service in the party organization appears to take place. Of at least equal importance are the favourable conditions which civil servants enjoy for their political activities. Party political commitment is facilitated by adjusted working hours, often a proximity between work and party issues. Civil servants who take on full-time party offices and become, for example, parliamentary delegates, are entitled to return to their employment without loss of status, income, or pension rights. Until a recent ruling of the Constitutional Court, civil servants were even entitled to draw half their salary in addition to the remuneration for their political or parliamentary work. Similar advantages are not available to other occupational groups. Those who can only pursue party work in their spare time and face the insecurity of losing their jobs, of curtailing their pension rights and forfeiting claims to their posts, have little chance of competing efficiently with civil servants who risk nothing by plunging into party politics. The trend towards a parliament of civil servants reflects these advantages and is unlikely to be reversed.[87]

FOOTNOTES

1. Dietrich Staritz, Sozialismus in einem halben Lande, Zur Programmatik und Politik der KPD: SED in der Phase der antifaschistisch-demokratischen Umwälzung in der DDR, Berlin (Wagenbach), 1976.
2. Theo Pirker, Die SPD nach Hitler, München 1965. Useful overview in Franz Osterroth and Dieter Schuster (eds), Chronik der deutschen Sozialdemokratie, Bonn (Dietz), 1980.
3. A good discussion of Schumacher's influence and policies in W.E. Paterson, The SPD and European Integration, Lexington Books, 1974.
4. See Lothar Albertini, Politischer Liberalismus in der Bundesrepublik Deutschland, Göttingen (Vandenhoeck & Ruprecht) 1980; Heino Kaack, Die F.D.P. Grundriss und Materialien zu Geschichte, Struktur und Programmatik, Meisenheim (Hain) 1979; dto "The FDP in the German Party System", in K.H. Cerny (ed), Germany at the Polls, Washington 1978, pp.77-110.
5. Geoffrey Pridham, Christian Democracy in Western Germany, Croom Helm 1977; Helmut Pütz, Die CDU, Düsseldorf (Droste) 1978; Also Alf Mintzel, Die Geschichte der CSU, Opladen (Westdt. Verlag) 1977; Günther Müchler, CDU:CSU, Das schwierige Bündnis, Munich (Vögel) 1976.
6. Richard Stöss and Horst Schmollinger, "Die soziale Basis der Parteien I" in Prokla 25, 1976 p.21 and p.27. Also Peter Hoschka and Herman Schunk, "Regional Stability of Voting Behaviour" in: Max Kaase and Klaus von Beyme (eds), Elections and Parties. German Studies III, Sage 1978, p.33.
7. For an extensive survey see Kurt P. Tauber, Beyond Eagle and Swastika, Middleton 1967, vol. I.
8. See Kaack, Geschichte und Struktur, ibid. also Timothy Tilton, Nazism, Neonazism and the Peasantry, Indiana Univ. Press, 1975.
9. Bernard Schäfer, "Grundzüge des sozialen Wandels in der Bundesrepublik" in Gegenwartskunde Sonderheft 1979, p.15.
10. In detail: Eugen Lemberg and Friedrich Edding (eds) Die Vertriebenen in Westdeutschland. Ihre Eingliederung und ihr Einfluss, Kiel (Hirt) 1959 esp. vol.I.
11. Wolfgang Jacobmeyer, "Die Niederlage 1945" in Westdeutschlands Weg zur Bundesrepublik, Munich

(Beck) 1976 p.19.
12. Dietrich Hilger, "Die 'mobilisierte' Gesellschaft", in Richard Löwenthal and Hans-Peter Schwarz (eds), Die Zweite Republik, Stuttgart (Seewald) 1974, p.105.
13. Infas Report: Parteisoziologische Untersuchungen 1977. Zusammenfassung der Ergebnisse, Bonn-Bad Godesberg February 1978 no.140-8678, p.4 (repro).
14. Hans See, "Strukturwandel und Ideologieprobleme der SPD - eine empirische Studie" in Wolf-Dieter Narr (ed) Auf dem Wege zum Einparteienstaat, Opladen (Westdt. Verlag) 1977, p.98.
15. Infas Report ibid.
16. The membership fluctuations of the early years have yet to be studied in detail.
17. Stöss and Schmollinger, ibid. p.25 argue that the CDU became the major party within a Bürgerblock alliance and increased its share of this Bürgerblock from 66.1% in 1949 to 83.3% in 1965.
18. Hoschka and Schunk, ibid. p.37 show the relative stagnation of the CDU since 1953, i.e. a decline in its strongholds and some growth in so called diaspora regions. The SPD enjoyed consistent electoral gains during the fifties and sixties.
19. The SPD now calls itself an Arbeitnehmerpartei, a party for the salaried and waged, see Sozialdemokrat Magazin 4, April 1978, p.9.
20. Kaack, Geschichte und Struktur ibid. p.346 f. Also Infas survey of 1976 in Elections and Parties ibid., p.172.
21. See Gerald Braunthal, The Federation of German Industry in Politics, Cornell University Press 1965.
22. Paul Ackermann, Der Bauernverband im politischen Kräftespiel der Bundesrepublik, Tübingen (Mohr) 1970, pp.62-84.
23. Erich Andrlik, "The Farmers and the State: Agricultural Interests in West German Politics" in West European Politics 4, Jan. 1981, pp.104-119.
24. Gabriel Almond, The Politics of German Business. Research Memorandum. The Rand Corporation RM 15 06 RC, 20 June 1955.
25. Walter Wellner, Parteienfinanzierung, Munich (Bayrische Landeszentrale für politische Bildung) 1973, p.48.
26. Ossip K. Flechtheim (ed) Die Parteien in der Bundesrepublik Deutschland, Hamburg (Hoffmann & Campe) 1973, p.546.
27. Wellner ibid., also Flechtheim (ed) Dokumente zur parteipolitischen Entwicklung vol.

VIII, Berlin (Dokumenten Verlag), 1970.
  28. Rudolf Wildenmann, Gutachten zur Frage der Subventionierung politischer Parteien aus öffentlichen Mitteln, Meisenneim (Hain) 1968, p.13.
  29. Der Spiegel 45, 1959, pp.22 ff.
  30. Flechtheim, Dokumente VIII, ibid., p.532.
  31. Braunthal, "Der Bundesverband der deutschen Industrie" in: Heinz Josef Varain (ed) Interessenverbände in Deutschland, Köln (Kiepenheuer) 1973, p.279.
  32. Uwe Schleth, Parteifinanzen. Eine Studie über Kosten und Finanzierung der Parteitätigkeit, Meisenheim (Hain) 1973.
  33. Extensive documentation in Flechtheim, Dokumente VIII, ibid., pp.1-249.
  34. Flechtheim, Parteien ibid., pp.549-550
  35. Rolf Zundel, "Hochfahrend auf dem Schuldenberg" in Die Zeit 17, 20.4.1979, p.9 gives the following data:
  1949: DM 348,000   1977: DM 35 million
  1967: DM 4.3 million   1978: DM 39.3 million
  1976: DM 30.6 million   1979: DM 41.6 million
  36. Schleth, ibid. p.209.
  37. Wichard Woyke and Udo Steffens, Stichwort Wahlen, Leverkusen (Leske) 1980, p.36 f.
  38. Letter to the author dated 4.9.1980.
  39. Jochen Lorek, "Auch künftig knapp bei Kasse", Vorwärts 2.8.1979, p.5.
  40. Der Spiegel 30, 1969, p.39.
  41. Dialog no.1, 1969, p.39.
  41a. See Michael Pinto-Duschinsky, British Political Finance 1830-1980. American Enterprise Institute 1982; also The Times 26.2.82 p.9.
  42. Betrifft Verfassungsschutz 1979, Bonn 1980 (ed. Bundesministerium des Inneren) p.65.
  43. Jürgen Weber, Interessengruppen im politischen System der Bundesrepublik Deutschland, Stuttgart (Kohlhammer) 1977, p.313.
  44. Frankfurter Allgemeine Zeitung 29.11.1977.
  45. Zundel ibid.
  46. Dokumentation über die Werbekampagnen im Bundestagswahlkampf 1972, ed. Parteivorstand der Sozialdemokratischen Partei, Bonn, 1973.
  47. Bericht des. F.D.P. Präsidiums über die endgültigen Wahlkampfaufwendungen, Bonn, 1973.
  48. Dialog, ibid.
  49. Schleth ibid., p.61 compares patterns of election expenses in West Germany and the USA: broadcasting 18% (USA) 37%) advertisements 16%, printed matter 25%, posters 11% (USA 1%), rallies 13%, additional personnell 3%, films 8%, surveys 2%

(USA 12%) transport of voters nil (USA 12%).

50. The disappointing election results in 1976 generated a discussion paper by Börner and Koschnik on the problems of party organization and the weaknesses of the campaign. The authors also suggested that a detailed survey of the party should be commissioned; the SPD ordered two such surveys, Infas and Infratest, see chapters 2 and 3.

51. Interview with Herrn Esser, Referat Organisation bei der Bundesgeschäftsstelle der CDU, Bonn 24.4.1980.

52. Interview with Herrn Hartwig, Referat Öffentlichkeitsarbeit Bundesgeschäftsstelle der CDU, 16.3.1983.

53. See the ruling of the Federal Constitutional Court in March 1977; Karl Heinz Nassmacher, "Öffentliche Rechenschaft und Parteienfinanzierung" in Aus Politik und Zeitgeschichte 14-15, 1982, pp. 3-18.

54. e.g. "Partei-Spenden, 'Der unordentliche Weg'" in Der Spiegel 8, 1978 pp52-57; "Das ist ein einziger Skandal" Spiegel Report über das Finanzgebaren von Parteien und Parlamentariern", in Der Spiegel 27, 1978 pp.26-32; Arthur B. Gunlicks, "Campaign and Party Finance at the State Level in Germany" in Comparative Politics 12, 1980, no.2, pp. 211-223; "Political party finance. Why big money is a mixed blessing" in The Times 26.2.1982, p.9.

55. Nassmacher ibid. p.14.

56. Der Spiegel 6, 1983; also Nassmacher ibid. p.6.

57. Vorwärts 18.12.1980.

58. Der Spiegel 4, 1983, pp.17 ff.

59. Flechtheim, Dokumente IV, pp.183-185; also Dittberner, "Der Wirtschaftsrat der CDU e.V." in Dittberner/Ebbighausen (eds.), Parteiensystem in der Legitimationskrise, Opladen (Westdt. Verlag), 1973, pp.200-228.

60. Horst Schmollinger, "Gewerkschafter in der SPD" in Dittberner/Ebbighausen ibid., pp.229-276.

61. Der Spiegel 2, 1983, p.70.

62. See Das Parlament No.20/21, 21. and 28.5.1983: Zur Neuordnung der Parteienfinanzierung, p.13. Also: Bericht der Kommission zur Neuordnung der Parteienfinanzierung, Bonn, 1983.

63. Harald Siebert, "Neuere Entwicklungen in der Parteienfinanzierung" in Kaack/Roth, Handbuch des deutschen Parteiensystems I, Opladen (Leske & Budrich), 1980, pp.190-191. Also: Hartmut Klatt, "Wahlkampffuehrung und Wahlkampfkostenbegrenzung - Moeglichkeiten und Grenzen des Wahlkampfabkommens

1980", in Z Parl 1, 1981, pp.21 ff.
64. See Frank Pilz, Einführung in das politische System, Munich (Beck) 1977, p.51 and pp.223 ff.
65. Gerhard Lehmbruch, "Wandlungen der Interessenpolitik im liberalen Korporatismus" in Ulrich von Alemann (ed.), Verbände und Staat. Vom Pluralismus zum Korporatismus, Opladen (Westdt. Verlag), pp.50 ff.
66. A discussion of corporatist tendencies in European societies in Reginald Harrison, Pluralism and Corporatism. The political evolution of modern democracies, Allen & Unwin 1980.
67. Documentation in Verbände und Staat, ibid. pp.214 ff.
68. e.g. Klaus von Beyme, "Der 'Gewerkschaftsstaat' - eine neue Form der 'gemischten Verfassung'?" in Peter Haungs (ed.) Res Publica. Studien zum Verfassungswesen. Festschrift für Dolf Sternberger, Munich (Fink), 1977, pp.22-36.
69. e.g. Walter Simon, Macht und Herrschaft der Unternehmerverbände, BDI, BDA und DIHT, Cologne (Pahl Rugenstein), 1976, pp.176 ff.
70. After the outcry in the fifties about interest group power e.g. Breitling, -Herrschaft der Verbände, 1955, studies have become more analytical. Klaus Beyme, Interessengruppen in der Demokratie, Munich, 1974; Wolfgang Rudzio, Die organisierte Demokratie. Parteien und Verbände in der Bundesrepublik, Stuttgart, 1977.
71. Ackermann, Der Bauernverband, ibid. Braunthal, The Federation of German Industry, ibid.
72. Examples in Parteiendemokratie. Wahlen und Parteien in der Bundesrepublik Deutschland. Materialienband by Falk Esche et.al. (eds.), Hamburg (Hoffmann & Campe), 1978, pp.168-174.
73. Zeuner, Innerparteiliche Demokratie, Berlin (Colloquium), 1970, p.73.
74. Michael T. Greven, Parteien und politische Herrschaft Meisenheim (Hain), 1977, p.295.
75. Heino Kaack, Wahlkreisgeographie und Kandidatenauslese. Regionale Stimmenverteilung, Chancen der Kandidaten und Ausleseverfahren, dargestellt am Beispiel der Bundestagswahl 1965, Opladen (Westdt. Verlag), 1969, p.597. Data for 1980, own calculations.
76. In detail: Heinrich Josef Schröder, Die Kandidatenaufstellung und das Verhältnis des Kandidaten zu seiner Partei in Deutschland und Frankreich, Berlin (Duncker & Humblodt), 1971, pp. 97-116 and 151 ff.

77. Eva Kolinsky, "Elections and Political Change in West Germany" in Treffpunkt June 1981, pp.17-22.
78. Emil Müller, "Vertreter von Arbeitnehmerorganisationen im Deutschen Bundestag" in Z Parl, 2, 1977, p.186.
79. Gegenwartskunde, ibid. p.75. Also Gewerkschaftliche Monatshefte, 7, 1983, p.450 ff.
80. Klaus von Beyme, "The Changing Relations between Trade Unions and the Social Democratic Party in West Germany", in Government and Opposition Special Issue Trade Unions and Political Parties, Autumn 1978.
81. Kurt Hirche, Gewerkschafter im 7. Bundestag" in Gewerkschaftliche Monatshefte, 2, 1973, p.83.
82. Jürgen Weber ibid., p.282. Also Z Parl 4, 1982, p.437.
83. Weber, ibid., p.269.
84. Adalbert Hess, "Statistische Daten und Trends zur Verbeamtung der Parlamente in Bund und Ländern", in Z Parl 1, 1976. The same trend is apparent in Dietrich Herzog, Politische Karrieren. Selektion und Professionalisierung politischer Führungsgruppen, Opladen (Westdt. Verlag) 1975, pp. 94 ff.
85. Uwe Anderson, Dieter Grosser and Richard Woyke, Wahl 1976. Parteien und Wähler. Politische Entwicklung. Probleme nach der Wahl, Opladen (Leske), 1976, p.80.
86. Hartmut Klatt, "Das Sozialprofil des Deutschen Bundestages 1949-1976" in Gegenwartskunde, ibid., p.71. Data for 1980: Kürschners Volkshandbuch Deutscher Bundestag 9. Wahlperiode, Bonn 1981, p.235.
87. Z Parl 4, 1982, p.461 brings details on the Constitutional Court Ruling on civil service pay for parliamentary delegates: For the duration of parliamentary service, dual salaries are no longer paid.

SUGGESTED READING

Paul Ackermann, Der Bauernverband im politschen
    Kräftespiel der Bundesrepublik, Tübingen (Mohr) 1970
Ulrich von Alemann (ed.), Verbände und Staat,
    Opladen (Westdeutscher, Verlag), 1979
Gerald Braunthal, The Federation of German Industry
    in Politics, Cornell University Press, 1965
Jürgen Dittberner/Rolf Ebbighausen (eds.), Das

Parteiensystem in der Legitimationskrise, Opladen (Westdeutscher Verlag), 1973
Ossip K. Flechtheim, Die Parteien in der Bundesrepublik Deutschland, Hamburg (Hoffman & Campe), 1973
Government and Opposition: Special Issue Trade Unions and Political Parties, Autumn 1978
Heino Kaack, Geschichte und Struktur des deutschen Parteiensystems, Opladen (Westdeutscher Verlag), 1971
Heino Kaack/Reinhold Roth, Handbuch des deutschen Parteiensystems, (vols. I and II), Opladen (Leske & Budrich), 1980
Richard Löwenthal/Hans-Peter Schwarz (eds.), Die zweite Republik, Stuttgart (Seewald), 1974
Uwe Schleth, Parteifinanzen, Meisenheim (Hain), 1973
Jürgen Weber, Interessengruppen im politischen System der Bundesrepublik Deutschland, Stuttgart (Kohlhammer), 1977
Walter Wellner, Parteienfinanzierung, Munich (Bayr. Landeszentrale), 1973

Chapter Two

PARTIES AND SOCIETY (II): CHANGES IN PARTY SUPPORT

POLITICAL PARTIES IN THE SEVENTIES

In the most general and tentative way, party support refers to an overall approval of political parties as components of the political system. In the Federal Republic party support has been discussed as the choice between a one party state or a plurality of parties. About nine in ten West German adults now opt for more than one party.[1] A more specific measure is turnout at elections. Again, parties enjoy a high level of support. Between 85 and 90% of the German electorate vote for one of the registered political parties, in elections above the local level. The big three, SPD, CDU/CSU, and FDP gain well over 90% of the popular vote. This active party support contrasts markedly with the most concrete level of involvement, membership in a political party. In 1980, only 4% of the electorate were members of a political party, less than two million people. Until the end of the sixties, membership had been lower still, about one million overall. Since the late sixties, the major parties experienced considerable upheavals. The roles in government on the national level changed from a CDU/CSU led coalition to an SPD led coalition. On the land and local levels, the trend was reversed with the CDU displacing the SPD. Party memberships soared. The relegation of the CDU/CSU to the opposition benches brought an unprecedented influx of new members, an annual average increase of 8.95% for the CDU and 8.46% for the CSU.[2] In 1969 the CDU numbered 300,000 members. It more than doubled its size to 682,000 by 1979.[3] The CSU grew from 76,000 to 169,000 members in the same period.[4] Together, the Christian Democratic parties numbered 850,000 at the end of the seventies or 45% of total

Changes in Party Support

party membership in the Federal Republic. The SPD grew also, but less rapidly. Between 1969 and 1979, the party expanded by 3.14% per annum. In 1976 it reached the one million mark.[5] It has since declined to just under one million. Although the quantitative changes of the SPD seem modest compared with the CDU and CSU, the transformation in the social composition of its membership was considerable. The party itself stresses that this one decade brought more profound changes in its social structure than the previous one hundred years of SPD history.[6] The changes alluded to concern white collar employees and civil servants, the adaptation of the party to the modernization process in society. The question arises how the social composition of electorate and membership have been altered and of possible repercussions on internal party organization.

For the FDP, instability and lack of organizational cohesion continue to constitute problems. Although the party gained new members over the decade, some 25,000 in all, the FDP on a national basis is still only half the size of the CSU which operates just within Bavaria. The scanty organizational network makes it difficult to gain and to retain members. Despite the role of the FDP in government and despite some growth in the seventies, FDP party support and party organization appear fragile.

CLEAVAGES BETWEEN PARTIES AND SOCIETY: SOME RECENT DEVELOPMENTS

During the seventies, all major parties increased their membership, i.e. their manifest support in society. This membership growth obscures a detachment from political parties which also emerged in this period. The decade started with a peak in political interest. For electoral turnout, the peak is evident. In 1972, an unprecedented 91.1% of the electorate voted. Turnout has since fallen to 88.6%.[7] Abstentions in 1972 were lower than at any other election, 8.9%. In 1949 for example, 21.5% had chosen not to vote, in 1980, 11.4% abstained. The non voters have always formed the third largest group in the West German electorate, outnumbering the FDP.[8] Those least likely to use their voting rights are the youngest.[9] In 1972 the SPD fared well among the under 25's with a 10% above average share of the vote.[10] In subsequent elections, SPD support and support of established parties overall declined. While 97% of the older electorate cast their vote for one of the established parties during the 1978-1980 round of land elections, only 80% of the under 25's supported one of these parties.11

The detachment among the young from the major political parties has increased during the seventies. In his study on Youth and Politics, Karl Josef Does found that 76% of the under 23's identified with CDU/CSU, SPD or FDP in 1972. Four years later, only 60% thought that their interests were represented by one of these parties.12 An Emnid survey in 1978 found that 62% of all West Germans expressed doubts whether political parties were representing the interests of the citizens. 31% stressed their own interests were ignored by the parties.13 The impression that parties remained aloof from society and people had grown not merely among the young. In 1976, 40% of the West German population thought that not everybody was represented by the major parties and 16% felt they themselves were not represented. The detachment or the cleavage grew faster still among the younger age groups. Nearly two thirds of the 18-30 year olds stressed in 1980 that parties cared only for the votes, not for the needs of their voters.14 In a survey conducted on behalf of the Second Television Channel ZDF and incorporated into a series of programmes on youth in West Germany which was broadcast in April 1980, 48% of the young people under 25 declared that none of the major parties bore any relevance to them or represented any of their interests.15 The majority of these young people were interested in politics but found the existing parties and politicians unsuited ambassadors of their aims.

First signs of a somewhat oppositional undertone in the political commitment may be detected during the 1972 election campaign, when groups alongside and outside the established party structure entered the campaign on behalf of these parties.16 These so called Voters' Initiatives usually supported the SPD. Their refusal to be amalgamated into the election machinery suggests a tentative and independent support, a detachment amidst open and public commitment. The SPD subsequently integrated the unsolicited assistance into the party organization, equipped the voters' initiative with funds and a Bonn office and successfully curtailed independent and at times unwanted electoral assistance.17 The CDU did not experience a comparable upsurge of voters' initiatives. It seized the name to disguise associations which were launched

for fund raising purposes. In 1980, none of the
existing parties generated voters' initiatives.
Commitment then was Anti-Strauss rather than for a
specific party.[18] The upsurge of commitment for one
of the major parties which characterized the early
seventies, has been replaced by distance if not a
cleavage. Today, all major parties and particularly
the CDU and the SPD find it difficult to broaden
their social base into the new generation. The
chairman of the Westfalia CDU admitted in 1980, that
young people were no longer willing to join the
party and its affiliated youth organization, Junge
Union. From SPD quarters, similar complaints were
voiced even more forcefully. A former chairman of
the Young Socialists, the SPD youth organization,
stated despondently: "Every football club would
sack its manager if it had such an erosion of membership as we do."[19]

ELECTORATES IN TRANSITION

Two processes of change converge in the social composition of party electorates: the modernization of
the economic structure which generated a decline in
the blue collar and the self-employed sectors and an
expansion of white collar occupational groups. The
second process concerns the displacement of class
related interest parties by broadly based people's
parties with diversified social support. The
changes in the party electorates bear witness of
both processes. Although all parties experienced
significant restructuring of their electoral support, the changes are particularly far reaching for
the SPD (Table 2.1). The other parties changed
their emphasis, the SPD changed its character.

White Collar and Blue Collar Voting

In Table 2.1, fairly broad categories have been
chosen to define social groups. Blue collar, white
collar and self-employed give the basic social
positions and occupations. The changes in the
social structure in the population have not been
mirrored by the political parties. The self-employed
continue to form 32% of the CDU electorate while
their share among the working population has decreased from 26% in 1956 to 14% in 1976. The decline of the blue collar sector is less drastic in
the population as a whole than among the SPD
electorate. While 80% of the SPD voters in 1956

Table 2.1: The Social Composition of Party Support: Voters, 1956-1976[1]

Occupational Group	SPD 1956 %	SPD 1976 %	CDU 1956 %	CDU 1976 %	Working Population 1956 %	Working Population 1976 %	FDP[2] 1953 %	FDP 1972 %
Blue Collar	80	53	37	28	52	45	16	21
White Collar	11	42	31	40	22	41	34	66
Self-Employed	9	5	32	32	26	14	50	13
Total	100	100	100	100	100	100	100	100

1. Source: Feist, Güllner, Liepelt, Structural Assimilation, p.174.
2. Data for the FDP from Stöss/Schmollinger, Bundestagswahlen und soziale Basis I, p.33.

belonged to the blue collar occupational group - in other words were working class, just over half the 1976 electorate came from a working class background. Both SPD and CDU experienced an increase of white collar voters among their electorate which can be related to the increased importance of white collar occupations overall. The white collarization of the SPD electorate, however, was more pronounced than that of the CDU.

Table 2.2 indicates the gap between CDU/CSU and SPD in voters' preference. It confirms the strides of the SPD in the white collar and civil service sectors and the allegiance of self-employed and farmers to parties other than the SPD. The most interesting change which became apparent in the 1983 elections concerns the working class vote: although the SPD remains the strongest party here, the CDU has caught up and won a larger share of working class support than at any time during the sixties and seventies.

Table 2.2: Party Preferences for Federal Elections by Occupation, 1949-83 (difference SPD - CDU/CSU*)

Occupation	1949	1953	1957	1961	1965	1969	1972	1976	1980	1983
Workers	+24	+12	+13	+16	+17	+29	+36	+23	+32	+14
White collar and civil servants	-21	-36	-39	-15	-6	+8	+13	-5	+13	-4
Self employed	-30	-44	-57	-44	-45	-52	-42	-68	-50	-62
Farmers	-31	-56	-58	-66	-60	-78	-61	-87	-68	-73

* The don't-knows have been incorporated into the calculations.

Source: Gewerkschaftliche Monatshefte, 7, 183, p.417 (based on a number of Allensbach and Infas polls).

The FDP, a Middle Class Wedge

While the FDP started out as a party with a predominantly self-employed electorate, the party is today largely white collar. In 1976, it fared less well in constituencies with a high concentration of self-employed and did particularly well in constituencies with a high proportion of civil servants and white collar employees.[20] It has been argued that the political reorientation of the FDP in the late sixties generated an exodus of the self-employed, traditional FDP voters.[21] Taking the FDP electorate as a sector of West German society however, its overall characteristics have not changed: it continues to be middle class, highly qualified and educated, largely protestant. In a survey of the FDP vote in Baden Württemberg, Klingemann showed that these characteristics were true in the fifties and sixties, and are still true today.[22] The middle class occupational groups and the highly educated today tend to be white collar or civil servants, i.e. the FDP wins the same type of electorate as in earlier years although its precise social composition has changed. The special importance of the self-employed for the FDP electorate has decreased.

The Denominational Divide

For SPD and CDU, the detailed survey by Gluchowski and Veen shows further changes. Educational levels of the electorates of both parties have become similar and roughly in line with educational achievements in the population. Twenty years ago, the SPD attracted the less educated while the CDU had an above average number of voters with O level, A level or university education.[23] A similar catching up is evident for civil servants, for employees, and for women voters. In 1959, the CDU/CSU electorate consisted to 59% of women, the SPD electorate to 42%, while 54% of the population were women.[24] By March 1979, the electorates of both parties had levelled out at 53% women. The opposite process occurred for male voters where the CDU vote increased from 41% to about 50% between 1959 and 1979. The SPD has now the same proportion of male voters among its electorate after lying above average with 57% in 1959. Distinct differences have, however, remained in two areas: trade union affiliation and religious denomination. Trade union members are more likely to vote SPD, Catholics and also practising Christians of all denominations are more likely to vote CDU.[25] Despite a closer proximity of the social structure of the electorates of the two major parties which emerged over the past two decades, distinct social strongholds of the parties in society remain visible. In Table 2.3, the focus is shifted from the electorate of the parties to an analysis of electoral preference within specific groups. Until 1972, the SPD could increase its hold on the working class vote while the CDU emerged as the major party for the self-employed and the farmers. The 1969 elections constituted a turning point in the levelling between parties. SPD gains among employees and civil servants brought the two major parties very close together. The co-operation in government during the Grand Coalition appears to have mobilized the white collar vote for the SPD which was needed to broaden the social basis of the party. In 1965, 28% of white collar employees and 27% of civil servants voted SPD. In 1969, 45% of white collar employees and 38% of civil servants voted SPD.[26] The same elections brought greater gains for the SPD among women than among men for the first time in its history.[27] While it may be stated that the two large parties represent specific groups and converge around the white collar sector, Table 2.2 also shows that the strides of SPD expansion were halted in 1976, a stagnation which recurred in 1980 and determined the outcome of the 1983 elections. The denominational divide in West Germany which had lost its severity with catholic gains for the SPD until 1972, has again become prominent. CDU/CSU tend to attract catholic votes from all social groupings; SPD and FDP more frequently protestant votes. During the 1980 election, the intervention of the West German bishops and the attempt to recruit catholic voters into the CDU/CSU fold, alienated some protestant CDU voters and led them towards the FDP. For the FDP, the denominational issues brought a welcome strengthening in conservative and protestant areas. Overall, denomination appears to be more significant as a social divide in West Germany today than social class. The CDU enjoyed in 1976 the lion share of votes from catholic workers, catholic employees and civil servants, catholic self-employed and catholic farmers. The hold of the SPD on the various social groups is less compelling. It emerges as the main party for protestant workers, for just over half the protestant white collar sector, for one third of the protestant self-employed and one fifth of the protestant farmers. For the last two groups, the traditional conservative clientele, the denominational factor seems to be the least relevant.

The resurgence of religious denomination as a dividing line in politics is perhaps surprising in a society where religious observance has tended to fade. Nearly half the West German population are catholics. In the early fifties, about 80% could be classified as practising catholics who would go to church regularly at least once a month. In the mid seventies, only half the catholics could still be

Table 2.3: Electoral Decision by Occupation and Denomination

Electoral Decision	Total Vote						Catholic Vote						Protestant Vote					
	1953 %	'61 %	'65 %	'69 %	'72 %	'76 %	1953 %	'61 %	'65 %	'69 %	'72 %	'76 %	1953 %	'61 %	'65 %	'69 %	'72 %	'76 %
Workers																		
SPD	48	56	54	58	66	52	36	41	40	50	55	34	60	69	66	69	77	70
CDU/CSU	35	36	42	39	27	42	47	50	58	49	39	63	22	25	30	27	15	22
FDP	4	5	2	1	6	5	2	4	2	–	5	3	6	5	3	2	7	7
Others	14	3	1	2	1	1	15	5	0	1	0	1	12	1	1	2	1	1
White collar & civil service																		
SPD	27	30	34	46	50	46	22	21	21	38	42	33	31	36	44	52	56	54
CDU/CSU	49	50	54	45	33	41	61	64	71	56	45	60	40	41	42	36	23	29
FDP	14	18	10	7	17	12	8	12	7	1	12	7	19	21	11	11	20	16
Others	10	2	2	3	0	1	9	3	1	5	0	1	10	2	3	1	0	1
Self-Employed																		
SPD	11	14	18	17	23	30	7	7	13	10	22	24	15	21	23	25	25	35
CDU/CSU	53	62	58	75	62	62	66	74	72	87	64	74	39	47	46	62	59	52
FDP	20	23	19	8	13	8	14	17	9	3	12	2	26	30	28	12	15	14
Others	16	1	4	–	1	–	13	1	6	–	2	–	20	1	3	–	1	–
Farmers																		
SPD	4	8	–	16	10	16	–	7	–	27	9	11	8	11	–	7	10	20
CDU/CSU	58	77	92	72	82	79	68	90	97	73	88	89	48	54	85	71	77	70
FDP	12	13	8	4	8	5	4	3	3	–	3	–	20	30	15	7	13	10
Others	26	2	–	8	–	–	–	–	–	–	–	–	24	4	–	14	–	–

Changes in Party Support

Overall																		
SPD	30	36	39	46	52	46	22	25	26	38	43	34	37	46	49	55	60	55
CDU/CSU	45	50	52	48	36	45	58	65	68	59	48	61	33	37	40	36	26	33
FDP	10	11	7	4	11	8	5	7	4	1	8	4	15	14	9	7	13	11
Others	15	2	2	2	1	1	15	3	1	2	0	1	15	2	2	2	1	1

Sources: Stöss/Schmollinger, Die soziale Basis I p.132 and Franz Pappi, Parteiensystem und Sozialstruktur, p.199.

regarded as practising catholics.[28] Observance among West German protestants had always been lower and has been rated at 28% in 1965. By October, 1978, it had declined to about 18%.[29] These changes in the role of religious observance in society make it unlikely that the party support is generated by religious motives. Feist and Liepelt argue that differences of economic interest have receded among occupational sectors and social groups in a more affluent environment. Instead, ideological distinctions come to the foreground as social and political divides. Denomination has taken on this role in West Germany. The denominational divide has somewhat eroded social and economic categories of political identification in society.

The Middle Class Syndrome

Changes in the occupational structure do not, it appears, fully reflect the changes in people's social self-identification. Improved living standards for all sectors of the society, improved social services and the relative prosperity experienced in West Germany meant that the majority of West Germans see themselves as middle class. In 1954, 43% thought they were middle class, in 1976, 56% felt they belonged to the middle class. Identification with the upper middle class rose from 2% to 5%, identification with the lower or working class fell from 54% to 37% in the same period.[30] In 1975, one third of blue collar workers counted themselves to the middle class.

This tendency to regard oneself as belonging to the middle ground also applies to political self-identification. Of the West German adult electorate in 1975, over 80% saw themselves as middle-of-the-road, the extremes of the right and left received little support. When these estimates of the voters' own position are related to the place in politics allocated to the party of one's choice, interesting contrasts are evident. For the FDP supporters, the perception of their own position and that of their party are virtually identical, both firmly rooted in the middle ground. CDU and CSU supporters see their party a little to the right of themselves. The contrast between party image and political self-identification is largest between SPD supporters and the assumed position of the SPD left of centre. The common accusation that parties are all the same, does not tally with these contrasts. Parties in their political profile are identified more sharply

Changes in Party Support

with ideological positions than the electorate feel
they themselves endorse. Tnis contrast between
political stance and party position is most problem-
atic for the SPD whose position on the left does not
easily tally with the predominantly middle class
image of its electorate and the influx of new middle
class support. It appears that the extent of social
regrouping and the proliferation of middle class
expectations put pressure on the SPD to moderate its
position towards that middle ground. SPD marginal
voters are more clearly middle class in self-identification than the hard-core voters or sympathizers.
The pressures towards the centre are all the more
forceful in a situation of electoral stalemate between the big two and the uncertainties of coalition
agreements with the FDP.

Women and the CDU/CSU

In July 1969, the West German writer Heinrich Böll,
himself a catholic by birth and a native of the
Adenauer stronghold Cologne, appealed in an Open
Letter to German catholic women to discriminate between religious beliefs and political allegiance and
vote for a party other than the CDU/CSU. During the
fifties and early sixties, over 60% of the CDU vote
came from women and well over 60% of the CDU voters
were catholic. Böll's appeal was clearly geared towards the forthcoming elections:

> Since you, to whom I address myself freely
> and in public, belong to the statistical
> category 'catholic woman', I would like to
> assure you straight away that I am not
> interested in separating you from the
> religious category 'catholic woman'. I
> would only like to try and liberate you
> from the undignified position of acting as
> 'Stimmvieh' for the CDU/CSU. I am afraid
> that you at times against your will, from
> sheer force of habit make your cross in
> the wrong place, and I am also afraid that
> the last push for this only happens in the
> secluded cabin of the polling station, and
> I am also afraid that you innocently make
> this disastrous error because these parties
> put the word 'Christian' in front of their
> names.[31]

The predominance of women in post-war society
helped the CDU/CSU to ascend to power. In Bavaria,

the allegiance of women to the CSU remains. In the 1974 land elections, for example, over 60% of the 18-24 year old women and 61.7% of the 25-34 year olds voted for the CSU.[32] With increasing age, the female vote for the CSU and the CDU increases.[33] Men are somewhat less likely to vote for the Christian Democrats. This bastion of support among West Germany's women began to decline a little since the late sixties. At least in mixed religious areas, the CDU no longer controls the female electorate. In 1969, a survey of electoral behaviour in Cologne showed that one in three women who had voted CDU in 1965 had cast her vote for a different party four years earlier.[34] In 1972, there were no differences in the voting behaviour between men and women. Taking the average for the Federal Republic, 45.7% of women voted SPD, 46% CDU/CSU, and 7.7% FDP. Among men, the SPD gained the support of 46.9%, the CDU of 43% and the FDP of 8.8%. Subsequent elections modified this even distribution. As we had seen earlier, the denominational factors played a more divisive role with catholics returning to the CDU (they hardly left the CSU). In 1976, women constituted 53% of the SPD electorate and 57% of the CDU electorate. The denominational divide of the seventies has hardened the grip of the Christian Democratic parties on West German women.

Young Voters

If the CDU has remained relatively successful in securing female votes, it has experienced difficulties in mobilizing an arguably more important sector of the electorate, the young. In West Germany, the voting age was lowered to 18 with effect from the 1972 Federal elections. Since then, nearly 4 million or ten percent of the electorate tend to be young voters under the age of 25. As a general trend it may be stated that younger voters are more inclined to support the SPD or the FDP than the CDU. The CSU is an exception and has, as Alf Mintzel pointed out, been remarkably successful in broadening its votes into the younger groups in Bavarian society.[35] In 1983, 56% of the 18-24 year olds opted for the CSU, 28% for the SPD.[36]

The problems of winning the younger votes concern the CDU. In 1972, more than half the young voters under 25 voted SPD. Just under 35% voted CDU and about 9% voted FDP.[37] In the 1976 elections, the first and young voters of 1972 who had voted SPD four years before, remained on the whole loyal to this party (Table 2.4). The age group of 25-35 has since proved a stronghold of SPD support. The CDU made some inroads into the 18-25 and gained 43% in 1976. The SPD suffered some losses.[38] These gains and losses were short lived. By 1980, the young vote for the CDU had declined, but so did the young vote for the SPD, except a slight improvement among women. Only the FDP could consolidate its position.

Table 2.4: Electoral preferences by age and sex, 1972-1980 (in %)

	CDU/CSU		SPD		FDP	
	1980/76	1976/72	1980/76	1976/72	1980/76	1976/72
Men 18-24	-4.7	+5.5	-1.8	-4.9	+2.6	-1.1
Men total	-3.0	+4.2	-0.5	-3.3	+2.4	-0.7
Women 18-24	-7.2	+4.3	+0.1	-4.8	+3.3	-0.1
Women total	-5.1	+2.8	+0.8	-2.6	+3.2	-0.1

Source: CDU-Dokumentation 7: Das Wahlverhalten nach Alter und Geschlecht bei der BTW 1980 p.6.

The detailed analysis of the 1978-79 land elections conducted by Klaus Troitzsch allows further differentiation.[39] He confirms the relatively good position of SPD and FDP among younger voters. Yet both parties lost an average of 7% of the votes among the youngest voters (18-21). The CDU who, as we saw, tends to mobilize a good third of the young vote on a national level, remained unaffected by the exodus of young voters from big party loyalties. Troitzsch documents the advent of the green parties as political alternatives for the younger voters who formerly supported or might have supported the SPD or the FDP. Table 2.5 looks at voting for the young and for the electorate as a whole by region. The special position of Bavaria is confirmed. Here over half the young voters endorse the CSU. Elsewhere, younger voters tend to favour the SPD, as has been evident since 1972. Younger voters also favour, as Table 2.5 shows, the newly launched green lists and parties which competed in the 1978/79 land elections for the first time. In Hamburg and Bremen, one fifth of the under 25 year olds voted for a green party. Green parties win much of their support among the younger voters in all regions. For Baden Württemberg similar findings have been recorded.[40] While the CDU faces the difficulty of finding means

Changes in Party Support

Table 2.5: Voting in the 1978-79 Land Elections by Age

Land	Age Group	Vote in %			
		SDP	CDU	FDP	Greens
Hamburg	18/25	48.6	21.6	6.8	20.6
	total	51.1	37.6	4.7	3.7
Lower Saxony	18/25	46.0	37.1	3.8	11.7
	total	42.9	48.8	3.8	3.7
Hesse	18/25	50.0	35.6	6.7	6.2
	total	45.0	45.4	6.7	2.0
Bavaria	18/25	34.3	54.2	5.9	4.2
	total	32.5	58.3	6.0	1.8
Rhineland-	18/25	49.5	42.7	6.4	-
Palatine	total	42.6	50.1	6.1	-
Berlin	18/25	43.1	31.0	9.2	14.1
	total	42.5	44.9	8.0	3.4
Schleswig-	18/25	50.7	36.0	7.1	-
Holstein	total	42.4	47.5	5.7	-
Bremen	18/25	50.5	16.9	10.3	20.0
	total	49.7	32.0	10.8	6.1

Source: Klaus Troitzsch in Kaack/Roth I, p.248.

to mobilize and attract a larger share of the young vote, SPD and FDP appear to face difficulties in retaining their vote or gaining that of the first voters. It has been argued that alliances formed in first elections are an important pointer towards future loyalties. This observation was made in relation to the three major parties whose young voters often vote again for "their" party in subsequent elections. If it could be upheld for parties with a sting of protest against the established three, the future loyalties of the under 35's seem uncertain. The young voters of today may retain some of their detachment. The SPD would then lose the support among the 25-35 year olds which has become a mainstay of SPD successes in the seventies. In a long term perspective, the detachment of the young from the major parties as it is reflected in the rise of the green party vote, could jolt the reduction of the party system to those major three. The inclination among young voters to endorse a non-established party has also been regarded as a temporary phenomenon. Klaus Liepelt for example argues that the young who vote for a green party are only searching for their firm position in West German politics and will gravitate towards one of the major parties in due course.[41] At this state, there is evidence both ways. Voting loyalty for a small party is lower than for one of the big three. For the 1978 Bavarian land elections, the fluctuation of voting has been well documented. The CSU could count on 71% of its voters from four years before, the SPD on 63%, the FDP on 44% and other parties on 31%.[42] Green parties and minor parties overall have not been more successful than the established ones to break into the camp of non-voters.[43] The competition among parties seems to concern young voters who would in any case have gone to the polls. As we have seen, during the seventies their support would have benefited SPD and FDP more than the CDU. In Bavaria, the association between young voters and the CSU is more stable. The Liepelt argument that the young will eventually choose one of the established parties may overlook the element of conscious rejection of these parties. More specifically, a rejection of Social Democrats or Free Democrats in the late seventies and early eighties. The relatively high educational attainment of the average green voter makes it unlikely that the vote was cast in a merely tentative fashion. It is more likely that voting for the Greens and not voting for SPD or FDP is a political manifestation of a critical detachment from society and politics in West Germany among better educated young people of today. The problems of the parties to secure the votes of the young, have to be considered in the context of the broader question how West German young people assess their place and future in their society.[44] It seems the optimism of the early seventies that the social-liberal coalition could voice the concerns of the young and reshape society is no longer shared by the new generation who has matured into voting age during the decade.

FOOTNOTES

1. Greiffenhagen, <u>Ein schwieriges Vaterland</u>, Munich (List), 1979, p. 355.
2. Kaack/Roth, <u>Handbuch des deutschen Parteiensystems</u> I, Opladen (Leske & Budrich), 1980, p. 83.
3. Statistischer Bericht der Zentralen Mitgliederkartei, Stand 31.12.1979.
4. <u>CSU: Portrait einer Partei</u>, (CSU Landesleitung) n.d., p. 80 and Kaack/Roth I, p. 83.
5. <u>Jahrbuch der Sozialdemokratischen Partei</u>, 1975/76.

6. Sozialdemokrat Magazin 4, April 1978, p. 8.
7. Amtliches Endergebnis, Zeitschrift für Parlamentsfragen No.1, 1981, p. 47. In 1983: 89.1% turnout.
8. Der Spiegel No.39, 1976, p. 80 and Zeitschrift für Parlamentsfragen 1, 1981, p. 47.
9. Werner Kaltefleiter, Zwischen Konsens und Krise. Eine Analyse der Bundestagswahlen 1972, Bonn (Eichholz Verlag), 1973.
10. Ferdinand F. Müller, "Das Wahlverhalten der Jungwähler" in Zeitschrift für Parlamentsfragen 2, 1980, p. 256.
11. Müller op.cit., p. 259.
12. Karl Josef Does, Jugend und Politik. Discussion paper published by the Konrad Adenauer Stiftung, Alfter 1976, p. 8.
13. "Jeder Dritte: Ich bin schlecht vertreten". Der Spiegel 25, 1978.
14. Der Spiegel 13, 1980, p. 32.
15. According to "Generation ohne Hoffnung", part II broadcast by the ZDF channel on 1 April 1980, 48% of young people felt unrepresented by any of the existing political parties.
16. Heidrun Abromeit, "Wählerinitiativen im Wahlkampf 1972" in Aus Politik und Zeitgeschichte B 37, 1973.
17. Dirk Cornelsen "Von den Parteien werden sie diskret gefördert" in Frankfurter Allgemeine Zeitung, 11.9.1980.
18. Der Spiegel 26, 1980, pp. 26-28.
19. Der Spiegel 40, 1980, p. 76.
20. Heino Kaack, Die FDP Grundriss und Materialien zu Geschichte, Struktur und Programmatik. Meisenheim (Hain), 1979^3, p. 62.
21. Horst W. Schmollinger, "Abhängig Beschäftigte in den politischen Parteien der Bundesrepublik Deutschland" in Zeitschrift für Parlamentsfragen, 1974, p. 58 ff. argues that the FDP suffered an extensive regrouping of its electorate (Wähleraustausch).
22. Hans D. Klingemann, "Der Wandel der Bildes der FDP in der Bevölkerung" in Lothar Albertin (ed.), Politischer Liberalismus in der Bundesrepublik, Göttingen (Vandenhoeck & Ruprecht), 1980, p. 158.
23. Peter Gluchowski/Hans-Joachim Veen, "Nivellierungstendenzen in den Wähler - und Mitgliedschaften von CDU/CSU und SPD 1959-1979", in Zeitschrift für Parlamentsfragen 3, 1979, p. 315.
24. Data ibid., p. 319.
25. Ibid., pp. 320-21. Also Eva Kolinsky,

Treffpunkt, June 1981.
26. Bernhard Vogel/Dieter Nohlen/Rainer-Olaf Schulze, Wahlen in Deutschland. Theorie, Geschichte, Dokumente 1848-1970, Berlin/New York, 1971, p. 231.
27. Ibid., p. 232-33.
28. Ursula Feist/Klaus Liepelt, "Machtwechsel auf Raten. Das Parteiensystem auf dem Weg zur Mitte" in Wahlforschung. Sonden im politischen Markt, Opladen (Westdt. Verlag), 1976, p. 47, data used by Horst Schmollinger/Richard Stöss, Bundestagswahlen und soziale Basis Part I in Prokla Vol. 6 (1976), No. 25, p. 119.
29. Gluchowski/Veen, op.cit., p. 322.
30. Data from Ursula Feist/Manfred Güllner/ Klaus Liepelt, "Structural Assimilation versus Ideological Polarisation: on Changing Profiles of Political Parties in West Germany" in Max Kaase and Klaus von Beyme (eds.), Elections and Parties. German Political Studies Vol. 3, Sage, 1979, p. 179.
31. Heinrich Böll, "Offener Brief an eine deutsche Frau" in Die Zeit 25.7.1969, p. 13.
32. Alf Mintzel, Geschichte der CSU. Ein Überblick, Opladen (Westdt. Verlag), 1977, p. 435.
33. e.g. Zeitschrift für Parlamentsfragen 2, 1980, p. 193.
34. Ossip K. Flechtheim (ed.), Die Parteien der Bundesrepublik Deutschland. Hamburg (Hoffmann & Campe), 1973, p. 68.
35. Mintzel, Geschichte der CSU, p. 435.
36. B VII 1-5, 83 Statistische Berichte Wahl zum 10. Bundestag in Bayern, 1983.
37. Kaltefleiter, Zwischen Konsens und Krise, p. 165.
38. The SPD gained 47% among the age group 18-25 in 1976.
39. Klaus Troitzsch, "Grenzen der Stabilität des etablierten Parteiensystems: Wahlen, Wählerverhalten und politische Einstellungen" in Kaack/Roth I, p. 247-249 presents data on young voters in recent land elections.
40. Gustav Olaf Schulze, "Wahlerfolge der Grünen: Nur diffuser Protest?" in Zeitschrift für Parlamentsfragen 1, 1979, p. 57.
41. Infas Report Wahlen, Hamburg, 1978.
42. "Die bayrische Landtagswahl" in Zeitschrift für Parlamentsfragen 1, 1979, p. 57.
43. Ibid. and Schulze op.cit., p. 298.
44. These issues will be discussed in more detail in chapter 6.

Changes in Party Support

SUGGESTED READING

Klaus von Beyme/Max Kaase (eds.), Elections and
    Parties, Sage, 1979
Tony Burkett, Parties and Elections in West Germany,
    (Hurst), 1975
K.H. Cerny, (ed.), Germany at the Polls: The
    Bundestag Election of 1976, Washington,
    (Enterprise Institute), 1978
Peter Gluchowski/Hans Joachim Veen,"Nivellierungsten-
    denzen in den Wähler - und Mitgliedschaften
    von CDU/CSU und SPD 1959-1979", Zeitschrift für
    Parlamentsfragen 3, 1979
Heino Kaack/Reinhold Roth, Handbuch des deutschen
    Parteiensystems Bd. 1, Opladen (Leske & Budrich)
    1980
Ferdinand F. Müller, "Das Wahlverhalten der
    Jungwähler", Zeitschrift für Parlamentsfragen
    2, 1980
Bernard Vogel/Dieter Nohlen/Rainer-Olaf Schulze,
    Wahlen in Deutschland, Berlin/N.Y., 1971

Chapter Three

THE SPD IN TRANSITION: MEMBERSHIP TRENDS AND PARTY ORGANIZATION

Losses at elections seem to be needed to jolt parties into self-reflection. For the SPD, it needed the experience of 1976 and a discussion paper on the party's failings by its General Secretary at the time, Holger Börner and Hans Koschnik, the chairman of the Bremen land organization.[1] The Börner/Koschnik aim was twofold: on the one hand they wanted to specify the extent and reasons for the electoral disappointment, on the other hand they aimed beyond a mere election survey at the state of party organization and the problems of membership involvement. As criticism of the 1976 campaign the document is interesting enough. There are allegations that the party appeared too close to the CDU - 70% of the SPD electorate, Börner and Koschnik report - did not expect much change should the CDU win.[2] The "Model Germany" electoral theme was unknown to over 80% of the electorate at the start of the summer recess. At a time when 21% of the adult population felt threatened by redundancies the theme was ill chosen. The details of failure as enumerated by Börner and Koschnik are revealing. Compared with 1972, the newly mobilized support had not been consolidated. Vote losses were highest among women (5%) and among unskilled and semiskilled blue collar workers (6%).[3] On the other hand, the SPD managed to hold on to older voters. Here, Börner and Koschnik focus on a specific deficiency: while 27% of the electorate were over sixty and problems of old age and pension rights formed a significant part of the SPD campaign, old people had no institutionalized voice in the party organization. This has since been remedied.[4]

Other suggestions were less speedily implemented. Börner and Koschnik stressed how sluggishly party members had contributed to the campaign, a sluggishness which had been caused by the party and its performance in society. The election was overshadowed by allegations of corruption against long-serving SPD politicians in Hesse. This did not help matters. More significantly, information within the party did not filter down to the grass roots from higher centres of decision making. This deficit of communication inside the SPD bred passivity. So did the excessive size of local party branches.

SPD STUDIES

The Börner/Koschnik post-electoral reckoning touched upon disconcerting incongruities. The SPD who had from the outset favoured a mass organization and centralized decision making structures as a counterweight to other political forces in society, experienced in the seventies, that the force of numbers and the established organization alone ceased to be effective. Changes within the party membership and members' motivation to join the party rendered some modes of party organization obsolete. After the membership expansion since the sixties and the new "Volkspartei" basis, the SPD no longer knew enough about its membership to appraise the party's place in society and the commitment of members to the party aims. The immediate offshoot of the Börner/Koschnik discussion paper were two empirical surveys of members and office holders. The surveys by Infas and Infratest were conducted in 1977 and published internally in 1978. Some findings were communicated through the members' journal.[5] The bulk of the study remained under lock and key. Problems, it seems, were aired, but not solved. In 1980, the "Commission for Basic Values" was still moved to complaints about the quality of party life.

> It does not sufficiently attempt to inform the citizen, to interest him for the work of the party and to activate him. Party life gives the impression of a secluded business, where active members have long known each other. They hold meetings (which the majority of members does not attend) without lasting effect beyond the small group of party activitists. And very little is happening to integrate newcomers and stimulate them to active participation. Coordinated political education and information at the grass roots is rare.[6]

The "Communication Studies" may not have disentangled all problems of SPD organization. They provided however, up-to-date insights into the social composition of the party, the motivation of members and functionaries and their attitudes towards the organization and its aims. Both studies include comparisons with the CDU. Although it has been argued that the CDU sample is distorted in favour of the more committed CDU follower,[7] the side glances at the major rival party reveal interesting similarities and some significant contrasts. The other parties also conducted their "communication studies". The CDU began in 1971, in order to assess the party organization in relation to the opposition role. A follow-up study was carried out in 1977 within the Konrad Adenauer Foundation, the party affiliated Research Institute. This study is very much a CDU oriented effort, it does not include comparative data.[8] The CSU has not been included in this study as a separate entity. Beyond the extensive analyses, which Alf Mintzel conducted in the mid-seventies,[9] the CSU is sufficiently computerized to survey its membership and relevant trends for organizational and publicity purposes. The FDP joined the SPD in an effort to get a considered and detailed outside analysis of the party and its problems. It commissioned the Institut für Kommunikationsforschung to conduct a survey. The report was compiled in 1977, some figures were used in publicity materials on membership recruitment. The details, however, were not published and seem to be intended for internal use only.[10]

For the SPD, membership trends and social structure have not altered significantly since the late seventies. Trends which had been apparent then have continued rather than changed direction.

CHANGES IN THE SPD SOCIAL STRUCTURE: IN SEARCH OF THE WORKING CLASS

The notion of the SPD as a workers' interest party presupposes a homogeneity between the social position of voters, members, functionaries, and leaders. For the SPD this would mean that all layers of party followers and activists came from a cohesive German working class milieu. Already during the Weimar Republic, this harmony between voting public and party activists was not complete. The party was more middle class than its voters.[11] There is reason to assume that the party functionaries tended to be better educated than the average member or voter and more often recruited from white collar occupations. By 1930, about 60% of SPD members came from the working class. In the post-1945 period, the working class sector within the party has declined steadily.[12]

One of the difficulties in defining the working class component with percentage figures results from incongruities between the various surveys. In the summary account of its social structure in 1978, the SPD claims to have 22% working class members.[13] This figure has also been incorporated in a comparative analysis of the three major parties by Troitzsch (Table 3.1). He documents the relative strength of the working class sector among the SPD membership and also the similarity between the SPD and the other parties regarding white collar and civil servant following. The middle class weighting of CDU and CSU is centred around the self-employed, while the FDP emerges as a white collar based party. Troitzsch, however, lists pensioners as a separate category. For the SPD, many of its older members from the traditional working class clientele would be included here. The figure of 22% seems to be low if occupational backgroud is measured.

Table 3.1: Social Composition of Party Memberships, 1977

Social/Occupational Group	CDU %	CSU %	SPD %	FDP %	Total %	Pop I[1] %	Pop II[2] %	Members to electorate per 1000
Workers	11	14	22	5	17	22	17	33.1
Employees	27	20	24	30	25	19	22	57.3
Civil Servants	12	12	13	14	13	4	5	138.4
Self-Employed	26	32	5	19	12	7	7	77.2
Pensioners	5	6	18	12	12	19	18	28.3
Housewives	10	4	6	11	8	22	24	14.9
In training/education	6	4	5	9	5	7	5	34.0

Source: Klaus G. Troitzsch, in Kaack/Roth I, p. 95.
1. Data from Sozialdemokrat Magazin 4, 1978.
2. Data from Gluchowski/Veen, Nivellierungstendenzen.

The Infas survey of 1977 arrived at a total of 31% working class members, 20% skilled and 11% unskilled.[14] Here the observation is important that the higher skilled workers are more likely to join the party. In other words, that section of the working population which considers itself middle class and borders most closely in income and social position on the white collar and middle class strata constitutes the bulk of the working class segment in the SPD membership. As members, the party attracts, to put it casually, the working class aristocracy, not the humble labourer. Infratest does not distinguish between levels of skill. Workers here remains a somewhat amorphous category. Despite this lack of clarity, the findings are interesting since they show the difference between party membership, electorate and social origin of SPD members. Table 3.2 combines these data and also includes the Infas data on the social position of party officials.

Table 3.2: SPD Social Composition in 1977

Occupation of head of household	Pop[1] %	Voters[1] %	Members[1] %	Funct-ionares[2] %	Occupation of Father of Party Members
Worker	38	47	35	23	56
Employee	29	29	36	57	28
Civil Servant	12	11	18		
Self-Employed	14	6	7	7	15
Other	7	7	4	6	-
Not known	-	-	-	9	-

Sources: 1. Infratest p. 4.
2. Infas data p. 7.

Some differences and trends may be stated. The SPD electorate is more working class, the SPD membership less working class than the population as a whole. Since the mid-seventies, the proportion of workers in the SPD has declined further, the profile of the SPD as a party for the better-off and better-educated gained contour (Table 3.3). Overall, members tend to be social risers. More than half came from working class backgrounds in the seventies (Table 3.2). 43% saw themselves as working- or lower class, 48% thought they were middle class and 5% felt part of the upper class. Among functionaries, only 22% believed they were working class, 60% named the middle class and 15% the upper class as their place in society.[15]

In a discussion paper on the state of the party,

Table 3.3: Occupational Structure of SPD Membership 1977 and 1981

Occupation	1977 %	Balance of gains and losses 1977-1981	Estimates of social composition, end of 1981 %
Workers	22	-12,500	21
Employees	26	-4,300	27
Civil Servants	13	-500	14
Self-Employed	5	-3,000	5
Students, Pupils, Apprentices	5	-7,500	4
Pensioners	18	-17,900	17
Housewives	7	+4,300	8
Others	4		4

Source: Die SPD von innen, p. 59. The 1977 data are taken from the Infas study, the data on gains and losses from the EDV, statistical records, the 1981 occupational estimates are based on the impact of these losses and gains.

Peter von Oertzen called the prevelance of social risers, of people who had come from working class homes and were themselves no longer working class or who had improved their social standing during their working lives, a "structural problem" which the party had to face and digest:

> In the body of functionaries and in the active membership of the party those prevail who in their own life or in their political careers have enhanced their social status. Among factory workers, party- or trade union functionaries are also often not those who started as workers and will retire as workers. The voters, however, are not predominantly social risers, nor are the ordinary members.[16]

A detachment, even a rift between two layers of SPD supporters seems to loom, the presence of two parties under one name and organizational umbrella.

Inroads for the Better-off

The shift towards a middle class position of the party as a whole and SPD officials in particular is confirmed by other factors. The average income of party members is slightly, that of functionaries well above, the national average;[17] every second member owns a house or apartment, two in three functionaries own real estate.[18] SPD members are better educated and frequently recruited from public sector professions.[19]

Table 3.4: The Educational Background of SPD Members and Functionaries, 1977

Level of schooling	SPD members	SPD functionaries	Population
Basic schooling only	13	7	
Basic schooling and completed apprenticeship	49	41	70
Further and higher education	37	51	30
n.a.	1	1	-

Sources: Infratest p. 4, Infas p. 7.

In the mid-fifties, the SPD was a party for the less well educated. 91% had received only basic schooling. Twenty years later, 62% had basic schooling, while the segment of highly educated SPD members had grown from 3% in the fifties to 15% in the seventies.[20] In the early seventies, newcomers to the party were particularly well educated. 22% had A level or higher qualifications.[21] The various data on the social structure of SPD membership confirm the general claim that the party moved away from its working class focus. In a more specific way, the data also highlight some of the organizational and political consequences the SPD experienced in the wake of the growth and transitions since the sixties. The disparity between the social composition of the party electorate and the social composition of the party membership and leadership poses the question whether the SPD is on the way to becoming a divided party with a passive and powerless following and a leadership recruitment which favours the well educated, the white collar professions, and

and the civil servants who flocked into the SPD since it acquired government respectability.

PARTY ORGANIZATION AND PARTY FUNCTIONARIES

The day-to-day running of political parties relies heavily on honorary contributions. Salaried party workers are employed at the district, the regional and the national levels of all parties. In 1969, Bodo Zeuner collated information provided by the party offices in Bonn. Then, the SPD had about 405 paid officials, i.e. 0.05% of its membership.[22] At the same time, so called functionaries, unpaid party workers amounted to 10% of the party membership.[23] In 1982, the SPD had 64,000 such functionaries; this amounted to just under 7% of the membership. Organizationally, the SPD is divided into 22 districts (Bezirke), 250 sub-districts (Unterbezirke) and about 10,000 local branches. Perhaps the most significant right of the local branch in terms of influencing party affairs is the right to directly submit resolutions to the party congress. This right is used only sparingly and the organization of SPD party congresses makes it difficult for grass root initiatives to be successful.[24] Local branches also elect delegates to higher level congresses. They are involved in the selection process for parliamentary candidates and, of course, they elect their own local leadership.

A Platform for Leadership
On the macro-level of an interrelation between party organization and policy formulation in government or opposition, the limited impact of party goals and the principles agreed at congresses has received some attention.[25] The question of leadership is frequently linked with the question of policy formulation and mobilization of mass support.[26] In this broader perspective, the chancellorship of Brandt contributed significantly to the influx of students and grammar school pupils into the party, i.e. of young and highly educated new members. Schmidt as a Chancellor did not have a similar effect on the size and social composition of the SPD. The mid-sixties turning point when white collar and civil service support shifted the social balance of the SPD and its electorate can similarly be linked to the party's ascent to government.

A further dimension of party leadership concerns

the relevance of local party organizations and honorary party positions in the career patterns of politicians. Regarding parliamentary candidates we noted earlier that nomination largely depends on years of service at the grass root level. A study of front bench politicians in 1968 and their career patterns confirmed the place of honorary party work as a career platform. About half the SPD parliamentarians included in Herzog's study held positions as chairmen or members of the executive of local or district party organizations.[27] Local government is a further field of recruitment. In 1968, 55% of Herzog's leading parliamentarians had been in local politics prior to entering the Bundestag. This commitment to the grass roots of party politics is more than casual. Herzog arrived at an average term of office of ten years. Frequently, party functionaries are reelected year after year. Bearing in mind that Herzog's sample only included people who left the level of local party organizations and reached front bench positions in parliament, the slow pace of careers and the importance of grass root involvement are striking.[28] Herzog's data suggest that local party organization, the honorary party functionaries are the main segment for recruitment of political leadership in West Germany. Zeuner found in 1969 that the political influence of SPD party office holders on a local or district level was very high.[29] Although functionaries are honorary politicians, they can shape local party life and gain social and political standing in the community as a whole.[30] Grass root politicians in the SPD are an important group to shape the party and its place in society.

The Social Composition of SPD functionaries

SPD party functionaries in the late seventies tended to be better educated, more often in senior positions in the civil service or the professions than the rank and file members (Tables 3.2 and 3.4). They also tended to be younger and relatively new party members. 58% of the party functionaries of 1977 had joined the party since 1967, i.e. at a time when the SPD was broadening out into the white collar- and civil service sectors of society. One in ten functionaries had been a member of the party since 1950 or before. Most of the old guard occupied rather lowly position in the leadership hierarchy. A study for Northrhine-Westfalia showed that the few working class functionaries tended to collect the party dues. Through their regular visiting rounds they maintained good contacts with the members. In the party organization, however, their influence was small.[31] In Osnabrück, a similar survey rendered similar results. Working class origin was rare among members and even rarer among functionaries. Data for December 1982 suggest that nearly half the functionary positions in the SPD were held by technical or administrative staff, by teachers in secondary- or higher education. Their combined share of party membership at the time was around 20%. Functionaries with working class backgrounds often occupy the less important positions such as Beisitzer.[32] Women in the SPD suffer a similar fate. Overall, the party has about 23% female members; an estimated 15% of its functionaries are women. The positions of chairman or delegate or electoral candidate seem to be male middle-class prerogatives. Like workers, women rarely rise above the position of Beisitzer.[33]

A recent comparison of two neighbouring party branches in the Ruhr town of Mülheim highlighted the SPD transitions and internal differences.[34] One of the branches was located in the vicinity of the Mannesmann steel works. It had among its members a high proportion of workers, most active members and party office holders were also trade union functionaries or works councillors. They could be regarded as social risers among the working class, a workers' aristocracy perhaps. In this branch, members tended to locate themselves politically on the right (33%), and less frequently on the left (23%). In contrast, the branch Town Centre organized civil servants, employees, college students and drew on more residential areas. Here, women were more strongly represented (30% compared with 10%) and political opinion tended towards the left. 38% saw themselves as on the left, 10% as on the right of the political spectrum. In both branches, a displacement of ordinary working people was evident:

> Those from the Metal Workers' Union or from the Miners' Union, those from large industries with their high degree of unionization and - for those workers who still live in housing estates which belong to large industrial enterprises - with their cohesive social fabric and climate, all those people experience difficulties of orientation and problems of asserting themselves in the mixed social environment inside the party. Municipal employees,

teachers, civil servants have more time and
perhaps more inclination to perform in public.

In short, at best those workers who gained confidence and organizational skills through trade union work may have a chance to make a mark in the SPD and rise to office holders. With the disappearance of enclaves or working class culture such as works' estates or working men's social clubs, and with the gradual displacement of manual work by technical-, white collar- and administrative tasks in the economy, the social fabric of the SPD has undergone and is still undergoing a profound transformation. Organizationally and politically, the party has yet to face the consequences of this transformation and find answers to the social and political incongruities which now characterize its place in society.

MOTIVATIONS FOR MEMBERSHIP: BEYOND WORKING CLASS TRADITIONS

The feeble representation of working class members in the SPD body of party functionaries is not just a matter of polished speech and an ability to state one's case in public. A shift in membership motivations and attitudes of members vis-a-vis their party contributed towards the transformation of the SPD and accelerated the entrenchment of the middle class segment in the party leadership structures. Two surveys of membership structures and membership goals in the late sixties showed that traditional SPD loyalties based on family tradition and focused on the party organization as the main lever for political influence were still relevant for just under half the members.[35] More individualized motivations for party membership and more individualized intentions to shape the political process were on the increase.[36] Comparisons with the CDU suggested at the time, that most of the CDU members had such an individualized motivation for membership and were more ready than their SPD counterparts to hold an office in the party or in organizations or associations on the local level. The commitment of the traditional SPD supporter, it seems, breeds loyalty but also little push to hold office and fulfil a leadership role in the community or in the party. The upsurge in party membership since the mid sixties brought significant shifts of emphasis. Today, traditional loyalties may still be relevant for one third of SPD members,[37] the majority however combine personal aspirations of gaining influence and shaping the party or democracy as a whole according to their own interests. The political focus changed from the party and loyalty to the organization to the individual and his motivation for participation and involvement. The influx of members from social strata not traditionally affiliated to the SPD made the individual motivation of gaining political influence in and through the party more relevant. While it was quite sufficient for a recruit from an SPD environment to join the party, the middle class newcomers tend to strive for office within it. Active SPD members, whether functionaries or regular attenders of party meetings or campaign helpers are particularly interested in gaining political influence through the party.[38] Of the members in 1977, 20% were active in terms of holding posts, acting as delegates or contributing on a regular basis to party activities. A further 5% participated fairly consistently to party matters. This active sector of 25% is to a large extent shaped by the white collar and civil service segment of the party. The traditional SPD support seems to feed into the bulk of passive membership, the 65% who only want to belong and pay their dues.[39]

Several factors could influence this internal division. The differences in motivations for membership might result in two types of members and aid the white-collarization of the SPD. The activity/passivity divisions might also point to an alienation of the more traditional sectors of SPD support, the working class members. More detailed studies would have to explore whether formerly active members have withdraw from party involvement in the last decade or so. At present it seems the remaining working class elements in the party are pushed to the margin. Within the SPD, differences in membership motivation and activity seem to correspond with social position. The white-collarization of SPD functionaries might produce a divided party, a party dominated and run without really involving the working class sector. The distance is also growing between the day-to-day organization of the SPD and its electorate in West German society. Although it could be argued that these tendencies show a successful adaptation of the SPD to the major changes in the social structure of post-war Germany, the extent of the transition created new imbalances.

Some Practical Moves

In the wake of the Börner/Koschnik report and the two communication studies, the SPD has articulated this danger and generated several drives to improve the link between local party organizations and the communities they serve. Extensive publicity materials on membership recruitment and especially looking after members once they joined were intended to broaden the social spectrum of SPD activities. On a more pragmatic level, a reduction of resignations from the party might also have been intended. The SPD maintains that the old pattern of party loyalty where leaving the party was unthinkable is still in force.[40] This assumption does not tally with further evidence.

The Infratest study found 5% of SPD members ready to leave the party with even more voicing criticism that their hopes for political involvement had been blocked by the way the party operated.[41] The SPD does not publish details on resignations and reasons for resignations of membership. Crude estimates are possible from the material on membership development and the SPD yearbooks. Between 1975 and 1977, about 5% annually resigned. These could be compensated for at the time by new admissions.[42] Since 1978, resignations outstripped admissions, and SPD membership began to decline. The change of government seems to have halted this process. In January 1982, the SPD recorded a deficit of 5,610 members or 0.6% compared with the previous month. In January 1983, membership rose by 719 or 0.9%. Party workers referred to packing crates full of membership applications after the collapse of the coalition in September 1982. In June 1982, the SPD had reached a low point for the late seventies and early eighties with 925,933 members. By January 1983, figures had climbed back to 926,866.[43]

In addition to the membership drives on the local level, community relations have been emphasized. Party organizations are encouraged to publish district newspapers and involve themselves in local issues. <u>Stadtteilzeitungen</u>, it seems, are popular with SPD members since they show their party as a locally relevant political force. Distributing the papers tends to draw the active members more closely together and give room for casual participants to play a part. More important, however, is the competition on the community level from citizens' action groups and citizens' initiatives which proved the most outspoken campaigners on issues of planning and community care in recent years.[44] Rather than reach

the passive sectors of its own membership, the SPD
is trying with the Stadtteilzeitungen and similar
efforts to not lose touch with the local scene and
local topics. Community related topics, which always ranked highly among CDU members, have emerged
as an important focal point for the SPD as well.
There is some evidence, however, that the restructuring of the party's activities is only slowly
catching up with the shift in political orientation
of its membership over the last decade. The mainstay of SPD party meetings in the fifties and early
sixties was the lecture on major aspects of national
politics. Membership involvement was limited to a
summary answer to questions after the lecture. In
any case, the lecture normally took place after the
event. Its function was to inform the members of
decisions taken. The assumption that the SPD had a
role to play in educating its members politically
and keeping them informed, if not instructed, might
have been appropriate to a more traditional pattern
of SPD support. The new party clientele does not
rely on the party and its various organs for political information but makes ample use of the ordinary
media, not least the mass circulation tabloid Bild
Zeitung.[45] The new format of party work has still
to be created. It would have to satisfy the need of
the SPD traditionalists to identify with their party.
It would also have to satisfy the need of the politically motivated newcomer looking for ways to involve
himself in decision making and democracy to shape
events through the party organization and within it.
These dual aims have not been reconciled. In addition, the high regional diversity might create quite
disparate SPD organizations. The only apparently
successful format of party involvement seems to be
the social gathering which enjoys the highest turnout. But even here, members report it is always the
same closed circle which meets and socializes. A
blueprint for unifying the social camps in the party
needs still to be discovered.

Membership integration and an emphasis on grass
root organization have been advocated as partial
answers. In the late seventies, a series of handbooks was compiled to assist honorary party workers.
Focal points were looking after new members and re-
thinking social and political programmes to ensure
maximum impact and audience participation,[46] In
addition, a compendium to bring new members more
effectively into the party was published in 1982 by
the Education Department of the SPD headquarters.
Personal contacts, discussions and less formal

settings for party meetings are increasingly recommended.[47] Organizational matters also occupied the party congress at Munich in 1982 as one of its core themes. To highlight the importance of local branches and their work, an exhibition was mounted and a prize awarded under the heading <u>Lebendiger Ortsverein,</u> living local branch.[48] Critical analyses of the internal disparities of the SPD preceded their public airing. In January 1982, a discussion paper by the Commission for Organizational Policies warned of impending conflicts in the party between different social and political camps and between members and functionaries or activists. Membership losses of 10-20% were reported for urban areas, and an overall low ebb of motivation to work for the party and its goals. In large branches, membership contacts were mostly neglected, a small executive circle run affairs and remained quite detached from the rank and file.[49] The challenge to instil new life, even enthusiasm, into an ailing SPD did not merely arise from a search for more members, more revenue, a better atmosphere within the party or better performance at community level. It also arose from the organizational reforms which had changed the CDU during its spell in opposition from a rudimentary framework for elections to an efficient party machinery with a large and active membership. The challenge for the SPD in opposition may be called a challenge of revitalization. Addressing his fellow parliamentarians in the Bundestag, Hans Jochen Vogel, the luckless contender for the chancellorship in 1983, appealed to intensify contacts within the party, in particular with SPD branches and representatives on local and regional levels.[50] He called for <u>Schulterschluss</u>, a walk shoulder to shoulder to strengthen the party internally and improve communications. With opposition, the integrative force of government, providing the chancellor and making national policies, has disappeared. More depends on the party and its organization. Opposition may well provide the incentive for the SPD to tackle the problems of membership disparities and social transformations which accompanied the period in government and burdened the party with their political and organizational side-effects.

The SPD in Transition

IMPULSES FROM THE YOUNG

Like all parties, the SPD sees the recruitment of young people as a yardstick of the party's appeal among the new generations and its capacity to rejuvenate membership and leadership. Looking at recruitment alone, the SPD has done well. In 1972, just under one third of its members were under thirtyfive.[51] In the boom year of 1972 when it gained over 100,000 members in this age bracket; later the SPD reported 30-40,000 new members under 35 per year. On average, two thirds of the new recruits to the party have belonged to the post-war generations.[52] In 1979, as at the beginning of the seventies, one third of the SPD members were under 35 years old.[53] Since then, the proportion of young people in the party has declined. In December 1980, it accounted for 26% of the SPD membership, by December 1982, to 24%. The decline was most pronounced among the under 30s, from 16.5% in 1980 to 13% at the end of 1982.[54] We saw earlier that younger members are well represented among party functionaries. They seem to be ready for active participation and for the "Ochsentour", i.e. the years of service through the party to rise to higher office and to elected positions in the community or in parliaments. There is little evidence yet that the rejuvenated body of party functionaries launched new initiatives and generated impulses into the party which improved its cohesion and the participation rate of its members. On the contrary, various warnings about a crisis within the party, of dwindling members' involvement and cleavages between the rank and file and the functionaries at the local level and above suggest that the integration of the younger members into the SPD honorary bureaucracy did not by itself bridge the inner-party divisions analysed earlier.[55]

    A youth wing, an association or party sector where the young could articulate policies and test new approaches to party organization does, of course, exist. The Young Socialists are open to young people from 16 to 35. Membership in the SPD is not required although active and passive voting rights within the Young Socialists depend on party membership.[56] The SPD in 1977 had some 300,000 members in the age groups under 35, 80,000 of these stated to belong to the Young Socialists, 35,000 claimed to be active members.[57] The figure of 44% active participation in youth organization, however, or 12% of

all young SPD members does not stand up to scrutiny.
In November/December 1977, Dieter Stephan conducted a
survey among Young Socialists to assess the activity
ratio and changes in the social structure. He found
that at best 16,000 Young Socialists could be called
active, i.e. they attended meetings about once a
month.[58] Participation was high in 1972 and has
since fallen by about 40%.[59] Apathy spread between
1974 and 1976, which corresponds to a slackening in
SPD recruitment overall and the resignation of Willy
Brandt as Chancellor. The unwillingness of young
SPD members to involve themselves with the Young
Socialists is highest in those areas where academics
hold the positions of functionaries.[60] Yet, the
Young Socialists today are largely an association for
young academics and grammar school pupils in the SPD.
An average of 48% are in higher education.[61] There
are some regional variations. Dortmund, for example,
had a relatively high proportion of workers in 1977
(18.4%) and fewer pupils and students (21.9%). Overall, the Young Socialists have become a party section which is strongly dominated by the academically
trained or the highly educated. Among the functionaries, and particularly at the district and higher
levels, workers are not represented. The impact of
academics increases with the level of activity.
Among members who are regulars at meetings, 52% are
academics, among the executive on the lowest organizational level 53%, at district level 86%, among
delegates to the national congress 81% are fully
qualified academics.[62] If one were to include students and grammar school pupils as potential academics, the take over of the Young Socialists by academics would prove even more complete. Youth in the
Young Socialists has come to be a synonym to academic
youth. The white collarization of the youth sector
has outpaced that of the SPD as a whole. The working young now ignore the Young Socialists as an inroad into the party. At present, they appear to
stay away from the SPD altogether. If they join
anything, it would either be their relevant trade
union section or the youth group "Falken", Hawks
which has emerged during the seventies as the forum
for the working class youths.[63]

The segregation between academic and non-academic sectors of West German youth and the transformation of the Young Socialists into a student/academic association occurred in the mid sixties.
Contrary to the student sector which had a series of
conflicts with the main party, Young Socialists had

been loyal adherents to the party line.[64] The SPD ditched its original student group, the SDS[65] for refusing to follow the moderate course after Godesberg. The successor organization SHB[66] became radicalized in the mid sixties under the dual impact of Grand Coalition and student unrest. The party again dropped the unwelcome appendix and has since been without a formal student organization. This organizational void might have been one reason for academics to come to the Young Socialists. More relevant perhaps was the feeling of <u>Machtwechsel</u> and the desire spurred by the failure of extraparliamentary politics to participate in and through an existing organization, the SPD.

The newcomers were better educated and more committed to left wing politics than the earlier Young Socialists and the party as a whole. In a series of clashes in the seventies, the Young Socialists emerged as propagators of anticapitalist theories and political concepts which were ill matched to the efforts of the SPD to expand towards the middle ground.[67] The political stance of the Young Socialists was clearly out of line with the party although academics and white collar professions set the tone. In other words, the Young Socialists emerged as an opposition of highly educated middle class elements in the party, an inner party opposition of the left.

The influx of the highly educated did not necessarily spell moderation. The correlation between protest potential to the left and high educational achievements which has been established for West German society is also relevant for young members of the SPD and in particular for the activists in the Young Socialists. There is little evidence that the inner party opposition of the young creates new impulses in the SPD. Recruitment to positions of leadership from the ranks of the Young Socialists is rare.[68] The former student organizations were platforms for leadership training. Helmut Schmidt had belonged to the old SDS; Wolfgang Roth and Volker Hauff, to name just two prominant younger politicians, came from the successor organization SHB. Today, the SPD no longer has a student wing as such and the Young Socialists took over some of the functions of a student organization - save that of leadership training. Young people today advance in the party as party functionaries from the lower level upwards. Their incorporation into the party machinery seems to be more intense and prolonged than that of their predecessors, the first generation of post-war politicians and party leaders had been.[69] Career chances for Young Socialists exist in and through the party branches. In their search for influence and advancement in politics, Young Socialists have been reported to aim for control of branch proceedings and selection procedures. Some incidents have become known of Young Socialists, as a group, ousting established party workers and of young functionaries maintaining a distinctly left-wing profile in contrast to the majority views in the ward or branch in question. The radicalism of the Young Socialists intensified discussions within the party on organizational reform. While the SPD was in government, criticism centred on the inability of the party to transfer party goals onto government levels. In the face of government constraints, party initiatives always seemed to fizzle out. "Never in the history of the SPD were party congress decisions ignored as cynically as they are now by SPD parliamentarians".[70]

While the SPD was in government, the Young Socialists spearheaded the opposition from within the party. They became the voice of a leftist intelligensia with little echo in the party of other youth organizations of the labour movement. The Young Socialists' middle class radicalism seemed to alienate the very wage earners whom they so emphatically wanted to reach. The academic takeover of the SPD youth association also isolated the party from trade union youth and from ordinary young people. The SPD, as we saw earlier, faces a problem of transition where leaders and activists seem detached from the party rank and file, and from the mainstream of political thinking in society. The radical left-wing profile of the Young Socialists and their academic orientation aggravate the problems of transition from a party of the labour movement to a party of contemporary German society. Yet, some adjustments of style have been apparent after the collapse of the SPD/FDP coalition. The Young Socialists have been less critical of the party, less entrenched in their role as inner party opposition than they were at times of government.[71] They may in fact attempt the <u>Schulterschluss</u>, the shoulder to shoulder position to which Vogel hoped to commit the SPD and its politicians. The newly found party loyalty does, however, not compensate for the marginal place of Young Socialists in the SPD today.

The SPD in Transition

SPD AND OPPOSITION

Nearly sixteen years in government left their mark on the SPD. We discussed earlier how a new generation of members, party leaders and politicians has emerged who never experienced the SPD outside government. Their commitment may undergo some changes, quite apart from the need for party political appointments in the state administration to find new openings, or for former members of the Bundestag who were not re-elected in 1983, to look elsewhere. While the CDU in its period of uninterrupted government from 1949 to 1969 practiced a format of political decision making which granted priority to the government level and had the party follow loyally, the SPD never recinded its role as a policy creator. Party congresses attempted to sketch the guidelines for SPD chancellors and their ministers. Conflicts within the SPD about priorities and orientations continued. Helmut Schmidt as Chancellor displayed a tendency to regard the party as an appendage to his office. This provoked opposition and counter-pressures. Between 1976 and 1980, public eruptions of opposition were kept at bay by the slender majority in the Bundestag and by repeated warnings that rocking the boat and contradicting government lines would serve to erode the already shaky government support. The handsome gains in the 1980 elections, even if won by the FDP, gave more leeway to voices of dissent, and some parliamentary factionalism emerged in public, for instance, over the issue of armament policies. The SPD reacted as always: it expelled the offending members and tried to deter future dissenters. While this approach worked reasonably well in the Bundestag, other party levels could not be cajoled into submission to a government inspired unison.

The issues of disarmament and of stationing nuclear missiles on German soil created perhaps the fiercest rift between sections of the party on one side, and Chancellor and government on the other. Within the party, opposition to all types of nuclear weapons and specifically to the additional weapons systems Pershing II and Cruise had gathered momentum since 1980 in line with opinions and views in society. The Nato Twin Track Decision gradually unleashed what has become known as the Peace Movement. Large groupings in the party from Young Socialists to whole districts, branches and individuals endorsed it. The party congress in Munich in April 1982 had to formulate a policy commitment in this matter. It proceeded cautiously. Congress found a compromise formula which committed the party to hold an extraordinary congress in the autumn of 1983 (scheduled for November) which should assess the outcome of the negotiations in Geneva and then decide whether or not political agreement had made it superfluous for the party to take a definite stand against stationing nuclear missile systems in West Germany.72 In Munich, Young Socialists and other groupings from within the SPD staged a torch-light procession against nuclear arms and against the policies of their own party's chancellor. Since then, the SPD has entered opposition. The tightrope walk between supporting the chancellor and responding to pressures from below is no longer necessary. Schmidt himself has renounced the ill-fated formula which links armaments to the outcome of talks. Party chairman Willy Brandt who in Munich had to use all his charisma to pacify dissenters, could ease up and hint at a newly gained political scope:

> I was of the opinion that if one has the chancellor and he comes in a difficult area to the result to which he came, then one has to give him support. This at least was my duty as the chairman of the party. And it was my duty, at the Munich congress, to ensure that the Chancellor would not be deserted. And in such a situation one puts one's own preferences a little into the background - at least in the function which I held then and which I still hold at the moment ... What does this mean for today where we no longer provide the chancellor? For today, it means firstly, that we have to honour what we stated at the time. And it means secondly, that we have to remain able to conduct politics (politikfähig bleiben).73

Brandt's cautious hints highlight the dilemma for the SPD: the backing it provided for its own chancellor left it with a congress commitment to further reflect upon the nuclear weapon issue and evaluate it calmly in the light of the Geneva talks. This fails to satisfy the mounting oppositional pressures from within the part and elsewhere in German society. Yet, congress decisions cannot simply be ignored. More awkwardly, the political momentum of the so called Peace Movement is extra-parliamentary, prone to articulate policies by means of demonstrations, protests, civil disobedience. Brandt's plea

to remain <u>politikfähig</u> also means that the SPD
should not be sucked into the temptations and irregularities of extra-parliamentary protests as a replacement of more conventional political routes.
The new tightrope for the SPD in opposition spans
between taking up the issues of the Peace Movement
and its own left wing without succumbing to object-
ionable styles of action or all too rigid priorities.

In June 1983, the SPD executive finally ruled
that the party was in overall agreement with the
themes and issues of the Peace Movement. Directives
to local and district branches recommended to keep
SPD activities around the peace and disarmament
themes clearly separate from those of other Peace
campaigners. By that time, a week of protest actions had already been scheduled by the Peace
Movement for late October 1983, a tide had begun to
role which the SPD was unable to stem. By mid
October, most party districts had voted at their
conferences to reject nuclear arms. Some even rejected explicitly the NATO Twin Track Decision. All
proclaimed that they would join into the action week
in October.[74] One year after the step into opposit-
tion, the SPD has swung against a cornerstone of its
own government policy on defence. More accurately,
decisions against these policies snowballed within
the SPD from the lower organizational levels and
urged the party to adopt a more flexible approach.
The heavy losses during the 1983 elections and the
experience that younger voters had not immediately
found their way back to the SPD from the Greens,
have speeded up the reorientation. The SPD cannot
afford to leave the peace issues and related themes
of disarmament to the self-styled Peace Movement.
The party is now attempting to become the most respectable, albeit moderate voice from the left, and
regain those voters from the multifaceted opposition
who were disenchanted with the SPD in government or
who never considered voting SPD because it was in
government and on the wrong side in matters of peace
and similar issues of the "new politics".[75]

A second thrust of SPD opposition relates to
the social and economic conditions in West Germany:
the experience of unemployment or the fear of unemployment had persuaded a considerable segment of the
better-off working population to change sides and
vote CDU. At the same time, the long standing SPD
promise of full employment and state measures against unemployment have gained new drive. Most SPD
parliamentary activities since September 1982 were

aimed at unemployment.[76] Most of the preliminary programmatic statements in opposition concerned unemployment and how to fight it with public investments.[77]

Since the trade unions also mounted a campaign against the dismantling of the welfare state and against unemployment, party and unions seem to have arrived at a more cohesive approach in opposition than they were able to pursue while the SPD was in government and had to accomodate the social market reservations of the FDP in all labour- and economic policy matters.

Opposition, it may be concluded, has stimulated innovation and readjustment in key areas of policy and in matters of party organization. Some expect a revision of the Godesberg programme. Others predict a revision of the Orientierungsrahmen of 1975 which had been written as a long term perspective for government and was strongly influenced by the views and priorities of Helmut Schmidt. A programmatic clarification of SPD goals and policy landmarks for the eighties and nineties is on the cards. Opposition has returned the policy making initiatives to the party. It has also created the opportunity for the dissenting voices and diverse motivations in the SPD to contribute to its new political profile. This could be the Schulterschluss or the revitalization from within, for a transformed and destablized SPD.

FOOTNOTES

1. Holger Börner/Hans Koschnik, Bundestagswahlkampf, 1976: Analyse und Folgerungen für die SPD. Unpublished manuscript n.d. (1976), SPD archives.
2. Ibid., p. 13.
3. Ibid., p. 6.
4. An Office for Senior Citizens (Beauftragter für Seniorenarbeit beim Parteivorstand) has since been established at the Bonn SPD headquarters.
5. "Röntgenbild einer Volkspartei", Sozialdemokrat Magazin 4, April 1978.
6. Zur politischen Kultur in der Demokratie. Ein Diskussionspapier der Kommission Grundwerte beim SPD Parteivorstand, Januar 1980. Reihe Theorie und Grundwerte, Bonn 1980, p. 16.
7. This was stated by Dr. Wolfgang Falke, then Director of the Social Sciences Research Institute of the Konrad Adenauer Foundation in St. Augustin, near Bonn, during an interview on 25 April 1980. The SPD studies referred to are: Infas Report. Parteisozio-

logische Untersuchungen 1977. Bonn Bad Godesberg, February 1978. Ref No 1407/8678: Zusammenfassung der Ergebnisse and: Infratest Sozialforschung. Kommunikationsstudie zur SPD Organisation. Zusammenfassung, 1978.

    8. For the CDU: Wolfgang Falke, Die Integration von Parteimitgliedern. Eine empirische Studie zur Teilnahme und Kommunikation der Mitglieder in der Organisation der CDU 1971-1977. Berlin (Duncker & Humblodt), 1982.

    9. Alf Mintzel, Anatomie einer Partei: die CSU Opladen (Westdt. Verlag) 1976 and Mintzel,"The Christian Social Union in Bavaria. Analytical notes on its development, role and political success". In Elections and Parties, German Political Studies III, op.cit., pp. 191-226.

    10. Institut für Kommunikationsforschung (IfK): Situationsanalyse zur Ermittlung der Voraussetzungen für methodische Öffentlichkeitsarbeit innerhalb der Mitgliederstruktur der FDP. Meinungsumfrage bei FDP Mitgliedern. Abschlussbericht I 1977. Unpublished manuscript in the FDP archives in Bonn.

    11. See Richard N. Hunt, German Social Democracy 1918-1933, New Haven/London 1964, p. 129 f. Also Jürgen Harrer, "Die Sozialdemokratie in Novemberrevolution und Weimarer Republik 1918-1933" in Jutta von Freyberg et.al., (eds.), Geschichte der deutschen Sozialdemokratie 1863-1975, Köln (Pahl Rugenstein) 1975, pp. 94 ff.

    12. Marie-Christine Zauzich, Parteien im Wandel, München (Bayrische Landeszentrale für politische Bildung) 1976, pp. 84-92.

    13. Sozialdemokrat Magazin, ibid., p. 9.
    14. Infas, p. 7.
    15. Ibid., p. 8.
    16. Peter von Oertzen, "Die organisationspolitischen Aufgaben der SPD" in Organisationspolitik, Ergebnisse einer Fachkonferenz des SPD Bezirks Mittelrhein 20.5.1982 in Köln, p. 45.
    17. Infratest, p. 5.
    18. Ibid., p. 7.
    19. Gluchowski/Veen op.cit., p. 325 compare SPD and CDU.
    20. Ibid.
    21. Infratest p. 4, also the Jahrbücher published bi-annually by the SPD.
    22. Bodo Zeuner, Innerparteiliche Demokratie, Berlin (Colloquium) 1970, p. 86.
    23. Ibid., p. 76.
    24. So Jürgen Dittberner, "Die Rolle der Parteitage im Prozess der innerparteilichen

Willensbildung" in PVS ii (1970), no. 2/3, also: "Party Congresses" in German Political Studies I., p. 19.

25. Gerard Braunthal, "The Policy Function of the German Social Democratic Party" in Comparative Politics 9 (1977), no. 2, pp. 127-145.

26. Paterson for example analyses the SPD from the perspective of the Brandt/Schmidt leadership: "The German Social Democratic Party" in W.E. Paterson/A.H. Thomas (eds.), Social Democratic Parties in Western Europe, Croom Helm 1977, pp. 176-212.

27. Dietrich Herzog, "Karrieren und politische Professionalisierung bei der CDU/CSU, SPD und FDP" in Dittberner/Ebbighausen (eds.), Parteiensystem in der Legitimationskrise, Opladen (Westdt. Verlag) 1973, p. 118.

28. Ibid., pp. 114-115.

29. Zeuner, op.cit., p. 83.

30. Ulrich Lohmar, Innerparteiliche Demokratie, Stuttgart, 1963, p. 51.

31. Feist/Güllner/Liepelt, in Parties and Elections, op.cit., p. 183.

32. Heinz Peter Platen, "Volkspartei oder was sonst? Zur Sozialstruktur der SPD in Osnabrück" in Neue Gesellschaft 24 (1977), no. 11, p. 937. Information for 1982 based on various interviews at the SPD Bundesgeschäftsstelle on March 17 and 18, 1983.

33. Infratest, p. 7.

34. Die Zeit 31, 29.7.83.

35. Armin Meyer, "Parteiaktivitäten und Einstellungen von CDU und SPD Mitgliedern" in Dittberner/Ebbighausen, Parteiensystem, op.cit., p. 67.

36. Nils Diederichs, "Zur Mitgliederstruktur von CDU und SPD" in Dittberner/Ebbighausen, ibid., p. 52.

37. Infratest, p. 23.

38. Ibid., p. 24.

39. Infas, p. 48.

40. Röntgenbild, op.cit., p. 10.

41. Infratest, p. 24.

42. Calculated on the basis of the figures in Jahrbuch der Sozialdemokratischen Partei 1975-77 and 1977-79.

43. Interview with Frau Doris Biesenbaum, Abt. Organisation beim SPD Vorstand, 17.3.1983. Membership data EDV - printout.

44. See chapter 9 below.

45. Röntgenbild op.cit., p. 12 and in detail in both Infratest and Infas.

46. See Parteiarbeit. Handbuch für die Arbeit in sozialdemokratischen Ortsvereinen; among the themes covered are Ortsverein, Organisation, Bildungsarbeit.

47. Neumitgliederschulung, zusammengestellt vom Referat für Bildung beim Parteivorstand der SPD, November 1982.

48. See Vorwärts Extra, 6.6.1982, pp. 1-8; also Wegweiser, Anschauen, Reden, Nachmachen, 1982; also SPD Parteitag 19-23, April 82, München Protokolle (Bd. I), Bonn 1982.

49. Vorlage für die Sitzung des Präsidiums 8.2.1982 (TOP 3d, manuscript) esp. pp. 1-8.

50. See SPD Bundestagsfraktion, Thema der Woche, 10.3.1982.

51. Jahrbuch der SPD 1970-72, p. 306.

52. Jahrbücher 1973-75, p. 296 f. dto 1975-77, p. 286 f. An annual recruitment of 20,000 members under 35 is mentioned in: Timothy R. Staines, The Young Socialists, MA thesis, University of Warwick, 1980, p. 87.

53. Jahrbuch 1977-79.

54. SPD - Mitgliederstatistik Stand 31.12.1980- 31.12.1982, provided by SPD Bundesgeschäftsstelle.

55. e.g. Hans Georg Kiera, "Wohin treibt die SPD?" in: Neue Gesellschaft 26 (1979), no. 8, p. 678. Resolution 448 which was submitted by the Niederrhein district organization to the 1979 party congress focussed on inner-party democracy and highlighted some of the problems of day-to-day party organization: "In fact, the party is so thin in its structure of activity in many places that only the tireless efforts of professional politicians, of delegates and of the executive of the local party branches and associations ensure that the most basic organizational tasks are carried out. The so-called ordinary member is less and less involved in party meetings and in party work". Quoted from Neue Gesellschaft Sonderheft Vertrauensarbeit 1979, p. 690.

56. A brief account and documentation of programmes in: Peter Pulte (ed.), Politische Jugendorganisationen, Leverkusen (Heggen), 1975. Also: Bilstein/Hohlbein/Klose, Jungsozialisten - Junge Union - Jungdemokraten, Opladen (Westdt. Verlag), 1972.

57. Röntgenbild op.cit., p. 10.

58. Dieter Stephan, Jungsozialisten - Stabilisierung nach langer Krise 1969-1979, Bonn (Verlag Neue Gesellschaft) 1979, p. 99.

59. Ibid., p. 100.

60. Ibid., p. 103.

61. Ibid., p. 105. Stephan gives the following details on the social structure of Juso membership for late 1977:

	%
Pupils	20.1
Students	26.2
Apprentices	8.2
Workers	7.4
White collar employees	16.4
Civil servants	14.3
Unemployed	2.8
Other n.a.	4.5

62. Ibid., p. 107.
63. Interview with the Representative for Youth Affairs (Beauftragter für Jugendfragen beim Parteivorstand), Herrn Eppe on 23 April 1980.
64. Völker Häse/Peter Müller, "Die Jungsozialisten in der SPD" in Dittberner/ Ebbighausen op.cit., p. 292.
65. SDS: Sozialistischer Deutscher Studentenbund.
66. Sozialdemokratischer Hochschulbund.
67. Klaus Dieter Edler "Konflikt mit den Jusos - Ausdruck einer Parteikrise?" in Neue Gesellschaft 24, 1977, no. 11, p. 911 ff. This article contains useful references to the evaluation of the Juso work in the SPD party press. Also Staines, ibid., pp. 74 ff.
68. Herzog/Karrieren, op.cit., pp. 116-117.
69. e.g. Joachim Raschke, Innerparteiliche Opposition. Die Linke in der Berliner SPD, Hamburg (Hoffmann & Campe), 1974.
70. Johano Strasser, "Vertrauensarbeit durch die Partei" in: Neue Gesellschaft 26, (1979), no. 8, p. 667.
71. Olaf Scholz u.a., "Auf dem Weg zum parteifrommen Jugendverband?" in Sozialistische Politik und Wirtschaft 16, September 1982, pp. 335-340.
72. Dokumente SPD Parteitag: Beschlüsse zur Aussen-, Friedens- und Sicherheitspolitik, 19-23. April 82 München (n.d.).
73. Information der SPD Bundestagsfraktion, Ausgabe no. 1345, 14.9.1983: Willy Brandt in der Fraktionssitzung.
74. See FAZ, 11.10.1983.
75. See below chapters 6 and 9.
76. A compilation of SPD opposition initiatives by Herbert Wehner as an appendix to Letter to the Parliamentary Party, 17.1.1983. Also regular

reports in Das Parlament. In detail: Stenographische Berichte des Deutschen Bundestages (9. und 10. Wahlperiode).
77. See Solidarpakt gegen Arbeitslosigkeit. In: Politik. Aktuelle Informationen der SPD No. 10, December 1982.

SUGGESTED READING

Horst Becker/Bodo Hombach et. al., Die SPD von innen. Bestandaufnahme an der Basis der Partei, Bonn (Neue Gesellschaft), 1983
Douglas A. Chalmers, The Social Democratic Party of Germany, Yale University Press, 1974
Jürgen Dittberner/Rolf Ebbighausen (eds.), Das Parteiensystem in der Legitimationskrise, Opladen (Westdeutscher Verlag), 1973
Richard N. Hunt, German Social Democracy 1918-1933, New Haven/London, 1964
Kurt Klotzbach, Der Weg zur Staatspartei, Programmatik, praktische Politik und Organisation der deutschen Sozialdemokratie, Bonn (Dietz) 1982
Wolf-Dieter, Narr. et. al., SPD - Staatspartei oder Reformpartei, Munich, (Piper), 1976
Franz Osterroth/Dieter Schuster, Chronik der deutschen Sozialdemokratie, Berlin: Bonn (Dietz), 1980
William E. Paterson/Alistair H. Thomas (eds.), Social Democratic Parties in Western Europe, Croom Helm, 1977
Theo Pirker, Die SPD nach Hitler, Munich, 1965
Marie-Christine Zauzich, Parteien im Wandel, Munich (Bayr, Landeszentrale) 1976
Bodo Zeuner, Innerparteiliche Demokratie, Berlin (Colloquium), 1970
Bilstein/Hohlbein/Klose, Jungsozialisten - Junge Union - Jungdemokraten, Opladen (Westdeutscher Verlag, 1972
Peter Pulte (ed.), Politische Jugendorganisationen, Leverkusen (Heggen), 1975
Dieter Stephan, Jungsozialisten - Stabilisierung nach langer Krise, 1969-1979, Bonn (Neue Gesellschaft), 1979

Chapter Four

PROBLEMS OF PARTY STABILITY: THE FDP

After more than thirty years in national and regional politics and after a succession of coalition alignments, the FDP is still a party of electoral instability. Less than half its voters are loyal regulars.[1] Since the early seventies, most stood closer to the SPD, earlier and again since 1980 the vote was closer to the CDU. The FDP seems to be accepted more for its alliances than for its own ideological and political profile. The constant proximity to the five percent hurdle has made it urgent to explore possibilities to mobilize more support. It has been estimated that the FDP can secure the votes of 60% of its potential electorate, SPD and CDU/CSU win about 80%.[2] The vexed question of political orientation and the most effective way of transforming potential votes into real votes and into parliamentary seats remains to be answered. Uncertainties and instabilities also permeate the party organization itself. Between 1969 and 1976, the FDP recruited 50,000 new members and lost 30,000.[3] The party appears to win members whom it cannot integrate. Membership potential has been estimated at 16% of the FDP electorate. This would bring the party to around the one million mark. Maximum membership to date has been 86,948 in September 1981, a considerable shortfall of the presumed potential.[4] Since the break with the SPD, the FDP lost members. At the end of 1982, it was down to 79,251, a drop of 7,500 within a few months.

The problem of stability is rooted in the political manoeuvring of the FDP to remain in governing coalitions. It is also rooted in the cavalier approach to party organization. Party organization as a precondition of cohesion and political effectiveness has never been fully accepted in the FDP. Membership figures have been centrall monitored since 1968 only. In 1974, the party computerized its files. Suspicions against a party machinery abounded. In 1976, when all established parties were well on the way to command effective organizations, the General Secretary of the day, Verheugen, still had to remind party members and functionaries: "Liberalism is not the opposite of organization".[5] The party itself refrains from presenting itself as an organization. In its publicity materials, it stresses ideology and attitudes, not organizational structure. It even avoids calling itself "party". The "liberals" appeals to beliefs, not to specific party commitment.[6] The instability at the grass roots seems to be matched by an uncertainty whether the FDP is a creed, a contemporary expression of timeless liberal ideals, or a distinct and organized political party. Josef Ertl, for example, the FDP land chairman of Bavaria, said in an address to the 1975 regional party congress in Augsburg:

> Democracy thrives on variety in major and minor affairs. And the variety, the minorities and the individual citizen have their only and true defender in liberalism! ... It is true, Germany needs Bavaria. But this Bavaria needs more liberals, needs a strong and cohesive liberal party.[7]

Remnants of an anti-party sentiment appear to hamper the FDP in its efforts to commit liberalism to party organization.

THE ORGANIZATIONAL FRAMEWORK

The FDP is structured in eleven land organizations and 349 boroughs (Kreisverbände). In 1980, Northrhine Westphalia had the largest regional FDP with just over 26,000 members, i.e. 32% of the total membership.[8] Hesse and Lower Saxony reported about 10,000 members each, Baden-Württemberg and Bavaria just over 9,000. Apart from the city states, the Saar region had the smallest organization with 3,800 members or 4.5%. In calculating delegates for the party congresses and the <u>Bundeshauptausschuss</u> which monitors the work of the executive, memberships and electorates for the regional parties are taken into account.[9] The lower levels of party organization are less straightforward. The basic organizational unit of the FDP is the borough office, which normally serves several communities. Nevertheless, group

Problems of Stability: the FDP

sizes are small. In 1978, 35% of the boroughs had less than 100 members on their books.[10] Sixteen per cent had even less than 50 members. Membership figures for the FDP have a direct bearing on election results. Districts with less than 100 members average less than 5% of the vote in their constituencies. Districts with up to 300 members average 7.5%, larger organizations manage 8.5% on average.[11] For a party on the brink of electoral defeat, these organizational links are significant.

This link between electoral reforms and party organization constituted one of the reasons to study the composition of the party and its organizational cohesion. In addition, the FDP experienced unprecedented fluctuations of membership.

These fluctuations cannot easily be connected with major political events such as elections or coalition alliances. While both SPD and CDU/CSU observed that new members are recruited in election years more readily than at other times, the pattern of the FDP in the seventies (Table 4.1) shows that gains and losses are not perceptibly caused by macro-political events. The instablility receded somewhat towards the end of the decade, not least because the inclination to join any of the political parties had decreased. An internal report produced by the FDP-affiliated Friedrich Naumann Stiftung warned in 1977 that, were these membership movements to continue unabated, every second FDP member would no longer belong to the party in ten years' time.[12] This instability further weakens a party which already suffers from lack of membership density and an all too patchy network of FDP party offices to produce much consistent party work. After the coalition switch in 1982, the instability increased when left-liberals expressed discontent or turned away from the FDP.[13]

The various studies the party commissioned to explore its changing structure[14] pointed to an intensification of grass root party work as a possible remedy. The task is a sizeable one. In 1977, 75% of the small party branches had no offices or opening hours for the public. Of the larger ones, 20% were not open to the public, less than one third were open for twenty or more hours per week.[15] In the meantime, the FDP opened 2,000 local branches, although judging from the modest size of its boroughs these must be miniscule.[16] With 9,000 towns and villages in West Germany, the Flächendeckung of the FDP, the area coverage, remains incomplete.

The FDP has also made an effort to equip its

Problems of Stability: the FDP

Table 4.1: FDP Membership Gains and Losses, 1969-1976

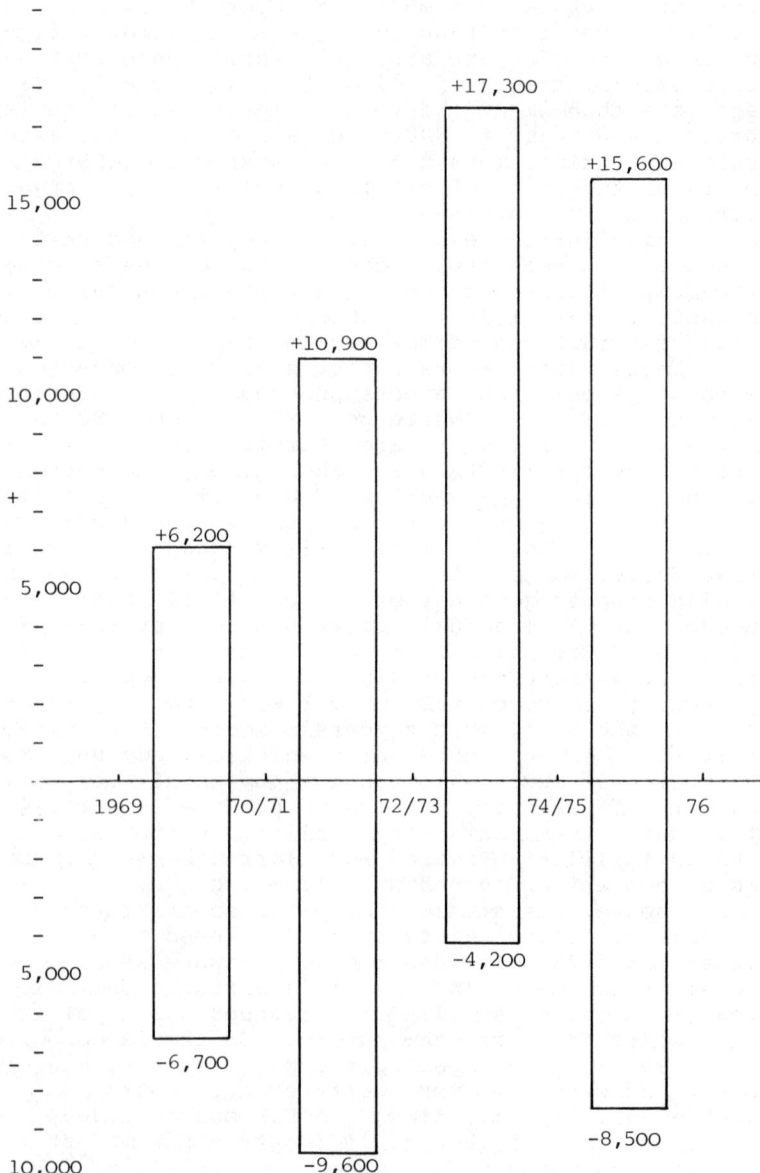

Source: FDP Mitgliederstudie, see footnote 19.

Problems of Stability: the FDP

party offices with at least rudimentary technical apparatus. As late as 1978 most branch offices (75%) lacked basic equipment like Xerox machines or film projectors. The smaller branches were the least likely to be mechanised beyond a typewriter and telephone. In his appeal to streamline the party, the FDP General Secretary, Verheugen, stressed that the district chairman who typed his own letters, printed from stencils, and licked his own envelopes ought to be relegated to the past. The appeal would not have been necessary if that district chairman was not a common feature. More important, the regional and local party organizations did not follow procedures which could be standardised. Even as late as 1980, some continued to use letter-heads with the old FDP black eagle which had been abolished as a party symbol in the opening to the left during the late sixties.[17] Whether such diversity is only due to disorganization or suggests political opposition and resilience to the reorientation of the party has to remain open.

What Party? FDP Studies

Insights into the social structure of the FDP and the integration of FDP members into their party have not been available until recently. Under the ausices of the Institute for Communication Research, questionnaires were sent to all FDP members between 1975 and 1976 and a first report published in March 1977.[18] The response was somewhat sluggish with only 36% of the questionnaires returned. More detailed information came from a series of 1,843 interviews with FDP members in their own homes during February 1977.[19] Ninety six per cent participated, 4% did not wish to be interviewed. The data have been presented under various headings with the intention of clarifying the social composition of the party, of finding the weak points and the strong points to guide future FDP recruitment and canvassing, and of arriving at some answer to the problem of fluctuating membership.[20]

The research on the party could draw on few preliminary efforts. In 1971, a brief overview of the membership structure was compiled by the Institute for Political Planning and Cybernetics.[21] It was preceded by a case study of Cologne which was published and for some time contained the only reliable data on the structure of the party.[22] The Baden Württemberg FDP commissioned its own survey, based on questionnaires in 1971. 17.4% of the questionnaires were completed and the significance of these early insights is somewhat doubtful.[23]

The findings of the 1977 studies jolted the FDP into action almost immediately. A project group "Organisational Reform" was constituted in order to draw organizational and practical conclusions. In August 1977 it published its report, a stocktaking of the disarray of the FDP at the lower organizational level and some possible remedies. The General Secretary who masterminded the quest for reform explained the dual purpose of creating an effective organization and retaining a bond of common ideals and a commitment to liberalism in the party:

> The proposals are an attempt to reduce the organizational deficit of the FDP without changing the character of the liberal party. The FDP does not wish to develop the self-identification of being a functionaries party instead it relies on the responsible contribution of the individual member. The lack of mighty centres in the FDP strengthens the democratic structure of the party.[24]

FDP MEMBERSHIP PROFILES

Any discussion of the FDP membership structures and transitions is hampered by the shortage of reliable data. The only information for the pre-1969 FDP was published in the Süddeutsche Zeitung, and refers to 1965 and 1967. These data have been used by Kaack, and recently by Zauzich,[25] in an attempt to locate the FDP in society. Table 4.2 presents these data and also the data derived from the two surveys conducted in 1977. Although the status of the latter data seems more authorative than that of the earlier ones, some reservations are called for. The survey by questionnaires seems biased in favour of the more active members. Criteria for the interviewing samples are not explained although it appears that the first survey was used as a pilot study to determine the sample. The limitations of the questionnaire-based survey would then also colour the more detailed examination of FDP membership.

Observations on changes in the social structure of the FDP membership need to be tentative. The impact of the Grand Coalition or the alliance with the SPD on FDP membership patterns cannot be measured adequately. Table 4.2 suggests some decline in the

Problems of Stability: the FDP

Table 4.2: The Social Composition of FDP Membership: Occupational Structure

Occupation	1965[1] %	1967[2] %	1971[3] %	1977[4] %
Workers	14	14	5[6]	5
White collar employees	25	40	33	36[8]
Civil servants	15	8	20	19
Self employed	31	22	27[7]	24[9]
Farmers	5	6	4	1[10]
Others[5]	11	10	3	15[11]

Notes:
1. Based on a survey of FDP membership published in the Süddeutsche Zeitung and reprinted by M.C. Zauzich, Parteien im Wandel, p. 104.
2. As for note (1).
3. Daten zur Mitgliedsstruktur 1971. See Footnote 20
4. Data based on 1977 surveys of FDP membership. See Footnotes 18 and 19.
5. Except for 1971, this category appears to include housewives, pensioners and young people in training.
6. Includes artisans in employment.
7. Includes professionals (Freie Berufe) - 10.2%.
8. Includes employees in the public sector - 7%.
9. 14% professionals. Data for self-employed from interview survey Vol. A. p. 6.
10. Data from Vol. A. p. 6.
11. The 1977 survey based questionnaires omit the self-employed and arrive at a high proportion of non-employed people: 11.3% housewives, 9.7% pensioners, 8.9% apprentices and pupils.

self-employed and a rise in the white collar component between 1965 and 1967. The low figure for civil servants, however, is not explained and seems out of line with later developments. Emphasis on the relatively high proportion of "workers"[26] in the FDP during the early sixties also seems hasty since this category appears to include people helping in the family business as well as artisans in dependent employment. The observation which does seem possible concerns the continuity within the party. With slight fluctuations between occupational groups, the FDP has started as a middle class party and has remained a middle class party. If middle class as a characterisation of social status is extended to those in white collar occupations, in the civil service, the self employed and the farmers, the middle class component in the FDP constituted 76% in the earlier years, 84% in 1971 and 79% in 1977. Bearing in mind that the vague category "others" is too large to allow reliable percentages, it may be stated that throughout the sixties and seventies, and despite the new coalition alliance, four in five FDP members followed middle class occupations. Of the civil servants, half were employed in senior positions in 1977. One third (6% of the total party membership) were teachers.[27] The majority of those listed as professionals were academics.[28] Among the self-employed, artisans, retailers and wholesalers predominated. Businesses tended to be small or medium size. Big businesses and industry were not attracted to the FDP.[29]

Among FDP members and voters, the highest income groups are over-represented, which confirms the position of the FDP as a party for the better-off. Table 4.3 groups together data from 1971 and 1976.

Table 4.3: Income of FDP Members and Voters

Monthly Income (DM)	FDP Members[1] %	FDP Voters[2] %	Population %
Under 1,000 DM	25	17	24
1,000-2,500 DM	49	59	65
2,500 DM and over	21	22	8
n.a.	5	-	-

Notes:
1. Adapted from FDP study 1971, p. 3-4.
2. Anderson/Grosser/Woyke, Wahl '76, p. 80. Data for voters and population from Wahlstudie '76, Forschungsgruppe Wahlen.

Income levels have risen considerably during the seventies, i.e. in 1971 the lower income groups were also underrepresented in the party. This is borne out by the data on low income groups in West

Problems of Stability: the FDP

Germany for 1971. 34.2% of the working population earned DM 600 or less. Just over 10% of the FDP members were in this lowest income bracket. About 20% of the working population had monthly earnings of DM 600 to 800, an income reported by only 6.2% of FDP members at the time.[30]

Educational achievements confirm the position of the FDP as the party for the "besseren Leute", the educated and well-to-do. In 1977, 49% of its members had obtained 'A' levels or a university degree. In the population as a whole, 13% were educated to this level in 1977.[31] On the other end of the scale, 26% of FDP members received only basic schooling (Volksschule) compared with 66% in the general population. Data on party workers and functionaries are not available. On the basis of our observations on the SPD, it may be expected that an even higher proportion of academics holds party- and electoral offices. Taking the parliamentary party in the 9th Bundestag as an example, 45 of the 54 members had obtained higher education at university or equivalent institutions, i.e. 83% of the FDP delegates who were elected in 1980.[32]

A further imbalance familiar from the SPD is repeated in the FDP. Women are poorly represented. In 1971, the FDP reported 15% women members, by 1977 the figure had risen to 22%, by 1982 to 24.9%.[33] This is higher than in the two big rival parties. Yet only 15% of the executive positions on the local or regional level were occupied by women, only 12% of the FDP local councillors were women. FDP women tend to be less well-educated and somewhat younger than their male counterparts. This might contribute to the disadvantage they experience in gaining office and positions in and through the party.[34]

Membership in the Seventies and Party Instability

At the time of the first coherent stocktaking in 1971, the FDP was a rather over-aged party. Sixty three per cent of its members were over forty years old, compared with 52% of the population as a whole. The shifting membership in the seventies adjusted the age balance. In 1977, nearly half the members were under forty.[35] The younger age groups still showed some deficits. Three per cent of FDD members were between 16 and 20 years of age and 6% between 21 and 25. Each of these age brackets accounted for about 10% of the population overall. However, the middle range, the age group 26-40,

Problems of Stability: the FDP

constituted 40% of FDP members and only 23% of the general population in 1977.[36]

The rejuvenation of the FDP during the seventies seems to have been based on recruiting members who had already established their careers and found their footing in life. A similar recruitment pattern has been observed for the CDU.[37] The integration into the FDP, however, appears to be tentative and fraught with problems. Between 1968 and 1972 the party won 17,000 new members and lost 16,300. Between 1969 and 1976 membership fluctuated by 30%. Despite the coalition alliance with the SPD and the government position, the FDP has not succeeded in holding its members. In 1971, one fifth of the membership had belonged to the party less than two years. About one third came to the party before 1969. There are considerable regional variations. The FDP in the Saar region had 41% members of ten or more years' standing, Rhineland Palatine 38%, Hamburg 31%. Hamburg was also among the land organizations with the highest share of members who had been in the FDP for less than three years, 31%. The Rhineland Palatine and Saar organizations in contrast, had only 17% and 18% of new members respectively. The duration of membership, i.e. the stability of the organizational and personal cohesion of the party, is directly reflected in satisfaction or dissatisfaction with party membership itself.

In Hamburg, 78% declared to be disappointed with the FDP and the possibilities of participating in it, 21% were satisfied. In the Saar region, 46% were disappointed, 43% satisfied. For the FDP overall the rate of disappointment is alarmingly high at 69% with less than one third (27%) expressing general agreement with the party.[38] The reasons for these detached views of their own party are varied and somewhat inconclusive. About half can be classified as criticisms of the FDP political line and the coalition commitments on the national and land levels, the other half concerns party organization itself and the possibility for members to make a meaningful contribution. Here, lack of chances to work within the party, lack of inner party communication and cooperation and the proliferation of cliques who scramble for posts and allocate offices amongst themselves are mentioned most frequently.

Beyond the array of reasons given in the interviews, the IFK Study does not attempt to specify

Problems of Stability: the FDP

which groups are discontented and why. There is some indication that young people are more prone to be critical than older members.[39] One third of the 16-20 year olds feel badly informed about internal policies relating to the FDP.[40] Yet, younger members see themselves as particularly active in the party. Only the age group 41-45 achieved a similar rating, 37% (average 26% active/very active members). Looking at the membership which is mobilised for party work, the FDP profile is similar to that observed for the SPD. About 40% of the members are passive and withdrawn from the organizational or political work.[41] For a small party such as the FDP this level of passivity is in itself an element of instability. It means that half its local and borough organizations can rely on less than 100 active members, a number which had been confirmed as a viability threshold for party organization and electoral results. There might be a connection between disappointment with the party, passivity and the high fluctuation rate in the membership. Such a connection cannot be established conclusively from the data available.

The motivations for joining the party give also inconclusive evidence. Forty per cent stress they wish to strengthen liberalism as an important creed in modern society. Such an answer either corresponds with an idealised reason for joining a political party or it could mean that the highly-educated FDP clientele has a more considered approach to political participation than for example the SPD members.[42] Whatever the answer might be, the reference to overall liberalism hides more mundane aims for joining, such as gaining positions in the party or in the community. This dimension is of considerable importance in the FDP. Thirty seven per cent of its 1977 members held an office or had held an office at some time before. One third occupied party positions within the land organizations, 18% at the local level. Five per cent of the FDP members were local party chairmen. A further 13% of FDP members held electoral position, 11.2% in their communities, 0.2% in the Bundestag. The IFK Study did not probe into a possible link between office and satisfaction with the FDP. In a post-intensive organization such as the FDP it cannot be ruled out that a major expectation on joining the party is to hold office.[43] Identification with the party would then be a means of furthering individual career ambitions. Identification would be less with the goals or organizational structures of the party than with the status openings it can create. Here, the FDP is likely to generate other disappointments. There is little evidence that the office of branch chaiman wields much political influence within the party. A career in politics is less frequent from the local levels for the FDP than for both its rivals.[44] The grass roots of FDP party organization have yet to be consolidated and they have yet to assume weight as a training ground for party and political leadership roles.

The instabilities of the FDP cannot be fully explained by the change of coalition partner in the sixties and cannot be remedied by coalition loyalty alone. The membership fluctuations also bear no direct relationship to electoral performance or even to election campaigns. The FDP seems to attract a sector of the highly educated middle strate intent on gaining status and political office in an through the party. Some of the instability suffered by the FDP in the last decade can be ascribed to frustrated career expectations. The FDP also wins some support from younger people who are motivated to be active but whose zeal is thwarted by the impenetrable groups who tend to control the small local organizations. The fluctuation rate is highest among the younger FDP members. A third dimension of instability concerns the ambiguous attitude towards organization and party integration itself. FDP members tend to find their way into the party through personal contacts and friends. A major aspect of integrating new members and binding them into the party consists of personal, individualised political counselling. In concrete terms, new and potential members need and expect visits, talks, discussions, personal attention. Since FDP membership cannot usually be built on a family tradition of liberalism or activism in a liberal party, the motivation is personalised and individual. The reservation against identification with a party organization and the emphasis on creed and beliefs, which was apparent in the reasons for joining the FDP, make it necessary for the existing party organization to shape and strengthen an inclination into a commitment.

On this level, the FDP has not been successful. Local party organizations are too small to cope properly with the task of recruiting and retaining members. The anti-centralisation slant in the party fostered a regional and local diversity which made it impossible to discern a cohesive party line and develop strategies for membership recruitment and

Problems of Stability: the FDP

organizational reform. Since the mid-seventies, the problem has been recognised and more initiatives are attempted by the head office in Bonn to train party workers and increase the efficiency and cohesion of the party. It is too early to say whether the FDP has managed to enter the eighties less rent by instabilities in terms of membership and in terms of policies than it experienced in the previous decade.[45] There is no evidence that the loyalty towards the party even among those who became members increased.[46]

The lack of continuity, of experienced party workers, of stable membership support for publicity efforts and election campaigns, remains an unsolved legacy. With well over half the members relative newcomers who joined the party during the last five years, not much continuity of support is evident. The permeation of disenchantment which is said to hit the established parties as a whole appears to affect and destabilise the FDP membership in particular.[47]

POLITICAL FOCUS AND SURVIVAL IN POLITICS

In its governmental roles, one of the policy aims, which the FDP has pursued over the years, concerned the economy. True to its backing from medium and small business and true to its strong liaison with the relevant interest groups,[48] economic liberalism has been a focal point of FDP policies since the foundation of the Federal Republic. Other issues of social reform came into the foreground after the 1971 party congress in Freiburg and the departure into left liberalism.[49] But the primacy of economic policies was never fully renounced. It was reasserted at the congress in Kiel in 1977. The earlier programme envisaged a moderating influence of the state. Now a more traditionally liberal play of market forces was advocated.[50]

The primacy of economic policy might determine the macro level of FDP policies. On the micro level of members' interest and involvement in the party, economic policy scores low. Only 14% in the 1977 survey thought the economic policy of the FDP met their expectations and was successful.[51] The assumption that economic issues concerned members most intensely does no longer apply to the new middle class sector the FDP mobilised in the seventies and eighties. This is confirmed by the distribution of working parties at district level. Like all parties,

Problems of Stability: the FDP

the FDP offers the possibility for members to pursue their particular interests in <u>Arbeitskreisen</u>, working parties on a variety of issues. In 1977 15% of these working parties were concerned with economic matters. The most popular topic proved to be local government, <u>Kommunalpolitik</u>, which occupied 44% of the working parties.[52] In the traditional grooves of the FDP, community level politics has little room. In 1971, 70% in the Baden Württemberg party felt it was relevant to help with national or land elections. Local government elections did not seem worth the trouble. Chances of the FDP at this level were regarded as poor and involvement looked upon sceptically. "This allows only to conclude that the self-confidence of party members is very low and they accordingly lack confidence in the ability of the party to convince and do well".[53]

We saw in relation to the organizational structure that the FDP tends to bypass the small community and stress participation in land and national governments. It could be said that the discovery of communal politics as a key area of FDP members' interests and readiness to participate came as a surprise to the party. It posed the problem of extending the political aims of the FDP onto the lowest level of West German politics and concern itself with community issues. As a model, the FDP referred to the British Liberals and their successes in Liverpool. The FDP General Secretary published a brochure on Liverpool as an example for organizational reform. Here the "sidewalk politics" of the Liberals in Liverpool are presented. Informal chats with citizens about little everyday grievances gain status as effective means of electoral canvassing. Verheugen is at pains to underline that these issues and approaches are no "banalities"[54] but initiatives which relate to a community and give the party specific, local relevance. "The secret of Liverpool's success is of course no secret on closer inspection, but a long known remedy applied with devotion: very hard work 'at the coal face', permanent and untiring concern for the problems of the citizens, bringing about improvements and talking about them".[55]

The urgency of local politics was accelerated by the emergence and activities of citizens' initiative groups in West Germany. As we shall discuss later, all parties had to come to terms with these groups and their implication that established parties might have ignored problems in the communities. Problems which parties would not concern themselves

Problems of Stability: the FDP

with, generated local action groups of people who were affected by planning decisions or tried to influence or remedy specific ills in their environment.[56]

Pressure on the FDP came from two sides. In electoral terms, the transformation of action groups into green lists and parties posed a threat to a party close to the 5% hurdle. In those Lander where the FDP was voted out of parliament after 1978, the losses to the Greens were sufficient to be fatal. The second threat arose from within and concerns the instable FDP membership. Citizens' action groups and FDP draw their members from similar social strata and are in direct competition as frameworks for active participation in local affairs. Eight per cent of the FDP members belonged to citizens' initiatives groups in 1977. In the age group 31-45, membership was near 12%.[57] Nine out of 10 FDP members who also worked in a citizens' group were publicly active for that group. Potential participation was considerably higher than de facto participation. On average, 59% of the FDP members of 1977 would have liked to join a citizens' initiative group. Among the under 35s, well over 70% were interested. Again, economic issues figured low on the list of priorities and concerns. Matters of urban planning, education, and leisure facilities for the young ranked top, followed by environmental interests and the question of atomic energy.[59]

The question of atomic energy can also show the detachment in the FDP of the leadership from the party rank and file. The majority of citizens' groups in the environmental sector are also opposed to the uses of nuclear power as a source of energy production. FDP members who are active in these groups can also be considered opponents of nuclear energy in the Federal Republic. Within the party anti-nuclear voices have been frequently heard. At the 1977 party congress a resolution was passed to control and to limit the use of atomic energy.[60] The four FDP ministers subsequently ignored the party line and proceeded to support the government in its plans to expand the nuclear sector. The ministers also forced the FDP parliamentary party to override the congress resolution and to endorse atomic energy.[61] FDP top level politicians do not seem to be bound by party positions. Such a segregation of views and initiatives coming from the membership and through congress on the one hand and on the other a leadership who follows the law of political expediency of the day does not allow for a revitalization of the FDP from below, a German Liverpool or such like. The lone decision by the FDP party leader Genscher, the Minister of Economic Affairs, Lambsdorff and possibly one or two others to end the governing coalition with the SPD and to plunge the party into a new gamble for a more secure place at the top is a further example for the relative insignificance of the FDP party organization and membership for the drift of its political decisions. For a short while, the party remained in disarray with some tentative moves to secede and form a new left-liberal party.[62]

They faltered, and the party seems to have settled to the new course i.e. it has done what it always had to do: endorse in retrospect the decisions the handful of top politicians took.[63] The coalition coup also shows that the FDP continues to stake its political survival by a place in government, not by a strengthening of its party organization. The remedy for the crippling instability with fluctuating memberships, virtually defunct party offices and an unsteady electorate may have been to give more weight to the grass roots, to communal politics, to membership participation. The leap into the new alliance has once again postponed substantive changes in the FDP. Its problems of stability and survival have yet to be remedied.

The dominance of the leadership over FDP party members has not survived 1982 unscathed. An extraordinary party congress in Berlin in January 1983 which was called to sanction - in retrospect - the single handed policy making of the FDP leadership, in particular of Genscher and Lambsdorff, endorsed the new coalition. It also insisted on an amendment of the party statutes; in future, the leadership has to obtain the consent of the party membership before entering into any political realignment.[64] This innovation may, for the first time grant FDP members a voice in deciding the political alliances on which the FDP has depended so long and which have come to characterize its place in West German politics. At the same time, the FDP lost most of the prominent advocates of left-liberalism who broke away to form a new party or to join the SPD after the coalition realignment.[65] Those who remained, like the former Minister of the Interior Gerhart Baum, lost their leadership status. In November 1982, the youth organization Young Democrats finally declared itself independent after prolonged controversy over its leftist orientation and after attempts by the party leadership to starve it of funds.[66] In 1981, a rival grouping was set up under the sponsorship of the FDP right-wing, the Young Liberals. They have now gained official recognition.[67] The separation from the Young Democrats and other adherents to the left liberal principles of the seventies, leaves the party without an effective opposition to the new political course alongside, even right of the CDU. Ties with the middle, in particular small and medium business interests have ostensibly been strengthened.[68] Politically, the FDP reverted to is place in the party system of the early sixties, even the fifties, prior to the reform drive which gave birth to the SPD/FDP coalition. In the changeover, the FDP lost about one third of its members, among them many local and district functionaries who had joined in the seventies when the party seemed to stand close to the SPD. It will take some time to assess the organizational disarray and its effects. Politically, the FDP has abandoned the feeble attempts at organizational reform and decision making from below. Once again, it seems to stake its survival on being the battering ram in government for the partisan economic and social interests of that conservative middle strata on whose electoral and financial backing the future of the FDP in parliaments and politics depends.

FOOTNOTES

1. A 1972 survey showed that 72% of the respondents tended to vote regularly for a particular party. Of these, 40% voted SPD, 28% voted CDU or CSU, only 4% voted FDP. Of those who identified with the FDP, only 12% did so "very strongly" (SPD: 26%, CDU/CSU: 23%). See Manfred Berger, "Parteiidentifikation in der Bundesrepublik", <u>PVS 14</u>, 1873, pp. 218-19.
2. H-J Beyer, <u>Ammerkungen zum Wählerpotential der FDP</u>. Bonn 15.6.1977, unpublished manuscript, FDP Archives, p. 10.
3. Members who joined and left during this period are not included in these figures. <u>Bittere Bestandaufnahme</u>: Der Wahlkampf der FDP ist die politische Arbeit zwischen den Wahlen. Bonn n.d. (1978) p. 21. Also: FDP Bundesgeschäftsstelle:FDP Mitgliederentwicklung 1972-1981.
4. Data for 31.12.1979, EDV Zentrale Mitgliederkartei provided by Bundesgeschäftsstelle, Bonn.

5. Wahlkampf, ibid., p. 24.
6. e.g. a brochure entitled "liberal" which elaborates on possible meanings of the word and historical connotations of liberal and liberalism. Ed. Friedrich Naumann Stiftung, Bonn n.d.
7. Perspektiven liberaler Politik, Landesverband Bayern 1976, p. 16.
8. Stand 28.1.1980. Data from Bundesgeschäftstelle 1980-81.
9. Heino Kaack, Die FDP, p. 70. Also: Delegiertenrechte der Landersverbände zum Bundesparteitag 1982 und 1983 compiled by the FDP General Secretary Fritz Fliszer, Jan. 1982.
10. Ibid., p. 69.
11. Wahlkampf, ibid., p. 24.
12. Wissenschaftlicher Dienst der Friedrich Naumann Stiftung. Mitgliederbewegungen der FDP Stand, April 1977, Archiv der FDP.
13. "Nur 5% forderten Genschers Rucktritt", in Generalanzeiger 29.9.1982.
14. See pp. 109 ff.
15. Michael Buse, Organisation und Aktivitäten der Kreisverbände. Unpublished manuscript 1977, p. 12.
16. Kaack, p. 70.
17. Interview with H-J Beyer, 21.4.1980
18. H-J Beyer, Erste vorläufige Ergebnisse einer Mitgliederbefragung von 1975-1976, Bonn 23.3.1977, Archiv der FDP.
19. Michael Buse, Ergebnisse der Mitgliederbefragung von Februar 1977, 31.5.1977 Archiv.
20. Situationsanalyse zur Ermittlung der Voraussetzungen für methodische Öffentlichkeitsarbeit innerhalb der Mitgliederstruktur der FDP. Abschlussbericht I - 1977. Vol. A No. 0004, Vol. B No. 0108 Zahlenwerte zur Auswertung nach Strukturkriterien, Vol. C No. 0112 Auswertung nach Zielgruppen.
21. Daten zur Mitgliederstruktur der Freien Demokratischen Partei. Stand, September/Oktober 1971, Archiv der FDP.
22. e.g. Marie Christine Zauzich uses data from this study.
23. Mitgliederbefragung im FDP Landesverband Baden-Württemberg April 1971, IpK unpublished manuscript, Archiv der FDP.
24. fdk (Freie Demokratische Korrespondenz) No. 195, 25.8.1977 p. 1 f.
25. kaack, Geschichte und Struktur, p. 493. Zauzich 104 ff.
26. thus Zauzich p. 104/105.

27. Vol. A, p. 9.
28. Ibid., p. 8.
29. Ibid., pp. 7-8.
30. Jürgen Roth, Armut in der BRD. Über psychische und materielle Verelendung, Frankfurt, (Fischer) 1974, p. 77.
31. H-J Beyer, Daten zur Mitgliederstruktur. Comparative data for population from the survey material in Gluchowski/Veen, ibid., p. 325.
32. Kürschners Volkshandbuch, Deutscher Bundestag 9. Wahlperiode, p. 238.
33. Data for 1971: Mitgliederstruktur Vorbericht, p. 2. Data for 1977: Buse, Ergebnisse.
34. Vol. A, p. 6 and p. 10.
35. Ifk 1971 and Friedrich Naumann Stiftung, Mitgliederbewegungen 1977.
36. Buse, Ergebnisse.
37. Nils Diederich, "Zur Mitgliederstruktur" ibid., p. 48 found that 50% of the CDU members in his survey had joined the party after having accomplished a secure position in their job or profession. This applied to only 33% of SPD members.
38. Vol. B, pp. 44-46.
39. Wahlkampf 22.
40. Vol. C, p. 24.
41. Vol. B, p. 53 and Vol. C, p. 25.
42. These critical points raised by H-J Beyer in an interview 21.4.1980. Beyer thought the tendency to idealise membership according to a stereotype was the more appropriate explanation of FDP idealism.
43. See also Zeuner, p. 86. In 1969, the FDP had 148 full-time paid officials to the SPD's 405, despite much lower membership.
44. Herzog, ibid., p. 114.
45. See Geoffrey Roberts, "The FDP in Crisis", ASGP Journal 1, Summer 1981, pp. 1-8.
46. The Delegiertenschlüssel 1980-81 shows losses in 4 lander, gains in 7. The uneven electoral performance of the FDP underlines the uncertainties. It lost its parliamentary seats on a land level in Hamburg, Lower Saxony, Schleswig-Holstein and Northrhine Westphalia, and made its largest gains during the 1980 elections precisely in these lander.
47. Norbert Lammert, "Das Phänomen der 'Staatsverdrossenheit' und die Strukturdefekte der Parteien". Aus Politik und Zeitgeschichte 25, 1979.
48. In the 9th Bundestag 12 of the 53 FDP parliamentarians were representatives of their economic interest groups. Berufsstatistik der Mitglieder

des 9. Bundestages, Stand 15.5.1981, p. 2, Reg. No. 1-22, 81. Unpublished manuscript.
49. Die Freiburger Thesen. Programm der liberalen Gesellschaftspolitik, beschlossen auf dem FDP Parteitag vom 25-27 Oktober 1971 in Freiburg. Bonn n.d. (1971).
50. Kieler Thesen, ... Bonn 1977.
51. Vol. B, p. 44 f.
52. Buse, Organisation und Aktivitäten der Kreisverbände, p. 13.
53. Mitgliederbefragung im LV Baden-Württemberg, p. 25.
54. Gerd Rauhaus, Erfolge liberaler Arbeit. Zum Beispiel: Liverpool. Ed. Günther Verheugen, Friedrich Naumann Stiftung, Bonn n.d., p. 25.
55. Ibid., p. 1.
56. A good overview in Michael Buse, Bürgerinitiativen. Dokumentation ed. Friedrich Naumann Stiftung, Bonn, 1978.
57. Vol. C, p. 1.
58. Vol. A, p. 21.
59. Ibid., pp. 24-25.
60. Beschluss zur Energiepolitik des 28. Ordentlichen Bundesparteitages der FDP in Kiel, Bonn, n.d.
61. FAZ, 8.1.1979.
62. For full documentation of the problems and excerpts from the Bundestag debate see Das Parlament 4.10.1982.
63. e.g. "In Freiburg will die FDP sich wieder sammeln" in FAZ 28.1.1983; "Die FDP in Freiburg geschlossen und friedlich" in FAZ 31.1.1983.
64. FR 31.1.1983.
65. Reports in Generalanzeiger 29.2.82; FR 16.11.1982. Also "Liberale gegen die Rechtswende - gegen den Wahlbetrug der FDP Spitze", Informationsblatt NRW Landesverband der deutschen Jungdemokraten, 20.9.1982.
66. ppp no. 128, 9.7.1982; also Westfaelische Rundschau 19.8.1982; Rheinischer Merkur/Christ und Welt 23.7.1982 ("Etikettenschwindler der FDP").
67. FAZ 3.11.1982; FAZ 31.1.1983, for the background Der Spiegel 30.8.1982 and William Borm, "Jungdemokraten - Freie Demokraten" in liberal no. 4, April 1979.
68. e.g. "Liberales Aktionsprogramm für den Mittelstand" in neue bonner depesche 2, 1983, pp. 18-21; also the slogan "Handwerk statt Mundwerk", artisans instead of big mouths' nbd 5, 1983 p. 42 and reports on connections between FDP and representa-

tives of small business and their interest groups in neue bonner depesche since 1982.

SUGGESTED READING

Lothar Albertin (ed.), Politischer Liberalismus in der Bundesrepublik, Göttingen (Vandenhoeck & Ruprecht), 1980
Herbert Bertsch, Die F.D.P. und der deutsche Liberalismus, 1789-1963, Berlin (Ost, VEB Verlag der Wissenschaften), 1963
Karl-Hermann Flach, Noch ein Chance für die Liberalen. Eine Streitschrift. Frankfurt (Fischer) 1977 (2nd. ed.)
Jörg Michael Gutscher, Die Entwicklung der F.D.P. von ihren Anfängen bis 1961, Meisenheim, (Hain) 1967
Heino Kaack, Die F.D.P. Grundriss und Materialien zu Geschichte und Struktur, Meisenheim (Hain) 1979 (3rd revised edition)
Kurt J. Körper, F.D.P. - Bilanz der Jahre 1960-1966, Köln (Wison Verlag), 1968
Naumann-Stiftung, Literaturmerkblatt zur Geschichte und Programmatik des Politischen Liberalismus in Deutschland, Bonn, 1979
Marie-Christine Zauzich, Parteien im Wandel, Munich (Bayr. Landeszentrale), 1976
Rüdiger Zülch, Von der FDP zur F.D.P. - Die Dritte Kraft im deutschen Parteiensystem, Bonn, 1972
Rolf Zundel, Die Erben des Liberalismus, Freudenstadt (Eurobuch Verlag Lützeyer), 1971

Chapter Five

THE CHRISTIAN DEMOCRATS: PARTY ORGANIZATION AND MEMBERSHIP DEVELOPMENT

GOVERNMENT AND PARTY, THE CHANGING PLACE OF THE CDU

For the first decade or two of its history, the CDU attached little significance to organizational matters or membership recruitment. The party had emerged from a variety of local and regional groups, bracketed together by a Christian approach to politics, and more important still, by holding the senior position in the West German government. Indeed, the "union" never had to hammer out precise policies before it assumed government responsibility. The government role then provided and defined the aims and also held the various segments and regional organizations together. CDU party organization reflected this dependence on the government position. The first party congress took place in 1950, after a CDU Chancellor had taken office; it was later still until the first administrative headquarters of the party were set up. For the era Adenauer at least, the CDU relied on the position of Chancellor to unify the party. Party congresses provided major occasions for the Chancellor to make policy speeches, to unite the party behind government aims and achievements and project to the outside world an image that CDU and Federal Government were virtually identical. Inner party debate had no place at congress; congress applauded its political leaders, and the Chancellor in particular.[1] Such conflicts as there were, articulated themselves in inter-regional rivalries and the relatively separate development of CDU land organizations.

The equilibrium between party and government function was somewhat disrupted in the sixties. In 1963, Adenauer had to step down as Federal Chancellor and give way to the former Minister of Economic Affairs, Ludwig Erhard. On the surface, it appeared as if the CDU had retained the office of Chancellor and the mechanism to blend party and government. The 1965 elections confirmed Erhard as a vote puller. The hidden change, however, concerned the amalgamation of political and party leaderships.[2] Under Adenauer, the Chancellor was also chairman of the party. When Adenauer resigned as Chancellor, he retained his office as party chairman for a further three years. For the first time in the CDU history, the Chancellor did not also control the party. Thus the factions which opposed Erhard could not be mollified and brought into line. Erhard attempted to compensate his lack of support from the CDU by basing his office on the popular support of a Volkskanzler, a people's Chancellor. In the wake of economic recession, this support began to waver. Although Erhard was elected chairman after Adenauer resigned in 1966, he could now swing the party. Once the recession had started to bite, all factions in the CDU plotted to topple Erhard and hoist their own representative into office. When the coalition government finally collapsed after the FDP withdrew its backing, Erhard had already lost his popular appeal and his slender support in the CDU.

An identification of chancellorship and party organization became even more difficult under the subsequent government, the CDU headed Grand Coalition with the SPD. The Chancellor, Kurt Georg Kiesinger had risen to power as the Minister President of Baden-Württemburg, as one of the Landesfürsten, the influential leaders of CDU land organizations. He was also regarded sufficiently mid-stream to appease the warring factions and restore the Chancellor image in the party and in public. He encountered none of Erhard's difficulties. At the 1967 party congress in Brunswick he was duly elected as CDU chairman and once again combined the leaderships of party and government.[3]

The scene might have been set for a restoration of the old harmony between party and state, but for two problems. The first problem came from the partnership with the SPD. The junior partner succeeded in generating important government initiatives such as Ostpolitik, an extension of the welfare state, co-determination.[4] Most of the government momentum between 1966 and 1969 seemed to originate from the SPD. The CDU took once again to stating its policy principles. It published a new party programme in 1968 which rephrased the well tried themes of the fifties. The 1969 party congress reflected the unease over losing political control and committed

the CDU in an unprecedented public debate not to
enter any further coalition with the SPD after the
1969 elections.[5] These elections were to bring an
SPD/FDP coalition government and until 1982 deprived
the CDU of a place in government on the national
level. For over a decade, the primacy of the government role to the CDU party line could no longer
apply. The party had to adjust to opposition, it
had to create a party organization separate from the
office of Chancellor and in particular it had to
undertake a policy formulation without a government
position.

The second stumbling block which prevented
Kiesinger from recapturing the old harmony between
party and state lay in the organizational changes in
the party itself. The need to cooperate and to compete with the SPD pushed the question of party organization into the foreground. While the SPD could
rely on a long tradition of centralized party organization, the CDU seemed to be defunct at central
level and coherent only in the regions. The SPD
head-office seemed to deserve its name and leave
little room for regional autonomy within the party.
By contrast, the CDU had only rudimentary organization. From the outset, organization had been be-
littled in the name of freedom.[6] A party which professed freedom as one of its key aims could not, it
was argued develop a party machinery to control its
members. The loose and casual reliance of party
organization on the traditional networks developed
by "Honoratioren", citizens of renown and influence
in their communities proved a useful device to hold
the party together while the office of Chancellor
and the role in government provided the focal point
and the unifying force.[7] Until 1971, the head-
office in Bonn was housed in sixteen different buildings scattered all over the town. The impression
was one of improvisation rather than organization.
"The rooms (are) stuffed with materials to the
ceiling ... The teleprinter is to be found in the
bathroom and the archives are overflowing".[8] One
of the steps to stress the place of organization in
party matters was the move into the Konrad Adenauer
Haus in 1971, which allowed the CDU to run well-
appointed and prestigious headquarters equipped with
up-to-the-minute technical aids and resources.[9]

Organizational Adjustments

The shabbiness of the old head office signified a much deeper problem. As an appendage to government, the party appeared to function only at times of elections, as a Chancellor's Election Association, a Kanzlerwahlverein. In 1966, for example, a delegate complained at the regional party congress of North Badenia:

> District party executives and business managers should not allow the situation to continue whereby there are local branches which are not active between election campaigns. Also, those communities in which our party has not organized a group should not be forgotten. In cooperation with the Bundestag deputies, the Landtag deputies and the municipal representatives, consideration must be given as to how work at the district level and the localities of the district can be made more lively. Our party must be like this outside election campaign times, so that every man should remain actively in his place.[10]

The first move to reduce the weight of elections for the CDU and to increase the weight of party organization dated back to 1956 when the Baden-Württemberg regional party fought successfully for an amendment of the CDU statutes concerning delegates to the party congress.[11] Initially, the number of delegates a regional party could send depended solely on the number of votes that party won at the last election. Party organization and membership were overshadowed by the vote catching power - a mechanism which tended to generate passivity between elections and activity at election times. Until 1956, the regional party could send one delegate to congress for every 25,000 CDU voters within its boundaries. This formula was amended to allow for organization and membership to be also considered. Since 1956, regional parties could claim one delegate to congress for every 75,000 voters and one for every 1,000 members in their area. Today, the CDU congress consists of 750 delegates, 600 of these are selected by the regional parties in proportion to the share of the vote they obtained at the last federal election. The remainder is elected on the basis of regional party membership.[12]

A further move to involve members and to stress the place of the party over and above winning votes accompanied the preparation of the new party

programme in 1968. The CDU had not been a party of
programmes which would lay down policy objectives.
Early attempts such as the Ahlener Programme of 1947
which pressed for a degree of socialization, were
brushed aside by the political realities under
Adenauer's leadership.13 The 1949 <u>Leitsätze</u> never
were a programme in the sense of having been passed
and agreed upon by a full party congress. They were
guidelines published shortly before the elections.
The 1953 programme repeated government policy objectives as those of the party. 1968, then, provided
the first challenge for the party to create a framework for the future.

    The 1967 Brunswick Congress had spelt out the
task to prepare a party programme, and discuss
policy priorities throughout the party.14 Some
10,000 meetings took place and generated some 30,000
proposals which were submitted to the Bonn head
office. This unprecedented membership involvement
came at a time when complaints especially from
younger CDU politicians about insufficient representation in positions of leadership started to gather
momentum; when the party needed a forceful political
platform to fend off the SPD challenges in
government;15 and when the political principles
which served the CDU so well in the Adenauer era had
become stale. The programme was also, as mentioned
earlier, designed to keep the party together and
once again state its common and unifying aims. It
was not a new political platform, just a re-state-
ment of familiar points, an assurance that reorientation was not needed. Whether the flood of suggestions was incorporated and guided the programme towards the well-tried principles, or whether they
were ignored and are gathering dust in the party
archives has yet to be investigated. The onset of
opposition forced the CDU to further revise the
Berlin Programme. In 1971, a second version was
agreed again with membership involvement and about
7,000 suggestions.16 This has since been superseded
by the new Basic Programme of 1978 which was preceded by several years of discussion within the
party on policy aims and the scope of the CDU in
opposition.17 Here, the CDU presents itself as the
mouthpiece of those who are ignored by other parties
and by mainstream social agencies, the old, the poor,
the housewives for instance. This so called New
Social Question, which was hotly contested within
the CDU, is intended to underline the ability of the
party to respond to social needs and mend social
ills. The purpose of these programmes was to hold

the regional organizations together and to present a unified image to the public even in opposition. Within the party, the programme activities had an additional effect: they strengthened the office of General Secretary of the party. One of the legacies of the diversified history of the CDU as an organization was the weakness of the party head office. In 1967, the post of General Secretary was created because the CDU felt the need to establish more cohesion in its rivalry with the SPD in government and the competition of a well functioning party apparatus. The post of General Secretary was to be the central position in the party; his impact was greatly strengthened by the coordinating function he assumed for the programme work. All party branches and land organizations had to communicate their programme ideas to the General Secretary who sorted them out and deliberated on their use. Since the purpose of the position of General Secretary was to establish organizational links with the regional parties, the district organizations or below, communications around the programmes were an important breakthrough to restrict the autonomy of these party levels. In the long run, creating the post of General Secretary was perhaps the most important innovation in giving the CDU independence from a place in government and more organizational backbone. Different General Secretaries had different degrees of influence on the party. As a general principle it is important that since 1967, the Bonn head office had a full time administrator whose task it was to establish links with the party organization in all regions and also directly from Bonn to the district levels throughout the Federal Republic. In the fifties and sixties, the Bonn head office was only permitted to approach the regional CDU organizations, who would themselves be in charge of all contacts with their district- and local branches. Effective control of the orientation of the party lay with the regional offices. The establishment of post of the General Secretary which also involved the right of the Bonn office to directly work with district organizations, strengthened the central dimension in the CDU and modified the regional traditions a little. At the 1975 CDU congress in Mannheim the CDU district was declared the smallest organizational unit. Local branches had to relate to their districts and communicate through their districts. Districts in turn were in overall charge of their affiliated branches. The CDU statutes were altered accordingly. This move confirmed the connection between the Bonn head office and the district level. By raising the status of the districts, an attempt seemed to have been made to strengthen the central administration at the expense of regional autonomy.[18]

The increased weight of central CDU administration since the mid sixties can also be shown in relation to the budget which the Bonn headquarters had at their disposal. In 1968, the first year of annual reports on party finance, the main source of income for the office in Bonn appear to have been the reimbursements of campaign costs provided by the state. Regional parties also paid a share of membership dues - about one quarter - to the central office. The readiness of CDU members, however, to regularly pay their subscriptions seems to have been low. In 1964, an estimated 50% did not pay any subscriptions at all.[19] The readiness of the regional parties to distribute sufficient resources to the Bonn office was also questioned.

To avert the financial drought at Central Office, plans were drawn up to put that office in charge of collecting all membership dues and then transfer the appropriate amounts to the regional parties. They highlight the predicament. Needless to say that they were never put into practice.[20] The financial resources of CDU regional parties in the fifties and sixties were much more plentiful than membership figures would suggest. In 1959 for example, the North Württemberg CDU reported that it obtained half a percent of its annual income or DM 900 from membership contributions. The remaining 99.5% came from a network of donors committed to this particular regional party, and of course, state funding.[21] The same applies to other regional CDU organizations who were financed by regional industries and businesses who had formed loose alliances in so called Citizen's Associations (<u>Staatsbürgerliche Vereinigungen</u>) or similar groups to pool and distribute funds. By comparison with the regional parties, the Bonn CDU was poor. In 1968, regional parties raised over twenty million Mark between them, the CDU in Bonn just 447,000.[22] Creating a viable network of donors which was committed to the CDU head office and would channel its funds that way, was very important if the CDU wanted to modify regionalization and increase central organizational control. The treasurer since 1971, Leisler Kiep succeeded in creating just such a network and tightened up control over regional party finance. The financial support of the CDU via the <u>Wirtschaftsrat</u>

also benefits central control in the party since the funds are provided for the Bonn office.23 In 1974, about one quarter of membership dues, nearly seven million, were paid by regional parties to the Bonn office. In 1977, the Bonn office scooped up 12 million in donations, it had caught up with the combined financial strengths of the regional CDU organizations. Organizational remodelling was helped by this financial emancipation of the Bonn offices from the regional party organizations and their networks of party income.25

The CSU Challenge

The drive towards organizational reform was intensified by the rise of the Bavarian sister party, the CSU. Since the fifties, the CSU had streamlined its organization secured an absolute majority in Bavaria and become strong enough to claim more influence within the Christian Democratic camp. The rivalry of the successful partner had to elicit some CDU response. What had happened?

One of the founding principles of the CSU had been to create a party organization as strong and effective as that of the SPD. The CSU was intended as a competitor to the SPD, a political force which would unify Christian voters and which could develop a well functioning network of party branches throughout Bavaria.26

Initially, the dual emphasis on political conservatism with a Christian prefix and an effective party machinery worked well. By 1948, the CSU had gained an absolute majority in the Bavarian land elections and formed the government. It had created an extensive system of district and branch organizations and a membership of well over 80,000. The licencing in 1948 of the Catholic Bavarian Party was a major blow.27 The CSU lost about half its membership and suffered such a drop in popular support and income that it had to abandon its drive for an efficient party machinery in Bavaria. Until the midnineteen fifties, the CSU relied again, as its sister party CDU, on local dignitaries and small town elites. The Honoratioren party structure made it virtually impossible to generate political initiatives through the party. The party was instead a mirror of traditional local patterns of influence. When jolted into opposition by a coalition of four parties in 1954, in the Bavarian land parliament, the CSU retrenched with organizational restructuring and reform. Under its new chairman Hanns Seidel, the party resumed the earlier approach of building an efficient party machinery. In 1955, the CSU created the position of General Secretary. The importance of the Munich headquarters grew. From 14 salaried employees in 1955, the so called <u>Landesleitung</u>, land-leadership, expanded to over 200 in 1972. The CSU used constituencies as organizational grid for the party and appointed at least one full-time functionary for each of them. Mintzel estimated a budget of DM 200,000 for the party headquarters for 1957.[28] Ten years later, it exceeded 2 million; in the seventies, well over 3 million were allocated. These budget estimates only included personnel and running costs and excluded the increasing publication sector. The weekly <u>Bayernkurier</u> for example is the CSU membership paper; it also developed into a national paper with an impact well beyond Bavaria. The CSU <u>Landesleitung</u> was equipped with modern technological aids to facilitate its task of supplying the district- and branch offices throughout Bavaria with materials for their political work. The restructuring of the party organization had two tangible results: membership started to grow very fast. From an estimated 35,000 in 1955 the CSU expanded to 43,000 at the beginning of 1957. By 1961, it had reached 58,000 members. At the time when the CDU began to consider party organization, the CSU had at least 73,000 members. From one tenth of the Christian Democratic camp, CSU membership had grown to about one quarter.[29] By December 1972, the CSU had 106,000 members; by 1980, about 170,000; at the end of 1982, 175,000. The old aims of outpacing the SPD had been accomplished. In 1972, the Bavarian SPD has a total of 74,000 members, at the close of the decade about 70,500.[30]

Electoral results told a similar story. While the SPD stayed around the thirty percent mark and the FDP barely survived the five percent hurdle, the CSU emerged as the strongest party, commanding an absolute majority in Land and Federal elections (Table 5.1). The CSU as "party machine of the modern type"[32] proved a challenge to the CDU in its uncertain state between government and party.

The alliance CDU/CSU had always had its difficulties. Early attempts to arrive at a unified Christian party for all regions had to be abandoned when the Bavarians continued to insist on their name and identity as Christian Social Union.[33] The organizational separation did not preclude a standing arrangement that the CDU does not campaign in

The Christian Democrats

Table 5.1: CSU Election Results, 1946-1983

Land elections		Federal elections in Bavaria		% for CSU on national level
Year	% CSU	Year	% CSU	%
1946	52.3	1949	29.2	5.8
1950	27.4	1953	47.8	8.8
1954	38.0	1957	57.2	10.5
1958	45.6	1961	54.9	9.6
1962	47.5	1965	55.6	9.6
1966	48.1	1969	54.4	9.5
1970	56.4	1972	55.1	9.7
1974	62.1	1976	60.0	10.6
1978	59.1	1980	57.6	10.5
1982	58.3	1983	59.5	10.6

Source: Zehnte Landtagswahl in Bayern am 10 Oktober 1982. Die Landtagswahl von A bis Z. Ed. Statisches Landesamt und Landeszentrale für politische Bildung, München 1982, p. 119 und 137. For 1982: FAZ, 11.10.1982; Sonderdruck SZ Dokumentation BTW März 1983, pp. 1 & 5.

Bavaria, the CSU not outside Bavaria, and that the representatives of both parties form one parliamentary party in the Bundestag. This cooperation in the national parliament and the ban on political competition between the two partners created the impression that there was only one Christian Democratic Party. Matters are not as simple.

Despite cooperation in Bonn, the CSU established its own parliamentary group, the Landesgruppe within the joint parliamentary party CDU/CSU. The Landesgruppe enjoys an apparatus and leadership structure similar to other parliamentary parties. At various times, the liaison between Landesgruppe and the main CDU has been questioned and a continuation of the alliance queried. The CSU in fact insisted on a renegotiation of the terms of cooperation at the onset of every legislative period. Several times it challenged this cooperation or even threatened to break away from the alliance. A vociferous split of this nature occurred in 1976 when the CSU leadership pronounced an end to joint parliamentary work.[34] Although the alliance continued after a renegotiation of terms the point was made that the CSU considered itself strong enough to break away and go it alone. The expansion of membership, the close ties between the party and Bavarian industry and business, the electoral dominance of the CSU within its area of influence and the dense network of party offices with powerful headquarters in Munich, all these factors have combined to make the CSU into a strong and challenging partner. The lesson of organization, which the CSU learnt in the fifties and the electoral successes which seemed to follow could not fully be ignored if the CDU wanted to remain dominant in the alliance. The nomination of Strauss as the candidate for the office of Chancellor in 1979 reflected the weight the CSU had accumulated. It also reflected the fact, that despite organizational restructuring and remodelling, the CDU continued to look for a leader figure who might restore the equilibrium of party and state.[35] Back in government since 1982, the CDU seems to rely on the FDP to fend off all too direct pressures from the CSU and its leader, Strauss.

Membership Party CDU
During the thirteen years in opposition, the CDU began to rise to the challenge to become an "Apparat-Partei". It also grew in terms of membership.

The so called "Machtwechsel" in Germany, the change from a government headed by the CDU to a SDP/FDP coalition, seemed to have boosted interest in politics. All political parties enjoyed unprecedented growth. The Christian Democratic parties which had remained relatively small throughout the fifties and sixties grew faster than the others. The CDU had around 300,000 members in 1969, and 720,000 in 1982.[36] The expansion of the CSU from 350,000 members at the end of the sixties to 175,000 had already been mentioned.

If we take the Christian Democratic Camp rather than the separate parties, membership today amounts to about 895,000 or 48% of all party members. In 1968, CDU/CSU had 31% of all party members in the Federal Republic. In order to estimate party affiliation, membership in associations close to the CDU should also be considered. The association in the economic and youth sectors are open to people who are not paid up CDU members but may be counted as CDU oriented.

The <u>Wirtschaftsrat</u> and <u>Mittelstandsvereinigung</u>, the associations organizing larger and smaller businesses respectively, had an estimated 10,000 members without CDU membership cards in 1978.[37] The <u>Junge Union</u> totalled about 25,000 in the same year.[38] CDU membership seems to vary in different parts of the country. In Baden-Württemberg, 18% of the Junge Union members in 1977 also belonged to the CDU.39 In Bavaria, the proportion was 60%.40 In the sixties, two thirds of Junge Union members were at the same time members of the party.41 Today, dual membership has been estimated at 40%. By affiliating young people to the party, the Junge Union has an important recruitment function. Most young members join the CDU or the CSU through their membership in the youth association.42

If we take all party sectors and associations together, Christian Democracy in West Germany had about one million members at the end of the seventies. There is nothing to suggest that membership figures have changed much since then. The formerly small and somewhat diffuse Christian Democratic camp may not have fully overcome its organizational disparity. In terms of membership development, it has more than caught up with its old rival. The SPD fell below the one million mark in 1978 and is slow to recoup its losses from the days of government.43

CDU Studies
The influx of new members and the transition to a mass membership party made the CDU into an unknown quantity. Who were the newcomers? What made them join, what did they expect from membership? Could the party accommodate so many new members, did it have enough outlets for involvement - what kind of involvement did these members hope for? How was party stability affected by the membership changes? These were some of the questions facing the CDU in the seventies. The major question in the background, of course, concerned the rise of the CDU into government once again.

Similar to SPD and FDP, the CDU commissioned a "communications" study in order to penetrate the unknown quantity "mass party" and to ascertain how the facilities provided by the party were used by the membership and how they helped to consolidate the policies and positions of the CDU. The CDU entrusted its own research institute, the Konrad Adenauer Foundation, with the work. In 1977, a survey based on a representative sample of party members was carried out.44 It was supplemented by interviews with district managers and an assessment of the circulation of party publications. This study was preceded in 1971 by a first survey of party members, district managers and CDU representatives in parliament. A further survey, in 1975, looked at new members of the party.[45] Gluchowski and Veen used some material from the 1971 and 1977 surveys in their comparison of voters and members of CDU and SPD.[46] While SPD and FDP published selected information for their members, either to reassure them about the secure state of their party or - as was the case for the FDP - warn them about the difficulties and remind them about the potential that might be realized with sufficient effort, the CDU did not use the data in a direct membership approach.[47] The CDU seemed to have envisaged to obtain a better understanding of the social composition and the membership participation in the newly expanded party without directly translating the findings into advice for recruitment or party organization.

THE SOCIAL COMPOSITION OF THE CDU MEMBERSHIP

The CDU has been hailed as a "model for a genuine Volkspartei", a trendsetter in the West German party system, a non-ideological melting pot of social groups.[48] The scramble for a broad appeal and maximum electoral impact has persuaded all parties to formulate policies and devise sections in their party programmes for various groups in society. It has become virtually compulsory to give special mention to pensioners, to the young, to women. The nuts and bolts of party politics, and the selection of leadership personnel and parliamentary candidates through the parties seem to be untouched by the niceties of caring for everybody which rings so forcefully in public pronouncements. Here it matters who joins as a member, who is nominated and rises through party membership to positions within the party or in the elected bodies on a communal, regional or land level; or even who represents a political party in the Bundestag. On this concrete level of members' contribution to politics and society, the CDU remains a far cry from a people's party.

The Middle Class Party
The membership expansion during the seventies confirmed the position of the CDU as the party for the conservative middle class (Table 5.2). Taking new and old middle class together, i.e. the occupational

The Christian Democrats

Table 5.2: Changes of the CDU Membership: Occupational Structure

Occupations	1955[1]	1964[2]	1966[3]	1971[4]	1973[5]	1977[6]	1979[7]	Population overall 1977[6]
Workers	15	15	13	11	11	9	10.5	17
Employees	18	20	21	22	26	26	27.5	23
Civil Servants	9	11	12	16	13	14	12.5	5
Self-employed incl. Farmers, professions	38	37	30.5[8]	32	28	26	25.5[9]	7
Pensioners	7	–	10	16	6	13	5	18
Housewives	13	–	8	4	8	8	11	24
In training/education	–	–	2.4	3	5	3	6	5
Unemployed	–	–	0.02	0	–	1	0.23	2
Others/n.a.	–	17	3.6	–	3	–	1.7	–

1. Heidenheimer 1957 quoted in Gluchowski/Veen, Nivellierungstendenzen bei CDU/CSU und SPD, Z Parl 3, 1979, p. 329.
2. Data from CDU Annual Report, ibid.
3. Data from central membership files 31.8.1966 (274,037 members) quoted in Falke, Die Mitglieder der CDU, p. 77.
4. Data from Konrad Adenauer Foundation survey, quoted in Gluchowski/Veen, p. 329 and Falke p. 78.
5. dto.
6. Konrad Adenauer Foundation Survey, quoted in Falke p. 113.
7. EDV print out dated 31.12.1979 (684,445 members).
8. Includes 0.5% helpers in family business.
9. Includes 0.43% helpers in family business.

groups of employees, civil servants and self employed as applied in Table 5.2, 65% of the CDU members in 1955 and 65.5% in 1979 were middle class. The self-employed today hold a less prominent position in the CDU than twenty years ago. Their share decreased from 38% in 1955 to near 25% in 1979. Still, the CDU includes considerably more self-employed than the West German population overall. The new middle class, i.e. employees and civil servants combined grew from 25% in 1955 to 40% in 1979. Similar to SPD and FDP, the CDU had a relatively large civil servants' component. Table 5.2 lists pensioners, housewives, trainees, and students separately. It can be assumed that their social backgrounds correspond to the CDU membership overall and are mainly middle class. At the end of the seventies, an estimated four in five CDU members held middle class occupations or came from middle class backgrounds.

There is some evidence that the CDU attracts members with higher incomes and higher social status. In the model of social stratification of the Federal Republic, the self-employed occupy the upper ranges of the middle class with income levels well above average.[49] Civil servants also enjoy above average incomes and a high degree of status security through promotions and index linked pensions. The Infas study which compared SPD and CDU memberships suggested that the CDU included a larger proportion of higher civil servants and top level employees in the managerial brackets. Of the few workers in the CDU most are skilled and tend towards a middle class status. Although numerically the CDU today has nearly twice as many working class members than in 1955, 70,000 compared with about 33,000, workers now constitute a smaller sector of the total CDU membership than twenty or so years ago.

The links between the social structure of society and of the CDU membership, are not easy to determine. Table 5.2 includes figures from the 1977 survey which have also been used by Gluchowski/Veen and Troitzsch in their evaluations of the social composition of parties.[50] On the basis of these figures, the CDU does not mobilize workers or unemployed in accordance with their place in society. Women and pensioners are also underrepresented. The party is quite successful in attracting employees; it performs well regarding civil servants. The sector of self-employed however is the most clearly overrepresented. If one compares the CDU social structure with the data on occupational positions published by the Federal Statistical Office, the discrepancies appear sharper still.[51] In 1976, 42.6% of the labour force were workers. The CDU in 1977 had only 9% workers among its members. Civil servants and white collar occupations combined amounted to 43.7% in the Federal Republic, to 39% in the CDU; self-employed and family members helping in the business constituted nearly 14% of the work force, 26% in the CDU.

Whichever way the calculations and comparisons are carried out, the findings point in the same direction: the CDU is a party with a strong middle class bias. As in other parties, the new middle class sectors have expanded. Contrary to other parties, the self-employed constitute about one quarter of the party membership at a time when their share in society has decreased to around 9%.

It is impossible to determine recruitment patterns among certain occupational groups since the data basis is insufficient. The self identification of the members who joined in 1975 confirms the position of the CDU as the party of the middle and upper strata in West German Society, 14% of the new members classified themselves as workers, 66% as belonging to the middle strata in society (Mittelschicht) and 20% saw themselves as upper or upper middle class.[52] Only 54% of the original sample of this study completed the questionnaire. The findings, therefore, cannot be taken as hard and fast numerical values, but only as indicative trends. Although the occupational structure of CDU membership changed over the last decade and seems to be still changing, the position of the party in the middle ranges of society, among the Mittelstand in terms of self-identification and social values has been maintained through the membership growth and the adjustments to the role of opposition.[53]

The Denominational Balance

The membership growth during the seventies modified the denominational character of the CDU. Although intended to bridge the gap between denominations as a Christian party, the CDU has been predominantly catholic. In 1971, three in four (73%) members were catholics. Six years later, 65% were catholics. Over the same period the share of protestants rose from 25% to 33%.[54] In 1982, 59% of CDU members were catholic, 34% protestant. A broadening of the denominational base may be under way. Among new admissions in 1982, 47% were catholics, 41% protestants.[55] Regional differences of denomination must not be overlooked. Denominations in West Germany are largely regionalized. The Northern areas tend to be protestant, the centre regions and the South West mixed, the South and the Rhine regions catholics. In most regions, the CDU attracts a disproportionately high share of catholics among its membership. In the Saar region, for example, 90% of the CDU membership and 75% of the population were catholic in 1969. In Hanover, the CDU included at the same time 50% catholics among its members while the population had 18%. The only land organization with a protestant majority in 1979 was Schleswig Holstein, with 34,000 members, one of the smallest in the CDU. The region had 87% protestants and 6% catholics, the CDU 82% protestants and 7% catholics.56 In the denominationally mixed regions of Westfalia Lippe and Rhineland, four in five CDU members were catholics in 1979 and both regional parties grew fastest of all CDU Land organizations.57

Despite the slight increase of protestants in the CDU membership, the party remains largely catholic. In the light of our earlier observations about the place of the CDU in society, we can be more specific: as a membership party, the CDU is the political party for the catholic middle class, with a modest sector of conservative protestants.58

CDU Educational Profile

The character of the CDU as a party for the middle class is underlined by the educational profiles of its members. The CDU has never been a party for the poorly educated. In 1957, 16% of its members were educated to University level or beyond, 20% in 1969 (see Table 5.3). Although the precise numerical value may be doubtful since the data are based on partial surveys of the CDU membership, an overall contrast between educational attainment of the population and of CDU members is apparent.

For the seventies, the data base is more secure. The membership explosion shifted the educational profile even more towards the higher levels. In 1977, 28% of the CDU members belonged to the top educational bracket; 54% compared with 42% in 1971 had been educated at least to O Level. This development reflects the improved educational qualifications in the population as a whole; it also reflects the inclination of the higher educated to become politically active by joining a political party. Both factors have been observed for SPD and FDP as well.

The educational profiles of newcomers to the CDU have not been published. Data relating to the occupational structure of the youth section Junge Union, however, indicate that the better educated form a strong contingent among the new recruits under the age of 35. In 1969, 15% of the Junge Union members were students or grammar school pupils.59 Taking these two categories together as the better educated, a clear trend emerges for the seventies: the highest educational group grew to 45% of the Junge Union membership in 1978.60

The Christian Democrats

Table 5.3: CDU Educational Profile

Educational level	CDU Members				Population	
	1957[1] %	1969[2] %	1971[3] %	1977[3] %	1969[2] %	1977[1] %
Abitur (A Level) and/or University	16 }	20 }	19 }	28 }	5 }	13 }
Mittlere Reife (O Level)	39 } 23 } 34 }	54 23 }	42 26 }	54 26 }	31 17 }	30
Basic Schooling (Volksschule) and apprenticeship	{ 35 } 61	41 } 38	37 } 57	46	44 } 78	41 } 66
Basic Schooling only	{ }	3	16	9	34	25
N.A./None	–	8	1	0	0	1
	100	100	100	100	100	100

Sources: 1. Data from Hartenstein/Liepelt quoted in Gluchowski/Veen, p. 325.
2. Marie Christine Zauzich, Parteien im Wandel, p. 67.
3. Wolfgang Falke, Die Mitglieder der CDU, p. 67.

Another factor may influence the educational profile of the CDU. Members tend to come to the party when they have reached a certain career level: in 1968 Diederichs found that members normally held secure professional positions by the time they joined. They tended to be older than their counterparts in the SPD and financially somewhat better off. CDU membership seemed to be a step after reaching a respectable place in one's life and in the community.

In Diederichs' survey, 50% of the CDU newcomers had reached a secure position in their career, 25% had already started a family.[61] Recruitment was frequently through neighbourhood contacts: membership seemed part of a lifestyle. The CDU, then emerges as the party for the accomplished and the middle aged.

The Age Structure
Through the decade of CDU growth, the age structure

has remained remarkably constant. Some four in five members were 35 years or older, i.e. above the age officially classified as "youth" in party politics. There have been some shifts within this range: the proportion of over-sixties declined, that of 35-45 year olds increased. Among the young, the CDU seems to have achieved little. In 1977, only 6% of its members were under 25, 5% in 1971 (Table 5.4). If the data for 1968 are numerically reliable, the CDU did a little better among the youngest group during the seventies. In the seventies, under 35s constituted roughly one fifth of the party membership, yet one third of the population.[62] The EDV data for 1978 and 1979 show a slightly less favourable picture and suggest that CDU recruitment among the young has slackened further. At the end of December 1978, 9.9% of the CDU membership were under thirty years of age, at December 1979, 9.7%. About the same proportion were over seventy.[63]

Table 5.4: Age Structure of CDU Membership

Age	1968/9[1]	1971[2]	1977[2]
Under 25	2	5	6
25 - under 35	21	15	16
35 - under 45	}	24 }	28 }
45 to under 60	76	31 80	31 78
60 and over	}	25 }	19 }
n.a.	1	-	-

1. Data based on Diederichs p. 43,
2. Gluchowski/Veen, p. 325.

Since then, the party has been a little more successful among the younger age group. In January 1983, 12% of its members were born in 1951 or later i.e. they were roughly under thirty. Among newcomers, 27% belonged to the under 30s. Still, the CDU encounters difficulties in winning young people as members.

PROBLEMS OF STABILITY

With a fast growing party, stability needs to be examined. We have seen that the CDU has retained its social composition and its place in the upper middle class range of society, that it has retained its denominational orientation towards catholicism, and despite the influx of some younger members, its overall age structure with a predominance of middle aged. Yet, the problem of stability can be discussed on another level: do individual members join and stay or are they easily moved to leave the party again? Do memberships last, does the CDU enjoy membership loyalty?

Did the entry into the opposition role alienate old and attract new members, albeit from the same social segment? Did the return to government affect the party organization?

Gains and Losses
First, we shall examine membership fluctuations. Between December 1969 and December 1977, the CDU gained 553,343 members, an average increase of 15.48% annually.[64] In 1977, three in four members had joined the party after it had become the opposition party (Table 5.5). Only 13% were old-timers from the forties and fifties.

Membership gains tend to be highest around election times.[65] The general emphasis on parties and political positions and the media exposure may motivate people to join. The ubiquitous posters in German streets certainly ensure that parties and their leaders make themselves known to the broader public.[66]

Table 5.5: CDU Membership Duration, 1945-1977

Year of Entry	% of membership	Duration of membership
1945-1953	5	25 years or more
1954-1961	8	17-24 years
1962-1969	17	9-16 years
1970-1977	68	1-8 years
Unknown	2	-

Source: Falke p. 65.

In the late seventies, gains for all political parties slowed down. The CDU recorded an increase of 22,000 between December 1969 and December 1971, which would be an annual increase of just under one percent.[67] In the mid seventies, the party gained 6.7% annually, in the early seventies near ten percent. The return to government seems to have boosted membership. Between 1980 and 1982, the CDU registered a monthly increase of 1,400 members, 34,000 altogether. Between January and February 1983, the increase was 2,823.[68]

Over the period 1970-1978 membership losses averaged 4.9% per annum. At the start of the opposition period, the loss was somewhat heavier: 7.5% of the members in 1970. Falke suggested that about 26% of membership losses can be attributed to death, there are also usual delays in adjusting files and updating records. Overall, about 60% of membership losses seem to reflect a political decision and disappointment with the party. Specific reasons, however, are rarely given.[69] Of the 300,000 or so members of the CDU in 1969, 106,000 were no longer in the CDU in 1978. Thus, the CDU lost through natural causes or political dissatisfaction, one in three of its old-time members. Yet, at the end of the seventies two in three of these old-timers were still in the party. This points to a considerable degree of party loyalty. Of the members who had joined between 1970 and 1977, 16% had left the party again within that period. Troitzsch stressed that in the early seventies, the CDU had twice as many gains than the SPD and about the same proportion of losses.[70] Despite the rapid influx of new members, membership fluctuation has been low. The CDU is a stable party.

Membership Motivations

Membership has become altogether more important in the CDU of the seventies and eighties. Recruitment and integration of new members has been emphasized as one of the key roles of local branches. Since 1974, the Bonn head office has produced handbooks and guidelines to assist branches and individuals in the recruitment task.[71] It is difficult to determine how successful these efforts have been and can be. The first major drive took place in 1974, a year in which CDU membership leapt up 15%.[72] In Falke's survey only one in five party members mentioned recruitment campaigns or contact with the local party branch as the reason which made them join. More important seem to be meetings with well known politicians (26%), one's own initiative (34%), and contacts with friends (35%).[73] For the new members between 1970 and 1972, individual motivation (39%) and the impact of a meeting with a politician (29%) seemed to have been particularly important. CDU membership is also influenced by family commitment.

About one in five newcomers to the party mentioned the family as the major influence. The family and the political traditions in the immediate social circle are, however, more important still. In 1975, 86% of the new members came by their own admission from CDU orientated families. Four out of five had never been interested in a party other than the CDU. In 1971, 38% of the CDU members had other CDU members in their family. Party affiliation appears to intensify among office holders. Of the CDU delegates to land parliaments, 73% had other CDU members in their family, so did 78% of the delegates to the Bundestag.

The importance of family background and social networks like neighbourhoods, associations, clubs, friends for the recruitment to the CDU has already been observed by Meyer in the sixties.[74] For SPD members, the cohesion of working class culture and its influence on party membership is gradually losing ground; yet SPD recruitment is strongly indebted to the work place and the working environment. For the CDU, a less explicit interrelation between party and social environment seems to exist. Members tend to come from a CDU oriented middle class segment of society. Families are either directly or indirectly affiliated to the CDU. The CDU emerges as the natural political choice, the political home. Choosing and joining the CDU is for most members the party political consequences of their social status, their position in the community, their identify in society. The CDU, then, is accepted as the only party to articulate one's interests.[75]

Liepelt observed that CDU members consider themselves as in the political middle ground and their party slightly to the right. This discrepancy seems to be slighter than for the SPD, the consensus between the party and its followers seems to be high.[76] Another of Liepelt's observations throws some light on the membership motivation and the cohesion of the CDU: he argued that in West German society today, denominational criteria have taken on the function of class distinctions. For the CDU this would mean that the identification as catholics has a social and political weight similar to the identification of the SPD supporters and members of the early years with the working class. In short, the consensus among environment, social expectations, and political interests emerges as the major factor in motivating for CDU membership. Party efforts may count little compared with a CDU-bound background and environment.

A Party of Potential Office Holders

Meyer's study noted a willingness of CDU members to hold office in the party or in the community. The inclination towards an office was clearly higher than in the SPD, CDU members in the sixties seemed eager to take an active part. 58% had already competed for a post (SPD: 35%), 39% held a party post at the time of the survey (SPD% 21%), 35% an electoral office at local government - or at a higher level (SPD: 14%). Over half the CDU members (54%) stressed they would accept an office if it was offered to them, only 18% did not wish to become actively involved, even if they were approached personally.[77] With the membership growth in the seventies, this readiness to actively work for the party and hold an office seems to have somewhat abated. In 1977, 40% of the CDU members declared that membership in itself was sufficient support for the party. This is an attitude familiar from the SPD. The remaining 60% however, envisaged a more active role. One in four (25%) intended to hold an office and become party functionaries in some way. The remainder, 33% were prepared to play an active part without necessarily expecting to actually be elected to an office. The CDU traditions of active involvement and potential office holding created new bottle necks in the seventies. The party has more ambitious candidates than positions. Taking only those who openly declared that they aspired to an elected office in the party or in an assembly or parliament, the CDU had 166,054 such members in 1977, and only 108,000 office holders. In the mass party, obtaining an elected office has become more difficult. In 1971, 74,000 CDU members i.e. 22% had positions, in 1977, 17%.[78]

The organizational reforms which the CDU introduced in the interest of tighter control of the party and a degree of centralization, reduced the number of elected offices while membership figures and the number of potential candidates rose. The major reform consisted in strengthening the district level and establishing a connection between districts and the Bonn headquarters which would by-pass the regional parties. In streamlining the party, districts were enlarged and reduced in number from 350 to 261. The number of party positions i.e. district executives was reduced from 10,000 to 8,500.[79] While the relatively influential functions at district level became scarcer, the CDU broadened its branch level and decided at the 1975 party congress to increase local elected offices from 52,000

to 98,000. Most of these posts were so called
Beisitzer, additional members of the branch executive who would have little political influence.
Since the importance of local branches in the party
was weakened at the same time in favour of district
offices, the possibility to contribute politically
in the CDU had not been expanded in substance.
   For the rank and file members, local branches
are the most normal points of contact with their
party. Yet, the CDU district offices have become
the focal points of activity in the party. Elected
CDU representatives communicate most frequently with
the district offices. CDU delegates to communal
assemblies, to land parliaments and to the Bundestag
tend to regard the district office as the lowest
level of CDU organization, as the grass roots.[80]
The districts, in return, dominate the political
activities of local branches. The strong connection
between the district levels and the CDU parliamentary party in the Bundestag enabled the *Fraktion* in
1979 to push through its own candidate for the
Chancellorship and command sufficient support from
the rank and file via the district offices to go
against the choice of candidate by the CDU party
congress and the nomination of the party chairman,
Kohl. The backing of the *Fraktion* through the districts and the direct link between central CDU administration and districts affords a considerable
power basis to the CDU parliamentary party for which
the procedure of nominating Strauss and the acquies-
cence of the party to overruling conference decisions
is an instructive example. Local branches with
their enlarged number of office holders have little
substantive impact on the direction of inner party
decision making. In the seventies, the liaison between CDU districts and parliamentary representatives emerged as the backbone of political power in
the CDU.
   This organizational constellation may cont-
tribute to the experience of disappointment articulated by CDU members with the workings of their
party. If we accept that CDU members are highly
motivated to hold office and wield some influence in
the party or through their party affiliation in the
community or at a higher political level, the shortfall of openings and the relative marginality of the
numerous local branch positions are obstacles for
these potential office holders. Falke found in 1977
that 40% of the CDU membership expressed disappointment with the party, 35% expected more when they
joined, 5% declared themselves thoroughly disillus-

ioned.[81] Despite such disillusionment, these people were still members of the party. Disillusionment in the CDU seems to follow frustrated ambitions towards an office and frequently leads to members' passivity. Falke determined the Ämterneigung as the major force motivating CDU members and generating disappointment. By comparison, an identification with the party was hardly relevant. As "a human and loyal community"[82] the CDU did not have visible value for its members. Social get-togethers played virtually no part in CDU party work. We saw earlier that socials were the most popular party function in the SPD, especially for the older and the passive members. The CDU seems to be regarded by its members as providing inroads for advancement and political influence for the most active segment of a CDU orientated middle class layer in West German society.

The pockets of disappointment in the CDU do not generate an inner party opposition. They are not in any way organized or present a challenge to the CDU party organization. Opposition and discontent in the CDU remain individualized, they emerge as grumbles and as haggling over nominations and posts. Overall, the party is characterized by the high motivation to be active and take responsibility. According to Falke's data, the CDU in the seventies had 30% passive members, 50% who took part occasionally in meetings and functions, 20% could be classified as active.[83] This active fifth predominated the party and the elected offices in politics. It also predominated the associations and the positions there. All CDU office holders were actively involved in CDU associations, three in four active members were also active in these associations. This shows that active members and office holders accumulate multiple opportunities of influence. It also shows the close integration of party and associations in the Christian Democratic camp. Within the party, the participation of active members and office holder in one and often in several associations reinforces the standing of the party activist and creates multiple opportunities to obtain electoral positions. The associations clearly strengthen the position of party functionaries who often hold several positions. In the youth associations, Junge Union, active involvement feeds directly into career prospects in politics. Of the CDU Bundestag members in 1977, 48% had started as Junge Union office holders, 42% in the Landtage. The CDU does not seem to have a pattern of advancement from local branch chairman into political office as observed for the SPD.

The CDU - A Membership Party?

Despite the expansion in the seventies, the social place of the CDU as a party for the middle classes, as a stronghold of the old middle class and the self employed, as a predominantly catholic party remains unchanged. Newcomers to the party are hardly converts to conservatism. They tend to come from a CDU orientated environment; joining the CDU may be induced by an election campaign or mobilizing political event, it frequently expresses the wish of the new member to actively involve himself in the party and to obtain an office in and through the party. This inclination towards holding an office has been singled out as the most frequent cause for disappointment with the party which provides proportionately less posts now than it did in the sixties. More important still, the channels of influence within the party seem to preclude ordinary members and office holders at local level from making much impact in the party or beyond. Despite the mass membership, the grass root level of the branch or local CDU has lost in importance. The CDU is run from the district as the lowest relevant organizational layer. This constellation of inner-party influence had already been observed by Zeuner in 1969, who found that the importance of local branches for the nomination of candidates in the CDU was very small, with district associations and their leaderships playing a major role.[84] The heritage of the fifties that the parliamentary party of the CDU and the CDU delegates in parliament were the nucleus of party power seems to have change little. Falke found that the direct link between Bundestag delegates and district organizations remains crucial. In addition, the districts maintain close links with the central CDU administration in Bonn. By comparison with district offices, the branch level is secondary in the CDU. This lack of influence at the lowest level of party work may be a factor in the scramble for offices and electoral functions. Only in the higher party functions and as members of assemblies or parliaments can CDU activists wield influence and fulfil their membership motivation to shape West German politics through participation in the CDU.

OFFICE HOLDERS IN THE CDU

In 1971, a number of prominent CDU members left the party with a public gesture of protest against the way in which the CDU found its policies and its political representatives. Although the voice of dissent did not alter anything, it still is an interesting comment on some party practices usually screened from the public eye.

> The interest of those ten percent of the population who earn and make as much as the remaining ninety percent put together, continue to steer the decision making process of the party leadership and determine the ranking of candidates on the party's election lists.[85]

With their grumbles about selection procedures and about the close association of the CDU and a slim social strata in West German society, the dissenters of 1971 did not tread new ground. The selection of candidates for the party lists has been shown to reflect the links of CDU regional organizations with the relevant industries and businesses and their interest groups.[86] Increasingly, direct candidates who are nominated by the district- and land parties are secured by a list place. The land organizations enter outsiders from the interest sectors less freely today than they seemed to have done in the fifties. One of the issues of the 1971 protests, concerned the transition and remodelling of decision making and leadership recruitment in the party. In the Honoratioren phase in the fifties and early sixties, the days of the CDU as Kanzlerwahlverein where local dignitaries defined policies in the CDU between elections and congresses, the membership was hardly involved in party organization and work. Personal influence and regional practices shaped the party at the lower levels. Once the CDU entered into opposition, the drive towards a higher degree of centralization and political control, was, as Pridham has shown, one of the most important processes of readjustment. Questions about the suitability of established party practices reverberated the pressures for change. In 1971 the CDU had also began to expand its membership. The broader social base could be expected to leave it's mark on the party, on the nomination and selection of office holders and leaders. The 1971 dissenters implied that the membership growth left no such mark.

From Membership to Political Office
Looking at the openings for newcomers to gain a party office or an electoral office, the general

complaints of the 1971 dissenters were not fully justified. In 1977, about half the office holders and 68% of the party members had joined the CDU after 1969. The other half of the CDU office holders and one third of the CDU members had already belonged to the party before 1969. With the duration of membership, the chances to hold an office at any level increase.

Table 5.6 shows the importance of party offices as a starting point into political office. Newcomers to the party were more likely to obtain an office in the party than get themselves elected to assemblies or parliaments. The successes of the CDU in local and land elections in the early seventies, however, provided more electoral offices and enabled newcomers to obtain positions. One quarter of the office holders who joined between 1970 and 1972, were only in an assembly or parliament, one fifth of those who joined later. Among the old timers, the combination of electoral and party office was more frequent than among the other groups. Those combining the two types of offices can be considered the leadership segment in the party. Beyme found in his study of West German elites how party office in the CDU frequently led to local government positions which could, in turn, become stepping stones into regional (land) politics.[87] Within the CDU, advancement from land politics to a seat in the Bundestag is a common career pattern. Experience of Bundestag delegates in land politics is more frequent in the CDU than in any of the other parties.[88]

The Social Composition of the CDU Leadership

The hierarchy of positions and posts is confirmed by the social composition at different levels of leadership. Taking the Bundestag as the highest and the party functionary as the lowest level of leadership, a growing detachment from the social composition of the membership may be stated. The higher the office the narrower the circle of persons who have access to such office. Table 5.7 compares the social basis of the party with that of offices holders and Bundestag members.

Women, already poorly represented among party members, were less likely to hold office - in the CDU as in other parties - than their place in the membership would suggest. The spiral of disadvantage makes it difficult for women to attain the highest level, Bundestag membership. The changes

Table 5.6: CDU Office Holders and Duration of Party Membership

Total Membership 1977	Date of joining the CDU		
	Before 1969 %	1970-1972 %	1973-1977 %
Proportion of office holders	20	21	12
Of these: Electoral office only, no party office	12	26	20
Only party office	49	45	66
Both	39	29	14
	100	100	100
Office holders 1977 and duration of membership	46%	25%	29%

Source: Falke, p. 86.

during the eighth legislative period also show that women tend to be on reserve lists and might enter the Bundestag as replacements for other retiring members. The less educated in the CDU, however, are even less likely than women to hold an office. Only three CDU Bundestag members in 1980 had only basic schooling, 98% had achieved 0 level or higher, 78% university. The educational achievements of office holders are not quite so far removed from those of the rank and file members, but a tendency towards better education is evident. As we observed for SPD and FDP, educational attainment is a distinct advantage in contemporary German politics in the competition for political office. Academics seem to be particularly successful in obtaining positions of leadership; they have also been shown to be more interested in competing for such positions than less educated members.

The differences in social structure between the membership and the leadership indicate that certain groups - men and the better educated, in particular politicians with university education - have better chances to obtain influence in the CDU than their place in the party membership might suggest. In a party where policy decisions happen at district level or above, the distance in the social structure points towards a detachment of leadership and party

The Christian Democrats

Table 5.7: The Social Composition of the CDU Membership and Leadership

	Members[1] %	Office holders[1] %	Bundestag delegates[2] %
Sex			
Male	77	83	92
Female	23	17	8[3]
Age			
Under 35	29	31	8.5[5]
35–59	49	62	83[6]
60 and over	22	8	8.5[7]
Education			
Basic schooling only	40	25	1
Grammar school or higher	59	74	98
University ed.[4]	no data		78
n.a.	1	1	1
Denomination			
Catholic	68	62	no data
Protestant	30	33	
n.a.	2	5	

Notes:
1. Data from Infas p. 7, also include CSU.
2. Chronik des Deutschen Bundestages pp. 186, data for the end of the VIIIth legislative period.
3. 8.3% = 21 women. At the beginning of the legislative period, 19 CDU MdB were women, two entered through their list places. Average for women members of the Bundestag 7.9%.
4. Grammar school includes education to at least O level. University education data or only available for BT. For the CDU women in the BT, 89.5% went to university, only 47.4% finished. Of the men 77.4% went to university, 68% finished. See Chronik 194.
5. CSU: 3.8% BT average 7.7%
6. BT average 74.2%.
7. BT average 8%; CSU 15.1%.

rank and file. The denominational divide has not been monitored for Bundestag representation. For the party functionaries, it appears that those protestants who join the CDU are more active and successful in achieving party office than could be expected from their place in the CDU membership. In its body of functionaries, the CDU seems to be a slightly less manifestly catholic party than in its membership composition. This question of denominational balance, however, would have to be followed up on a regional and district level in the light of the denominational balance and leadership pattern in each case.

The data in Table 5.7 on the age structure confirm the character of the CDU as a middle aged party. Nearly two thirds of party functionaries and four in five of Bundestag members belonged to the middle age group 35-59; this accounts for about half the membership. In the Bundestag, this age group was particularly strongly represented while the youngest and the oldest together constituted half the membership and less than one fifth of CDU Bundestag members. Table 5.7 also shows that among party functionaries the old play little part, but the young seem to do well. About one third of the CDU functionaries, more even than for the general membership, belonged to the youngest age group. It can be assumed that many of these young CDU functionaries hold positions in the party affiliated Junge Union. This has a network of branches at local, district, regional and at national level with a complete network of posts for the under 35s.[89] In 1980, the JU comprised 3,800 local branches, 328 districts, 27 regional and 14 land organizations.[90] In addition, a so called Schüler-Union, Pupil's Union was launched in 1972. In 1979 it consisted of 2,000 groups and about 260 districts.[91] Altogether, a sizeable number of junior positions appear to be available in the CDU in addition to the regular party offices. The Junge Union constitutes an important element in the CDU leadership and an expansive training ground for politics. The role of the youth section as a seedbed of criticism and as an avantgarde seems, by comparison, muss less developed.[92] The influx of young members in the CDU leadership through the Junge Union may also explain the relatively high proportion of young members in the CDU parliamentary party. Although the youngest group, as Table 5.7 shows, is underrepresented compared with the membership structure, comparisons with other parliamentary parties are more favourable. In the CSU Landesgruppe, only 3.8% were under 35, in the SPD parliamentary party, 7.1%. The FDP fared a little better: 12.5% of its delegates at the end of 1976 were under 35.[93]

If the average CDU office holder seems to be a

Table 5.8: The Occupational Structure of CDU Members and Office Holders

Occupation	Members[1] %	Members[2] %	Functionaries[3] %	Local Govt[4] office holders %	CDU/CSU members of the Bundestag %
Self-employed	23	24	20	37.8	33.4[7]
Workers	9	9	6	6.7	1.1
White collar employees	26	39[6]	44[6]	26.5	33.9
Civil servants	}40 14	}52 13	}60 16	21.0	35.8
Pensioners	13	–	–	1.2	–
Housewives	8	–	–	3.2	1.6
In training/students	3	2	4	1.7	1.6
Unemployed	1	–	–	0.2	–
Others	–	5	4	0.3	–
n.a.	–	8	6	1.5	–

Notes:
1. Falke 1977, p. 113.
2. Infas p. 7. This only reached the politically active CDU members.
3. Infas ibid.
4. Gegenwartskunde SH, p. 85.
5. Chronik, p. 197, also Z Parl 2, 1981.
6. The Infas survey used the classifications: Higher employees and civil servants (13); other employees and civil servants (39).
7. Of these: 19.3% self-employed, 14.1% in professions.

male, middle aged, catholic, with higher education a look at the occupational profile of the CDU leadership can specify the social positions and origins further (Table 5.8). Workers, who already counted little among CDU membership, were weakly represented among the functionaries. Housewives were similarly by-passed in the leadership selections. For students and young people in training, the observations on the role of the Junge Union are again valid. They did relatively well among the functionaries with Junge Union and Schüler Union positions. They did much less well in elected offices outside the party organization. The self-employed point to an interesting problem: they are underrepresented among party functionaries, but overrepresented compared with their place in the membership in local government positions and in the Bundestag. The sector of the self-employed comprises the old middle class and the professions. It maintained considerable influence in the political system for its specific interests and within the party through the unbroken importance of the Mandatsträger, the elected members of assemblies and parliaments. Finally, a tendency towards Verbeamtung, the predominance of civil servants in politics is also visible in the CDU. Well over one third of the parliamentary party in 1980 consisted of civil servants compared with 14% of the party membership.

    Civil servants seemed to be particularly well placed to achieve local government offices. This may be related to their high motivation to contribute actively in the party. Falke found that civil servants were potentially the most active group in the CDU.[94] They also frequently have first hand experience of local government administration or have legal knowledge. Both assets make them strong contenders for political office. The observations we made earlier about exemptions from work and special provisions for those civil servants who wanted to become politically active are also relevant to this context.[95] The combination of job security for civil servants, specialist knowledge, administrative proficiency and often a background of legal studies fosters the Verbeamtung of German politics. The CDU as a party and in its leadership is no exception.

Between Membership and Leadership Party
The membership explosion of the CDU in the seventies has not altered the social bias of the leadership towards the self-employed and towards the civil servants. As we saw, the new membership came from the same social sector as established CDU members; the organizational structure of the CDU does not directly reflect membership diversities in the party leadership. The voices of dissent in 1971 suggested that segments in the party expected a new flexibility. At the end of the decade, a new bout of criticism hit harsher and more precisely at specific leadership structures. The voice of protest this time came from the organized student group of the CDU.[96] It did, as before, not generate a wider debate, but it does highlight some incongruities in the development of the CDU towards a membership party.

The Christian Democrats

We discussed earlier, that the numerous local party offices are quite insignificant as far as political influence is concerned. The important level is the district. Here, it seems, district chairmen usually hold an elected office in an assembly or in parliament in addition to their party post; they are doubly powerful; doubly limited according to the critics. They attack a "cartel of mediocrity" (<u>Kartell der Mittelmässigkeit</u>) which allegedly permeates the CDU. Sitting politicians tend to be reselected for their positions, because their political standing and their livelihood have been tied up with that position. More important still, between elections, the energies seem to be spent largely on canvassing for re-selection at beer evenings etc, rather than pursuing the party's interests through their elected offices. The paper implied that only the CDU leadership, not the members, determine who is reselected and how the nominations for office are handled. It also suggests that the half-hearted work in the assemblies and in parliament with one eye at least on the mood of the party and among the relevant leadership clique makes for inefficient representation. Real politics, then, is left to those few who hold the strings of party political nominations and re-selections: and to the leadership groups within assemblies and parliaments. "The executive, in particular a small leadership circle within the parliamentary party, determine the policies".[97] The oligarchic tendencies and nomination practices are, of course, revealing and have a familiar ring from other parties. The new element in the critical attack of 1980 is the new importance attached to the CDU membership: it has become the critical yardstick for change of the party and its organization. "The overlap of offices may be a straight question of power for the individual. For the party, however, as well as for the tasks in parliament, it brings many disadvantages".[98]

The emergence of the CDU into a membership party has so far accompanied the leadership structures and decision making processes: it has not influenced or altered them. The voices of discontent from the CDU students seem to indicate that some groups in the CDU wish to remodel the party and provide more scope for the members, more outlets for participation and a relevant political role for the rank and file. On the whole, the CDU does not experience a participation debate. In this respect, it is clearly different from the SPD. The

established roads towards holding office still tend
to be accepted and the established ways of making
decisions and of formulating policies have not been
seriously challenged. The new and broadened social
basis as a membership party, which the CDU proudly
celebrates in its name "the big people's party" does
not seem to have remoulded inner party democracy.
On the contrary, expansion occurred at a time when
the political need for more streamlined party organization had been recognised and attempted. The
trend towards more central party control resulted in
strengthening the districts at the expense of party
grass root organizations. The remodelling of the
CDU, it appears, did not take its priorities from
the membership development and look for increased
chances to allow participation. The priorities were
largely organizational and, of course, aimed in the
long run at winning elections and leading the government once again. In Falke's research, this perspective of efficiency comes through clearly: he
regards the membership expansion with its increased
costs and efforts of communication and its limited
returns in terms of activity, involvement, commitment for the party, as a largely wasteful exercise
and implies that the CDU would be better off with
less members - its policies could be as effective
and the cost and time of running the party could be
reduced.[99] This is not the official CDU line.

   The differences in assessing the place of members in the party may have prevented publication of
the Falke studies under CDU auspices. In a longer
term perspective, the CDU seems to be in transition
still: the transition from <u>Honoratioren</u> party to
streamlined party apparatus has not been completed.
The parliamentary party retained much of its weight
as a policy formulating body. Central office gained
importance alongside the regional parties, but has
not replaced them in their autonomy. The cacophony
of political announcement preceding the 1981 CDU
congress in Hamburg confirmed that the transition
remains incomplete. Through the media, regional
leaders, the business manager of the central office
as well as the <u>Junge Union</u> launched conflicting
views. At the congress, a policy debate did not
take place, instead the CDU leader made a general
and unity-inspiring speech. The fact remains, that
policy formulation is still diversified, and that
the membership, through party congress or through
local party organizations has little voice in it.[100]
The same congress, however, articulated the theme of
interrelationship between "basis" and leadership in

a new vein. Following a campaign of the Junge Union which called for leadership of the CDU in policy matters, the Hamburg congress proceded to invite five hundred young people as guest delegates and observers. The congress adopted the slogan "with the young: our country needs a new beginning" and held workshops on four major issues: education, the Social Market Economy, peace and the relationship of citizens and state. There were no heated debates, just calm deliberations and public agreement. The controversies which had flourished before the congress and re-emerged afterwards, were not even audible. Nothing could suggest that the extended participation at the Hamburg congress meant an extended franchise for the CDU rank and file or even its sympathisers and supporters. The demonstrative inclusion of young people had a different purpose: signalling to the public that the CDU does have an active approach across the generations, and, of course, underlining the theme of unity within the party and the promise of unity through the party for the country. The concluding phrases in Kohl's speech to congress confirm that no new initiatives and forms of participation were intended:

> We have to establish the solidarity between generations once again. This solidarity, the guarantee of peace within as well as personal and social security - has been endangered today more than ever before. The awareness of needing each other and depending on each other tends to get lost. We have to start here. We have to become aware again that the generations of a people become a community of fate, which nobody may dissolve.[101]

The message to the young culminated in an appeal to support the CDU, to accept it as the party which will bring about a great "Wende", turning point in all matters. Or as the General Secretary of the CDU Geissler put it in his address:

> We have to carry the torch of hope into these times: the belief and the hope that one day freedom and social justice will be realised everywhere. For this, we can enthuse young people ... We, the Christian Democrats have to become and to remain the torch bearers of hope for one hundred million people. A new confidence should emanate from here and from today, a new belief, a new will for action: we, the

CDU, allow ourselves to be challenged by the young, and we challenge them: do not sit in the comfy corners of private happiness or of resignation, come and help build a new and better world![102]

The return of the CDU to government will show how important the party has become in formulating policies. There is nothing to suggest that the phase of opposition, of membership growth, of organizational reform has generated a party which derives its policies and directives from the whole of the membership and has developed substantive and workable forms of participation that could enfranchise all the members even on the humblest levels of party work. Despite all the changes in the seventies, the CDU in opposition seems to have retained its tendency to make politics as a Chancellor's Party.

FOOTNOTES

1. Jürgen Dittberner, Die Bundesparteitage der CDU und der SPD von 1946 bis 1968, Augsburg 1969. Also dto. "Die Parteitage der CDU und SPD - Ideal und Realität" in Ossip K. Flechtheim (ed.), Die Parteien der Bundesrepublik Deutschland, Hamburg (Hoffman & Campe) 1973, pp. 44-58.
2. Geoffrey Pridham, Christian Democracy in Western Germany. The CDU in government and opposition 1946-1976, Croom Helm, 1977, pp. 142 ff.
3. Ibid., pp. 169 ff.
4. See Gerard Braunthal, "The Policy Function of the German Social Democratic Party" in Comparative Politics vol. 9, no. 2, Jan. 1977, pp. 134-137.
5. For a detailed study of different organizational strands see Hans Georg Wieck, Die Entstehung der CDU und die Wiedergründung des Zentrums im Jahre 1945, Düsseldorf (Droste) 1953. Also: Paul Ludwig Weihnacht (ed.), Die CDU in Baden-Württemberg und ihre Geschichte, Stuttgart (Landeszentrale für politische Bildung), 1978.
6. Good discussion in Pridham, ibid., Chapter I.
7. Arnold J. Heidenheimer, Adenauer and the CDU. The rise of the leader and the integration of the party, The Hague 1960. Also Günter Müchler, CDU/CSU. Das schwierige Bündnis, München (Vögel) 1976.
8. Quoted in Pridham, ibid., p. 252.
9. Peter Radunski, "Die CDU und ihre Vorsitzenden" in CDU im Bild. 30 Jahre Politik für Deutschland, Stuttgart (Rüber & Denzel) 1975, p. 23.

10. Franz Gurk, the CDU chairman for North-Baden at the 1966 congress for the region, quoted in Pridham, p. 249.
11. Ibid., p. 250, also Weihnacht, "Die Ausstrahlung der süddeutschen CDU auf die Bundespartei" in Die CDU in Baden-Württemberg, ibid., p. 293 ff.
12. The CDU statutes are reprinted in Kaack and Roth, Handbuch I, p. 29. The so called CDU in Exile, i.e. in the GDR is entitled to send 30 delegates to the congress. They have no voting rights.
13. See A.R.L. Gurland, Die CDU/CSU. Ursprünge und Entwicklung bis 1953, Stuttgart (EVA) 1980, esp. chapters II-IV.
14. Good account in Pridham, ibid., p. 179-182.
15. Helmuth Pütz, Die CDU. Entwicklung, Aufbau und Politik der CDU, Düsseldorf (Droste), 1978, p. 6.
16. Ibid., p. 102.
17. Richard von Weizsäcker (ed.), CDU Grundsatzdiskussion. Beiträge aus Politik und Wissenschaft, München (Goldmann), 1977. Also: Die Programme der CDU. Der Weg zum Grundsatzprogramm, ed. Bundesgeschäftsstelle der CDU, Bonn n.d. (1979) no.3869. This publication omits the 1968 programme altogether.
18. Pütz, ibid., p. 54 ff. Also Wolfgang Falke, Die Mitglieder der CDU. Eine empirische Studie zum Verhältnis von Miglieder - und Organisationsstruktur 1971-1977, Berlin (Duncker & Humblodt) 1982, p. 80.
19. Walter Wellner, Parteienfinanzierung, München, 1973, p. 44.
20. 34 Thesen zur Reform der CDU, discussed in Pütz, ibid., p. 72.
21. Karl Schmitt, "Die CDU in Nordwürttemberg" in Die CDU in Baden-Württemberg, ibid., p. 226.
22. Kaack and Roth I, pp. 186-187.
23. Pütz, ibid., pp. 68-72.
24. Kaack and Roth I, p. 178.
25. The role of the Wirtschaftsrat der CDU e.V. would need to be examined in relation to the financial independence of the central CDU office.
26. See Alf Mintzel, CSU. Anatomie einer Partei, Opladen (Westdeutscher Verlag), 1976, esp. Ch. III, pp. 139-165.
27. Mintzel, Geschichte der CSU. Ein Überblick Opladen (Westdeutscher Verlag), 1977, pp. 94-112.
28. Mintzel, Anatomie, p. 277.
29. Data supplied by the CSU Landesleitung, Munich.
30. For 1972, see William E. Paterson, "The

German Social Democratic Party" in Paterson and Thomas (eds.), Social Democratic Parties in Western Europe, Croom Helm 1977, p. 211. For 1978: SPD Jahrbuch 1977-1978, Bonn 1978, pp. 265.

31. Porträt einer Partei, ed. CSU Landesleitung Munich n.d., p. 72.

32. Mintzel coined the Phrase "Apparatpartei modernen Typs" in Geschichte der CSU.

33. An excellent discussion in Müchler, Das schwierige Bündnis, ibid.

34. Mintzel, "Der Fraktionszusammenschluss nach Kreuth: Ende einer Entwicklung?" in Z Parl 1, 1977, pp. 58-76.

35. Mintzel has extensively analysed the CSU and, at this state, little new could be added. This chapter concentrates on the CDU with some reference to joint developments.

36. Data supplied by the Bundesgeschäftsstelle der CDU, Bonn, EDV printout dated 31.12.1982. See also Kaack and Roth, ibid., pp. 82 ff.

37. Wolfram Höfling, "Die Vereinigungen der CDU. Eine Bestandaufnahme zu Organisationsstruktur, Finanzen und personaler Repräsentanz" in Kaack and Roth I, p. 129 and p. 133.

38. Ibid., pp. 38-39.

39. Bericht des Landesverbandes Baden-Württemberg für die Wahlperiode vom 4.10.1975 bis 22.10.1977, Offenburg 1978, p. 54.

40. Mintzel, Geschichte ibid., p. 187.

41. Ulrich Grasser, "Die CDU und die Junge Union" in: Dittberner and Ebbighausen (eds.), Das Parteiensystem in der Legitimationskrise, Opladen (Westdt. Verlag), 1973, p. 329.

42. Manfred Dumann (ed.), 25 Jahre Junge Union Deutschlands: Werdegang, Grundlagen, Aufgaben, Bonn 1972, p. 95.

43. Good compilation for all parties in document Hr/Ht - 0023 d, Bundesgeschäftsstelle der CDU, 15.9.1982.

44. Falke's data are based on written questionnaires, 62% of the original sample took part in the survey, 195 of the 261 district managers were interviewed.

45. Both surveys were also conducted by Falke under the auspices of the Konrad Adenauer Foundation, see Falke, ibid., pp. 42-43.

46. Peter Gluchowski and Hans-Joachim Veen, "Nivellierungstendenzen in den Wähler- und Mitgliedschaften von CDU/CSU und SPD 1959 bis 1979", in Z Parl 3, 1979, pp. 321-331, also Holger

Thielemann, "Neuere Daten zur Sozialstruktur von CDU und SPD" in Gegenwartskunde SH 1979, pp. 81-86.
  47. Wolfgang Falke, Die Mitglieder der CDU, ibid., typescript in 1980, published in 1982, see footnote 18; Interview with Dr. Falke at the Konrad Adenauer Foundation on April 25, 1980.
  48. Gordon Smith, Democracy in Western Germany, p. 86.
  49. Cleassens/Klönne/Tschoeppe, Sozialkunde der Bundesrepublik. Grundlagen, Strukturen, Trends in Wirtschaft und Gesellschaft, Düsseldorf (Diederichs) 1981, pp. 295 ff. Also: Klassen - und Sozialstruktur der BRD 1950-1970 Part II/2, Frankfurt/M (Marxistische Blätter) n.d., p. 48.
  50. Gluchowski/Veen, ibid.
  51. Gesellschaftliche Daten 1977, ed. Presse- und Informationsamt der Bundesregierung Bonn, 1978, p. 113 ff.
  52. Falke ibid., p. 106 table 14 and own calculations.
  53. Of the new admissions in 1982, 9% were workers, about 80% belonged to the middle class segment with 19% self-employed. EDV printout 15.1.1983.
  54. Pridham ibid., p. 277, also Troitzsch in Kaack/Roth ibid., p. 101 and 108.
  55. Statistischer Bericht der zentralen Mitgliederkartei 31.1.1983.
  56. Pütz, ibid., p. 43.
  57. FAZ 23.6.1979. At that time, Rhineland had 131,779 CDU members, Westfalia-Lippe 127,781.
  58. Geoffrey Pridham "The 1980 Bundestag Elections: A case of 'normality'" in WEP 4 no. 2, May 1981, p. 116.
  59. Up to 1971 the minimum age for JU members was 18, since 1971 it has been lowered to 16. The large majority of pupils' organizations of the CDU Schülerunion, are in the high-school and grammar school sectors.
  60. Data from Höfling, ibid., p. 140.
  61. Nils Diederich, "Zur Mitgliederstruktur von CDU und SPD" in: Dittberner and Ebbighausen ibid., pp. 35-55, esp. pp. 40-48.
  62. Falke ibid., p. 57.
  63. Statistische Berichte der Zentralen EDV Mitgliederkartei, dated 31.12.1978 and 31.12.1979.
  64. Falke ibid., p. 56 and Troitzsch ibid., pp. 88-89.
  65. Falke ibid., pp. 48-56. Also the interviews with Dr. Falke and Herrn Esser on April 25, 1980.

66. See Elisabeth Noelle-Neumann, "The Dual Climate of Opinion. The Influence of Television in the 1976 West German Federal Elections" in Kaase/Beyme (eds.), Elections and Parties, German Studies III, Sage 1978, pp. 139-169.
67. EDV data provided by the CDU Bundesgeschäftsstelle.
68. Jan.-Feb. 1983 compiled by Herrn Hartwig Referat Öffentlichkeitsarbeit.
69. Details in Falke ibid., pp. 58-65.
70. Troitzsch ibid., p.87.
71. From November 1975, the CDU Bundesgeschäftsstelle has published and distributed a series Regiebuch with special emphasis on relations between community and party and new members and party, e.g. Regiebuch 1 Mitdenken, Mitarbeiten, Mobilisieren: Mitgliederwerbung. Regiebuch 2 Mitdenken etc. Neubürgerbetreuung.
72. Kaack/Roth I, ibid., p. 82.
73. For these and the following data see Falke pp 96-110.
74. Armin Meyer, "Parteiaktivitäten und Einstellungen von CDU- und SPD-Mitgliedern", in Dittberner/Ebbighausen ibid., pp. 58-59.
75. Falke ibid., p. 97.
76. In Elections and Parties ibid., p. 179.
77. Meyer ibid., p. 64. In the SPD, 27% of the members could not be activated at all.
78. For this and the following see Falke ibid., pp. 77-81.
79. Pütz ibid., p. 55, Falke ibid., p. 113.
80. Falke typescript (1980), p. 243 f.
81. Falke, Die Mitglieder ibid., p. 166.
82. Falke, typescript, p. 214.
83. Falke, Die Mitglieder ibid., p. 172.
84. Bodo Zeuner, Innerparteiliche Demokratie, Berlin 1969, p. 83.
85. Reprinted in Ossip K. Flechtheim, Die Parteien der BRD, ibid., p. 473.
86. For a summary see Jürgen Weber, Interessengruppen im politischen System der Bundesrepublik, München, 1976, pp. 187 ff.
87. Klaus von Beyme, Die politische Elite in der Bundesrepublik, Stuttgart (Kohlhammer), 1975 p. 74.
88. See the collection of data by Heino Kaack in Z Parl 2, 1981, p. 186.
89. JU functionaries can remain in office beyond 35, provided they were under 35 when they were first elected.
90. Höfling ibid., p. 138.

91. Wulf Schönbohm, CDU - Porträt einer Partei, München (Goldmann) 1979, p. 103.
92. Grasser ibid., pp. 327 ff. calls the JU a "Nachhut" while Höfling shows that the JU have developed some links with the workers' wing of the CDU and have mapped out a course of their own (ibid., p. 181 ff).
93. Chronik. Gesetze, Statistik, Dokumentation. Deutscher Bundestag, 8. Wahlperiode, 1976-1980, ed. Presse-und Informationsamt der Bundesregierung, Bonn 1981, p. 185.
94. Falke, ibid., pp. 92-93.
95. See Ch. I.
96. See Stefan Dingerkus et.al., "Gedanken zur Lage der Union im Herbst 1980" in Sonde 4, 1980, pp. 64-77.
97. Ibid., p. 74.
98. Ibid., p. 75.
99. Falke, obd p. 255-259.
100. See FAZ 2.11.1981; FR 4.11.1981; Vorwärts 5.11.1981.
101. Rede des Parteivorsitzenden Helmut Kohl vor dem 30. Bundesparteitag der CDU in Hamburg, 3.11.1981, brochure Bonn n.d. p. 13.
102. Heiner Geissler, "Mit der Jugend: Eine Allianz für Frieden und Freiheit", Rede auf dem 30. Bundesparteitag der CDU, 3. Nov. 1981 brochure Bonn n.d. p. 10.

SUGGESTED READING

Wolfgang Falke, Die Mitglieder der CDU, Berlin (Duncker & Humblodt) 1982
A.R.L. Gurland, Die CDU/CSU Ursprünge und Entwicklung bis 1953, Stuttgart (Europäische Verlagsanstalt) 1980
Arnold J. Heidenheimer, Adenauer and the CDU, The Hague 1960
Alf Mintzel, CSU - Anatomie einer Partei, Opladen (Westdeutscher Verlag) 1976
Alf Mintzel, Geschichte der CSU, Opladen (Westdt. Verlag) 1977
Günter Müchler, CDU/CSU. Das schwierige Bündnis, München (Vögel) 1976
Geoffrey Pridham, Christian Democracy in Western Germany, Croom Helm 1977
Helmuth Pütz, Die CDU. Entwicklung, Aufbau und Politik, Düsseldorf (Droste) 1978
Wulf Schönbohm, CDU - Porträt einer Partei, München (Goldmann) 1979

Ludwig Weihnacht (ed.), Die CDU in Baden-Württemberg und ihre Geschichte, Stuttgart (Landeszentrale f. politische Bildung) 1978

Hans Georg Wieck, Die Entstehung der CDU und die Wiedergründung des Zentrums im Jahre 1945, Düsseldorf (Droste) 1953

Richard von Weizsäcker (ed.), CDU Grundsatzdiskussion. München (Goldmann) 1977

PART TWO: OPPOSITION AND SOCIETY

Opposition and Society

Politics in West Germany have increasingly become the realm of the educated. Of course, there is nothing to prevent open access to parties. Party membership can be taken out regardless of social standing and educational accomplishment. In the established three - as we saw in the first part of this study - this is not happening. Political parties tend to mobilize a slim segment of society. Willingness to join a party and educational attainment go hand in hand. Within party organizations, advancement to leadership positions even on the lower levels again discriminates in favour of those with a grammar school or university background. In short, none of the established three can claim to reflect society within their own organization. Although West German voters give overwhelming support to these parties in elections, the less educated - the majority who did not receive further or higher education - have no foothold in the parties. Recruitment for leadership and the representation in parliaments and in society which is effected through the parties leaves out the average citizen. The spectre of a largely passive population, loyal in elections but without influence in the parties and in political decision making processes on the one side and on the other side some educated few who run political affairs raises its head.

The parties have yet to develop patterns for membership recruitment and involvement to counteract such trends. If the mainstay political parties are operating in an increasingly narrow social network, do other groups, movements, trends outside the established parties involve a broader spectrum of West German society? There appears to be a task for opposition to break into the educational - and class barriers of politics today. Although opposition

Opposition and Society

from various political directions left its mark on West German politics and society in the seventies and eighties, it has hardly faced up to this challenge. The anti-system legacy, which has marred opposition since the days of Imperial Germany, still penetrates the self-awareness of the left and of the right. At the same time, the political cleavage between the educated and active and the passive masses has not been bridged by political initiatives outside and in opposition to the established parties.

Chapter Six

YOUTH AND POLITICS

The thirtieth anniversary of the Federal Republic was marked by a good number of summary evaluations and political reminiscences on the state of the nation. Many familiar themes were mentioned. The relative strength of the economy, the stability of the party system, of governing majorities, the democratic loyalties of interest groups and elites. Other familiar themes had a slightly critical edge. The average West German was reproached for a lack of attachment to his society, a lack of citizen's pride in his political environment.

> The collective mentality which was dominant in the era of the economic miracle and of political and social reconstruction, did not leave much room for the gradual unfolding of the public virtues which are so important for the social climate in a democracy.[1]

Given time, West German citizens might develop a more active commitment to democracy. Their loyalty to democratic institutions goes unquestioned in any case. By contrast, the intellectual fringe of West German society, university staff and students, some writers, some journalists are reprimanded for the negative view they hold about the success of West German democracy. Rainer Lepsius concluded that this opposition was detached from the major trends of political culture, a futile and destructive opposition emanating from a social segment which should better contribute constructively to the political and social process.[2] In a similar vein, Kurt Sontheimer castigated the intellectuals for voicing opposition where the political realities do not warrant it. The "weakness of democracy in West Germany" appears to be an

"alienation of spirit and power" (Geist und Macht), a
"discongruity between the relatively untarnished
functioning and stability of political institutions
and the critical approach of political awareness".[3]
The reprimand of intellectuals for futile dissent
dates back to the sixties and the experience of
student protest. It is a lasting theme, not a new
one. The concern about uncalled-for disagreement
with a basically sound society found a more sensitive
and arguably more contemporary target in the stocktaking exercises after thirty years: West Germany's
young people. "The emaciation of the Republic - does
this idea generate fear among the young? Does it
create the will to defend democracy - I do not know.
I rather suspect, it does not".[4]

The integration of the younger generation into
the society, the politics and the values of the
Federal Republic seems no longer certain.

> The younger generation has difficulties to
> identify with this Republic as its own state.
> Although they would hesitate to identify with
> another system, socialism for example ... they
> lack interest to continue in the footsteps of
> their fathers, and they lack, which is perhaps
> more important, the confidence that the values
> that guided the war generation when they
> constructed the Federal Republic, remain valid
> to this day.[5]

The uncertainty surrounding the political allegiance and the social place of West Germany's young
generation, contrasts with the expectation that the
children of post-war democracy who are now reaching
maturity should have absorbed democratic political
culture and grown into democratic institutions as
their natural and congenial environment. The older
generation, it could be argued, whether ordinary citizens or holding positions of leadership, were converts to democracy. Many had already established positions of eminence before 1949, during the Weimar
Republic and even during Nationalsocialism. The major
socializing agents for their professional careers and
their political outlook predated the democracy of the
Federal Republic. After thirty years, the products of
that democracy, the new generation should emerge and
begin to shape the country according to the awareness
of democratic politics and society in which they grew
up. The unease about the detachment of young people
from the issues and channels of established politics
stems from a feeling that this new generation might

not continue the established structures once it rises to power or it might reveal hidden shortcomings of German democracy in a wider sense. The gap between the political status quo and the young has been stated again and again. The young are reported to write off official programmes, declarations, intentions as "waffle and nonsense", "Gesabere, Geseiere und Gellale".[6] One of the youngest former government ministers, Volker Hauff, admitted: "They sit and listen silently, then they say politely: you have not convinced us".[7] Willy Brandt pleaded for communication and contact in an electoral address to a young Berlin audience:

> We are trying to understand what concerns you, we have readjusted our areals. We are thinking things over and we need the dialogue. Please believe us: again and again we want to tend and care for the liberal and social core of our democracy. We need the young to contribute and to help. Those who remain on the sidelines will not change anything. On the contrary, they strengthen regression, corruptors, reaction. If we all give our best together, we can set things in motion. We are already correcting misguided developments and we want to make it clear that our democracy needs self-confident and critical democrats. We do not wish distrust to spread. We never wanted rewards for cowardice and spinelessness. We want to encourage those young people who feel listless and discouraged. I pledge the readiness to listen well and to help, as much as we still can, or as much as we will again learn to help.[8]

Brandt's protestations of goodwill point to the problem of communication. When Gerhart Baum, West Germany's former Minister of the Interior, talked with students in Bochum to dismantle some of their reserve, the danger of a communication breakdown became apparent. In his effort to reach his audience, Baum had abandoned a prepared speech. The impromptu discussion centred on the relationship between youth and state. Baum denied that a separation between them and us, between the state and West Germany's youth could be made. His ejaculation "we all are the state" aroused little understanding. One member of the audience summed up the general feeling: "We are excluded from all real participation. Our alternative ways of living only receive two responses: discrimination and police".[9] Heated retorts in a discussion or the wooing of politicians keen to secure an electorate may illuminate a problem, they do not help to clarify its size and origins.

That there are troubles with the young in West Germany has become apparent in forceful ways. Challenging speculation on the housing market to save old buildings or cheaper rental accommodation, the 'occupation' of houses has become common practice.[10] Most of the occcupiers are under twenty five. To stop the construction of nuclear power plants, sites have been invaded and blockaded. In Gorleben for example, the place selected as a nuclear dump, a temporary settlement of protesters remained for over one year, the Free Republic of Wendtland.[11] Most of the inhabitants were under twenty five. In October 1981, Bonn witnessed one of the largest demonstrations of the post-war period. About 300,000 people marched to express support for a peace movement, an end to the nuclear arms race in the world and the stationing of nuclear arms in the Federal Republic in particular.[12] Many followers of this peace movement are young people under twenty five. In Nuremberg, the youth centre Komm entered the headlines when police moved in and arrested over one hundred young people for suspected breach of the peace (Landfriedensbruch).[13] In Bremen, young people protesting against conscription clashed with police.[14] In Frankfurt, the dismay of local residents in the small community of Mörfelden over a planned extension of Frankfurt airport generated a protest movement and occupation settlement at Startbahn West. As far afield as the Ruhr area and North Germany the issue Startbahn West won followers, a symbol of protest against the sacrifice of forests, the extension of military facilities and the destructive potential of modern technology.

If the detachment of young people from the mainstream of political decision making in West Germany were only a detachment in issues, nobody would pay much attention. The political parties, however, are concerned about electoral support from the young. A broader concern still arose from the conflict with law enforcement agencies, notably the police, which has accompanied some of the young people's dissent. At times, this conflict escalated to street battles or a series of clashes over a number of weeks. The gap between generations seems to involve more than a disagreement over aims and intentions in politics. It concerns the means chosen to voice dissent and the tolerance of society and social authorities towards dissent. The forcible eviction of squatters, the storming of the makeshift settlement at Gorleben, of the protest camp at Frankfurt's Startbahn West, the mass arrest of the Komm people in Nuremberg, underline the urgency of the problem with West Germany's young. On the one hand, the question needs to be asked whether the police are too obsessed with prevention of a new wave of terrorism to scale down their methods and approaches to the protest they actually encounter. Court cases and legal evidence suggest that police procedures were not always in line with the offence and the use of force had perhaps not always been warranted.[16] On the other hand, one has to probe somewhat deeper into the problem of what type of dissent would erupt as a defiance of legal strictures and violent protest, and who would join it. Amidst the spectacle of protests and clashes, the full scope of the youth issue has been obscured. It includes a detachment from the state, from the goals of the war generation who built the Federal Republic, an aggressive and challenging protest. It also includes passivity, withdrawal, resignation. Both sides of the youth problem shape the place of the young generation in West Germany today.

YOUNG PEOPLE IN WEST GERMAN SOCIETY

In the 1980 federal elections about 4 million first voters joined the electorate, i.e. they had reached the voting age of eighteen since 1976. The segment of first voters had increased by about one million between elections and will continue to increase until the late nineteen eighties.

The young generation today is sizeable - 16.4 million or 24.3% are under 18; 9.8 million (16%) are between 18 and 29 years.[17] The baby boom of the sixties which peaked in 1964/1965 now inflates the ranks of young people. To be more precise: one legacy of Nazi social policy was a rise in the birthrate which in turn pushed up the number of live births in the Federal Republic in the sixties.[18] The generation born into the affluence of the sixties, those who are now between fourteen and their early twenties, were also born as members of the largest post-war generation yet. At a time when they reached their teens, the economic optimism of the fifties and sixties had given way to circumspect crisis management. The oil crisis in 1973 drove home the lesson about the insecurity of economic progress and expansion. Unemployment started to bite even in Germany. Rationalisation and investment in countries where production was cheaper, structural crises of primary industries and the decline in the coal and steel sector shook the German labour market. The pressures to cut costs and to stay competitive were met by increased productivity. In 1960, forty workers could produce goods to the value of one million Deutschmark in one year. In 1978, only nineteen workers were required to produce the same quantity.

Through rationalization and modernization, places of employment have disappeared. In 1960, the Federal Republic had a work force of over 26 million, in 1976, it had decreased to 25 million.[20] Between 1970 and 1976, over two million places of employment were abolished, about 700,000 newly created, leaving a deficit of 1.3 million. These figures point to a contraction and a significant restructuring of the labour market from the primary and secondary sectors to service industries and the public sector.[21] An estimated 250,000 posts are abolished or significantly altered in the Federal Republic every year. With an average investment of DM 160,000 per worker, new places of employment are costly, not readily attempted in a climate of high wage costs and a labour legislation which protects against dismissals.[22] All in all, employment has become sparse at a time when the number of young people looking for work or for apprenticeships is larger than ever before.

Prospects for School Leavers
The Federal Republic has a compulsory system of state education up to the age of eighteen. The general school leaving age is sixteen. After that, pupils attend vocational schools part-time for a further two years or so. Vocational schools and other further education courses want to ensure that young people acquire vocational skills and a sufficient degree of literacy and numeracy to cope with the requirements of a high technology labour market in a changing world. De facto, the accomplishments are somewhat tarnished by the high rate of absenteeism and truancy among pupils in basic schooling (Hauptschule) and vocational schools, up to 40%.[23]

In 1980, about half the young people who completed their education had attended a basic or special school. Ten years earlier, over 60% achieved only basic schooling, over 70% did so when the Federal Republic was founded. Educational qualifications in the Federal Republic have improved over the years with more young people accomplishing some form of higher or further education.

On leaving school, about 12% of each school year do not take up an apprenticeship or further training. The others extend their education or learn a trade. The system of apprenticeships in West Germany appears well regulated. Under the general supervision of the Chambers of Commerce and Industry, firms are permitted to train apprentices towards examinations which are administered by trade on a regional basis under state supervision to control standards. Vocational schooling and practical training go hand in hand. While this system seems to rule out an abuse of apprentices as cheap labour, the German model has shortcomings. Of West German apprentices, 48% learn in artisan firms. These are normally small, with less than twenty employees, many have less than five. Only few are equipped with high technology machinery and use up to the minute processes of production. Most are outdated, relatively little mechanized. The artisan sector employs 19% of the West German labour force and provides nearly half of all training places. The industrial sector employs 45% and trains just under 30%; the tertiary sector employs 36% and trains 22%.[24] The discongruity between training and employment creates insecurities. Having learned a trade, young people frequently find themselves out of a job and forced to retrain or to work in semi-skilled occupations which do not fully utilize their qualifications.

The pressure of numbers further aggravates this situation. Between 1977 and 1983, the large generation born in the sixties will reach the school leaving age of sixteen. An estimated 750,000 pupils will come onto the labour market and compete for 400,000 training places and apprenticeships. In the decade 1975-1985, about 9.7 million pupils will leave or have left school at sixteen. In the scramble for openings, 1.4 million will remain unsuccessful. Together with those who normally fail to train for a trade or profession, one quarter of the young people of working age will be without sufficient occupational or employable skills by 1985.[25] The sixties seemed to hold the promise of multiple opportunities. Educational qualifications increased; there was no apparent shortage of apprenticeships or jobs in trade or industry. The seventies were marred by the constraints of recession. While educational levels continued to improve, the promise of matching career opportunities no longer existed. For the first time in the history of the Federal Republic, youth unemployment became a problem. In 1977, 26% of the unemployed were under 25. The unskilled and untrained were most likely to lose their jobs. In 1980, youth unemployment had fallen to 10%, only to rise again in 1981 and 1982 with no sign of recovery.[26] Youth unemployment is expected to rise since young people are less well protected against dismissal than older workers. The shock of youth unemployment prodded the SPD/FDP government into action and new apprenticeships were created in the late seventies.[27] In view of the demand for apprenticeships and in view of the need for qualifications in the modern working environment, such measures may ease the repercussions of economic stagnation. They cannot restore the confidence of the young school leavers that they might be able to train in the trade of their choice, that they might find a job suited to their qualifications and that the type of training provided would be of any use in their future working lives. On all these counts, insecurities and uncertainties remain and are likely to grow.

The Scope of Higher Education

In the founding days of the Federal Republic and well into the sixties, higher education was accessible to a small segment of the younger generation and carried a guarantee with it of leadership positions and social status. The elitism and the solid career prospects in higher education are no longer applicable. In the sixties, Georg Picht sounded his warning of an impending education catastrophy, of West Germany becoming a country with an educational deficit, unable to maintain the pace of modernization. Since then, the educational qualifications of young West Germans have changed significantly. In 1950, 4.7% of the nineteen year olds had completed grammar school education, in 1970, 9.6%, in 1980 15.5%.[28] In its initial stages, this educational advance coincided with the entry of the "birth mountain" into formal schooling and education. An expansion at primary and secondary levels was matched by new openings in universities. In 1968, 358,000 students attended West German universities, in 1977, 906,000. For 1980, student numbers have been estimated at about one million.[29]

The rise in student numbers does not mean that a larger proportion of grammar school leavers is proceeding to university. West German students tend to remain longer at university, between five and eight years on average.[30] Overall student numbers are high because students spend a long time completing their courses and taking examinations. For grammar school leavers, it has become more difficult during the last decade to gain a university place. In 1972, 90% of young people completing their Abitur (A level equivalent) intended to study at university. In 1980, only 69% of grammar school leavers wished to study. Several factors combined to constrict access to higher education at a time when demand for places was rising with the size of the generation leaving schools. To stem the tide of applications and to control student numbers, a numerus clausus was introduced in the seventies. Regardless of demand, the number of places offered in certain subjects was limited. Admissions were competitive and depended on the average grade achieved at Abitur. Waiting lists were opened. The overall time of training and education can be unduly long if waiting times are added to the already extensive period of study.

With an average of six or seven years at university and an additional one or two years waiting for a university place, young people would be in or near their thirties before entering employment. The uncertainties about finding a suitable position, in line with the level of education and the expectations attached to it, proved a further deterrent to young people to venture into university studies.[31] Instead, an increasing number of grammar school leavers pushed into the labour market from above. In a situation where training places and apprenticeships are short, the influx of well educated applicants will make it more difficult for the lower qualified to be successful. In German, this has been called "Verdrängungswettbewerb", a displacement by competition. Apprenticeships are harder to come by; in a long term perspective, prospects for the lower educated to rise through training and experience into positions of leadership in their firms or enterprises have decreased.

The Norm of Success - Leistungsdruck

Competition at the bottom end of the labour market is one side effect of the shortage of university places for grammar school leavers. Another concerns the competitive atmosphere in the schools. University access in the popular subjects rests to a large extent on the average mark achieved at Abitur. German universities do not run their own entrance examinations where students could show qualities not reflected in their school reports. They also do not hold interviews which would allow candidates to be assessed on personality or general intellectual calibre. The all important marks relate to a set of final examination papers and also the grades achieved during the last three years at grammar school. The pressures to ensure prime performance and to obtain top marks at all times are considerable. Career prospects appear to rest on every test, every mark, every piece of work. For those who decide to compete for university access, the <u>Leistungsdruck</u>, dictates the pace and the contents of learning. Heinrich Böll expressed a fear shared by many in the Federal Republic, that the pressure to succeed will produce a defaced generation, "a generation who has been made insecure, a generation of opportunists and unquestioning followers".[32]

    The scramble for firsts does not begin during the last years of schooling. High expectations in education and high norms of learning are already a major factor at primary level. The expectations originate from schools and from parents. In a study of pupils aged eight to ten, Does and Motz found that none of the parents of eight year old children expected these children to attend a <u>Hauptschule</u>, the German equivalent of a Secondary Modern School at 11.[33] In fact, one in three West German pupils aged eleven to twelve attend such schools.[34] On the other end of the educational ladder, 59% of the eight to nine year olds were seen by their parents as able to complete their <u>Abitur</u>. Yet, only about 15% of the age group can expect to do so. A similar discrepancy between expectations and achievements is evident for performance. While parents tend to stress that school work is well within reach for their child, the children tend to feel they do not cope well.[35] Psychosomatic difficulties are on the increase. Headaches, stomach pains and nausea have been diagnosed as side effects of apprehension or even fears about school.[36] The mechanism of rejection which is operated throughout the German school system underlines the pressures to cope and to succeed. In 1976-1977, about 330,000 pupils had to repeat their school year. While "Sitzenbleiben", having to repeat a year, can happen at any point in a pupil's career, it occurs most frequently during the first two years of primary schooling.[37] Roughly eight out of ten demoted pupils attend first or second grade of West German primary school. At a time when abilities are just shaping up and learning potentials are developing, children are stigmatized as failures and placed in a hopeless position for future educational advancement. The recent government report on youth pointed out that the lion share of young people who leave school without a qualifying certificate, have in fact not completed the full number of classes and were held back during the first two years of their schooling.

West Germany also screens six year olds to assess whether they are of sufficient maturity to attend school. Annually over 30,000 prospective school beginners are held back and have to wait one more year before entering school. They were deemed incapable of coping with syllabus and learning requirements stipulated for the first grade of German primary schools. About 5% of any age group are placed in special schools, often because they are deemed to be slow learners who would not stand the pace of a normal state school.[38]

The pressures of performance which emanate from the schools and from the parents have been linked with signs of acute distress among children and young people. Between 1950 and 1978, the suicide rate of children aged between 5 and 15 doubled to over 500 per year.[39] Attempted suicides are much more frequent and often go unreported. It is difficult to arrive at figures in an area deliberately obscured by those affected, children, parents, schools. Estimates range from 15,000 to about 100,000 attempted suicides annually among the under eighteens.[40] Drug taking reached 10% among the age group 10-19 in 1978.[41]

More data could be collected, more aspects explored to illuminate prospects and constraints of the young generation in West Germany. The children of affluence and political stability experience inflated pressures for success. Schools earmark potential failures early. The shortfall of openings for training and apprenticeships on the labour market make it uncertain that school leavers can follow a training of their choice or take up a career. The transition from grammar schools to universities has become more difficult, putting further demands onto the labour market and the limited openings for training programmes. In the competition for advancement, the lower educated seem bound to lose out. Yet even higher education no longer provides a guaranteed route to the top.

A DISENCHANTED GENERATION

In 1979, the German weekly magazine Stern published data based on a survey conducted by the Allensbach Institute on young people in West Germany.[42] This in itself is not unusual. Youth and various findings provided by an array of demoscopic institutes made the headlines several times. Die Welt reported in 1978 that Willy Brandt as an "idol" of the young had been replaced by John Travolta. Some months later, the same paper claimed young people adored above all Konrad Adenauer, Helmut Schmidt, John F. Kennedy.[43] Quick, a picture review with a conservative political edge to it, announced the demoscopically confirmed fact that young people are again and above all guided by their parents, not by idols from politics or entertainment.[44] The German Press Agency distributed this insight as relevant news item to its subscriber papers. A recurrent theme in the jungle of figures and sensationalist reports is the claim that young people are keen to get on in life. "Youth does not drift to the right or to the left. It looks for the way to the top".[45] The norms and pressures to succeed are apparently accepted, the uncertainties of finding work or training places taken into one's stride. The unusual element about the Allensbach survey and the report in Stern was its critical focus. Instead of a further confirmation that basically things were going well with West Germany's young generation, the paper sounded a warning note about disenchantment. An Emnid survey had mentioned disenchantment as a problem area some years before.[46] Only since the report in 1979 has disenchantment become a key word for a controversy whether or not West German democracy bred in its midst a group of people who no longer endorse it, who opted out.[47]

Disenchantment - A Closer Look
What is at issue? The Allensbach survey and the Emnid study before it had asked a series of questions to ascertain how young people related to political and social institutions, to their work, their

environments, the whole gambit of social traditions and conventions. 700,000 or 13% of the 17-23 year olds regarded all these areas with indifference and attached no value or significance to them. These 13% were called disenchanted.

> They no longer fight this state, they do not press for reforms, they ignore the state wherever they can. Most of them retreat from society (schotten sich ab). They cannot identify with them and expect nothing or little from them.[48]

Some forms of retreat are visible beyond the analysis of attitudes. Drug addiction and alcoholism are on the increase. Between 50,000 and 80,000 young people in the Federal Republic are heroin addicts. Seventy per cent of registered drug addicts are under the age of eighteen. Crimes connected with addictions are on the increase. It has been estimated that one quarter of West German school children drink alcohol regularly and get frequently drunk.[49] Pseudo-religious sects, so called youth religions offer another uncanny form of retreat. In 1981 over 150,000 young people were members of such a sect.[50]

Opting out into drugs, alcohol, sects leaves the structure and the priorities of contemporary society unchallenged. The retreat into a ghetto-like subculture of alternative living has a more critical and political edge. In Berlin alone, over 100,000 young people live in the alternative "scene". There are many more in other big cities in West Germany. The "scene" includes "alternative" workshops, agricultural units which abide by ecological and organic principles, food shops, cafes, newspapers, meeting places and group living in communes. Fichter and Lönnendonker reported from Berlin that many young people took pride in not communicating with anybody outside the subculture for weeks or even months.[51] Many names have entered the German language to describe facets of this retreat: <u>Spontis</u>, <u>Stadtindianer</u> (city indians), <u>Kajoten</u> (the chaotic ones), <u>Tunix</u>. A <u>Tunix</u> congress in Berlin in January 1978 attracted over 20,000 participants who met to articulate their distrust.

> We no longer want to do the same kind of work over and over again. They ordered us about long enough. They controlled our thoughts, our ideas, our homes, our passports and slapped

us in the face. We do not want to be taken for a ride any more, we do not want to be shoved aside and we do not want to be made the same as they are.52

In addition to the 700,000 disenchanted young people, a further 2 million were identified in the Allensbach study who expressed dissatisfaction with state and society.53 Of the 5.4 million young people, about half were dissatisfied or disenchanted with conditions in the Federal Republic. At times, dissatisfaction was linked directly to certain difficulties. In the Allensbach survey, 70% feared unemployment, 73% were afraid they would not be able to choose a career, 39% thought expectations were so high that they were unable to meet them, 40% felt they could not live the way they wanted to and another 40% could not detect any purpose in their lives. A study in Berlin found that young people accepted the principle of free speech and expected it to relate to their lives. Yet only 26% of a sample of 13 to 25 year olds felt they could make full use of free speech at any occasion and on any topic. 51% were sure speaking their minds freely would incur disadvantages and was not possible, 22% declared they did not know.54

The sense of disappointment rests on an emphatic endorsement of democratic principles among West Germany's young generation. In comparative analyses of democratic values among younger and older people, the young score high. They are in favour of political opposition (60%), of free competition among parties to form the government (57%), and free speech (71%).55 Jennings and Jansen compared political attitudes across the generations and took as the hallmark of democratic awareness whether or not the principles of plurality and change in society were accepted.

Table 6.1 suggests that young people are in favour of change and plurality. By the terms used in the study, the political attitudes of the young are more democratic than those of older people. A similar result emerged in the research by Bürklin. He divided his sample into the under thirties and the over thirties with a special section for students (Table 6.2). Since the criteria of classification are at variance, direct comparisons are not possible. A trend does, however, emerge. In Bürklin's study, self classification on a right-left scale was used to ascertain political attitudes. Young people were somewhat further to the left than the older ones.

Table 6.1: Democratic Attitudes Across the Generations

Support for change and plurality	Youth (15-20) %	Adults (21 and over) %
Low	30	53
Medium	33	28
High	37	19

Source: M. Kent Jennings/Rolf Jansen, Die Jugendlichen in der Bundesrepublik, PVS 17, 1976, No. 3, p. 321.

Table 6.2: Self-Identification on a Left-Right Scale

	Students 1979 %	Population 1979 18-29 %	30 and over %
Left	60	27	17
Middle or neither nor	27	45	47
Right	10	22	30
No answer	3	6	6

Source: Wilhelm P. Bürklin, Links und/oder demokratisch? PVS 21, 1980, No. 3, p. 228.

Students emerged distinctly further to the left than both other groups.

Leaving aside the special problems related to students, the materials on political principles and political attitudes do not confirm the alarm signal, that large numbers of West Germany's young are disinterested, disenchanted, detached from society and politics. Attitudes and self-identification suggest, on the contrary, that the young are more forceful democrats than their elders. They are less likely to confuse political change with instability.[56] They are less likely to mistake economic prosperity and growth for the essence of democracy.[57] They tend to score high on democratic principles and beliefs. The notion of disenchantment and disinterest does not appear to relate to the attitudes and beliefs. Here, democratic commitment seems to be high.

Disenchantment may have a critical sting and relate to a discrepancy between these beliefs and experiences of social and political life. Disenchantment would then articulate the disappointment of democrats whose expectations and hopes were faulted.

Interest or Retreat: Some Recent Trends

Nothing as drastic as faulted hopes and pent-up disappointments shape the young generation as a whole. Overall young people seem to be as content with democracy as older ones. There are no staggering differences. An Emnid survey from 1980 for example, found 69% of the 18-30 year olds and 70% of the general population in agreement with democracy and its institutions.[58] With 6%, open dissatisfaction among the young was marginally higher than average (3%). Slightly different results emerge from the material compiled by Veen and Hansen for the Konrad Adenauer Research Institute. They focussed on the age group 14 to 21 and further differentiated by education and social class. Dissatisfaction seemed to be more pronounced among the 18-21 year olds. With 10% of the young people in the survey stating they were dissatisfied with democracy, the negative fringe was clearly larger than in the broader study mentioned earlier (Table 6.3).

What is measured and meant when people say they are dissatisfied, is somewhat open and points at best to a general tendency, not a hard and fast fact of consolidated dissent. Other tendencies may be extracted from the Veen/Hansen comparison (Table 6.3). Dissatisfaction - whatever it might mean - appears to peak at the extremes, at the highest and the lowest levels of formal education and at the highest and the lowest social group. Those with basic schooling and those with further or higher education may take a negative stand. Young people classified as workers were similarly dissatisfied as those classified as upper strata, (Oberschicht). Dissatisfaction, it seems, peaks at the extremes of the social and educational divide. The notion of dissatisfaction and some of its possible meanings need to be explored further.

In the early seventies, young people seemed to be well integrated into their political environment. Electoral support for political parties, especially for the SPD was high. Political interest had reached unprecedented levels.[59] In 1972 three out of four young people between the ages of 18 and 23 felt

Table 6.3: How Satisfied are you on the Whole with Democracy in the Federal Republic?

Total	Very satisfied	Quite satisfied	Not satisfied	No answer
Total	21	67	10	2
Male	22	67	10	2
Female	21	68	9	2
14-17 years	21	70	7	2
18-21 years	21	65	12	2
Schooling, education				
Special and Secondary Modern	18	69	13	1
Technical Schools (Real/Fach)	24	67	8	2
Grammar School	16	71	12	1
University	17	62	20	1
Social Strata:				
Workers	20	65	14	1
Middle Strata	22	68	8	2
Upper Strata	22	63	15	0

Source: Stephanie Hansen und Hans Joachim Veen, Auf der Suche nach dem privaten Glück, Die Zeit, 5.9.1981, p. 61.

they could identify with one of the existing political parties. Only one in four (24%) thought that there was no party which could be relevant. The early seventies were of course, a somewhat unusual period in German post-war history. After years of CDU dominated governments, the SPD had become the senior partner in a coalition with the FDP. Policies of detente and cooperation with Eastern Europe, Ostpolitik, had finally broken the stalemate of anti-communism, West integration and Hallstein doctrine. Ostpolitik caught the political imagination of younger people and seemed to suit their hopes for re-orientation. In 1972, Ostpolitik formed the core of the CDU attempt to topple the government and return to power. Willy Brandt opened his second period as Chancellor with a pledge to "dare more democracy". The political climate was teeming with promise to enhance the quality of democratic life in the Federal Republic. Over the next four years, the hubbub died down. Plans towards more democracy were bogged down in practicalities of political compromise and coalition bargaining. Ostpolitik showed few tangible results. The opening towards East Germany was halted by <u>Abgrenzung</u> from the East and the challenge in the Constitutional Court whether the Basic Treaty could be in line with the Basic Law and its perspective on reunification. The return of political sobriety seemed personalised when Brandt was succeeded by Helmut Schmidt as Federal Chancellor. In line with the changed political climate, the interest of the young in political matters waned. Those who had been keen in 1972 became more passive. The younger ones started at a lower level of commitment altogether. In 1976, only one in four, 25% of the 18-23 year olds declared an interest in politics, three in four remained indifferent.[60] Does found for 1976 that only 40% of 18-23 year olds could identify with one of the political parties. Survey materials incorporated into a ZDF series on youth suggested that in 1976 32% of the under 24 year olds felt detached from all parties, 48% did so in 1980.[61]

In the study by Does, interest in politics was defined as interchangeable with party identification. The research interest seemed to have been the freak success of the CDU among young people in 1976 which the party could not sustain. Interest in politics and the view that one of the existing parties articulates these interests do not necessarily go together. The data from the ZDF survey confirmed that indifference had increased since the early seventies. In 1980 40% of the age group 16-24 professed themselves indifferent to political matters, 60% remained interested. The same survey had found 48% of the young detached from established parties. While two thirds of the young people in the ZDF studies took an interest in politics, nearly half could not relate this interest to the conventional grooves of political participation.

Taking an interest in politics implies the confidence to be able to make an impact by personal commitment. Of the young people interested in politics, just under one quarter named "big politics", parties, parliaments, as the field of action they had in mind. For the majority of the potentially active young, an impact seemed possible only closer to home: in their own environment, their community, through ad hoc groups or individual efforts. 76%

The Politics of Personal Involvement

At the core of an authoritarian approach to politics, is the powerlessness of the individual. The small man, the ordinary citizen seems to wield no influence, has to take things as they come, as they are decided by those in charge. Thomas Mann aptly spoke of "machtgeschützte Innerlichkeit", a private realm, sheltered by the power structure, the existing forces of politics and state. Young people today have also been described as privatizing, of being in search only of their personal, private happiness.[62] It would be rash to talk of a new edition of "machtgeschützte Innerlichkeit", of an ego-trip away from society and politics. The new stress on private matters reflects a change in political awareness. The individual has gained political stature. The subject in German politics has given way in some measure to the citizen, who is willing and confident to take a stand. Young people are more confident than their elders that personal efforts could be useful. Table 6.4 shows the contrast between generations and the increase of political confidence during the last two decades. In 1959 nearly 30% of the young people under 30 felt nothing could be done against an unjust piece of legislation. Fifteen years later, pessimism had declined to just under 20%. A similar boost in confidence seems to have occurred in the age group under fifty, while the over fifties appear a little more despondent.

The pessimism of the older generation points to their more traditional political attitudes. A relatively conservative electorate may also feel that little impact is possible at a time when a social-liberal coalition is in government, as was the case at the time of the surveys. For the younger generation, the decrease of passivity suggests that disappointment with the parties, and the political despondency which grew during the seventies did not produce a generation of privateers. The confidence to make an impact matches the keen political interest discussed earlier. The scepticism about conventional organizations, parties, and institutions however channels this interest and confidence into new forms.

Young people tend to support activities and

Table 6.4: Citizens and Politics - "What can a citizen do against a law he finds unjust of damaging?

Answers:	Nothing (by age)			
Year	Age			
	18-30	31-50	51 and over	
1959	29.8	30.3	39.1	100
1974	19.4	21.3	43.0	100

Source: Kaase/Marsh in Barnes/Kaase, Mass Participation in Five Western Democracies, Beverley Hills 1979.

initiatives off the beaten track. Signing petitions, joining public demonstrations, collecting funds for charitable or neglected political causes, are favoured forms of involvement.[63] Over two thirds think that joining a citizens action group would be an effective way of gaining influence. In contrast under 20% would join a political party, 25% a trade union.[64] Compared with the adult population the willingness to organize is high. It is much higher than actual party- or union membership. As a facet of political interest, this willingness to organize and the hesitation to do so complement the inclination towards non-conventional activities and groups. Hans Eckehard Bahr found a suitable formula for the discongruity between political interest and disinterest in parties: a contempt of functionaries.[65] Joining a party tends to be discarded as becoming just another number.[66] Being absorbed and possibly thwarted by an established organization, being unable to see issues through and making a personal and noticeable contribution appear to be deterrents for the young against joining large organizations with general policy concerns. The immediacy of the locality, the community, are regarded as the political seedbed by the majority of West Germany's young people who have not retreated into disenchantment and passivity. The critical disenchantment seems to have generated a new kind of political interest. This interest attaches itself to activities and groups which can give a feeling of personal involvement and the confidence of making a personal and relevant contribution. These new modes of politics and the contempt of functionaries harboured by the young might act as a challenge to established political parties to broaden their concerns and to losen their hierarchies.

FORMS OF DISSENT

In 1981 the daunting question "Does Youth leave our society" occupied the Bundestag and generated a special commission on youth.[67] At a series of hearings for the interim report in December 1981, and a concluding report in 1982, several West German professors elaborated on the problem.[67a] Youth, it was said, could not be reached by ordinary community work, their distance to society was neither left nor right protest but fear of excessive technification and rationalization in industrial society; another expert contradicted and claimed young people followed no detectable ideology; others still were more practical in their comments. Kurt Sontheimer pleaded for common sense and determination to stem the tide of youth problems. Society he stressed, should not shirk confrontation. An "alternative" researcher from Berlin demanded an amnesty for house occupations. The young, he argued, were at least not inclined to occupy foreign countries as their fathers had done.[68] Despite the multitude of views and observations, one explanatory concept seemed acceptable to all. The concept of postmaterialism was taken to provide an analytical framework which could explain the rifts between youth and older generations. The American researcher Ingelhart introduced the notion of postmaterialism into the political debate. He argued that young people who were socialized under conditions of affluence and political stability developed a new set of values, different from their parents'.[69] Instead of emphasising economic prosperity and material success, these children of prosperity focus on aspects of individual fulfillment and satisfaction, on issues which could be summarized as "quality of life". This theory of a change of values led to a theory of new politics. Hildebrandt and Dalton[70] argued that political priorities like economic growth, defence spending and combatting inflation have given way among the younger generation to new orientations: the participation of citizens in decision making, equality of income and equality of rights for minorities in society.[71]

These concepts of new values and of new politics have penetrated the wider political debate in West Germany. Detached from the strictures of the original research design, they seem to provide ready answers to a new variety of the generation gap. Germany's problems appear embedded into general trends in Western industrial societies, at least in those societies which were economically successful and combined political democracy with material prosperity for their citizens. From this perspective the present problems of youth are a side-effect of achievement, not a legacy of neglect. The new values pursued by the young and asserted in deliberate disregard of conventions and established institutions, suggest that a gradual reorientation within society is under way and might gain momentum once the youth of today advance to positions of leadership. Inglehart himself suggested that the new values were directly correlated to educational qualifications.[72] Young people who did not reach university standard were less likely to adhere to the new values or pursue the new politics. Jaide, in his surveys on youth, found a correlation between lower educational achievement and a preponderance of authoritarian or rightist attitudes.[73] Bargel showed how traditional values of good manners, modesty, obedience, have remained important for the lower educated while independence, critical facilities and inquisitiveness are coveted at higher educational levels.[74]

The notion of new values and new politics can throw some light on the academic segment of West Germany's youth and help to explain a student based dissent. The remainder of the young does not readily fit into postmaterialism.

Dissent as Passivity: the Unskilled and Uneducated

The Emnid survey of 1975 which first sounded the warning cry about disinterest and disenchantment singled out two groups as particularly affected: those most and those least educated.

Although the occupational classifications in Table 6.5 are rather broad, the data show discontent to be linked to integration into a working environment. The unskilled who experience the lowest degree of job security, have few opportunities for advancement and frequently the lowest educational qualifications are more likely to feel discontented and dissatisfied than any of the other groups.[75] In the economic and social conditions in the Federal Republic where employment is scarce, competition for work exacerbated by the size of the generation coming onto the labour market, where unemployment

Table 6.5: Discontent and Disinterest by Occupation (18-25 year olds)

Occupation	Discontent/disinterest expressed in %
White collar	28
Skilled workers	30
Pupils, students, apprentices	42
Unskilled	69

Source: Bussiek p. 17.

has been endemic since the early seventies and is bound to rise in the next few years, social uncertainties for the unskilled are high.

Discontent among the student population has long been taken as a normal by-product of higher education. Scheuch argues that the role expectation itself implies that students would question established ways and engage in protest actions. The role expectations for students from middle class homes where at least one parent went to university include dissent and protest, to question familiar values and to engage in protest conforms with these expectations.[76] For the non-academic young no such role expectations exist (Table 6.6). At best, the social stereotypes about young people being rash in judgement and thoughtless in action create some leeway to be different from the adult population. Protest, discontent, dissatisfaction are not part and parcel of youth. There is a social divide which separates the discontent of the educated from the discontent expressed by the young at the bottom end of the social ladder.

Table 6.6 makes the social divide more concrete. Those with rudimentary education do not consider dissent or protest a normal or even necessary behaviour for youth. While the first statement in Table 6.6 partly probes into tolerance, the second focusses on the overall role expectation and highlights the contrasts. Questioning the established structures is not considered part of growing up among the lower educated. Discontent does not erupt in protest and a challenge to society, rather the reverse: "These young people live in a socio-cultural no-man's land, switched off, secluded, passive, senile, troubled by mishaps to an extent that they lost confidence and are virtually unapproachable".[77] A study by Gangnus of unskilled youth on special opportunity schemes

Youth and Politics

Table 6.6: Dissent and Educational Achievement

Statement 1: "If young people go too far with their protests, this is quite understandable".

	Basic schooling	Secondary and University education
Agree	15	62
Disagree	85	38

Statement 2: "Youth should radically question existing values".

	Basic schooling	Secondary and University education
Agree	0	38
Disagree	100	62

Source: Erwin K. Scheuch, Die Jugend gibt es nicht - Zur Differenziertheit der Jugend in heutigen Industriegesellschaften, Konfliktfelder in der Gegenwart p. 152 quoting survey material from Klaus Allerbeck.

confirmed the passivity.[78] It also confirmed a leaning of the lower social strata to conservative or more right-wing views. Compared with a control group of apprentices, the unskilled stood politically on the right, they were sceptical and distant towards social and political institutions. They seemed to expect little from anywhere or anybody. In Gangnus' sample a small number had broken through their passivity and joined youth groups or trade unions. These tended to be more active and also more radical in their outlook than the apprentices with whom they were compared. Given the overall political disposition of the lower skilled and educated, passivity and disenchantment are common. Radicalization appears to be linked to playing an active part in a group or organization. Where it does occur, it is most likely to be a radicalization to the right. The back of the educational and occupational queue seems closer to Neo-nazism than to the radical left.

Numerous studies have attempted to trace political attitudes to the socializaiton processes, to the impact of parental values or to learning and teaching in West German schools.[80] For those in lowly skilled occupations, the need to submit to processes outside one's own control, the lack of responsibility and creativity at work, to name but a few aspects, have also been seen to contribute to political passivity, or rightist leanings. Scepticism and disinterest are linked to a deadlock of expectations. For the political retreat of the lower skilled the discrepancy between expectations and possible achievements is as relevant as the influence of home and school.

The average young West German strives for personal and social well being.

> At the age of twenty, he wants to own a car, with twenty-four, he wants to have a flat, with twenty-five a wife, with twenty-eight a child.. All this he wants to own, and with thirty seven, he wants to have achieved everything there is to achieve.[81]

Young people with only basic schooling seem more eager to accomplish a high living standard than the better educated.[82] The 1979 survey of the Deutsche Shell among young people in employment showed the wish to earn good money used to be the most prevalent aim. Today, anxieties over training and career prospects have assumed priority.[83] The economic recession coupled with a rise in unemployment have rendered the goal of a settled and financially secure life more doubtful. Those with further education tend to stress training and qualifications as a means to reach the top, i.e. they respond to the constraints of employment and advancement by looking at the social institutions and the starting positions attainable through them. Their response has an institutional, not a personal focus. The less educated and unskilled, on the contrary tend to see advancement and success often in terms of personal efforts and individual qualities.[84] In other words, those at the humblest entry point into occupational life are less likely to consider institutional access routes and objective possibilities. Instead of evaluating the disadvantages incurred by educational inequalities and shortfalls in training provisions, the lower skilled place the onus on the individual to make or break his success.

The discrepancies between expectations and opportunities of social advancement rarely generate demands for change and reform of unsuitable conditions. Disinterest, detachment, passivity are common responses. Young unemployed are more visibly still unable to cope with a framework of values where work leads to personal worth and dignity, where prosperity breeds social status and acceptance. Unemployment is experienced as personal failure.[85] Only few challenge the political or social system which perpetuates these values.

Dissent as Protest: Perspectives on Student Politics
In an international league table comparing conventional and non-conventional approaches to politics, West Germany emerges as a country with many inactive citizens and also with many who are ready for action and protest.[86]

Educational achievement tends to alter the mode of dissent from passivity to protest potential. Protest here means a readiness in principle to engage in non-conventional activities such as signing a petition, taking part in an unauthorized demonstration, refusing to pay rents or rates which are deemed unfair, occupying offices or factory premises.[87] Younger people are more inclined towards such protest actions than older ones.[88] Table 6.7 shows the different attitudes towards squatting which has become known as the 'occupation' of houses in the German language.

Support for squatting as a form of protest is highest among the youngest age group, lowest among the oldest. But even among the 18-21 age bracket, over half object to squatting. Overall, nearly one third of the electorate, i.e. West Germans aged eighteen or over are in favour, the remainder against squatting (Table 6.7). The willingness to participate in political activities outside established channels and parties increases with educational attainment. In 1979, Kaase and Marsh reported a protest potential twice as high among West Germans with at least grammar school education than among those with merely basic education. For university students protest potential was higher than for any other group.[89] A survey of political allegiances of students which was carried out by the SPD affiliated Friedrich Ebert Stiftung found in 1981 that about half the students were critically opposed to the political status quo. About 12% could be called "alternative" students, i.e. committed to priorities and values which were completely different from the West German conventions and social expectations.[90]

Student protest potential seems to have increased since the days of student unrest. In 1978, the Allensbach Institute published a survey with comparative data of 1967. Agreements or disagreements to political evaluations were used to measure the viewpoints of the student population. Although it can be argued that the questions are too suggestive, a change of views can still be observed. For instance, the statement: "The Basic Law is increasingly undermined and distorted in a reactionary and authoritarian way" drew 15% agreement in 1967, 27% in 1978. The sentence: "Government and parliament no longer represent the interests of the people" obtained 12% agreement in 1967, 21% in 1978.[91]

Similar changes have been observed by Bürklin. He compiled a synopsis of various studies on political attitudes among students between 1968 and 1979. The notion that opposition should support the government of the day met with less approval in 1979 than a decade earlier. Conversely, students in the seventies were more inclined to accept demonstrations as legitimate means of expressing their political interests than a student generation earlier. In 1979, 30% endorsed demonstrations even if they might endanger public order. In 1968, 18% held this view.[92] Students into the eighties seem to be more radical in their political beliefs and their principles of political action than the so called radical students of the sixties. They are clearly more radical than the average West German. When asked to place themselves on a left/right spectrum, students regard themselves more often on the left than young people or the general population (Table 6.2). Klingemann showed that self-classification on the political spectrum does not normally mean that a specific ideology or set of political priorities is accepted or shared. The terms "left" and "right" are used to indicate that one feels closer to one of the established political parties which is commonly looked upon as situated on the left or the right whatever the case may be. This proximity has been shown for students who regard themselves as "right": the statements they endorsed are close to pronouncements by the CDU/CSU. Numerically, the students on the right and the students organized in the Christian Democratic student group RCDS are very similar.[93] Today it is much more common for students to call themselves "left". In Wildenmann's 1979 study, 60% say they are on the left, 5% claim to take a position on the extreme left (Table 6.2). This self-classification must not be misunderstood as an identification with any of the political

Table 6.7: Protest Potential by Age: Attitudes Towards Squatting

Age	For	Against	No Answer	Total
18-21	45	54	1	100
22-25	46	51	3	100
26-29	34	66	–	100
30-39	32	64	2	100
40-49	24	74	2	100
50-64	26	72	2	100
65-and over	18	79	3	100
Electorate	28	69	3	100

Source: Der Spiegel 50, 1981, p. 99

parties, be it the SPD, be it one of the communist parties. It can only be taken to suggest that students hold views that they themselves would call left according to their understanding of the political divisions and party orientations in the Federal Republic. A further 27% would consider themselves moderates or liberals. Similar political allegiances have been shown for students regarding concepts, themes and political issues. For the first time in German history, a student generation identifies towards the left. In Imperial Germany, in the Weimer Republic and continuing during the Nationalsocialist period, universities had been strongholds of nationlist and rightist views. Students were the first group to be swept towards Nationalsocialism well before Hitler came to power. In this historical perspective, the political reorientation of West German students and their inclination towards the left is an important and welcome change. It shows on the one hand that today, higher education no longer feeds into right-wing or right extremist positions. Most students who declare to stand on the right are followers or members of CDU affiliated organizations or of the party itself. The proliferation of left-wing self-identifications shows on the other hand a distance of the higher educated from the mainstream of West German politics and the political positions of the general population.

The left-wing orientation of students tends to mobilize residual fears about communism. The stigmatization of the left as anti-democratic has been a virulent aspect of German political culture since the foundation of the nation state.[94] After the

Table 6.8: Violence and Student Politics

Type of violence	Student Total %	Political position			
		Right %	Moderate %	Moderate left %	Far left %
Violence against person and things	8	6	2	6	46
Violence against things only	25	10	18	35	29
No violence	62	81	74	52	22
Don't know	5	3	6	7	3

Source: FAZ 2.10.1978.

student unrest of the sixties, left-wing opposition also produced political terrorism in West Germany.[95] Since then, the concern about the left focussed on the question to what extent dissent and protest incorporated the use of violence. In his international comparisons, Kaase found West German students more inclined than those of many other Western countries to use violence. The 1978 Allensbach survey argued that 33% endorsed the use of violence, 62% opposed it. Those on the extreme left appeared more prepared to legitimize violence than students of other political orientations (Table 6.8).

The Diversity of a Generation

From the survey material on young people and politics in West Germany, a number of conclusions may be drawn, albeit in a tentative way. The disenchantment which has aroused trepidations among politicians, researchers and commentators is visible in the young as a diminished interest in political parties and political participation through established channels. Confidence in these channels has declined since the early seventies, while sceptical detachment and signs of disenchantment became more frequent. Disenchantment follows a social divide: for the lowly educated, it means passivity, even apathy and possibly a commitment to right-wing political beliefs. For the well educated, it tends towards protest and the use of unconventional, at times violent means to articulate that protest. Students in West Germany emerge as a group in German politics, whose confrontation with society seems sharper today than in the days of student unrest. The two-tiered detachment from status quo politics seems to be rooted in an overall endorsement of democratic values. If anything, young people in West Germany are more emphatically democratic than their elders; the discontent with political opportunities and realities seems to stem from a contrast of democratic principles and a poor realization of such principles in the everyday world of politics and society. The economic and social development in the seventies also contributed to foster scepticism and detachment at a time when the number of young people burst all the seams of common expectations and former generations. Opportunities for these young people have sharply declined. For the lower skilled and educated, the transformation of the labour market and the disestablishment of positions generated the threat and the reality of unemployment. At the end of basic schooling, training places are no longer certain, the possibility of securing a place in society, achieving a respectable position, making one's way have become more and more uncertain. This uncertainty for the lower end of the social spectrum tends to create passivity, and disenchantment.

Uncertainty has also begun to dominate the highest educational sector with social prospects for students no longer assured and career openings more doubtful. Across the social divide, the young generation in the seventies and eighties grows up under conditions of uncertainty and insecurity. Disenchantment is a reaction also to this aspect of their social position. This disenchantment articulates itself in different modes. The young unskilled, uneducated, the workers and apprentices on one side of the social divide seem to move towards Neo-nazism. On the other side of the social divide, the highly educated and the students move towards left-wing views. How right-wing and left-wing groups succeeded or failed to mobilize the protest potential among West Germany's young people under the straitened circumstances of the seventies and early eighties shall be explored in the next chapters.

FOOTNOTES

1. Kurt Sontheimer, "Die Bundesrepublik und ihre Bürger" in Walter Scheel (ed.) <u>Nach dreissig Jahren. Die Bundesrepublik Deutschland - Vergangenheit, Gegenwart, Zukunft.</u> Stuttgart (Klett/Cotta), 1979, p. 183.
2. Rainer Lepsius, "West German political culture", Paper delivered at the Goethe Institute, October 1980, published in Herbert Döring/Gordon

Smith (eds.), *Party Government and Political Culture in Western Germany*, Macmillan 1982.

3. Kurt Sontheimer, *Die verunsicherte Republik. Die Bundesrepublik nach 30 Jahren*, München (Piper), 1979, pp. 11, 37, also: ibid. *Das Elend der Intellek-tuellen. Linke Theorie in der Bundesrepublik Deutschland*, Hamburg, (Hoffmann & Campe), 1976.

4. Hans Jürgen Benedict, Was ist die Republik den Jüngeren wert? in *Die Aussichten der Republik*. Frankfurter Hefte Extra 2, 1980, p. 126.

5. Sontheimer, "Die Bundesrepublik und ihre Bürger", ibid., p. 184.

6. Jürgen Leinemann, "An uns denkt kein Schwein", *Spiegel* 40, 1980, p. 62.

7. Ibid., p. 67.

8. Documented in Lothar Balluseck, Zum Exodus Jugendlicher, in *Aus Politik und Zeitgeschichte B 30*, p. 17.

9. Eckehard Bahr, "Du hast keine Chance, aber nutze sie", *Die Zeit* 10.4.1981, p. 43.

10. See Bundesministerium für Jugend, Familie und Gesundheit, "Zur alternativen Kultur in der Bundesrepublik" in *Aus Politik und Zeitgeschichte* 39, 1981, pp. 12-14.

11. See the extensive debate of youth protest with ample references to various events in *Das Parlament* 12.6.1982, pp. 1-7.

12. On October 19th 1981 an estimated 250,000-300,000 people marched in Bonn.

13. Hermann Glaser, (ed.) *Die Nürnberger Massenverhaftungen*, Reinbek, (Rowohlt), 1981 dto "Ein Jahr danach. Zum Psychogramm der Nürnberger Massenverhaftungen" in *Frankfurter Hefte* 37, no. 4, April 1981, pp. 40-49.

14. See Hans Lisken, Gegen Bundeswehr und Polizei? Zur Opposition der Jugend heute" in *Frankfurter Hefte* 37 no. 8, August 1982, pp. 39-48.

15. Full reporting in Frankfurter Rundschau, also documentation on the decision of the land government to stop a referendum on the Startbahn issue FR 8.12.1981.

16. See Hans Schüler, Angeklagt: die Ankläger. Komm Prozess in Nürnberg. *Die Zeit 50*, 1981 Dossier p. 9-10; Gerhard Spörl, "Brokdorf Prozess: Sie fühlen sich überfahren", *Die Zeit 50*, 1981, p. 15.

17. *Spiegel 40*, 1980, p. 62 and p. 73. Also: Horst Poller, *Politik im Querschnitt. Zahlenspiegel 1981/1982*, Stuttgart (Verlag Bonn Aktuell), 1981, p. 17/18.

18. See Bernhard Schäfer, *Grundzüge des sozialen Wandels in der Bundesrepublik*,

Gegenwartskunde Sonderheft 1979, p. 17 (Table 2).
19. Ludwig Kippes/Gerhard Marino, Jugend-Arbeitslosigkeit. Vom Kräftemangel zum Stellenmangel München,(Bayrische Landeszentrale für Politische Bildungsarbeit), 1979, p. 39.
20. Ibid., p. 40.
21. Ibid., p. 27.
22. Poller, ibid., p. 86.
23. Bericht über Bestrebungen und Leistungen der Jugendhilfe-Fünfter Jugendbericht BT Drucksache 8/3685, 20.2.1980, pp. 70 ff. Also Johannes Esser, Wohin geht die Jugend. Reinbek (Rowohlt), 1979, p. 119.
24. Kippes, ibid., p. 218.
25. Ibid., p. 49.
26. Kippes pp. 75/76; Bundesanstalt für Arbeit: Jüngere Arbeitslose Mai 1980, Nürnberg August 1980 (report); Bundesanstalt für Arbeit: Jüngere Arbeitslose September 1980, Nürnberg December 1980 (report).
27. FR 8.12.1981 p. 1; Bericht des Bundesministeriums für Arbeit und Sozialordnung an die OECD: Der Übergang von Jugendlichen in die Berufsausbildung und das Erwerbsleben, Bonn 1979, p. 4. Also: Regierungspolitik 1977-1980. Press- und Informationsamt der Bundesregierung, Bonn, 1976, p. 19.
28. Data from Gegenwartskunde, ibid., p. 23; Poller, p. 56.
29. Spiegel 24, 1980, p. 87.
30. Poller, p. 58.
31. On unemployment among academics see Kippes p. 102 ff.
32. Quoted in Quick 28, 1979.
33. Karl Josef Does/Johann K. Motz, "Auf dem steilen Weg nach oben. Denn sie dürfen nicht was sie wollen", in Bild der Wissenschaft. Sonderdruck 1979. Kind und Umwelt Teil I, p. 48.
34. Gesellschaftliche Daten 1977, Presse und Informationsamt der Bundesregierung, Bonn 1978, p. 63 ff.
35. Does/Motz, p. 49.
36. Ibid., p. 54 ff. Also Johannes Esser, "Die Schule als Angstinstanz und öffentliche Anstalt für Angsterlebnisse", in Esser (ed.), Wohin geht die Jugend? Gegen die Zukunftslosigkeit unserer Kinder, Reinbek (Rowohlt), 1979, p. 130-132.
37. Bericht über die Bestrebungen und Leistungen der Jugendhilfe. Deutscher Bundestag 8. Wahlperiode. Drucksache 8, 3685: Fünfter Jugendbericht, p. 46 ff.

38. See also Klaus Hurrelmann, "Lernen, lernen, lernen. Trotz schlechterer Berufschancen streben Schüler und Eltern immer höhere Schulabschlüsse an", Die Zeit 50, 1981, p. 33.
39. The Times, 12.7.1978.
40. Herbert E. Colla, "Schülersuizid", in Esser ibid., p. 145.
41. See special issue of Das Parlament: Die Flucht in die Sucht, No. 33, 15.8.1981, pp. 6-7.
42. Stern 38, 1979.
43. Die Welt, 22.12.1978; Die Welt, 25.9.1979.
44. Quick 28, 1979, Survey conducted by Kehrmann Institute.
45. Stern 44, 1976; also Quick 34, 1978; Bild am Sonntag 34, 1978.
46. Emnid: Jugend zwischen 13 und 24. Ed. Jugendwerk der Deutschen Shell. Bielefeld 1975, see Walter Jaide, Achtzehnjährige zwischen Reaktion und Rebellion. Politische Einstellungen und Aktivitäten Jugendlicher in der Bundesrepublik, Opladen, (Leske) 1978, pp. 124-25.
47. For opposing views see for example: Rainer Lepsius op.cit., and Reimar Oltmanns, Du hast keine Chance, aber nutze sie. Eine Jugend steigt aus, Reinbek (Rowohlt), 1980, who takes "disenchantment" as the starting point for his discussion of youth while Lepsius claims there is no such thing as disenchantment.
48. Oltmanns, p. 38.
49. Dieter Baacke, "Krisen und Probleme des Jugendalters", in Claus Richter (ed.), Die Überflüssige Generation. Jugend zwischen Apathie und Aggression, Frankfurt, (Athenäum), 1979, p. 25; also Oltmanns pp. 41-44.
50. For details see: Michael Mildenberger, Die religiöse Revolte. Jugend zwischen Flucht und Aufbruch, Frankfurt, (Fischer), 1980. Henri Nannen (ed.), Die himmlischen Verführer. Sekten in Deutschland, Hamburg, (Goldmann, Stern Buch), 1980.
51. Sigwart Lönnendonker/Tilman Fichter, "Von der Apo nach Tunix", in Die überflüssige Generation, ibid., p. 137.
52. The last sentence reads in German: "Wir lassen uns nicht mehr einmachen, kleinmachen und gleichmachen". Quoted in Oltmanns p. 85. There are also case studies of various projects.
53. Stern 38, 1979, Oltmanns p. 38 and p. 48. Good summary of problems and research findings in: Bundesministerium für Jugend Familie und Gesundheit

(ed.). Jugend in der Bundesrepublik heute - Aufbruch oder Verweigerung, Bonn 1981.

54. Hendrik Bussiek, "'Saturday Night' - Philosophie, oder: Eine Jugend auf der Flucht", in Die überflüssige Generation, ibid., p. 73.

55. See Martin und Sylvia Greiffenhagen, Ein schwieriges Vaterland, München, (List) 1979, p. 356. For the over 25s: 57% for political opposition; 56% for competition among parties; 62% for free speech.

56. An Infas study from November 1971 quoted in M. Kent Jennings und Rolf Jansen "Die Jugend in der Bundesrepublik. Der Wunsch nach Veränderung und Meinungsvielfalt in der Politik - Der Einfluss von Sozialstruktur und Famile" in Politische Vierteljahresschrift (PVS), 1976, No. 3, p. 319.

57. Greiffenhagen p. 359.

58. Spiegel 13, 1980, p. 32.

59. Karl-Josef Does, Jugend und Politik 1976. Tendenzen und Perspektiven. Sozialwissenschaftliches Institut der Konrad Adenauer Stiftung, Alfter 1976, pp. 20 and 25.

60. Ibid., pp. 4-7.

61. Jugend 1980: Generation ohne Hoffnung, ZDF programme in 3 parts March/April 1980. Part II broadcast on April 1st, 1980 included the survey materials.

62. Recently Stephanie Hansen/Hans-Joachim Veen, "Auf der Suche nach dem privaten Glück, Jugend heute: Ergebnisse repräsentativer Studien zu den Wertorientierungen und der politischen Kultur Jugendlicher", in Die Zeit 37,5.9. 1980, p. 16.

63. Jaide, Achzehnjährige pp. 173-175.

64. Ibid., pp. 177-178. Also Bernd Guggenberger, Bürgerinitiativen in der Parteiendemokratie, Stuttgart, (Kohlhammer), 1980, p. 27 f.

65. Bahr, ibid.

66. Jaide, Achtzehnjährige p. 178.

67. Hauch (SPD) during the Bundestag debate on youth in May 1981. See Das Parlament 20, 12th May 1981, p. 1.

67a. Jugendprotest im demokratischen Staat. Schlussbericht der Enquete Kommission des 9. Bundestages Bonn (Zur Sache 1/83), 1983.

68. Reports in FR 1.12.1981; 2.12.1981; 3.12.1981.

69. On postmaterialism see in considerable detail: Helmut Klages/Peter Kmieciak (eds.) Wertwandel und gesellschaftlicher Wandel, Frankfurt, (Campus), 1979, especially Tino Bargel,"Überlegungen

und Materialen zu Wertdisparitäten und Wertwandel in der BRD", pp. 146-184; Max Kaase, "Legitimationskrise in westlichen demokratischen Industriegesellschaften: Mythos oder Realität", pp. 328-350.

70. Kai Hildebrandt and Russell J. Dalton, "The New Politics: Political Change or Sunshine Politics", in Beyme/Kaase (ed.) Elections and Parties. German Studies III, Sage 1978, pp. 69-96.

71. Good summary and exploration of the concept in Hermann Schmitt/Oskar Niedermeyer/Kurt Menke, "Etablierte und Grüne. Zur Verankerung der ökologischen Bewegung in den Parteiorganisationen von SPD, FDP, CDU, und CSU". Paper prepared for discussion in the DVPW (Deutsche Vereinigung für politische Wissenschaft) workshop "Parties, Parliaments, Elections", Berlin, April 1981, Preprint No. 57, p. 17. Since published in Z Parl 4, 1981.

72. Ronald Inglehart,"Wertwandel in den westlichen Gesellschaften: Politische Konsequenzen von materialistischen und postmaterialistischen Prioritäten", in Wertwandel ibid., p. 298. Also Inglehart, The Silent Revolution. Changing Values and Political Styles among Western Publics,Princeton 1977; Inglehart, "Socioeconomic Change and Human Value Priorities" in Samuel J. Barnes/Max Kaase et. al. Political Action, Mass Participation in Five Western Democracies, Beverly Hills, 1979.

73. Walter Jaide, Jugend und Demokratie. Politische Einstellungen der westdeutschen Jugend, München, (Juventa), 1970, pp. 40-45: excerpts from the questionnaires, pp. 122-126.

74. Bargel ibid., pp. 166-175.

75. Similar: Jaide, Achzehnjährige, pp. 124-125.

76. Erwin K. Scheuch, "Die Jugend gibt es nicht - zur Differenziertheit der Jugend in der heutigen Industriegesellschaft". In Scheuch, Konfliktfelder der Gegenwart, p. 152.

77. Quoted in Greiffenhagen, p. 261.

78. Wolfgang Gangnus, "Politische Einstellungen von Jugendlichen ohne Ausbildungsvertrag" in Barbara Hille/Burkhardt Röder (eds.) Beiträge zur Jugendforschung. Sozialpsychologische Befunde zum Jugendalter in beiden deutschen Staaten, Opladen, 1979, pp. 77-92, esp. p. 87.

79. Greiffenhagen p. 260; also Walter Jaide, "Rückt die Jugend nach rechts?" in Evangelische Kommentare 1974 No. 9: "Jugend und Politik heute" in Aus Politik und Zeitgeschichte B 39/40 1976, p. 2-24.

80. An overview of research approaches in: Politischer Protest in der Sozialwissenschaftlichen Literatur. Eine Arbeit der Infratest Wirtschaftsforschung GmbH, Stuttgart, (Kohlhammer), 1978; also Friedhelm Neidhardt, Die Junge Generation, Jugend und Gesellschaft in der Bundesrepublik, Opladen, (Leske), 1970 esp. Chapter II.

81. Hendrik Bussiek, Bericht zur Lage der Jugend, Frankfurt, (Fischer), 1978, p. 13.

82. Scheuch, p. 147, Question 4.

83. Die Einstellung der jungen Generation zur Arbeitswelt und Wirtschaftsordnung 1979. Studie im Auftrag des Jugendwerkes der Deutschen Shell durchgeführt vom Institut für Jugendforschung, Hamburg 1980, pp. 47-48.

84. Scheuch, p. 146.

85. e.g. Klaus Heinemann, Arbeitslose Jugendliche. Ursachen und individuelle Bewältigung, Darmstadt/Neuwied, (Luchterhand), 1978; Sybille Laturner/Bernhard Schön, (eds.) Jugendarbeitslosigkeit. Materialien und Analysen zu einem neuen Problem, Reinbek, (Rowohlt), 6th edition 1979.

86. Kaase in Wertwandel p. 341 includes the table "Typology of political action by country" which shows relatively large numbers of inactives and protesters for West Germany:

Types	Netherlands	GB	USA	West Germany	Austria
	%	%	%	%	%
Inactives	17.9	30.1	12.3	26.6	34.9
Conformists	11.1	15.4	17.5	13.5	19.2
Reformists	19.8	21.9	36.0	24.6	20.9
Activists	19.3	10.2	14.4	8.0	5.9
Protesters	31.9	22.4	19.8	27.3	19.1

87. M. Kaase/H.D. Klingemann, "Politische Ideologie und politische Beteiligung" in: Mannheimer Berichte No. 11, 1975, p. 332.

88. See Greiffenhagen, pp. 364/65.

89. Ibid., p. 366.

90. "Sie fühlen sich von keinem vertreten. Auszüge aus einer Untersuchung des Ministeriums für Jugend, Familie, Gesundheit", FR 3, 12.1981, p. 10.

91. FAZ 2.101978; critical evaluation by Friedhelm Heubel et.al. "Studenten im Ghetto?" In Liberal No. 9, September 1979, pp. 646-655.

92. Wilhelm P. Bürklin, "Links und/oder Demokratisch? Dimensionen studentischen Demokratieverständnisses" in PVS No. 3, 1980, pp.

224/5.
93. Heubel et. al., p. 654.
94. See Kenneth H.F. Dyson, "Left-wing Extremism and the Problem of Tolerance in Western Germany" in Government and Opposition 3 1975, pp. 306ff.
95. E.g. Iring Fetscher, Terrorismus und Reaktion. Frankfurt, (Europäische Verlagsanstalt), 2nd edition 1978, Chapters I and II; also: Shell, "Extraparliamentary Opposition in Postwar Germany" in Comparative Politics No. 4, July 1970, pp. 653-680.

SUGGESTED READING

Hendrik Bussiek, Bericht zur Lage der Jugend, Fischer (Frankfurt), 1978
Die Einstellungen der jungen Generation zur Arbeitswelt und Wirtschaftsordnung, Jugendwerk der Deutschen Shell, Hamburg, 1980
Johannes Esser (ed.), Wohin geht die Jugend? Reinbek (Rowohlt), 1979
Kai Hildebrandt/Russell J. Dalton, "The New Politics: Political Change or Sunshine Politics" in Beyme/Kaase (eds.), Elections and Parties, Sage 1978, pp. 69-96
Barbara Hille/Burkhardt Röder (eds.), Beiträge zur Jugendforschung, Opladen (Leske), 1979
Walter Jaide, Achtzehnjährige zwischen Reaktion und Rebellion, Opladen (Leske), 1978
Jugend '81. Lebensentwürfe, Alltagskulturen, Zukunftsbilder, Jugendwerk der Deutschen Shell, Opladen (Leske), 1982
Jugendprotest im demokratischen Staat. Zwischenbericht der Enquete Kommission des Deutschen Bundestages, Zur Sache 1/81, Bonn, 1982. dto Schlussbericht, Zur Sache 1/83, Bonn, 1983
Ludwig Kippes/Gerhard Marino, Jugendarbeitslosigkeit, München (Bayr. Landeszentrale), 1980, (2nd. ed.)
Helmut Klages/Peter Kmieciak (eds.) Wertwandel und gesellschaftlicher Wandel, Frankfurt (Campus), 1979
Reimar Oltmanns, Du hast keine Chance, aber nutze sie. Eine Jugend steigt aus, Reinbek (Rowohlt), 1980
Claus Richter (ed.), Die überflüssige Generation, Frankfurt (Athenäum), 1979

Chapter Seven

OPPOSITION FROM THE LEFT: COMMUNISM, STUDENT MOVEMENT, TERRORISM

In the Federal Republic of Germany, Communist or Socialist ideologies encountered a number of obstacles. As in all advanced industrial societies, living standards and wage levels no longer confirmed the Marxist prognosis of an impoverishment of the labour force.[1] The expansion of the white collar sector and the changes in the structure of employment have obliterated or at least obscured the social sector which was to spearhead revolution and fundamental change: the proletariat. Left-wing opposition to contemporary politics and society could either turn Marxism into an orthodoxy and proclaim its principles regardless of discrepancies with social realities today, or they could try to rephrase their aims and reconsider their approaches in the light of new experiences. The rapid economic recovery in the Federal Republic made such a restatement particularly urgent: after a slow start in the forties and early fifties, wage levels, living conditions, the general level of prosperity in West Germany rose sharply, overtaking most European countries.[2] Even among the lower paid, ownership of cars, washing machines, televisions, savings have risen. West German workers no longer see themselves as "proletariat" and adhere to a separate working class/proletarian culture or consciousness.

The pace of social change was only one factor to influence the prospects of left-wing opposition or Communist alternatives in West Germany. There are also historical and political obstacles. In the late twenties, the Communist Party had enjoyed a good deal of electoral support which grew as the unemployment crisis worsened. Yet, the party's dependence on the political directives from the Soviet Union paralyzed it at the time and prevented it from making a relevant contribution against the advance of fascism and towards economic stabilisation.[3] Then, the political energies of the KPD were directed against so called "social fascists", in other words against the Social Democratic Party. They were also directed against "the system", the political institutions and the constitutional principles of the Weimar Republic. The legacy of opposing the wrong groups and tacitly aiding the destruction of political democracy in the thirties, remained with the KPD although it had suffered at the hand of Nationalsocialism and had been treated as a major political enemy after 1933. Prospects for Communism or radical Socialism after World War II were further stifled by the impact of the Cold War. The division of Germany into a Western and an Eastern state, affiliated to opposing political blocks, gave the question of a KPD and its dependance on Moscow new topicality. In West Germany, West Integration went hand in hand with a resurgence of anticommunism.[4] In the wake of west integration and anticommunism, the KPD was banned by the Federal Constitutional Court in 1956.[5] By that time, it had lost all seats in the Bundestag and in land parliaments. In 1950, it had held fifteen seats in the Bundestag and a total of 133 seats in land parliaments, although its programme advocated a revolutionary overthrow of the Adenauer regime.[6] By the time the party was banned, five years after proceedings had been started, the electoral demise of the KPD had already happened. The ban confirmed rather than caused the disappearance of Communism from West German parliamentary politics. Ten years later, when discussions about a new Communist party were in full swing, an opinion poll once again confirmed that such a party would be unable to win seats in West German parliaments, i.e. take the 5% hurdle.[7]

Since the mid-fifties ban of the KPD, opposition on the left and from the left generated several movements and parties. The KPD itself retained a skeleton albeit illegal organization. An estimated 7,000 of the 78,000 members at the time of the ban remained active into the sixties.[8] In 1960, a new party, the <u>Deutsche Friedensunion</u>, Peace Union, was founded with two political targets: in the short term, this party was to compete in the 1961 elections on the left-socialist spectrum; in the longer term, it was to provide a political base for socialists disenchanted with the SPD and its move towards the centre in and after Godesberg. There was also the less open intention to provide a political

Opposition from the Left

frontage for Communists which was respectable, legal and apparently non aligned with the Moscow communist doctrine.[9]

An uneasy amalgamation of intellectuals searching for an alternative to the SPD, and Communists searching for an effective camouflage, the DFU failed on all counts. It could not compete successfully in elections and never entered land parliaments or the federal parliament; the political left remained splintered, and the Communists also failed to fully control the newcomer. Without a unifying force on the left, opposition became more diverse. A new approach to Marxism beyond obedience to Soviet Communism or its East German vassal and a workable response to the challenges and changes in affluent societies had yet to be developed. In the stalemate of the sixties, the opposition from the left was stirred up from a different angle. In 1961, the SPD decided to expel its Socialist fringe, the student organization SDS (Sozialistischer Deutscher Studentenbund) who had refused to endorse the Godesberg programme and tow the party line. The SDS remained intransigent in its Marxist principles and in rejecting the political orientation of the SPD. It remained equally intransigent in rejecting Communist orthodoxy. It subsequently developed into the core of the new left and the motor of the student movement. At the same time, the campaign against proposed emergency legislation in the Federal Republic unleashed a further tier of opposition. Emergency legislation was drawn up under the Erhard government to cope with possible crises. This involved suspending parliament and authorising a form of executive government. The erosion of the Weimar Republic by Emergency Powers was conjured up in people's minds as a warning that a so called "legal" step from democratic to anti-democratic government was imminent. The opposition against Emergency Legislation stretched from sections of the Social Democratic Party and the Trade Union Movement to the non parliamentary left of all persuasions. Once the Grand Coalition had approved the legislation in parliament, the diffuse alliance of mass demonstrations dispersed. For some, the issue remained a symbol of the dangerous course of authoritarianism on which society had embarked. Democracy itself was regarded as suffering a state of emergency which would warrant new forms of opposition and new initiatives for political change.[10] A further issue of opposition from the left concerned atomic weapons.[11] The devastation caused by atomic bombs at the end of the Second World War had given rise to protest - and peace movements in Western Europe. In the Federal Republic, the question of atomic armaments became politically inflammatory when the equipment of the Bundeswehr with atomic weapons was considered. The so called <u>Ostermarsch Bewegung</u>, modelled on the Aldermaston marches of the British CND, embraced protest against atomic bombs, against an escalation of atomic weapons in the Federal Republic and against military and armament policies of Nato and the Western Alliance. Similar to the protest against the emergency legislation, a diffuse following was mobilised; and more important still, the issue of atomic weapons soon detached itself from its concrete political starting point, the Bundeswehr and the use of atomic weapons. The Bundeswehr was never equipped with such weapons but the atomic theme came to symbolise the dangerous and destructive intentions which were ascribed to political leaders in West Germany, to "the system".

The protests against emergency legislation and the Easter marches were a multifaceted opposition, ranging from SPD supporters and trade unionists, churchmen, academics, writers, journalists, to the so called "homeless" left of SDS and similar leanings, radical Socialists, Communists, pacifists, antimilitarists. Alongside this varied opposition on the left, functionaries and activists of the illegal Communist party tried to manipulate events, prevent the formation of any party which might rival their influence or curtail their control over issues and actions of the West German left.[12] The drive to re-establish a Communist party was in itself largely motivated by the determination to retain control over developments on the left. The pace and pattern of left-wing opposition since the mid-sixties no longer fitted the straight-jacket of orthodox Communism. Other brands of Communism: Maoist, Leninist, Stalinist reared their heads and clambered for attention; the protest waves around emergency legislation, atomic weapons and not least the Grand Coalition of the two major parties since 1966 gave rise to a new phenomenon on the left, which professed Socialist or even Communist ideas and defied orthodoxy of a Socialist or Communist variety: the so called new left. The SDS, the cast off from the SPD was to become the most volatile part of this new left. The duality of opposition on the left, Communism and a non-orthodox left commenced in the sixties and has continued into the eighties. To-

THE DKP IN SOCIETY AND POLITICS

The new German Communist Party, the DKP was founded in September 1968[13] at a politically sensitive juncture. The liberalisation in the CSSR under Dubzec had been halted by a Russian invasion one month before. Anti-Soviet sentiments and anti-communism ran high in West Germany and elsewhere. The DKP started into politics as a staunch and unflinching supporter of the Soviet course. This course had few friends even among the political left. Conflicting views on the CSSR had led to the breakdown of an alliance between the illegal KPD and the so called Socialist Office which had begun preparations for a new Socialist political party. The trade union movement, the SPD, most intellectuals and university teachers who were affiliated to the Easter marches or the campaign against Emergency Legislation also condemned the Soviet invasion of the CSSR and the political submission of orthodox Communism under the prescribed doctrine.

In the situation of mounting distrust against Communism and the course of Soviet policies, one of the tasks of the DKP was to keep some sort of foothold in West Germany and in particular among the West German left. The party was to be a mouthpiece to articulate and endorse Communist views which would otherwise fall victim to the dismay with Communist political practice from the left and from the right. One of the founders of the DKP expressed the interrelation of the party and political situation in retrospect:

> The demand of broad strata of the population for necessary changes in interior and foreign policy are met by the governing circles with intensified anti-communism. They use in particular the events of August 1968 in the CSSR, which ended in the downfall of the counter-revolutionary attempts to discredit the demands for normal relations with our Socialist neighbour states, to bring divisions and confusion into the democratic movements and to discredit the aims of political and social change.[14]

Opposition from the Left

Behind the jargon, the intention to rectify the situation by injecting a pro-Communist, orthodox voice, is clear. It would not have had any effect, had not the principle of admitting a Communist party been accepted in West Germany well before September 1968. In October 1967, the Conference of Interior Ministers of the Länder had already indicated that such a party might be founded, provided it did not contravene the constitutional requirements.[15] In July 1968, Gustav Heinemann who at that time was Minister of Justice, stated vis-a-vis a delegation of functionaries that it was constitutionally impossible to legalise the old KPD, yet not impossible to found a new Communist party.[16] The KPD itself attempted to break out of illegality. It created an "initiative committee" for the re-legalisation (Wiederzulassung) of the KPD in March 1967 with the aim to force the West German government to reconsider the ban of 1956. This committee rejected any suggestions of setting up a new party; this was said to have "no teeth".[17] In short, the efforts of the old Communist party were directed towards legalisation of the former organization. Offers which would have led towards a new party and an altered political format of Communism in West Germany began to come forward in the mid sixties, but were flatly rejected. When a "Declaration about the new constitution of a Communist Party" was published in 1968, the document which eventually led to the founding of the DKP, it was not backed by the old KPD, the initiative committee nor by the majority of functionaries and members who had remained in the illegal KPD. The Declaration was issued by a "circle of 31 functionaries" five of them members of the central committee, but it was phrased without consultation in and through the party.[18]

    The timing and clandestine approach suggest that the prime intention was to establish a voice within the German left to represent orthodox Communism. The varied moves to retain the old Communist party remained without influence. In the Socialist camp, the continuation or recreation of a Communist party was in any case a contested issue after the events in the CSSR. Communist and Socialist left were deeply divided over the need for a Communist party and over the acceptable course of left-wing politics.[19] The Socialists who were loosely affiliated to the Socialist Office in Offenbach pursued their own plans to launch a party and continued to do so even after the DKP was founded. Within the Communist camp, the differences and disagreements soon faded. In November 1968, the founding committee was extended to include fifteen of the most senior functionaries of the illegal KPD. Three had been members of the Politbureau, another had been a candidate. All had actively campaigned for the legalisation of the old party and opposed the idea of a modified Communist party which would have to endorse the Basic Law. They now moved into the DKP leadership at national and regional levels.[20]

Until October 1971, the KPD continued to exist, albeit illegally, as a separate organization - at least on paper. The demands for lifting the KPD ban were also kept alive, as if the new Communist party had not been founded or would not be accepted as organizational umbrella for orthodox Communism in the Federal Republic. The charade of the two Communist parties side by side had, of course, some political purposes: the attempt to conceal the overlap of the two parties was also an attempt to conceal the identity of the leadership. The new party was to appear different, untainted by illegal Communism.

Having the two parties was also intended to protect the DKP from a possible ban as a successor party of the KPD. The double play ended only after the Central Committee of the SED finally pronounced in 1971 that the new party, the DKP, was the rightful Communist party in West Germany.[21] Only then did the First Secretary of the illegal KPD, Max Reimann, join the new party and become its honorary president.[22] The dependence of the political status of the DKP on the green light from East Germany underlines the orthodox obedience to the official Communist line of the Soviet Union and its East German vassal state and party. Even the experience of illegality and the decline of Communist opposition in West Germany did not generate new thinking, new approaches, political initiative; the subservience which had already characterised the German Communist Party in the twenties and in the forties and fifties continued after 1968.

Communist Continuities
The DKP was founded from above and with rapidity. The first organizational tier to be created was the party executive and a nine-man working committee to head the party until its first congress in April

1969. All of the leaders of the first hour had occupied functionary positions or had even been in the top leadership of the KPD.[23] By December 1968, less than three months after the declaration to form the DKP had been issued, regional offices were established in all Länder except in West Berlin where the SEW, the Western sister party of the SED coninued to exist. There was some organizational depth: the DKP had two hundred district offices and about sixty shop floor committees at the end of 1968. The KPD apparatus which had survived illegally and the party functionaries were merely reactivated for the DKP. Of the 336 members of the land executives at the time of the first party congress, 278 or 80% had been members of the KPD, most of them prior to 1956.[24] Continuity between KPD and DKP seems to have been higher at the top than at the lower levels of party organization. Seven of the thirteen KPD Politbureau members were again in the DKP Politbureau. In 1968, forty members of the 1956 KPD executive were still alive, sixteen of them held leadership positions in the DKP in 1968.[25] The first ten years of DKP development did not modify the dominance of former KPD activists. At the sixth congress of the DKP in Hanover in May 1981, the newly elected, i.e. largely confirmed party leadership consisted of a total of 109 people. From the KPD came 87 of these or 80%. For the rank and file, reliable estimates of party continuities are not available. After the ban, the illegal KPD had 7,000 active members; most of the leadership had sought refuge in the GDR or had been imprisoned in the Federal Republic. The leaders flowed back into the new party. The members who had been active between 1956 and 1968, in illegality, remained loyal. The old target of 78,000, however, had never been reached again. By December 1968, the DKP had 22,000 members; at the time of the first party congress in April 1969, 34,000. Since then, membership rose fairly steadily to 40,000 in 1975. In 1981, the DKP claimed to have 48.856 members.[26] Official estimates point to a membership of about 40,000 which has stagnated since 1975.[27] During the first decade, the DKP established a broad organizational network, twelve land offices and 200 district offices. Special emphasis has been placed on contact with local people and their concerns. In 1980, the DKP maintained 1,300 so called <u>Basisorganisationen</u>, grass root organizations where local and community issues are meant to be pursued: nine hundred of these were in residential areas, three hundred in factories and on the shop floor, one hundred in West German universities.[28]

Directives and decisions about the political activity and the scope of lower organizational levels of the party are formulated at the top and merely carried out at the lower levels. The DKP statutes which were ratified at the first congress in 1969, clearly state:

> The decisions of the party congress and of the party executive elected by it are obligatory for all organizations and members of the party. All sub-divisions of the party are required to develop an optimum of own initiative and independent activities on the basis of the policies decreed by the party congress and in line with the decisions of the party executive.[29]

Members are entitled, even expected, to approach congress with resolutions and points for discussion. In this way, it is claimed, every communist member can influence the political line of the party. These discussions would feed into the policies decided at party congresses which are, in turn, compulsory for members.[30] This model of welcome membership initiative suggests an interrelation between grass roots and leadership. The congresses themselves show few signs of such discussion and an active role of the rank and file. DKP congresses seem to have a similar function to CDU congresses in the fifties: to demonstrate publicly and for the members the unity and strength of the party. This means acclamation, unison votes for the one and only candidate for electoral offices, not discussion, dissent, conflict of policy aims and opinions. Congresses stifle possible dissent and intend to forge membership loyalty and an unchallenged primacy of the leadership.

The 1978 DKP congress in Mannheim seemed to divert from this well-trodden path. At this congress, the first Basic Programme of the DKP was to be discussed and adopted, a task which had been decided upon by the previous congress in 1976. During the two year interval - the normal spacing between party congresses - some 1,300 resolutions and amendments to the draft came from within the DKP and were placed before the congress for discussion. The draft, of course, had been formulated and approved

by the DKP executive and the many voices from the
grass roots, the many divergent political ideas indicated that perhaps the principle of obedience to
the decrees from above was no longer fully accepted.
Despite the large number of suggestions and resolutions, the programme was at no stage publicly discussed. At the 1978 congress, the DKP adopted the
programme without debate, just with the customary
applause. In an explanatory note, the chairman of
the DKP, Mies, claimed that all the proposals had
already been incorporated.[31]

This demonstrative consensus is also evident in
leadership elections. Nominations are made by the
party executive; for top positions, only one name is
put forward. To date, voting in the DKP for these
proposed candidates has been unanimous. At the
first party congress, a move had been attempted to
give more influence to party branches and members.
A resolution was forced through to allow branches
some say in the nomination and election of congress
delegates who would then represent branch interests
and be their spokesmen. Although the resolution was
accepted in 1969, it was again reversed in 1973 and
proved too feeble to break through the predominance
which the old Communist garde had already established in the DKP. Since 1973, the task of selecting
delegates to the party congress has rested with the
district and land organizations without involving
the grass root level at all.

DKP and Parliamentary Democracy

Control of the DKP leadership over the political
orientation of the party is paramount. Official
proclamations and programmes may therefore be taken
as statements which map out the overall aims and
purposes of the party. They also highlight the
strategic approach of the DKP between revolutionary
rejection of the political system of the Federal
Republic and democratic consensus as stipulated by
the Basic Law and the Constitutional Court sentence
of 1956. The 1969 Declaration of Principles for
example had replaced the notion of revolutionary
change and a dictatorship of the proletariat with
the more docile reference to peaceful and gradual
change towards socialism.[32] The determination of
the founders to adhere to the constitutional guidelines for political parties is evident. A discussion paper on the interrelation of bourgeois and
Socialist democracy articulates the ambiguity to aim

at fundamental change and at the same time not openly call for fundamental change:

> The DKP operates on the basis (auf dem Boden) of the Basic Law. It accepts the democratic principles which are contained in it. We defend the democratic rights and liberties, and fight for their expansion. Our aim is Socialism. It provides a stable basis for the democratic rights which the working people already won under capitalism. Socialist democracy raises democracy to a qualitatively new level.33

This cautious endorsement of the Basic Law, at least of those elements which are deemed acceptable and democratic in Communist eyes, shows the concern of the party to demonstratively accept the constitutional framework. The revolutionary radicalism of the twenties or even of the early fifties has abated. Now, there is just a vague hint at "change towards democratic and social progress".34

Politically, this modification means that the DKP presents itself as a parliamentary party which aims at parliamentary representation. It does not only want to be the voice of orthodoxy among the left, it also wants to be heard inside assemblies and parliaments on all levels.

> Everywhere in our country, wherever workers and employees, intellectuals, farmers, women and young people are fighting for their social and political demands, members of the DKP are to be found in the front row. Experience has shown: Communists are reliable. It can therefore only benefit working people, indeed all democrats, if after all this time consistent workers' representatives will hold seats and have votes in the Bundestag, if DKP delegates enter parliament.35

The pledges of parliamentary loyalty have yet to be tested. As we shall discuss later, the DKP has sent some seventy delegates into local assemblies. It never surmounted the 5% hurdle to win seats on a land or on the federal level. The main thrust of the party does not seem to be parliamentary. It is the push towards a working class base, towards working class organizations - the trade unions in particular - and towards workers in general. The DKP

Opposition from the Left

strives to be a workers' party as a political priority.

A Workers' Party?
Under the heading of Aktionseinheit, unity of action, the DKP regards itself as the most active component of the labour movement. This embraces also trade unions and Social Democrats. Both repeatedly rejected any cooperation with the West German Communists or the notion of a special alliance with the DKP.[36] Matters are straight forward enough for the SPD: the two political parties have no overlap and compete in the electoral field. For the trade unions, who are not aligned to any particular party in the Federal Republic matters are not quite so clear cut. As we saw earlier, the West German trade union movement as a whole and individual unions are more closely associated with the SPD than with any other party. Yet members of CDU, FDP, CSU are also members of these trade unions, although less frequently so; minority parties and groups may also be represented within the trade unions. Since the West German trade unions are party politically neutral, political allegiances within the movement may be varied. In fact, adherents of the centre or the right are less active in the trade unions, at least not those affiliated to the West German Trades Union Federation. For parties and groups of the left, this does not apply. There are some indications that West German Communists have joined trade unions and often achieved functionary positions. In 1981, Eugen Loderer, at the time chairman of the Metal Workers' Union IGM, sounded a warning of so called strong room Communists, i.e. of people who held Communist views but had become members of one of the established parties in order to successfully infiltrate that party and from there also the trade union organization. Loderer articulated a widespread fear of a possible march through the institutions from a determined and well organized left. He also attempted to defend himself and the trade union movement against the allegation that the march of the DKP into the movement had already taken place. There is no doubt that trade union links are regarded highly by the DKP. The majority of its party members, about 75% - belong to a trade union; most of them also hold a trade union post in local or shop floor organizations. This in itself is not surprising since the motivation to be politically active and join a political party frequently goes together

with union membership. This had been evident for
the SPD and may likewise be observed for the DKP.
The interrelation between SPD and trade unions has
several facets. A key aspect is that the party can
act as an amplifier of trade union concerns in parliament and throughout the political institutions in
the Federal Republic. Relations between trade
unions and DKP - or better the intentions of the DKP
concerning the trade unions - are the reverse.

The party tries to secure influence in the
unions, not the unions in and through the party.
DKP members who also belong to the trade unions are
above all delegates and spokesmen of their party,
they "articulate the opinions and positions of their
party in the trade unions. They not only do this,
they have to do this, if they do not want to defy
party discipline".[38] Whether ordinary member or
functionary in the trade unions, the activist seems
to be charged with working for the party and increasing DKP support among the workers. There are
some indications, however, that the role designed
for DKP activists is not easily played. Elections
to union posts and in particular to shop floor
representation seems to depend in the first place on
the union work of the candidate, not on the political message which might be behind it.[39] Conversely,
union positions are important for advancement within
the DKP. The reports presented at party congresses
on the background and organizational ties of delegates are the most reliable source of information
about the social composition of the party and the
relevance of trade union affiliation for DKP leadership positions.[40] At the first congress in Essen in
1969, 847 or 85% of the 994 delegates were trade
union members, 86% of these held some kind of union
office. At the second congress in Düsseldorf in
1971, a similar picture prevailed: of the delegates
87% were trade union members, about three in four
were functionaries.[41] Ten years later, the overlap
had become more apparent still. At the 1981 congress, 95% of the delegates belonged to a trade
union, 89% occupied trade union functions in the
organization or on the shop floor.

This trade union affiliation of DKP party congresses makes it appear as if the DKP was in fact a
"workers' party". The same impression is conveyed
by the data on social composition of the congress
delegations. The party does not grant access to
files and public accounting at congresses becomes an
important source of information. As in other parties, it has to be assumed that the social composi-

tion of congresses and the social background of functionaries does not reflect the composition of the party overall. While the established parties have a middle class bias and a civil service bias among their functionaries and leaders, the data from the DKP conform to the self assessment of the party as a workers' organization: of the 1981 delegates, 81% were "workers".[43] Estimates for 1977 suggested that only 35% of the DKP members were workers.[44] In 1980, the figure of 20% was mentioned.[45] In 1979, an intensive campaign got under way to recruit industrial workers.[46] There is no evidence that this has been successful. The DKP has not, despite the drive towards the unions, emerged as a workers' party. There are some indications that the DKP membership consists to 75% or more of intellectuals, students, pupils, educated people.[47] These are the cadres who also operate in the unions and whose influence tends to be seen as the dawn of a workers' mass movement by the DKP, as a threat to democratic unionism by others. DKP influence has become particularly noticeable in trade union youth work and in the educational sector. People who may be DKP members or who may be merely "ideologically at home in the DKP"[48] have become opinion leaders in local union branches and shop floor groups because the majority of union members remain passive, apathetic and "politically naive".[49] The upshot were various resolutions of youth congresses of the trade unions and publications in defence of Soviet practices and policies and also a glorification of the GDR and of Soviet society.[50] Whatever seems to be moving within the trade unions in their youth and educational sectors, is most unwelcome. One union chairman advised his functionaries to ignore as much as possible the views published by the left wing factions:

> I would like to beseech you to make it quite clear that the matters which are presented in this booklet are nothing but half-truths, allegations and blind suspicions. Perhaps it it best to ignore this booklet altogether and ensure that it receives no attention and no recognition in our organization.[51]

Some criticised this alarm as "hunting down left-wing colleagues",[52] others took it as evidence that the West German trade unions were indeed pursuing Communist aims or were used by Communists to pursue these aims.[53] The trade unions themselves tend to bury the whole question in silence.[54]

The measurable and tangible influence of Communism and the DKP in particular on the trade unions and through the trade unions is, however, miniscule. Of the 200,000 works councillors who are elected in all but the smallest enterprises in West Germany, about one thousand, or 0.5% also belong to the DKP.[55] In 1980, the party had three hundred shop floor groups, one hundred less than ten years earlier.[56] About half their number were in the metal industry.[57] One of the main tasks of those shop floor organizations concerns the publication of shop floor papers. In 1980, the DKP published 400 such papers. The shop floor papers are regarded by the DKP as an effective means of communicating with the work force since shop floor issues and political evaluations can be merged.[58] Only about one fifth of these papers are actually produced by DKP factory groups; the efforts of the party to find workers with sufficient standing and influence to be editors and contributors to these papers, shop stewards, foremen, workers in the upper wage brackets have not been accomplished. Instead, the local and district DKP offices produce the majority of so called shop floor papers. While this might point to a shortage of grass root activists, it may also mean that the DKP deliberately maintains tight control over the publication sector. The party runs six press agencies in the Federal Republic which supply articles and information to editors and contributors.[59] By monitoring the contents of the contributions, and keeping maximum involvement in the production of shop floor papers, the DKP can determine the political line among the topical and situational news items.

Overall, the publication sector and political influence through publications is an important aspect of the DKP work; the conundrum of weaving the political message into seemingly apolitical, neutral themes and concerns applies for all grass root efforts. In the late seventies, the DKP published about 1,000 grass root periodicals for the shop floor, for a neighbourhood, for a community.[60] In addition, the party controlled one daily paper with an edition of 30,000 on weekdays and 60,000 at weekends. For the smaller papers, editions have been estimated at between 250 and 9,000 copies per issue. In total, the DKP appears to publish about 500,000 copies of its papers per week. The small papers who want to penetrate to the non-Communist reader, the neighbour or fellow worker as well, have to disguise their political edge. In a note of advice, contributors are reminded to use a dual strategy. It is considered a mistake to "use marxist terminology and vocabulary which is familiar from the GDR".[61] Contributors are to

> first of all take into account the way ordinary people are thinking and adjust the shape of your statement to their level. Only later, after anti-communism has been broken down and the information in the shop floor papers has reached a high degree of credibility is it possible to disseminate among colleagues a higher level of knowledge and awareness.[62]

The publishing activities of the DKP reveal two important aspects: the party reaches a much larger number of people than membership or electorate would indicate. Secondly, the costly publishing ventures can only be maintained because the DKP does not rely on income from party membership to finance its work. Since it does not qualify for a reimbursement of election costs with results below 0.5%, the DKP funds itself largely through donations. Party accounting for 1980 showed that the DKP had an income of about 15 million, 32% from membership fees, 32% from the sale of publications and from entrance fees, the remainder through donations, nine of them amounting to over DM 20,000.[63] Expenditure for the DKP party apparatus, the publications and other aspects of party work outpaced the fifteen million income. The Office for the Protection of the Constitution has for years reported that the DKP also receives funding from the GDR. For 1980, a sum of DM 50 million was mentioned. Whether or not this figure is accurate, the access to additional funding permits the party to engage in a range of political activities - publications for example - which are normally well outside the reach of a small party with meagre resources. The funding from the GDR also points to the close liaison of the DKP with East German and Soviet Communism and the role of the party in West Germany as a mouthpiece of orthodox Communism. This role has remained unaltered since the beginnings of the DKP and even since the days of the KPD.

Opposition from the Left

The Party and its Members
In a party whose political purpose has been predetermined outside the organization, a party which is even financially not dependent on membership support, little scope seems to exist for members to influence events or for membership changes to make an impact on the party and its leadership. For the DKP, this detachment of the party and its apparatus from the membership can be shown from the outset. First surveys of the DKP in the early seventies revealed that this was a relatively young party.[64] About half its members were under forty years of age. One third were even under thirty, only 10% were 65 or over. At that time, the average age of the party executive was 42, only slightly higher than that of the party membership overall.[65] As mentioned earlier, 83% of those party leaders of the first hour had already been active in the illegal KPD. By 1981, the average age of the party executive had crept up to fifty, with many leadership positions still occupied by former members of the KPD. In the same period, the DKP membership overall appears to have become younger. At the 1981 party congress, well over half the delegates were under forty years of age. In the DKP, the youngest sector of the under thirties seemed to have expanded to well over one third of the total membership. Official pronouncements refer to the DKP as the party for workers and for the young.

> The DKP, as the party of the working class, is also as it has shown again and again in practical terms, the party of the young. It regards the struggle of the young generation the struggle for the realisation of the basic rights of the young generation as a joint task for all working people.[66]

At the top level of the DKP party organizations, the young are clearly not well represented and the old leadership has retained control. Lower down in the party, matters seem to be different. Recruitment of new members appears to be virtually restricted to the two youth organizations, the SDAJ, Sozialistische Deutsche Arbeitjugend, which caters for young workers, apprentices, pupils, and to the student organization MSB Marxistischer Studentenbund Spartakus. In 1981, SDAJ had 35,000 paid-up members, 40% of these also belonged to the DKP.[67] The student organization had 6,100 members, 70% of these were also members of the DKP. The party also maintains a children's organization, Junge Pioniere, with about 3,000 members. In the late seventies the children's section allegedly expanded to 4,700 members and 250 groups. Although the DKP has emphasised the place of young people in the party, the all important party leadership has remained in the hands of the KPD generation of Communists. For women in the DKP, the situation seems to be somewhat less unfavourable. With 29% of the membership, women are comparatively well represented in the DKP. With 22% of the DKP executive in 1981, women had advanced into leadership positions more visible than in other political parties. Most of the women executive members, however, were Beisitzer, members of the extended executive, not of the leadership circle itself. When the DKP compiled a volume to commemorate its tenth anniversary, the only DKP notable who contributed was from the academic world. The recognised dignitaries and DKP spokesmen were all men.68

There could be the makings of a clash of interests in the DKP between new West German Communists and old time orthodox Communists over influence and advancement beyond the lowest levels. It is in the nature of that party and the principle of 'democratic centralism' that such clashes would not become public and would not even materialise in the party. The only way to monitor possible discontent would be membership fluctuations. But here, data are not accessible and on can only surmise: while the KPD-origin wing is stable and entrenched in the party, membership recruitment and membership losses are amongst the young who join and desert the DKP in their search for a political opposition on the left.

Fringe parties without openings into political representation in assemblies or parliament tend to re-elect their political leaderships and close ranks against impulses and influences from below, even at the expense of disenchanting those members and supporters they wish to attract. Organizational conrol and cohesion are prone to override the membership dimension.

Not a Party for the West German Voters

The pledge of the DKP to aim for parliamentary influence has yet to be tested in political life. Since its foundation, the party has not entered the Bundestag or any of the land parliaments, in fact its percentage of the votes has been negligable. On a local level, the party had some minor successes. In 1980, it held 74 seats in 35 local assemblies in the Federal Republic. Most of these were in Northrhine Westfalia with the town of Bottrop, where the DKP scooped a 9% share, a well celebrated prize example. Most other seats were held in university towns.[69] In the context of local government, the DKP foothold is precarious. There are at least 80,000 electoral positions in local government[70] of which the DKP holds less than 0.1%. The failures in elections have not gone wholly unnoticed in the party.

> Stocktaking after ten years reveals a number of shortcomings and weak points. Now, as ever, there is a clear contradiction between the influence of the DKP and its role in society on the one hand, and the unsatisfactory results especially at federal and land elections. The key to overcome this contradiction lies in strengthening the party: in recruiting more members, in increasing the mass influence, in expanding the mass appeal, in popularising policies and principles of the DKP.[71]

Within the DKP, the few assembly members, about 0.18% of the total membership, do not appear to have a special role or influence beyond the local or branch level. A special leadership function for DKP members of assemblies at congresses or in the party executive is not apparent. Instead, full-time paid officials are the backbone of the party, also at local level. There is some evidence that local election campaigns attempted to play down the Communist identity and concentrate on small scale dissatisfactions, on local mismanagement and grievances. The DKP has eagerly embraced the topics of environmental protests and of anti-nuclear protests. It has been argued that in the light of the new protest movements in the Federal Republic, the DKP is attempting to redefine its policy of alliances and unity of action. Rather than extending only to the traditional working class organizations or shop floor activities, the alliance strategy of the DKP today is aimed at cooperation and support from a more varied protest sector.

> For a long time, the Communists did not have a chance to put a more comprehensive policy of

alliances into practice. But in the realm of
the peace movement they have most skillfully
taken over an issue which was ripe and in the
air. We are convinced that they will invest
hundreds of thousands into this, not so much
as direct finance, but through usage of
telephones, of offices and of the DKP organizational infrastructure.[72]

The involvement of the DKP with the peace movement
in the Federal Republic is a new departure. In the
first phase of anti-nuclear protests, the DKP remained aloof. In the 1981 Easter Marches and peace
rallies, it figured as a prominent participant,
even coordinator.[73] It seems, the old Communist
strategy of trying to keep control over all political initiatives on the left and ensure that they
take the direction which orthodox Communism would
wish, now applies to the political movements of the
seventies and eighties.[74]

The most successful branches of Communist activity today lie outside the conventional domain of
working class politics, in the university sector.
In the seventies, the student group <u>Spartakus</u>, emerged as the most successful facet of organized
Communism in West Germany. In 1980 it had 6,100
members. While membership elsewhere in the DKP had
stagnated since the mid seventies, MSB membership
had continued to grow. The MSB publication <u>Rote
Blätter</u> had a circulation of 30,000 in 1981 and
reached an audience far broader than the Communist
student sector.[75] At university elections, the MSB
was most successful getting its candidates into
student parliaments. In fact, in 1981 it held con-
trolling influence in most of these parliaments and
had a formidable voice in student and university
politics. Here, it seems to cooperate closely with
less orthodox formations on the left, especially the
former student association of the SPD, the Socialist
SHB, <u>Sozialistischer Hochschulbund</u>.

The pressures on the party to modify the stifled orthodoxy and embrace the political issues and
movements of the day come from the student and youth
sectors in the party. Although these pressures did
not yet manifest themselves on the leadership
levels, in the political style of the party and some
of the offical proclamations they have become evident. The 1982 conference of the youth organization
SDAJ for example lacked all the usual and treasured
paraphanalia of Communist pageantry. There was no

Opposition from the Left

solitary programme speech by the chairman, there was no wave of speechless applause. Instead, there was discussion about possible links between orthodox Communism and alternative culture, ecologists, peace protesters and other activists who were seen to work alongside the DKP in a similar direction.76 The new tone did not prevent the congress from confirming without dissent the acting leadership in their positions and endorse the one official candidate for every office as has become customary in the DKP. Yet the attempts to respond to new political impulses in West Germany are important. They may also be attempts to satisfy the political expectations of the young. About half the delegates to the 1982 SDAJ congress had only joined the organization during the past two years, an indication of membership fluctuations and of the challenge for the DKP to respond to contemporary political expectations of the young if that membership is to be retained, activated, integrated.77

In the eighties, the DKP finds itself in a situation that it has to try and join any kind of political activity, jump any kind of bandwagon in order not to lose political touch with non-parliamentary West German politics. The fear of being bypassed and losing grip seems to be particularly applicable to recruitment of the young, they constitute, as we saw earlier, the only relevant influx of new members into the DKP. A piece of SDAJ advice to its activists during the 1982 Festival of Youth in Dortmund highlights the predicament for the DKP today:

> In the youth centre, a group of young people discuss that they want to occupy an empty house. Do we turn away from such Spontis, anarchists, freaks just because we don't want to deal with them? no - we join them. We occupy the house with them. We help them to repair-occupy (Instandbesetzen) the damaged rooms, to print leaflets, and to distribute them. We have to be right in the middle of the movement and then travel with them to the festival, because we want to meet other house-occupiers and discuss with them how the whole thing shall go on.78

An educational pamphlet issued by the student organization Spartakus articulates matters more succinctly:

> We do consider the occupation of houses as an appropriate, correct and effective type of struggle. We reject the bourgeois notion of 'right' which regards violation of the private property of speculators and house owners as illegal. The occupation of houses is legitimate through and through, because it is directed against the violence which the owners practice against living space and people. The occupation of houses is, therefore, directed against concrete aims - the protection of living space, it is a radical form of protest and easily understood by the majority of the population. All this does, however, not apply to arson attacks or to throwing molotov cocktails and to aimless riots in cities.[79]

The DKP and its vociferous youth organizations are moving towards more activist forms of politics. The use of violence is deemed justified as long as it serves the "class interest".[80] The DKP chairman, Herbert Mies, included a cautious endorsement of violence and of an association with unorthodox protest movements in the key note speech at the 1981 party congress: "Greens, multi-coloured, non-established, protestors, rebels and alternatives" he cited as "evidence for an urge of a democratic citizens' will (demokratischer Volkswille) to be noticed, a democratic counter-force which strives to organise itself". The critique of political democracy in the Federal Republic has been the backdrop of Communist ideology. Today, this critique generates an activism which includes the use of violence among its approved means of political conduct. Mies found a formula in his congress speech which shows that the DKP has come to endorse the use of protest actions including violence. "Where right becomes wrong, where justice becomes injustice, resistance is a duty".[82] DKP Communism no longer calls the tune of movements and organizations on the left; the advances towards Spontis, alternatives, ecologists, occupiers and violent means of political conflict are attempts not to be outmanoeuvred and bypassed by the main swing of left wing politics.

UTOPIAS OF REVOLUTION: FROM STUDENT MOVEMENT TO COMMUNIST FACTIONS

The German Communist Party solved the dilemma of aiming for revolutionary change in a stable and

Opposition from the Left

prosperous society by retreating to the Marxist-Leninist doctrine laid down by the Soviet and East German Communist parties. The new left, which emerged during the sixties, chose a different path. The overall aim of abolishing the capitalist system was quite similar to Communism. Tactics and fields of action were not. Opposition on the left outside the tentative moves towards a new Socialist party and outside orthodox Communism began to become visible as a Student Movement. In the mid-sixties, conditions at West German universities had deteriorated. The need to expand universities towards mass education and allowing open and equal access clashed with the traditional teaching and research approaches and the organizational structures. Both had remained virtually unchanged since the nineteenth century. The predominance of professors - *Ordinarien* - and their far reaching controls over academic programmes and financial means proved too inflexible to cater for the student numbers and the occupational requirements of the day. Failure rates were high, study programmes disjointed, study periods vastly extended.[83]

The first group to publicise the issue of university reform and develop far reaching suggestions of restructuring higher education was the left-wing student group SDS.[84] In 1961, it had been expelled from the SPD for Marxist leanings. Since then it had survived as a student association with some 2,000 members and an urge to apply Marxist theory to contemporary industrial society. The university, as the immediate environment, seemed an obvious starting point. The fact that many politically motivated students also shared the complaints and experienced the constraints made for a potential political following.[85] In Berlin, protests were supported by several thousand students since the mid sixties. Some joined committees to discuss the introduction of more organized programmes of study, of compulsory introductory courses, of a system of co-determination in university decision making which would involve professorial, non-professorial and technical staff as well as students. These reform drives generated a multi-faceted debate and a considerable degree of change in study programmes and university organization. The principle of co-determination was introduced in some universities, but revoked by the Constitutional Court in 1973.[86] The drive for reform also helped to produce a framework for university legislation in 1976. Some of the liberalising innovations of the student reform

Opposition from the Left

debate were incorporated. By that time, students had abandoned the reform topics and pushed into broader politics. The university was regarded as a forecourt, perhaps a testcase for more substantive, even revolutionary transformations. Thus, the Institute of German Studies in Berlin was renamed Rosa Luxemburg Institute; the Goethe University in Frankfurt bore the name of Karl Marx. The message rang clear. Institutional reform in the university seemed futile and at best half-hearted. The real promise for change lay elsewhere. The war in Vietnam, the regime in Iran, guerilla warfare in South America, all became pressing political themes of the student movement. They were seen as examples where suppression and liberation in society were still clearly visible, where revolution could still take place.

A Mass Movement of Students?
Initially these politics remained the sole concern of the SDS and some affiliated groups on the left who searched for revolution outside Communist party orthodoxy. They were quite segregated from the majority of students. This segregation ended suddenly when a student demonstrator was shot and killed in Berlin.[86] The occasion was a protest against the regime of the Shah of Iran; the victim an ordinary participant who was not in the political forefront. This incident caused a wave of solidarisation among West German students. The shooting occurred in June 1967. For the next few months, a mass movement seemed to exist, based in the universities, a Student Movement. The nucleus consisted of political student groups, who had been active in the university area, most of them supported financially by government money and political parties as relevant for the political education of the student body. The most radical was the SDS; after June 1967, the SPD replacement student organization, Social Democratic University Association SHB, the Humanist Union, the student group of the liberal party, of the protestant church and others merged into a broad Socialist camp. The majority in the so called movement were students who did not belong to any of these associations and who were swept along by the tide of alarm. Several factors combined to give some cohesion to the loose formation of students. In the universities the debate had left the topics of reform. The subterranean politi-

cal aims of the left wingers had utilised the university issues for more generally aimed protests and introduced, with acclaim from fellow students, new methods of protests like sit-ins, teach-ins, go-ins; they had also taken to disrupting, boycotting and eventually publicly criticising the lectures and seminars of university staff. The demands for participation were no longer only demands but reinforced with the protest methods imported from the US civil rights movements: sit-ins in the university administrative offices for example, or go-ins into university senate meetings. The university administration in turn abandoned communication and discussion and drew on the police forces to secure buildings, protect personnel and evict protesters. The escalation of tension within the universities was matched by an escalation of hostilities among the general public. Students were frequently stigmatised as "criminals" in the press, who "deserved to be treated harshly" (BZ 3.6.1967). In the eyes of the Berliner Morgenpost, they were nothing but "Communist street fighters" (3.6.1967) who would be better off in the East. The hostility from the public was noticeable. While old ladies were reported to pour buckets of rubbish over the riot police during the May 1968 unrest in France, the old ladies who watched the protests from their windows in one of the West German cities or in Berlin would side with the police and pour their rubbish over the students. The tendency of the police to enforce law and order at any cost and deter students from further protests by harsh policing was a further factor in increasing political conflict and in forging a temporary cohesion among the students. Although the "movement" did not have a political aim and spread itself over the gambit of leftwing aims put forward by the activists, a kind of negative cohesion was achieved by rejecting the criminalisation through population, university hierarchy and police.[87]

In retrospect, it is doubtful whether the student protests of the sixties should in fact be called a movement. A movement does not need an organizational structure, but it needs an overall aim of some kind: the student movement seemed to be moved largely by the small political groups and associations which had been sucked into it and which pursued their own aims. Those who were the best organized and most active tended to be the ones setting the goals and calling the themes. Eventually, the political themes of SDS vintage prevailed, as did the self-styled leaders who came to fame through the student events.

Utopias of Revolution

From the perspective of the SDS, the events of 1967 and 1968 seemed to be a first stage of the revolutionary mass movement in West Germany. The flame which had been kindled in the universities had spread to the student body as a whole and was bound to spread to society as a whole if only the momentum of the movement could be maintained.

In February 1968, for instance, a Vietnam Congress was held in the Technical University of Berlin and attended by several thousand students from the Federal Republic, from the USA and some European countries. A huge banner was expanded across the hall: "It is the duty of the revolutionary to make the revolution"; the concluding resolution of the congress hit a similar note:

> The opposition stands at the point of transition from protest to political resistance. The representatives of the Socialist youth who have come together in West Berlin are agreed to make their anti-imperialist struggle more concrete and to harden it into active resistance.

The exclamation "long live the Socialist world revolution" ended the resolution and the congress.[88]

The revolutionary romanticism had two distinctly different effects: on the one hand, it alienated the diverse protest against conditions in university and society which had followed the shooting of the student in June 1967. With the political aims of the Student Movement sounding more and more Socialist and taking up the language and concepts of revolutionary Socialism, the ability faded to win the less distinctly political students. The Student Movement became increasingly a movement of the activist circles only. On the other hand, the misconception that a revolution was possible, even imminent, itself generated political activism and the use of violence. In 1968, the Student Movement fell under the control of groups and spokesmen who saw themselves in a Socialist tradition and who regarded the general situation at the end of the sixties as fraught with revolutionary potential.

Opposition from the Left

The campaign against the newspaper publishing house Springer is a good example for the displacement of student protest by Socialist aims. Dismay with press reporting about students and the hostile attitudes created by this reporting were widespread in student circles and beyond. In the late sixties, the Springer concern controlled most of the newspapers in Berlin, had nationwide influence through the daily <u>Die Welt</u> and had amassed a powerful and politically conservative publishing empire.[89] The most influential of its products, the <u>Bild Zeitung</u> had become the number one West German tabloid with a circulation of more than four million copies daily. For students to take up the issue of misreporting and distortion of news in the press could have been a way to alert the public about manipulation of news and public opinion. Even focussing the campaign on Springer could be explained since his newspaper empire was clearly hostile towards the students, their aims and activities. None of these general aims were evident in the campaign of 1968. It was organized under the slogan of Expropriating Springer, a congress duly passed a resolution to that effect,[90] it culminated in attacks on delivery vans and offices of the Springer concern and some of the fiercest street battles since the use of demonstrations by students in the mid sixties. The escalation of the Springer campaign into violence followed from the determination to generate revolution through resistance fighting, i.e. fighting against institutions and organizations in the Federal Republic.

The second shock in the short history of the Student Movement was also a catalyst of violence. In April 1968, only days before the Easter demonstrations against Springer, Rudi Dutschke, one of the SDS spokesmen from Berlin was shot and wounded. Already then, the determination of the SDS in particular to define Socialist aims for all student based activities and steer the presumed mass movement towards a revolution had alienated those who only wanted reform and more democracy. The political groups and activists developed their own orthodoxies with a ferocious debate over varieties of Communism and over the best way to find a mass following for the revolutionary aims. The students, whose support had given rise to the illusion of a mass movement, had turned away. Many found their way into the SPD as members or just as voters.

From Movement to Factions: New Orthodoxies of the Left

Since the early seventies, the active core splintered into several Communist factions, the so called K Gruppen; each adopted a specific brand of Communism, from Maoist to Leninist, from Stalinist to Albania oriented. None amalgamated with the orthodox Communist Party, the DKP which was created in September 1968. The disintegration of the active core of the student movement into warring orthodoxies has been seen as an indication that the critics of authoritarian practices in industrial societies were themselves authoritarian. Those who accused Springer for instance of criminalising opposition were themselves unable to practice democratic tolerance. Brentano sees the tendency towards dogmatism as the cause for the failure of the Student Movement. While students with their intellectual training and their social position outside full occupational and social integration might have been able to evaluate society astutely and initiate change, student acitivists took the shortcut of enshrining their own opinion as the prescribed view for all.[91] Shell shows that the centres which were created as umbrella organizations for a diffuse movement, the Republican Clubs, soon became battle grounds for various orthodoxies where official views were laid down.[92]

By the time the term Extraparliamentary Opposition was coined and suggested some unified force in society, some movement outside the parliamentary structures, the dissolution into warring orthodoxies had already begun. In Berlin alone, three different groups claimed to be the nucleus of a new political party on the left.[93] The catch phrase of the Extraparliamentary Opposition named a disjointed amalgamation: student activists from an SDS faction; Socialists in search of a political party and that mass following students seemed to constitute at the time; representatives of established parties who sought closer links to the student sector. The function of the Republican Club in Berlin had initially been to provide a meeting place for such an amalgamation, a grouping of people without parliamentary aspirations, an extra-parliamentary opposition. It soon assumed the function of a political command post to steer student activities and the conflicting political groups into one direction. Others abandoned the organizational and ideological drives towards a new party or a Socialist umbrella for the more mundane task to win working class support for the Socialist aims. The trade unions had been consistently adverse to student politics. In 1969, a Red Trade Union opposition began to set up red cells within West German unions. In 1980, some four hundred were known to exist with at least three members each.[94]

The push into the working class organizations was a sideline. The splintered Communism which developed from the student movement and the activist core around the SDS and similar student associations had an estimated forty thousand members in the early seventies.[94] Ten years later, membership had dropped to around ten thousand.[95] The upsurge of environmentalism and the wave of anti-nuclear protests in the seventies have been eagerly taken on board by the Communist factions. Activists from all groups joined demonstrations against power stations, often as protagonists of conflict with police. Their journals reflected the new orientation with headlines such as "Actions against the nuclear plans of Bonn"[96] "Occupation of the building site - no nuclear plant in Brokdorf" or "We shall come again: police terror against anti-nuclear protesters". The Green Party and the Peace Movement which emerged around the issues of nuclear energy and the use of nuclear weapons in West Germany in the eighties elicited support from most of the Communist factions,[97] who are still in search of a theme to mobilise the masses and generate the revolution which had seemed imminent over a decade ago. One of the successor organizations of the SDS, the KPD who began with 3,000 members in 1970, decided to disband in June 1980. It had declined to just 400 members, and the third party congress noted that the party had not been able to "live up to its claim to be an avantgarde". Since "the left was unable to give answers to the burning questions of our time", the delegates recommended to the remaining party members "to find another political home among the social-democratic left, elsewhere in the Communist camp, or in the green and coloured movement".[98]

In their drive towards revolutionary politics and a mass party, all new left and Communist groups or factions have been similar failures.

VIOLENCE AND OPPOSITION

The discrepancy between revolutionary utopia and a

society in which social change and democratisation are gradual, institutionalised processes - if they are accomplished at all - was experienced within the Student Movement as a frustration with established channels of participation in politics and society.

This impatience generated some fruitful innovations, in particular initiative groups which predated the citizens' movement of the seventies. In Berlin for instance an action programme envisaged factory cells in all working class districts and seminars about workers control, workshops with technicians in industry, groups for nursery nurses, teachers, rockers, social workers, apprentices. Talk was also of setting up legal advice centres on the resocialisation of prisoners, town planning groups to improve urban living and much more. Most of these ideas did not materialise or could not get enough support from the people they were meant to attract.[99] Some practical approaches were, however, accomplished. To compensate for the shortage of kindergarten and creche places in West Germany, so called <u>Kinderläden</u>, childrens' shops were created, staffed and run in conjunction with the mothers. In contrast to the British playgroup movement, the <u>Kinderläden</u> were training grounds in anti-authoritarian education. They wanted to provide offspring who would no longer adhere to conventional values and behaviour patterns. An announcement for an international childrens' day shows the vage and expansive political aims behind the child-care issue:

> As last year, we again want to organize an International Day of the Child with a children's demonstration and a festival after. Themes could be ... a strike of nursery nurses and the situation in state run nurseries, the situation of working mothers, a pupils' strike, the class oriented school system, teachers' training, working in the suburbs, cleaning up the cities etc.[100]

The red dot actions, against a rise in fares for public transport had a more immediate political sting: in order to force local authorities to keep their fares down, car drivers were asked to carry a red sticker and offer free lifts to dispense with buses and tubes. The campaign proved exceedingly popular and successful: the fare increases were reversed.

Opposition from the Left

Violence in Politics: Some Concepts
The impatience of waiting for change resulted in
other, more controversial refutations of accepted
social norms. In July 1967, Herbert Marcuse visited
a number of universities during a lecture tour of
West Germany. In Berlin, as elsewhere, he addressed
a huge and enthusiastic audience. People came to
hear the famous researcher who had come to speak in
the country which had forced him into emigration.
Some had come to hear words of guidance by a writer
whose theories of one-dimensional existence in the
modern world and in particular of a repressive tolerance which had to be exposed by the use of violent
means were readily short-circuited into a creed.101
Marcuse argued that profound change could only be
accomplished by a "guerilla fight in the big cities
(den Metropolen)". Political opposition which aimed
for change had to stand somewhere outside the established institutions.

> Opposition stands, from the very beginning,
> within range of violence. Right stands against
> right, not just as an abstract assurance, but
> as concrete action. Preaching to refrain from
> the use of violence at all cost only reproduced
> the violence which exists in the institutions
> and in the monopolistic industrial society,
> this violence is concentrated in an unprece-
> dented manner, concentrated in the structure of
> authority which permeates the whole of
> society.102

The message for opposition was to not enter any
alliance with the "system", but practice a "grosse
Verweigerung", a total rejection instead.
    Marcuse meant that such a rejection should gen-
erate a critical analysis of society, and contribute
to insights and enlightenment. This was obliterated
in the scramble for action. Some pushed for action
as Communist-tinted splinter groups: some began to
fight capitalism and industrial society in the guise
of urban guerillas. For them the use of violence
and a defiance of laws and conventions became preconditions of opposition. "Those in power use fear,
which they create through terror, in order to control the proletariat. Why should not the oppressed
also use fear, which they force on their enemies
through terror, in order to finally liberate themselves?"103 The amalgamation of terror, fear, and
liberation made a first public appearance in a number

of leaflets issued by a group in Berlin which called
itself Kommune I. They had annoyed the more orthodox activists by staging political happenings,
intended to ridicule society and those who held
demonstrations and protests. The Kommune leaflets
used a fire which destroyed a department store in
Brussels and killed many people to argue that here
the ordinary citizen could witness what it was like
in Vietnam.[104] To give that Vietnam sensations,
department stores should be set alight.

The Scope of Terrorism

Shortly after several literary critics had testified
in court that the leaflet and its absurd message
were satirical, a fire was in fact started in a
department store in Frankfurt; political rhetoric
and deliberations had given way to criminal activities with the vague political motivation of fright-
ening "the system" into change.[105] Armed struggle,
it was argued, had to precede and create a mass
movement for such change.

> It would be wrong to use armed struggle only
> once the agreement of the masses had been
> secured, since this would mean to dispense
> with the struggle altogether, because the
> agreement of the masses can only be created
> through armed struggle.[106]

The deviation of the Student Movement into terrorism
in West Germany has been well documented. Since
1970, guns were used first for the protection and
liberation from custody of other members of the
group which then adopted the name Red Army Faction
to stake its revolutionary claim. Soon, guns were
used for bank robberies, to resist arrest, and finally to abduct and murder prominent representatives
of West German society. The list of arson, bombings, shootings, murders, robberies and airpiracy is
breathtaking.[107] After training in Palestinian
camps and adopting the concept of urban guerilla
fighting as an approach suitable for the Federal
Republic, violence generated violence. Heinrich
Böll's early warnings that the political aims could
not possibly be achieved by terrorist means and with
weapons[108] was greeted with disdain. Helmut
Gollwitzers appeal to the students and to their
terrorist successors to bear in mind that a boundary
between violence against things and violence against

people could no longer be drawn once stones were thrown, was not heeded. The terrorist rejection of society developed its own momentum which betrayed its political roots and alienated those who had been sympathetic to the students' drive for reform. Gollwitzer, for example, called on the public to help apprehend the criminals after the murder of the President of the law courts in Berlin, Drenkmann in 1974: "The deceiptful and idiotic, politically and humanly equally disgusting murders must end".109 Others spoke out in a similar way and to no avail. For the RAF, events in the Federal Republic in the seventies had become a Volkskrieg, a people's war.

> The armed struggle is not influenced by the headlines in the press. The political military strategy of the urban guerilla reaches from resistance against the fascist nature of parliamentary democracy to the creation of the first regular units of the Red Army in the people's war. The struggle has only just began.110

At the time of writing, the author, Andreas Baader, with Ulrike Meinhof, Gudrin Ensslin, Jan Carl Raspe and a few others the initiator of West German terrorism, was already serving a prison sentence for four murders and other offences. The text was smuggled out of prison; it re-stated the aims and highlighted their inflexibility in a situation where support for a "people's war" was not forthcoming. The Baader text may also be read as an attempt at a pep talk to cement the unity of the co-fighters. Many of the terrorist actions were in fact centred inwards on terrorist factions and their members themselves. The first use of violence, for example, involved freeing Baader from prison in Berlin. Kidnappings and abductions which ended in murders were means to press free comrades who had been arrested or imprisoned. Even the abduction of the President of the Employers Federation, Schleyer, in 1977 was intended as a lever to free the RAF core, as was the hijacking of a Lufthansa plane by German and Palestinian terrorists. In the case of the Berlin politician Peter Lorenz, the blackmail was successful and terrorists were released. In other cases, the banker Jürgen Ponto, the Chief Prosecutor Buback, the abduction and blackmail went wrong and ended in multiple murders. The siege of the Stockholm embassy again was focussed on the group,

Opposition from the Left

the co fighters themselves. The same is true for the bank robberies which served to finance a fairly luxurious life-style, expensive cars and apartments, a well grommed and seemingly integrated appearance. This tendency towards an in-group seclusion seemed to be stronger with the so called second and third generations of terrorists than with the first who still came from the broader context of student politics. Their successors, who adopted names commemorating dead comrades or significant dates such as the Second of June when the student demonstrator was shot in Berlin in 1967, lacked the political - albeit diffuse - goals of Baader, Meinhof, Ensslin and others. Their starting point into terrorism was from the outset to defend and maintain that terrorism against society. Recruitment for that type of commitment seems to have come through various Communist sects and revolutionary cells.

There have been several attempts to explain why well educated and usually well-to-do young people and especially why young women abandoned West German society for terrorism.111 Horst Mahler, an ex-lawyer turned terrorist who began to move away from terrorism while he was imprisoned found a common motivation in a view of the state "as the absolute enemy".112 Gillian Becker suggested that the experience of a fatherless society after Fascism and the obsession with money-making and the economic miracle, bred a desire in some young people to belong to a closely knit group, find individual recognition as they challenge and negate social and political conventions. The confused politics of the left and the notion that opposition or substantive change could not be accomplished in the well organized and administered contemporary world might be more to the point. Revolutionary events, it seemed, could occur only elsewhere, in the so called wars of liberation of the Third World. The capitalist system revealed its true face and what the left called its fascist character through, for example, the American involvement in Vietnam. The craving for such a Vietnam and the craving for decisive events which could expose the "system" and make it collapse were two aspects of the same utopian politics. In practice, it bred terrorism and the endorsement of violence. In May 1972, for example, the RAF announced in Stuttgart that three cars would explode. The political background of this act was too indirect to be stated in a straight forward manner:

Opposition from the Left

> Nobody should be killed in this. The RAF wants
> to prove that it can hit whenever and wherever
> it chooses and remind the people of the bombing
> war of the US imperialists in Vietnam. There-
> fore, off the streets and into the houses ...
> open the windows and into the cellars for an
> hour. The people of Hanoi and many other
> towns do this every day for many hours and
> still have to die.113

Iring Fetscher concluded that German terrorism, its
message and intentions had no repercussions in the
population. They did not articulate anything which
the West German population or even the organized
political left could readily accept. They were
isolated. With slight exaggeration, Heinrich Böll
referred to the six against sixty million.114 They
were not quite so insignificant. Terrorism and the
broader experience of radical opposition on the left
made a considerable impact on West German society
and politics since the early seventies.

West German Democracy in Self-Defence

The left-wing push of the Student Movement, the
eruption of violent conflict with the police, the
challenge to key institutions in politics and
society, and especially the outbreak of terrorism
combined to put West German democracy on alert.
Danger to the democratic consensus seemed to come
from dyed-in-the-wool activists who were determined
to infiltrate and weaken social and political institutions. Danger more openly came from the random
terrorist attacks which might threaten everything
and everybody. Terrorism did not stop at the dozen
or so hard-core men or women, but embraced a network of supporters, suppliers of weapons, false pas-
sports, hired cars and hide-outs. West German
society seemed to be permeated with sympathisers,
people who had or would in principle have assisted
terrorists, without whom terrorism, as guerrilla
fighting, could not survive and who might well themselves turn into terrorists.

West Germany went on the defensive. The political leadership, with the SPD/FDP coalition in
government, devised measures to keep the threats at
bay and to defend the democratic system by an increased efficiency in policing and vigilance. In
1982, the Minister Presidents of the lander and

Opposition from the Left

Chancellor Brandt decided to halt the "march through the institutions" and keep radicals out of the civil service.[115] The Radikalenerlass, radicals' decree was, in principle, nothing more than a reaffirmation of the civil service code which required applicants to endorse the constitutional framework of the Federal Republic, the Free Democratic Basic Order as the Basic Law and the political realities it helped to create have frequently been called.

The measure itself was timed to soothe public concern about radical trends in West Germany. It gained untoward political momentum: the political left detected a Berufsverbot, a process of eliminating everybody from a settled career who ever ventured into protest or criticism of the established order. The apparent anomaly that left-wingers should wish for a pensionable existence in the service of the state is explained when one bears in mind that the whole teaching profession in schools, colleges and universities is staffed by civil servants of the lander.[116] In order to halt the march into the and through the institutions, the influence of radicals on the young, on children and students was to be halted. The sifting and screening methods were soon equalled to those applied by the National Socialists to weed out Jews and others who were unsuitable in Nazi eyes to serve the state. A great number of action groups and intitiatives to stop the Berufsverbot sprang up.[117] They avidly published cases to prove the detestable consequences of the decree and its application. The much quoted case of a Communist locomotive driver who was deemed unfit to perform his duties was only one of many chosen to show how unjust and arbitrary, how undemocratic at the core, the Radikalenerlass was. An important by-product of these protests was to give the radical left a common theme when it had been falling apart in ideological disputes. Berufsverbot became an above-group and above-party focal point which also gained the support of many who advocated tolerance in society without enlisting on the political left.

The German word Berufsverbot was one of the few entering foreign languages without translation, as a hallmark of an exaggerated even antidemocratic reglementation of the citizens by the state. The surveillance activities of the state grew considerably since the early sixties. In response to the student movement and to terrorism, expenditure for the policing rocketed. Police matters have customarily been lander affairs. Yet to answer the challenge of protesters and terrorists, the federal police and surveillance authorities, the Federal Criminal Office, the border police and the Office for the Protection of the Constitution were more generously staffed and financed and involved more directly into police matters and crime detection. Between 1969 and 1978, for example, the Federal Criminal Office grew from 933 posts with an annual budget of 22.4 million to 3,122 posts and a budget of 200 million.[118] The Office for the Protection of the Constitution, apart from moving to larger premises in which up to the minute devices for observation of suspects and identification of political activists were installed, more than trebled its annual budget from about 30 million in 1969 to 134 million in 1978. The border police enjoyed a similar boost. Its annual budget rose from 313 million in 1969 to 989 million in 1978; at the beginning of the seventies, West Germany had about 16,000 border police, at the end nearer 22,000. Special departments for terrorism were opened at the Office for the Protection of the Constitution and at the Federal Criminal Office to concentrate police efforts.

The apprehension of terrorists and other offenders was considerably speeded up by the introduction of computers. A network of data processing systems in the land police headquarters, at border posts, at the centre in Wiesbaden and at the Office for the Protection of the Constitution ensured instant correlation of observations and aided arrests. The advanced technology lent itself also to collect, store and recall data other than those pertaining to known law breakers. The intention to prevent terrorism and single out likely terrorists rather than just finding them after killings, bombings, robberies had been carried out, meant hording masses of data, to develop data banks which would include the majority of people living in West Germany. The danger of a Überwachungsstaat, a big brother state who would register anything a person might do or say which could be seen as critical or rejecting of the political status quo, alarmed many West German citizens and politicians.[119] The tables seemed to be turned: instead of information being produced to question the suitability of citizens for employment by the state, the citizens had to prove their innocence. Participation at demonstrations or protests, subscriptions to certain newspapers and journals, expression in public of radical political views and similar things became stumbling blocks in people's careers even if they lay years back and had never led to active involvement in terrorism or violent political protest.

Six years after its inception, Peter Glotz, former Senator for Sciences in Berlin and subsequently SPD manager, called the radical decree "our biggest mistake".[120] Ulrich Klose at the time SPD mayor of Hamburg complained that the fears of the computerised political scrutiny and the professional consequences bred passivity, apathy, cowardice in the young - or it made them unfairly negative and scathing about this state and its political purpose. Whichever, the radicals decree should be relinquished. The Federal Government moved in this direction in 1979 under the dual pressure of growing scepticsm of the young who regarded Berufsverbote and "Surveillance" as the hallmarks of a state which had nothing but contempt and illiberalism for its citizens;[121] the second dimension of pressure stemmed from the many cases of abuse and exaggerated use of an instrument which had been intended blunt enough to leave confidence in democracy and justice untouched - if anything, strengthen them in the face of terrorism. The backfiring, however, could not fully be mended. The states governed by SPD/FDP coalitions have lessened their practice of scrutiny. They no longer make a routine enquiry. Political activism during childhood or teens will no longer be regarded as a blackspot on the personal file. This lenience, however, has not been adopted by the lander under CDU or CSU governments whose confidence in the radicals decree as a viable instrument of securing democracy and shielding from radicalism of all persuasions has not faltered.[122] The division in the seventies between government and opposition also exacerbated the issues. For the CDU/CSU in opposition the eruption of terrorism, the radicalisation of the left into student movement and Communist groups, the existence of sympathisers in society all added up to prove that the SPD/FDP coalition government served to encourage the worst elements and run Germany to ruin.[123]

To overemphasise the occurance and impact of radicalism or terrorism from the left served to accuse the government of the day of incompetence and an affinity to Communism and Socialism. This opposition policy caught the SPD/FDP government in the dilemma that it could not moderate its appraoch without appearing to encourage terrorism. For possible supporters and followers among the political left and especially among the young, however, the inability of even an SPD/FDP government to do without Berufsverbot, radicals decree and surveillance was one of the factors to undermine the confidence of these groups in the political viability of the SPD or FDP as electoral parties. The strong currents of public opinion which favoured stricter measures and special legislation also left their mark.[124] The anti-terrorist legislation attempted to console public unease and sharpen the available legal and penal instruments.[125] For the CDU/CSU, none of the measures proved decisive enough. For the moderates and the left, they seemed oppressive and sparked off another wave of protest: the attempts to control contacts of convicted terrorists and political offenders were attacked as "Isolationsfolter", although more lenient types of punishment had encouraged imprisoned activists to communicate with the outside world and generate further terrorist actions. Perhaps, the construction of a special prison and court building in Stuttgart Stammheim to try the offenders, signifies the problem for West German democracy. In legal authorities and large segments of the public regarded existing institutions as unsuitable. The opposition from the right dismissed the new institutions as useless patchwork or window dressing, while those on the political left condemned them as proof that West Germany was reverting to the authoritarian and antidemocratic traditions of her past. There seemed to have been two winners from the ill-fated efforts to defend democracy, the CDU/CSU gained an opportunity to propound general principles of law and order and blame the SPD for endangering German society. Even the harsh measures which were taken could be dismissed as half-hearted and doubtful. The other winners were the radical and the extreme left who gained a new and contemporary perspective of rejecting government and opposition. They also gained a contemporary cause and a number of concrete examples to justify their rejection of political democracy, its institutions and conventions in West Germany.

FOOTNOTES

1. e.g. Ralf Dahrendorf, Class and Class Conflict in Industrial Society, London Weidenfels & Nicholson, 1965.
2. e.g. Statistisches Jahrbuch 1980, p. 432-433. Also: Facts and Figures. A comparative Survey of the FRG and GDR, Presse und Informationsamt der Bundesregierung (ed.) Bonn 1981,

pp. 44-45.
3. Ossip K. Flechtheim, Die KPD in der Weimarer Republik, Frankfurt, (Europäische Verlagsanstalt), 1964, pp. 264 ff.
4. Martin McCauley, "The Rebirth of Democracy. Political Parties in Germany after 1945-1949", in Döring and Smith (eds.), Party Government and Political Culture, Macmillan 1982, pp. 44 ff.
5. Christian Bockemühl, "25 Jahre nach dem KPD Urteil. Historische und aktuelle Überlegungen" in Aus Politik und Zeitgeschichte B 46, 1981 p. 6-7.
6. See Der Spiegel 23, 1977 pp. 157 ff.
7. Rolf Ebbighausen, Peter Kirchoff, "Der angepasste Klassenkampf: Organisation und Politik der DKP zwei Jahre nach ihrer Neukonstituierung" in PVS 11, 1970 p. 556.
8. Helmut Bilstein/Sepp Binder/Manfred Elsner/ Hans-Ulrich Klose/ Ingo Wolkenhaar, Organisierter Kommunismus in der Bundesrepublik, Opladen (Leske) 1975 p. 13; also Manfred Rowold, Im Schatten der Macht, Düsseldorf (Droste) 1974, p. 171. Ernst Richert, Die radikale Linke von 1945 bis zur Gegenwart, (Berlin) (Colloquium Verlag) 1969.
9. Rowold p. 136 f. Also Ossip K. Flechtheim. Dokumente zur parteipolitischen Entwicklung, Berlin, (Dokumenten Verlag) 1966 Vol. V. pp. 6-35.
10. e.g. Notstand der Demokratie. Kongress in Hannover 1967, Voltaire Flugschriften 1967. For the origins of the Notstand legislation see Carl Nedelmann "Die Gewalt des politischen Staatsschutzes" in Gerd Schäfer/Carl Nedelmann (eds.), Der CDU Staat. Analysen zur Verfassungswirklichkeit der Bundesrepublik vol. 1 Frankfurt, (Suhrkamp) 1976 pp. 174-210.
11. Summary in Innere Sicherheit 62, 1982 pp. 4 ff.
12. For details see the chapter on the DKP in Rowold, also Helmut Bärwald, Deutsche Kommunistische Partei. Die kommunistische Bündnispolitik in Deutschland, Köln 1970.
13. Herbert Mies, "Gedanken zum 10. Jahrestag der Gründung der DKP" in Max Schäfer (ed.) in Die DKP. Gründung, Entwicklung, Bedeutung. Verlag Marxistische Blätter, Frankfurt 1978 p. 16.
14. Kurt Bachmann "Die Konstituierung der Deutschen Kommunistischen Partei" in Die DKP ibid., p. 169.
15. Helmut Bärwald, "Die DKP. Ursprung, Weg, Ziel" in Aus Politik und Zeitgeschichte B8, 1969

pp. 9 ff.
16. Bilstein ibid., p. 14.
17. Manfred Kapluck, later district chairman of the DKP Ruhr-Westfalen in Sozialistische Hefte No. 3 1968, also Die Welt 30.4.1968.
18. For details see Bärwald, Die Kommunistische Partei; good summary in Rowold, ibid. pp. 165 ff.
19. See Berliner Extra Dienst 13.11.1968: here the purpose of the Socialist Office is defined as creating a new left-wing party. The new Communist party is not accepted as the bridgehead of the Socialist left.
20. Good summary in Bilstein ibid., p. 15.
21. Betrifft Verfassungschutz 1971, p. 65.
22. Bilstein ibid., p. 15.
23. Frankfurter Allgemeine Zeitung 12.12.1968.
24. Bilstein ibid.
25. Betrifft 1968, p. 61.
26. Innere Sicherheit 58, 1981, p. 3.
27. "DKP: Gewisse Stagnation" in Der Spiegel 25, 1977.
28. Betrifft 1980 p. 66, also Innere Sicherheit 47, 1979, p. 4. UZ 28.10 and 18.11.1979 mention 1,400 grass root organizations and 187 district organizations of the DKP.
29. Quoted in Bilstein ibid., p. 106.
30. Karl Heinz Nötzel, member of the DKP executive explaining the statutes at the party congress in 1969. Bärwald ibid., p. 68 f. reports that originally a centralized system of nominations and elections for party delegates had been envisaged. In an open controversy this had to be amended and decisions about nomination had to be left to the branches and grass root organizations. Four years later, the executive could abolish this innovation in democracy and regain control over nominations at all party levels. This effectively reduced the possible role of branches and the chances of members to gain nomination to party congresses through local party work.
31. Betrifft 1978. Also Der Spiegel 44, 1978 p. 60.
32. Rainer Kunz/Herbert Maier/Theo Stammen (eds.), Programme der politischen Parteien in der Bundesrepublik, München (Bayrische Landeszentrale für politische Bildung) 1975 p. 308 ff.
33. Bürgerliche oder sozialistische Demokratie. Pluralismus - Phrase und Wirklichkeit. Studienmaterial für das 3. Thema im Bildungsjahr der DKP 1977/78, ed. Parteivorstand der DKP, Düsseldorf

1977 p. 6.
  34. Siegfried Hergt (ed.) Parteiprogramme. Grundsatzprogrammatik und aktuelle politische Ziele von SPD, CDU, CSU, FDP, DKP, NPD, Leverkusen, (Heggen) 1978 p. 225.
  35. "Wahlprogramm 1972" in Kunz et. al. ibid., p. 316.
  36. See Betrifft 1971 p. 50.
  37. Eugen Loderer "Die DGB Gewerkschaften haben keine kommunistische Wurzel" in Handelsblatt 13/14.3.1981.
  38. Karl Hauenschild "Zur Situation und zur Diskussion in der und um die IG Chemie-Papier-Keramik" in Gewerkschaftliche Umschau 1, 1981, Dokumentation p. VI.
  39. See Spiegel 23, 1977 p. 165.
  40. Details compiled by the so called Mandatsprüfungskommission which reports on composition of every party congress. Figures included in the summaries in Betrifft, and in the accounts of party congresses in Innere Sicherheit.
  41. Gerd Walter, Theoretischer Anspruch und politische Praxis der DKP. Eine Analyse am Beispiel der Betriebsarbeit, Meisenheim (Hain), 1973 p. 26.
  42. Innere Sicherheit 58, 1981, p. 3.
  43. Ibid.
  44. Spiegel 23. 1977 p. 160.
  45. ibid.; Betrifft 1980 reported that about 35% of DKP members were workers, the others students, teachers, university lecturers and members of the professions. For the late twenties, Flechtheim suggested that the proportion of industrial workers among the membership was as low as 20-22% in 1931. Die KPD ibid. p. 317.
  46. See UZ no. 283, 6.12.1979.
  47. Betrifft 1980 p. 66.
  48. See Fritz Vilmar/Wolfgang Rudzio, "Politische Apathie und Kaderpolitik. Zum Streit um kommunistische Einflusstrategien und ihre Wirkungen in Gewerkschaften und Hochschulen", in Aus Politik und Zeitgeschichte 46, 1981 p. 37.
  49. In detail in Ossip K. Flechtheim/Wolfgang Rudzio /Fritz Vilmar et. al. Der Marsch der DKP durch die Institutionen. Sowjetmarxistische Einflusstrategien und - ideologien, Frankfurt, (Fischer) 1980.
  50. Vilmar/Rudzio, Politische Apathie und Kaderpolitik, ibid. pp. 32-33.
  51. Thus the chairman of the trade union for wood and plastics, Goergi in Informationsdienst

Junges Wort 8.4.1981 p. 1, quoted in Vilmar /Rudzio p. 33.

52. D. Staubert/H. Tornow, "Hatz auf linke Kollegen" in Der Stern 12, 1981 p. 220.

53. e.g. Kleine Anfrage der CDU, BT Drucksache 8/3070; answer reprinted in Innere Sicherheit 21, 1979 pp. 4-7; included in the Kleine Anfrage was a list of 28 people who at the time occupied party functions in the DKP and held union positions at various levels.

54. Walter, Theoretischer Anspruch und politische Praxis p. 27.

55. Rowold ibid. p. 172.

56. Betrifft 1980, also Betrifft 1972 p. 69.

57. Betrifft 1969 and from then on annually.

58. DKP Bezirksvorstand Rheinland - Westfalen (ed.), Kurzanalyse von Betriebszeitungen der DKP aus dem Bezirk Rheinland -Westfalen, Düsseldorf November 1970 p. 1.

59. Bilstein ibid. p. 33.

60. F.U. Breitspecher, Linksextremistische Betriebszeitungen Berichte des Deutschen Industrieinstituts no. 6, 1971 p. 54.

61. Bilstein, ibid., quoting from a DKP manual on Betriebszeitungen.

62. "So werden unsere Zeitungen besser. Arbeitshilfen für junge Leute" in Elan. Magazin für junge Leute, Dortmund, quoted in Walter, ibid. pp. 96-97.

63. Betrifft 1980 p. 68.

64. Rowold ibid. p. 172 f.

65. Kunz et. al. ibid. p. 306. Also regular reports in Innere Sicherheit and annually in Betrifft.

66. Hermann Gautier, "Die Partei der Arbeiterklasse, der Jugend - eine einigende Kraft" in Die DKP ibid. p. 203.

67. The SDAJ journal Elan has a circulation of 40,000; see Betrifft 1980 p. 70.

68. Jutta von Freyberg, from the university of Marburg; the volume also includes useful biographical notes on the DKP leaders of the first ten years, Die DKP pp. 324-327.

69. Data in Betrifft since 1971; for 1980 ibid. p. 86.

70. See Chapter 5; the calculations based on the data by Wolfgang Falke ibid.

71. Herbert Mies, "Gedanken zum zehnten Jahrestag der Gründung der DKP", in Die DKP p. 38.

72. In Kölnische Rundschau 5.6.1982 also

"Friedensbewegung: Kommunisten immer dabei" in Der Arbeitgeber No. 10/34, 1982 p. 626.
73. Report about joint actions in Innere Sicherheit 62, 1982 p. 4.
74. See below the chapter on the Green Party and the Peace Movement.
75. See Vilmar/Rudzio, ibid. p. 21; also Krause/Lehnert/Scherer, Zwischen Resignation und Revolution. Politische Grundströmungen, Alternativkultur und Hochschulaktivitäten in der Studentenschaft, Bonn 1980.
76. Report in Der Arbeitgeber 6/34, 1982 p. 280.
77. Bericht der Mandatsprüfungskommission, VII. Bundeskongress der SDAJ vom 6. und 7. März 1982, Kongress Information No. 13, Düsseldorf 1982.
78. Innere Sicherheit 59, 1982 p. 4.
79. Ibid.
80. Marxistische Blätter 2, 1982; also UZ 30.3. 1982. Innere Sicherheit 62. 1982, p.2 also brings material on Communism and violence: "For us marxists, violence means merely using pressure. In this sense, violence is a specific way or pursuing the class interest".
81. Protokoll des 6. Parteitages der DKP, Mai 1981, Düsseldorf 1981 p. 83; see Innere Sicherheit 62, 1982 p. 2 f.
82. Ibid.
83. See Dietrich Goldschmidt, "Psychological Stress: A German Case Study" in Julian Nagel, (ed), Student Power, Merlin Press London 1969 pp. 59-72.
84. In 1961, the SDS published Hochschule in der Demokratie; as a book in 1964 (Luchterhand).
85. Hans Schoeps/Christopher Dannemann, Die rebellischen Studenten. Elite der Demokratie oder Vorhut eines linken Faschismus? München, (Bechtle) 1968.
86. e.g. Hartmut Häussermann et. al. Die Rebellen von Berlin. Studentenpolitik an der Freien Universität, Köln,(Kiepenheuer & Witsch)1967; the ruling of the Constitutional Court in Horst Säcker, Das Bundesverfassungsgericht. Oberster Hüter der Verfassung. München (Bayrische Landeszentrale für politische Bildung) 1977 pp. 113-117.
87. See Wolfgang Zeidler, "Ausserparlamentarische Bewegungen. Demonstrationsrecht und Widerstand" in Aus Politik und Zeitgeschichte B 10/1969 pp. 3-13.
88. Februar 1968. Tage die Berlin

erschütterten. Europäische Verlagsanstalt (res novae provokativ), Frankfurt 1968 pp. 86-88. The congress is also discussed in Peter Mosler, Was wir wollten, was wir wurden. Studentenrevolte zehn Jahre danach. Reinbeck (Rowohlt) 1977 p. 46.

89. For Springer press see Hans Dieter Müller, Press Power. A study of Axel Springer, Macdonald & Co., 1969.

90. Materialien zur Diskussion: Springer enteignen? Presse- Arbeitskreis des Republikanischen Club e.V. Westberlin, Berlin, (Oberbaumpresse) n.d. (1968).

91. Margherita von Brentano, "Privilegierter Protest? Chancen und Gefahren einer studentischen Oppositionsbewegung" in Hans-Gerd Schumann (ed.) Die Rolle der Opposition in der Bundesrepublik, Darmstadt, Wissenschaftliche Buchgesellschaft 1976 pp. 348-357.

92. Kurt Shell, "Extraparliamentary Opposition in Postwar Germany" in Comparative Politics 2 No.4, July 1970 pp. 677 ff.

93. Betrifft 1969 p. 30.

94. Bilstein ibid. pp. 80-104.

95. Betrifft 1972, p. 55 and Betrifft 1980, p. 55.

96. UZ 218, 20.9.1977; KPD Rote Hilfe: Regionalkommittee Wasserkante 1977: Dokumentation zum Kampf gegen das Atomkraftwerk Brokdorf, KDP/ML 1977.

97. Innere Sicherheit 54, 1980 p. 13.

98. Innere Sicherheit 53, 1980 pp. 4-5.

99. Rüdiger Proske/Jörn Klamroth/Heiner Thoemen, Modelle und Elemente künftiger Gesellschaft Reinbek (Rowohlt) 1971 pp. 71-73.

100. Ibid. p. 40.

101. Good evaluation of the impact of Marcuse by Werner Birkenmeier, "Ist die Frankfurter Schule an allem schuld? Anmerkungen zum Verhältnis von kritischer Theorie und Terrorismus" in Hat sich die Republik verändert? Terrorism im Spiegel der Presse, ed. Arbeitskreis Öffentlichkeitsarbeit gegen den Terrorismus im Bundesministerium des Innern, Bonn 1978 pp. 112 ff.

102. Wulf Schönbohm et. al., Die herausgeforderte Demokratie. Deutschlands Studenten zwischen Reform und Revolution, Mainz (Hase & Köhler) 1968, quoting verbatim from Marcuse's Berlin speech pp. 75-76. See also Herbert Marcuse, "Repressive Toleranz" in Robert Paul Wolff, Barrington Moore, Herbert Marcuse, Kritik der reinen

Toleranz, Frankfurt (Suhrkamp) 1965 pp. 93-128 esp. 127.
103. Kollektiv RAF, Über den bewaffneten Kampf in Westeuropa, Rotbuch 29, Berlin (Wagenbach) n.d. p. 40.
104. Reprinted in Mosler ibid. p. 110 ff.
105. Iring Fetscher, Terrorismus und Reaktion, Frankfurt, Europäische Verlagsanstalt 1978 pp. 33 ff.
106. Ibid., p. 43.
107. Der Minister und der Terrorist. Spiegel Gespräch zwischen Gerhard Baum und Horst Mahler, Hamburg (Spiegel Buch) pp. 158-222. Also Manfred Funke, (ed.) Terrorismus. Untersuchungen zur Strategie und Struktur revolutionärer Gewaltpolitik, Bonn,(Schriftenreihe der Bundeszentrale für politische Bildung)1977 pp. 331-365.
108. In Der Spiegel 41, 1977 p. 40.
109. Ibid.
110. Der Spiegel 42, 1977 p. 52.
111. The government commissioned a research project on the curricula vitae of terrorists. See also Jillian Becker, Hitler's Children, Panther Books 1978.
112. Der Minister und der Terrorist ibid. p. 16.
113. Quoted in Walter Althammer, Bert Rombach, Gegen den Terror. Texte und Dokumente, Hans Seidel Stiftung, München 1977 p. 79.
114. Der Spiegel 3, 1972: "Ulrike Meinhof: Gnade oder Freies Geleit".
115. Reprinted in Streitbare Demokratie. Informationen zur politischen Bildung 179, Bonn 1979 p. 19; See also Phillip Hablutzel, Some Recent Developments in Civil Liberties in the Federal Republic of Germany: Radicals in the Civil Service. Paper delivered at the Conference Group on German Politics at the Xth World Congress International Political Science Association, Edinburgh 1976.
116. See Roger Tilford in WEP May 1981 pp. 149-51.
117. Several actions groups collected and co-ordinated information and campaigns about the so called Berufsverbote, e.g. Aktionskommittee gegen Berufsverbote in Berlin; Initiative Weg mit den Berufsverboten in Hamburg. The 2. Russell Tribunal was held about Berufsverbote in Frankfurt in 1978.
118. All figures Leistungsbilanz Innere Sicherheit 1969-1978, Bonn 1979 p. 16-33.
119. e.g. Jochen Bölsche, (ed.) Der Weg in den Überwachungsstaat, Spiegel Buch Rowohlt 1979.

120. Der Spiegel 43, 1978 p. 49.
121. Grundsätze für die Prüfung der Verfassungstreue. Neufassung vom 17.1.1979, Bulletin 6, 19.1.1979, p. 45-47. Also Bulletin 131, 14.11.1978 pp. 1221-1223: Verfassungstreue-Prüfung im öffentlichen Dienst.
122. An excellent summary of the controversy in Gegenwartskunde Sonderheft 1 1979 pp. 93-104.
123. See Heiner Geissler, Der Weg in die Gewalt. Geistige und gesellschaftliche Ursachen des Terrorismus und seine Folgen, München, (Olzog) 1978; also a collection of quotations issued by the CSU which linked prominent politicians, journalists, writers with terrorism in the Federal Republic, München 1978.
124. "Wen die Bevölkerung für einen Sympathisanten hält", in FAZ 17.12.1977 p. 4.
125. See Die Anti Terror Debatten im Parlament 1974-1978, Zusammengestellt und kommentiert von Hermann Vinke und Gabriele Witt, Reinbek (Rowohlt) 1978.

SUGGESTED READING

Helmut Bilstein et. al., Organisierter Kommunismus in der Bundesrepublik, Opladen (Leske) 1975
Jillian Becker, Hitler's Children. Panther Books 1978
Die Anti-Terror Debatten im Parlament. Zusammengestellt und kommentiert von Hermann Vinke und Gabriele Witt, Reinbek (Rowohlt) 1978
Die DKP. Gründung Entwicklung, Bedeutung, Frankfurt (Verlag Marxistische Blätter) 1978
Februar 1968. Tage die Berlin erschütterten, Frankfurt (Europäische Verlagsanstalt) 1968
Iring Fetscher, Terrorismus und Reaktion, Frankfurt (Europäische Verlagsanstalt) 1978
Ossip K. Flechtheim et. al. Der Marsch der DKP durch die Institutionen, Frankfurt (Fischer) 1980
Manfred Funke (ed.), Terrorismus. Untersuchungen zur Strategie und Struktur revolutionärer Gewaltpolitik, Bonn (Bundeszentrale für politische Bildung) 1977
Hat sich die Republik verändert? Terrorismus im Spiegel der Presse, ed. BMI, Bonn 1978
Hartmut Häussermann et. al., Die Rebellen von Berlin, Köln (Kiepenheuer & Witsch) 1967
Krause/Lehnert/Scherer, Zwischen Resignation und Revolution. Politische Grundströmungen,

Alternativkultur und Hochschulaktivitäten der
    Studentenschaft, Bonn (Neue Gesellschaft) 1980
Peter Mosler, Was wir wollten, was wir wurden.
    Studentenrevolte zehn Jahre danach, Reinbek
    (Rowohlt) 1977
Ernst Richert, Die radikale Linke von 1945 bis zur
    Gegenwart, Berlin (Colloquium) 1969
Manfred Rowold, Im Schatten der Macht, Düsseldorf
    (Droste) 1974

Chapter Eight

OPPOSITION FROM THE RIGHT: NEONAZISM IN WEST GERMAN SOCIETY

The shape and impact of opposition from the right within or against the political system of the Federal Republic is the theme of this chapter. We shall focus on the permeation of ideas, on the organization of groups and parties, who all advocate political alternatives which are in some way reminiscent of Nationalsocialism or which advocate the replacement of democratic government by a leadership state. It is not possible to extract a cohesive ideology of right-extremism. Nationalsocialism itself was a conglomerate of many sources and diverse aims.[1] Its successor ideologies are no different.

WHAT CONSTITUTES NEONAZISM?

For contemporary adaptations of Nationalsocialism and ideologies of the extreme right, two aspects seem to be central: nationalism and racism. The nationalist component is shared by extremists and conservatives on the right, racism is the hallmark of the extremists alone.[2] This distinction has often been blurred. When for instance political criticism equates the CDU or the CSU with fascism, the essential borderline between the right and the extreme right has been obliterated.[3] Case studies of the campaign against Ostpolitik in the early seventies and of periodicals of the right and the extreme right have revealed stunning similarities of argument and approach on issues of nationalism.[4] This does not apply to racism. The extreme right is nationalist, but it is also racist. The decisive focus on nation is complemented by a stigmatization of social groups which are typecast as enemies. Wehler argued in his theory of social imperialism that one of the hallmarks of German nationalism at the time of the Wilhelmine Empire was the mechanism of negative integration, i.e. singling out foreigners and in particular Jews as enemies of nation and state. The device of identifying enemies within - the proletariat and its political organizations also came into this category - helped to blur unresolved social and political conflicts within German society.[5] Nationalsocialism perfected the practice of negative integration into a policy of discrimination and persecution which culminated in the Holocaust, the mass murder of those who had been branded as enemies. The racist focus of Neonazism today is partly antisemitic and partly directed against foreign workers in West Germany, the so called guestworkers. To quote from a summary evaluation by the Office for the Protection of the Constitution:

> Right extremism uses a nationalism which refutes the ideas of coexistence among different peoples as a starting point for biased accusations and insinuations against foreign states and their members, denying their basic rights as human beings. The open or candid revival of antisemitism is incompatible with the dignity of mankind and other basic human rights. It is the obligation of the state to respect and protect these rights.[6]

It would be superficial to claim that Nationalsocialism were merely repeated in right extremism and in Neonazi tendencies and organizations in the Federal Republic. In the sense of direct succession, Nationalsocialism has, of course, been excluded from post-war developments. One of the few points the Allied Powers could unanimously endorse during their World War II cooperation concerned the destruction of the system of Nationalsocialist organizations and the principle of prosecuting those who had been perpetrators of Nationalsocialism.[7] The Basic Law incorporated the ban of any Nationalsocialist party although the principle of punishment of the perpetrators has been less avidly adhered to.[8] When the Federal Constitutional Court came into operation in 1951, one of its tasks was to scrutinize developments on the right and to prevent a reorganization of Nationalsocialist or similar antidemocratic groups. Since then, four organizations have been banned for right-extremist agitation.[9]

Opposition from the Right

The modest number of party bans might suggest that Nazism, Neonazism and related political positions do not have a place in the remade political culture of post-war Germany. From within Germany, the whole problem of right extremism has been resolutely attributed to the past as if 1945 had been a new leaf in history, a zero hour of society. Sontheimer characterized the determination to locate Nazism and related political practice in the past alone as one way to evade the question of continuities into the post-war democratic state.

> The Nazi state appeared as an accident of German history, a devilish abberation, which was really caused by Hitler alone, not by the German citizens, not by their political parties, not by the civil service, not by the universities, the churches or other social institutions which had contributed to the failure of the Weimar democracy and to the rise of Nationalsocialism.[10]

From outside Germany, the problem of continuity has been regarded with more concern. There was the question of a renewed acceptance of former Nazi activists and their integration as functionaries and dignitaries into the democratic state.[11] There was the further question of a new nationalism, even new racism taking shape in post-war Germany which could not easily be shrugged off as the desperate attempt of intransigent oldtimers to restore the past. Neonazism has recruited newcomers who are too young to have personally been involved in Nationalsocialism, young people who received their political education and their socialization in the new and democratic Germany. In short, the cries of alarm that West German democracy might be undermined by a network of old Nazis or succumb to an onslaught of the new, may be illmatched to the place of right extremism and its prospects. That right extremism survived and received new impulses as Neonazism warrants investigation, if only to explain why West Germany did not, as one of the lessons from the Nationalsocialist experience, develop a watertight political culture in which Nationalsocialism and similar ideologies are altogether discredited.

Opposition from the Right

THE ANTISEMITIC INCIDENTS OF 1959/60

In the winter of 1959/60, a wave of antisemitic offences forced public attention for the first time on the question of survival or revival of Nationalsocialist or related attitudes. At the time, antisemitic slogans were scrawled on synagogues, Jewish cemetaries were vandalized. The unheralded outburst was greeted with indignation and embarrassment. Chancellor Adenauer went on radio and television to emphatically condemn what had happened: "What was done is a disgrace and a crime. The Federal Government in whose name I speak, hopes that this will meet with rigorous pubishment by the courts".[12] In a similar vein, the Vice President of the Bundestag, Carlo Schmid, referred to "those abominable characters" who "brought disgrace on the country".[13] Although disturbing, the incidents did not seem to signify much. The culprits were dismissed as hooligans whose deeds could not reflect the views of the German people. Adenauer for instance concluded:

> The German people have shown that these ideas find no response among them. The majority of German people served Nationalsocialism during the period of its sway only under the heavy yoke of dictatorship. Every German was by no means a Nationalsocialist. I think that this fact should gradually become recognized in other countries. Neither Nationalsocialism nor dictatorship had any roots in the German people, and a few incorrigibles who still exist will not achieve anything.[14]

The detailed report about the offences and arrests which was published as a Government White Paper underlined the importance which was attached to the incidents. It also fails to confirm the view that a few incorrigibles had let fly, or that the occurrences could be aptly explained as hooliganism.
    Nearly seven hundred offences were reported, 234 people were arrested. Of these, more than half were under twenty years of age. Their participation in antisemitic offences cannot be explained as an old timer syndrome. These young offenders were not normally members of organizations or groups on the extreme right; searches of their homes, however, revealed that most had hoarded Nazi items, posters,

books, emblems. In other words, the "hooligans" of 1959/60 had hardly acted spontaneously. They were committed, if not addicted, to Nazi ideologies in a more fundamental sense.[15] Even without organizational ties, they can be identified as Neonazis.

The statistical account in the White Paper gave another unexpected insight: 41% of those apprehended were skilled or unskilled workers.[16] The sample is, of course, too small to arrive at reliable conclusions. Yet, it may be stated in a tentative manner that the social spectrum of Neonazism in the Federal Republic seemed to be slanted towards the lower status groups, the lower paid and lower educated. Compared with the NSDAP support of the early thirties, the appeal of Neonazism has shifted. Then, the better educated with middle class occupations and the old middle class of farmers, shopkeepers, artisans were in the forefront. In Neonazism, it seems, two strands overlap: the former Nazis who have been activated again and who may be more middle class in their social positions; and the younger age groups who frequently belong to the working class or similar status groups. Neonazism seems to be able to draw on a contingent of young, lower skilled followers, offspring of post-war Germany, who articulate their opposition to society and their own experience of society in a new-Nationalsocialist, a Neonazi mould.

THE NPD AND THE PROSPECTS OF RIGHT-EXTREMIST POLITICS

The determination of the Allies to obstruct anti-democratic parties through their licencing prerogatives made it difficult for the extreme right to organize. Before they could set up a political party, much of their potential electorate had already chosen other parties; only those who could not accept the political realities of the Federal Republic - former Nationalsocialist functionaries who had lost status and positions, some refugees who had been socially and economically demoted, were swung to the right. In the First Bundestag, for which a regional 5% clause operated, the right extremist DRP won five seats. It was strongest in the Northern region, Lower Saxony and Schleswig Holstein. The party was a makeshift alliance of various strands on the right and soon fell apart. It unleashed the Socialist Reichsparty, which refused to accept the political realities of the Federal Republic and campaigned for the continuation of the German Reich.[17] In the 1951 land elections in Lower Saxony, it gained 11% of the vote, but was banned one year later. Then, only the DRP remained as a party on the extreme right. It gradually declined in voting strength and political impact. Instead of competing in the political arena alone, right extremism moved more and more into publishing during the fifties. A network of book clubs and publishing houses was created, frequently headed by former SS officers or Nazi writers.[18] Since the fifties to this day, a steady stream of pro-Nazi literature, of reprints and hagiographies of war exploits and war heroes appeared in the Federal Republic. Initially, these publications were confined to their own distribution system. In 1966 for instance, one of these publishers was expelled from the Frankfurt bookfair.[19] Gradually the presence of that type of publication has aroused less alarm and in 1974, several right extremist publishing houses were represented at the Frankfurt book fair.[20] The borderline between the right fringe publishers and so called respectable ones has become increasingly blurred during the seventies. Books, records and facsimile reprints of Nationalsocialist materials and positions were produced more freely and marketed as historical documentations. Department stores, station bookstalls and newsagents have become popular outlets in addition to the bookclub network which still exists. Since the fifties, the booklet <u>Landser</u> has been published and enjoyed a mass circulation. By 1978, over one thousand titles has appeared, at least one hundred million copies altogether. <u>Landser</u> contains fictionalized accounts of war, its idealizes the deeds and the presumed courage of the German soldier, the superiority of German weapons and presents World War II as an exciting adventure and a great hour for the German nation.[21] Despite the demise of political organizations and the dismemberment of the SRP, Nationalsocialist and related ideologies had not fully disappeared. They had voices without tangible organizations. Politically the CDU had absorbed the former right-wing vote. Only organizational splinters remained.

    In this state of organizational weakness, a new party was founded as a so called "national opposition". The NPD, National Democratic Party of Germany, was created in November 1964 as a self-proclaimed "fourth big party" which was determined to shape "the future of Germany and Europe".[22] One of the intentions had been to bring under one political umbrella the splintered right, all those groups, factions, parties who stood to the right of the CDU/CSU.[23] This has not been achieved. The new venture consisted largely of two founder groups: the German Reichsparty DRP and the German Party DP. Both were in considerable disarray at the time of their merger.

NPD Origins and Organizations

In 1961, the DRP suffered a split when so called neutralists who endorsed political neutrality as a precondition of German national revival, proceeded to found a new party, the German Freedom Party (DFP). Although the competitor remained luckless, the DRP was weakened, not least because it had already lost some 20,000 members since the early fifties.[24] Electoral results were equally depressing. In the 1961 Federal Elections, the DRP polled only 0.8%. An even clearer signal of decline was the loss of half its electorate in the land elections of Lower Saxony in 1963. Lower Saxony had been a traditional stronghold of the party, i.e. it had been represented in the land parliament from the beginning. In the early sixties, political prospects of the DRP were visibly shattered. In contrast to the membership losses and electoral disasters, the party apparatus remained stable and functioning. The party leadership continued in office, unperturbed. The party paper <u>Reichsruf</u> continued to appear in 16,000 weekly copies. It was produced by the Schütz publishing house, one of the right-wing network with SS connections. Schütz, a member of the DRP executive, also published the <u>Deutsche Wochenzeitung</u>, a weekly which allegedly had no party leanings. It had a readership of about 12,000 per week and may have been read outside the DRP boundaries.[25] Despite the decline, the DRP retained a well functioning publishing sector in addition to the network of branches and offices. In short, while the political viability of the DRP was doubtful by the early sixties, its organizational machinery was intact.

The other partner of the NPD alliance, the <u>Deutsche Partei</u> was less well endowed. Originally, the DP started out as a regional party for Lower Saxony; it had to broaden its political scope once the five percent hurdle was based on the national rather than the regional vote. The hastily reoriented party called itself the German Party and cooperated with the CDU in government coalitions. Yet, its ideological proximity to the CDU made it a prime target for amalgamation; in the late fifties, all DP ministers and the bulk of the membership joined the CDU formally. The rump organization which was left behind, tried to survive by forming an alliance with the similarly decimated refugee party BHE under the name All German Party, Gesamtdeutsche Partei. This venture had little success, not least because only some of the German Party joined the new venture, others decided to recreate the original German Party in 1962.[26] When this old-new DP competed for votes in the 1963 land elections in Lower Saxony it suffered a crushing defeat with the vote plummeting from 12.7% to 2.7%. In Bremen, the DP tried to halt the tide of decay by entering into an alliance with the DRP. This liaison was relatively successful, the duo clinched 5.2% of the vote and four seats in the Bremen Senate in 1963. This was only one third of the DP's former representation, but clearly better than the Lower Saxony devastation.[27]

In retrospect, the cooperation in Bremen was praised as a "model" which paved the way towards a new political alliance, the NPD. The more conservative element, the German Party, seemed to have retained sóme electoral appeal while the extremist element had the apparatus, the press backing and the financial resources to mount a campaign and to run a party. The format of cooperation in the new party, NPD, followed the same pattern. The chairman of the German Party, Thielen, was elected chairman of the new party. In three of the eleven NPD land organizations, the German Party also provided the chairman. Despite a seemingly strong place in the NPD leadership, the German Party had little influence. In all land organizations and on the national level, party organization and control remained firmly in DRP hands. While the number one tended to be from a conservative or right-wing moderate group, i.e. politically not conspicuous, the number two everywhere, and most of the remaining party executive came from the tightly knit DRP body of functionaries. In the NPD directorate of 1964-1965, nearly half came from the DRP. The largest contingent, however, were former Nationalsocialists for whom the newly founded NPD seemed a suitable

Opposition from the Right

political platform. Of the NPD leadership of the first year, 72% had already been active in the Nazi party in functionary positions. 55% had joined before Hitler came to power, 17% after 1933. Only 28% of the founding fathers of the NPD did not have an active Nazi past.[28]

The Nazi affiliations helped to make the party relatively well known in a short time, since it attracted a great deal of comment, criticism and fear among political observers in Germany and in other countries. The mere re-labelling of the existing DRP organization also enabled the NPD to appear well established in a short time. By September 1965, it had organizations in all eleven lander, it maintained 66 regional offices, 336 district offices and 240 local branches. For the 1965 Federal Elections, NPD leaders undertook a whistle stop tour across West Germany, delivered model speeches and gave rehearsed model answers in an attempt to present a cohesive image to the public. The party paper <u>Reichsruf</u> of DRP times was now renamed <u>Deutsche Nachrichten</u> and appeared with the same editorial board in the same publishing house for the new party label.

The electoral defeat in 1965, when the newcomer only obtained 2% of the vote, seemed to herald the end of the shrewd efforts to re-launch the DRP under a new flag and to re-instate former Nazis into West German politics. In the communal- and land elections in 1966, the NPD began to record some gains, 3.9% in Hamburg, 10.6% in communal elections in Schleswig Holstein. In Hameln, Erlangen, Bayreuth, Nuremberg, NPD representatives entered local government. By the end of 1966, the party had 126 delegates in communal- and district assemblies. In Hesse, the NPD won 7.9% in the land elections, in Bavaria 7.4%. During 1967 and 1968, the party entered five more land parliaments. By 1969, it had 61 land delegates. In the Federal Elections of that year, it narrowly missed entering the Bundestag when it won 4.3%. By 1971, the NPD still held 426 local government seats. The decline, however, had begun (Table 8.1). In the course of the seventies, the NPD lost all seats in the land parliaments and all but a handful of local government seats. In 1980, it had just ten local government representatives.[29]

Since the mid-seventies, the NPD had fallen below the 0.3% mark in all but some local elections. This means that the party no longer qualifies for a reimbursement of campaign costs. The expectation

Opposition from the Right

Table 8.1: The NPD in Local and District Assemblies, 1971-1982

Year	1971	1972	1973	1974	1975	1976	1977	1978	1979	1980	1982
Seats	426	124	126	60	54	42	31	22	13	10	12

Sources: Betrifft 1969/70 - 1982

of a sizeable vote at the beginning of the decade and the rapid electoral decline left the party in debt. It owed nearly two million Deutschmark to the state and has so far been unable to pay this money back.[30]

In the late sixties, refunds for election expenses amounted to at least one third of NPD party income.[31] Donations could not compensate the loss of revenue incurred by the poor election results. It is an important feature of the NPD in West German society, that it has been unable to strike up an alliance with industry or business. Donations only come from the circle of committed right extremists and they are constantly requested in the relevant press. The association with a power elite, which has been identified as a precondition of the success of a fascist party, has clearly been absent from the NPD political history.[32] After its short-lived electoral gains, the NPD was thrown back on its own resources of membership and party organization.

Ups and Downs in Membership
It took the NPD just over one year to burst the banks of the old extremist formations and draw in new members. At the congress in Hanover in November 1964, some four hundred founding members came forward. In the following months, the core of the DRP membership, estimated at 3,500 had joined. In May 1965, the party had 7,500 members who came predominantly from the constituent groups and factions of right extremism which had come into the party.[33] At that time, about half the members had been in the DRP.[34]

This was soon to change. By September 1965, the NPD had recruited 11,000 members. As Table 8.2 shows, within two years, the party had expanded to 28,000 members. It held this level until 1969, when membership began to dwindle. By 1980, the NPD had declined to 7,200 members, with numbers still

Table 8.2: NPD Membership, 1964-1982

Year	1964	1965 (Feb)	1965 (May)	1965 (Sept)	1966			
Members	473	1200	7500	11000	25000			

Year	1967	1968	1969	1970	1971	1972	1973	
Members	28000	27000	28000	21000	18300	13000	12000	

Year	1974	1975	1976	1977	1978	1979	1980	1981	1982
Members	11000	10800	9700	9000	8500	8000	7200	6500	6000

Sources: Lowell Dittmer, "The German NPD in: Comparative Politics vol. 2 no. 1, Oct. 1969 p. 81 and Betrifft 1969-1982

falling.

During the late sixties, the NPD was the fastest growing political party in West Germany with an estimated gain of 1,000 members per month. Membership fluctuations were high. To be more specific: membership losses in the sixties and seventies seem to have occurred only among members who had joined the NPD without former commitment to the DRP. Of the 3,500 DRP activists who came into the NPD, 3,300 were still there in 1967 although the party had lost some 6,000 members during that year. In 1968, it recruited 7,500 and lost 8,500.[36] By 1971, the NPD had lost four times as many members as it could recruit. An estimated 30,000 people had belonged to the NPD at some stage in their life and left it again within five years. At the end of the seventies, 45,000 West Germans had at one point been NPD members.[37]

The NPD has never been deprived of new members altogether. It continued to attract newcomers even after election successes dried up. Yet, it seemed unable to retain many of these new members and honour the expectations which prompted them to join. The discrepancy of motivation for and experience of NPD membership has been stressed by a number of right extremists who had originally tried the NPD as a political base. While the oldtimers and the NPD leadership stayed unflinchingly in the party, the new recruits were looking for comradeship, for political action or for an effective opposition from the right and were much more easily swung to criticize the ineptness of the NPD. The party seemed unable to offer a platform and a degree of integration for which the newcomers were looking; the inability of the NPD to integrate newcomer members accounts for much of its transient membership and organizational stalemate.[38]

The Social Composition of NPD Support

A similar discrepancy is evident when the social composition of NPD support and the self-proclaimed political and social tasks of the party are compared. The NPD presents itself as a party for the middle class. In the light of a nationalist approach to social problems, the middle class is idealized as the most essential part of society, albeit threatened and endangered by the pace of social change and the political priorities in the Federal Republic.

> For generations, the middle class enterprises have formed the pillars of the German economy. More than three million self-employed artisans, traders, small manufacturers and members of the professions have been the foundation of social stability, the buffer against radicalization. They guarantee the stability of our social order.[39] The NPD demands: end price rises. The NPD demands the formation of property for all people in employment, security of the endangered livelihoods of the self-employed in farming, in the professions, in trade, in handicraft, and small business. Property creates freedom.[40]

The middle class focus of the NPD may appear as a broader historical observation or as a pressing political demand. Over the years, it has remained unchanged. Studies of the NPD electorate have, however, suggested that the NPD tended to attract a relatively high proportion of working class support (Table 8.3). In fact, the social composition of the NPD electorate does not indicate that it could be the party for the endangered middle class. It is more or less a <u>Volkspartei</u>, i.e. at the time when it could win votes, no middle class focus could be detected in the electorate.[41]

The diversity of social support did not filter through into the social self-identification of the party. This discrepancy between an awareness of the party as a middle class bastion and the heterogeneous following from all walks of life may have contributed to the inability to hold on to the voters. For initially winning electoral support, the unclear social position seems to have mattered little.

Table 8.3: NPD Voters, 1965-1967: Occupational Structure

Occupational group	NPD 1965 %	NPD 1967 %	Population 1967 %
Workers	42	45	49
Farmers	6	13	9
Professions	4	2	1
White Collar	26	23	23
Civil Servants	9	7	7
Old Middle Class	13	13	11
Total	100	100	100

Source: Elisabeth Noelle-Neumann, "Wer wählt NPD?" in: Die Politische Meinung 1967 no. 1, p. 25.

Liepelt found that NPD voters on the whole did not know which policies the party advocated in its programme.[42] The decision for the party was more in opposition to the other parties and in particular a reaction to fears of economic deterioration in the late sixties. The recession of 1966/67 had pushed unemployment over 700,000 after years of labour shortage and a buoyant economy. Growth stagnated, prospects for the future seemed uncertain. With the hindsight of the seventies and the eighties, the so called crisis of the sixties was a mere ripple of instability. At the time, it acted as a catalyst for the NPD. Liepelt estimated that about half the votes cast for the NPD in 1966 and 1967 were protest votes: votes were cast to the right as a deterioration of one's own economic position seemed imminent. Nagle's analysis also confirmed that those who felt that their personal situation was threatened were more likely to vote NPD than members of the same occupational or social group who were more optimistic about the future. The pessimistic outlook was particularly common among unskilled and skilled workers. Membership in large scale organizations such as the trade unions or the catholic church tended to generate a more confident outlook. Nagle suggested a proximity between lower levels of skill and support for the NPD. In line with low educational attainment, the unskilled were the least likely social group to have heared of the NPD. But those unskilled who had heard of it were above average inclined to vote for it.[43] This NPD affiliation of the lower skilled has been recognized by Warnecke, but has not been seen by Scheuch, by Kühnl and others who regard the NPD as a middle class party.[44]

While the NPD electorate was socially diversified, the membership of the early years was much more clearly middle class. Table 8.4 shows that in 1966, 56% of NPD members can be ranked as middle class, although some of the pensioners would also belong to this category. By 1969, the middle class component had declined to 52%, the working class component had increased slightly.

Tabe 8.4: NPD Members, 1966-1969: Occupational Structure

Occupation	1966 %		1969 %	
Academics	6	}	5	}
Self-employed	25	}	32	}
Civil Servants	7	} 56	4	} 52
Whit Collar	18	}	11	}
Workers in small business	14		19	
Workers in industry	13		15	
Housewives	6		6	
Pensioners	11		8	
Total	100		100	

Sources: Freimut Duve, Die Revolution entlässt ihre Kinder p. 21; Betrifft 1971 p. 39.

Data for membership development in the seventies are not available and conclusions have to be tentative. There seems to be a trend in the NPD membership from a predominantly middle class composition to a somewhat stronger representation of the working class, in particular workers in small enterprises. This tallies with Nagle's observation that the NPD is stronger in smaller communities; small enterprises also tend to have a low degree of unionization and often lower than average wage levels for their branch of industry. The trend of the lower educated towards the right which was observed for young people in West Germany earlier in this study also seems applicable to the NPD membership. Data on new admissions between 1969 and 1970 also indicate

Opposition from the Right

that recruitment from workers in small enterprises was better (23%) than for any other social group.[45]

These changes in NPD membership would seem to close the gap between electorate and membership somewhat. They were, however, not reflected in the party leadership which has been dominated by the founder generation or by its appointees from the outset. The rapid demise of the NPD confirmed that the party had been unable to transform the tentative support based on fear of crisis or decline, into political and electoral loyalties. Niethammer analysed the work of the NPD delegates in land parliaments and concluded that the party lacked a unified policy or an orientation on virtually any issue. Each delegate defined what he regarded as the party line. Conflicts arose even within one parliamentary party, let alone between lander representations.[46]

The end of the recession and the better prospects of secure living standards could quickly erode the NPD following. In addition, <u>Ostpolitik</u> dominated West German politics after Brandt became Chancellor in 1969. The defence of national integrity, of national borders and national unity, which had for a time been given over to the right fringe, emerged as the major focus of the CDU/CSU opposition in the first years of SPD/FDP government. The NPD suffered a fate similar to that of the small conservative parties in the fifties who endorsed reunification just as the CDU did - and were gradually swallowed up. The boundaries between nationalist positions of the NPD and the anti-Ostpolitik campaign of the Christian Democrats, the Refugee Organizations and similar bodies, were virtually non-existent. The NPD lost most of its electoral support to the opposition of which it was now merely a right fringe group.[47] Not a voice with a political identity of its own. It has been argued that voters may have withheld their support because they feared the NPD might not clear the 5% hurdle. In 1969, an investigation was pending whether the party should be banned as anti-constitutional. This could also have dissuaded voters.[48] Other factors seem to be more to the point. With the economic stabilization of the late sixties, the protest vote element no longer continued to exist. This had amounted to, as we saw earlier, about half the NPD support. Once the CDU/CSU was in opposition, the place of the SPD as opposition on the right also changed. In 1969, it had become an opposition party to the right of the established opposition which itself was to the right of the government. This constellation contributed to the poor results which the NPD obtained after the 1969 Bundestag elections and throughout the seventies and eighties.

NPD voting results cannot be seen as a yardstick to measure the existence or otherwise of right extremism. What they do show is that parties of the extreme right who stand in elections have little support. And this is a significant development. They cannot reveal right extremist potential in society which may not be translated into right extremist votes but rather shape attitudes and prospects for a future of right extremism. On this level, information has been full of contradictions. In the sixties, estimates of extremist potential on the right ranged from 4% to around 15%;[49] Kühnl argued in 1974 that this potential was as high as 30% in West Germany.[50] A 1981 survey conducted by the Sinus Institute on behalf of the Federal Government suggested that 13% of West German adults held views which should be classified as right extremist.[51] In France, a survey showed in 1977 that 49% of the French still believed that "a man like Hitler could again rise to power in West Germany". In West Germany, 18% thought this was possible.[51a]

The evidence on right extremist potential may be inconclusive. Yet, the NPD has been unable to mobilize whatever potential there might be on the right. It has made a few gestures in response to its political decline. At the 1976 party congress, the chairman since 1971, Mussgnug, informed the delegates that "a dissolution of the party does not apply".[52] Most of the NPD branches and districts which existed in the sixties, now appear to be defunct. An attempt in 1980 to streamline party organization and to appoint a business manager remained useless since the post was given to one of the oldest NPD leaders, the veteran chairman of the Bremen NPD from whom new initiatives or new departures could hardly be expected.[53] Similar to the DKP, the NPD has entered the phase of organizational inflexibility which seems to accompany fringe politics.

Stagnation and Radicalization: the NPD in the eighties
The opposition against Ostpolitik revealed for the first time two camps within the NPD: those who tried

Opposition from the Right

to mount a respectable campaign on the right, share platforms with spokesmen from the CDU, the CSU, the refugee associations on the one hand and on the other those who pushed for direct action and aggressive opposition. The leadership and most of the older members belonged to the first group, younger NPD members and a number of former SS activists to the second.[54] Unauthorized working groups and circles within the NPD began to launch their own protests against <u>Ostpolitik</u> in 1970. In October, an umbrella organization was founded, <u>Aktion Widerstand</u>.[55] It staged so called "freedom rallies along the bloodstained zonal border"[56] and spiced its attacks of <u>Ostpolitik</u> with slogans such as "Brandt to the wall, Resistance" or "Break the Red Front - Resistance".[57] Aktion Widerstand tried to prevent the visit to Kassel by the East German head of state, Stoph, it repeatedly burned East German flags, so called dividers' flags.[58] Soon, the party had lost control over its radicalized followers. Even the leadership of <u>Aktion Widerstand</u> had difficulties in keeping track of events and actions and warned - to no avail: "Public appearances and actions in the name of Aktion Widerstand are only permitted if authorized by the chairman".[59]

The radicalization of right wing politics within the NPD came from younger members. Initially, the NPD was a predominantly middle aged party, four in five members were middle aged or older.[60] New members tended to be younger. In 1970, one thousand NPD members under 35 organized themselves into a youth wing with a considerable degree of political and fiscal independance. At that time, the party had 21,000 members and the youth sector amounted to 5% of the membership. While overall NPD membership fell during the seventies, the young NPD wing held its place, even won a little more support. In 1980, <u>Junge Nationaldemokraten</u> JN had 1,400 members, the party 7,200. The youth sector now constituted about 20% of the NPD membership, and its most dynamic and most radical element. <u>Aktion Widerstand</u> and the youth wing JN subscribed to the same political principles of aggressive activism.

Within the NPD, this meant that the only challenges ever to be made to the party leadership and the domination of the former Nazi and DRP generations came from the young radicals of the JN. In 1977, for instance, a former JN chairman, Deckert, attempted - for the second time - to oust the leadership and swing the party in a more radical and openly aggressive direction. In a circular to all delegates to the 1977 party congress he revealed some interesting details about the desolate state of the NPD and the discontent of its young.

> The NPD as a national party is not in demand at present. It has declined to complete political insignificance. The party is not led, it is administered. The intellectual power has all but disappeared ... The few pence which are collected at the grass roots are used to line the pockets of the top brass.[61]

A similar attack was launched at the 1980 congress. As its forerunner, it remained unsuccessful. It changed neither the leadership nor the course of the NPD.[62]

Since the mid-seventies, the NPD has been under pressure from its youth wing to radicalize. The JN publish their own press, organize their own activities and have stopped, despite many reprimands, to coordinate their political actions with the party.[63] The politics which seem to attract young people and which appear to split the NPD ressemble terrorism from the right. Young Nationaldemocrats have been involved in campaigns of intimidation of Jewish citizens and of foreign workers in the Federal Republic, of criminal assault and of inflicting damage to property and places of worship.[64] In 1979 and 1980, several JN members were apprehended with weapons, explosives and home-made bombs.[65] In Northern Germany and in Berlin, JN groups have merged with extremist factions outside the NPD, so called Neonazi groups. In Hamburg, Young Nationaldemocrats were involved in bombing a hostel for refugees. Everywhere, hostility against <u>Gastarbeiter</u> has escalated. An Infas survey established in 1982, that 49% of West German citizens were more or less hostile towards foreigners.[67] The NPD tried to capitalize on these attitudes which tally with the racism and nationalism of Neonazi ideologies today. In 1980, the party organized a referendum in North Rhine Westfalia to obtain public support for a repatriation of foreign workers.[68] The Young Nationaldemocrats share these aims without using such conventional means. A defiance of conventional politics and an endorsement of illegal, terrorist and violent practices in right-wing politics seems to be the hallmark of young Neonazi supporters. In 1981, the 21-30 year olds committed the highest proportion of right extremist offences, 46%. Among militant activists, about 70% were young people.[69] The pressures on the NPD towards militancy come from its young members. The borderline between NPD and Neonazi activism, between politics aimed at elections and parliaments and the politics of racism and aggressive nationalism have become blurred. The Young Nationaldemocrats are shaping the NPD towards a radicalized right. It is true, the leadership made some efforts to cool things down, but only because it did not want to lose control to younger functionaries. In substance, the aims and intentions of NPD and its youth wing are compatible and similar. Despite the occasional threats to expell unruly members, the NPD needs them as the only remaining dynamic element, which might mobilize support for the party and which might get the NPD politically noticed. The NPD has become an umbrella for Neonazi acitivism alongside the stagnant body of oldtimers who still control the party, the leadership and the official party press.

NEONAZISM

In 1978, survivors of the Nationalsocialist machinery of persecution marched through Bonn, dressed in striped garments like concentration camp inmates and protested against a revival of Nazism in West Germany. A few months earlier, a rally in Toulouse had warned of a reawakening of Nazism among Germans, "the most reactionary people in Europe".[70] In 1979, the European Parliament debated "an alleged upsurge of racism, antisemitism and neo Nazism" with special emphasis on West Germany.[71] The Federal Chancellor at the time, Schmidt, pledged to stem any tide: "We firmly resist any dangerous revival of neo-Nazism in our midst".[72]

The diverse concerns about Neonazism seem to have been generated by a public reappearance of Nazi paraphernalia such as leather jackets, jackboots and other replica of stormtrooper or SS outfits.[73] Swastika and other Nazi emblems were often used, the infamous Horst Wessel song came out of cold storage and was sung in public. The same happened to the first two verses of the national anthem which had been shelved for their territorial claims and anexationist overtones. When the West German extreme right of the late seventies took to the streets, it had lost the cautious suit-and-tie approach of the established NPD and displayed a more assertive identification with the Nationalsocialist model. At the time, West German society as a whole went through a phase of re-living the past which has been called a "Hitler wave".

The "Hitler Wave"

The name was based on a flood of reproductions of Nationalsocialist originals which came on the market under the guise of historical documentation. According to the Basic Law, the use and display of Nazi insignia and emblems, the reprinting of Nazi sources etc. is only permitted for the purposes of research. The extreme right, in its publication network, had exploited this provision for some time to reproduce Nationalsocialist speeches, songs, and broadcasts to the forces in the original form from radio archive materials. These publications were called historical documents to sidestep the law. A company which published under the name Documentary Establishment from Liechtenstein produced profiles of all major institutions of the Third Reich, including the SS; portaits on record of all leading personalities including Goebbels and Himmler, with commentaries which came from the Nationalsocialist radio stations themselves. In 1978, most of the records produced under this label were indexed as endangering the young and can no longer be sold openly.[74] By that time, however, other publishers had taken up the profitable business with the past. The John Jahr publishing house started in 1974 to produce a series of twenty long-play records which sold over 30,000 copies each.[75] Four discs with Hitler speeches had higher sales figures still. One of West Germany's largest publishers, Bertelsmann, recorded Nazi originals on its Ariola label.[76] Their products have been distributed by department stores and by regular record shops. The political ethics of resurrecting materials from the German radio archives and assembling them into records are far from straight forward. It is simplistic to assume that the original sources would enable the audience to get a true picture of the past. The sources themselves were designed to present to the public an image of Nationalsocialism, the regime and the leaders which suited official requirements. Re-recording these sources, with all the prolonged shouts of "Heil" which seem to follow every statement by any leader, adopts the Nazi version of events. As one advertiser put it succinctly to recommend his

Opposition from the Right

product to prospective buyers: "The record is not interrupted by any post-war German commentary".[77] The voice of the state controlled radio, the Volksempfänger has been resurrected, "Goebbels was the real producer".[78]

Even the use of commentary does not break the vicious circle of interpreting Nationalsocialism by repeating the viewpoints of the Nationalsocialists themselves. The series of "historical collages", Ein Volk, ein Reich, ein Führer by John Jahr for instance opens with prolonged cheers of "Heil". The overview ends with the last army bulletin: "Thus, the heroic struggle of six years had ended. The German Wehrmacht finally succumbed with honour to the more numerous forces". These words are accompanied by the strains of the national anthem and interspersed with the recorded replies from the Nuremberg trials, "not guilty ... not guilty". This type of look at the face of Nationalsocialism has not been confined to the record market. A great number of books, inside accounts, biographies, diaries were published to communicate to the West German public those dimensions of their own past which serious historical research had hitherto ignored.[79] Many entered the best seller lists. Hans Joachim Fest's biography of Hitler was made into a film, based on newsreel, the cinematic account of the Third Reich about itself. In the Federal Republic, Fest's attempt to show what fascinated the masses and why they were prey to Hitler has been recommended for use in schools, and political education. The accounts from Nazi originals had an undeniable appeal to German audiences.[80] The proximity of this approach to the intentions of the extreme right has not gone unnoticed:

> The Führer has a new management and new fans. Like in the days of the political struggle, he strides from victory to victory, from appearance to appearance: Adolf Hitler. His public today is hardly smaller now than it was in 'his' Third Reich.[81]

The largest publication figures were reached by picture magazines. A so called document collection The Third Reich comprised over sixty different issues and sold an estimated one million copies. A Second World War series was launched at newsstands with huge swastika flags and posters as an advertising gimmick.[82] The same publisher, John Jahr,

273

reprinted the propaganda magazine of the German Army, Signal. Although Signal had been intended to show the acceptable face, even attractive face of Nationalsocialism and its army to the outside world, a Hamburg court ruled in 1978 that publication was permissible "since the character of the reprint as documentation is clearly stated and sensationalist advertising has been avoided".[83] It has since been listed as a publication which might endanger the young and cannot be sold over the counter; a reprint of the Nazi party publication for functionaries, Schulungsbriefe, has also been stopped in this way.

Other repeats of the past also blend into the Hitler wave and its glorification of history. A number of publishers have produced magazines, books, glossy pictorial accounts of German armaments, weaponry and World War II military equipment and battles.[84] Similar to the Landser romanticism, which was mentioned earlier, these glances at the allegedly technical and soldierly successes of Germany omit reference to the political context in which these arms were used. A sense of victory is communicated, of accomplishment in and through World War II.

Some of those who endorse and purchase the products of the Hitler-wave belong to the older generation who lived through Nationalsocialism and war. For them, the main incentive may indeed be political backwardness intermingled with nostalgia. The majority of purchasers, however, appear to be young people for whom these publications introduce rather than relive the past. The Motorbuch publishing house focuses on the young as a target group: "Young people who are free from the soldier romanticism of the literature and who are looking for factual information".[85] John Jahr claimed during a radio interview that about two thirds of the readers of his documentary histories and glossies were under thirty five, one third even under eighteen.[86]

The Hitler-wave is just part of a general tendency in West Germany to reappraise the past. The Weimar Republic has not lent itself to be rediscovered as genuinely German. The infatuation with Nazi leaders and the presumed rapport between people and leader did. Since the late seventies, a so called Prussia-wave has commenced. The newly awakened national consciousness in the Federal Republic seeks roots and justification in an acceptable, positive past. A commentary on the screening of the film Holocaust by German television sums up the new meaning of the past, whatever the historical period may be:

> Have not, in the last 35 years of our people's existence enough words been spoken to reveal the injustice against the Jews, have not actions followed to atone, if at all possible, for the mass murder? Just name me one other nation who has so consistently and repeatedly revealed the dark points in its own history. Young people who only hear negative things, who are only asked to see the shadowy side of things must become despondent. Has not the time come to try and show examples, positive deeds and good examples from the past, to encourage and to strengthen the young instead of bringing them up to be pessimists?[87]

Aims and Ideologies of Neonazism

The glorification of Nationalsocialism and its leaders, above all Hitler, which characterized the so called Hitler-wave in publishing and in the media, are dominant features of the Neonazism of the seventies. There is no coherent ideology or a conceptual discussion of ideological principles. In the aftermath of the NPD losses, the so called New Right made some short-lived efforts to develop a theory of nationalism. They wanted something as forceful and unified as political Marxism; this soon proved impossible and the theoretical wing of the extreme right fizzled out.[88] The principles of Neonazi ideology are easily summed up:

> There are a few strongly emotionalized basic principles such as a volatile German nationalism, which is accompanied by hostile attitudes towards foreign countries and foreigners. The decisive rejection of foreign workers is well known which is based on fear of 'cultural over alienation' (Überfremdung). The political left is regarded as the natural enemy within Germany.

This excerpt from a parliamentary reply by the former Junior Minister von Schoeler indicates the focal point and the scope of Neonazism.[89] A further common element concerns the rejection of the Federal Republic, and all democratic institutions. For some, the German Reich has never ended. The legality of the West German state is denied outright. So called <u>Reichstage</u> were staged in a number of towns to defy the political reality of contemporary Germany and also to demand the reinstatement of the Nationalsocialist Party. Most Neonazi groups voice this demand. They also use the expression "Nationalsocialist" in their name or programmes. From the right, the course of post-war German development is seen as a product of American re-education and as a betrayal of the German nation and the principles of national self-determination. Anti-Americanism and nationalism overlap with territorial claims about the size of the nation and the location of borders. Those who work for political democracy in the Federal Republic, all politicians and party representatives, have in the eyes of the right abandoned nationalism and therefore deserve punishment "Whoever serves the democratic holders of power (den Machthabern) does not deserve to live".[90] A similar view was expressed after the kidnapping of the President of the West German Employers Federation, Schleyer in 1977:

> What is all this talk about terror? The case is perfectly clear: He who sows wind will reap storm. He who has systematically destroyed all ideals for thirty years, reaps anarchy. He who incites the young against their parents reaps rebellion. He who was a professional terrorist in his youth, like Willy Brandt and Wehner, cannot in his old age demand loyalty to the state. This state has been created by the arbitrariness of occupying powers, not according to the will of the German people. Therefore, it remains unloved, and not even its functionaries are prepared to give their very best for it.[91]

The rejection of democracy seems to entitle Neonazis to any act of defiance or violence against that democracy, its institutions and loyal citizens. There are many versions of recapturing the Nazi spirit or reliving some of its principles. Beyond all superficial differences of emphasis, the rejection of political democracy and the West German state is shared by all groups and factions. "We are not democrats, at least not in the eyes of those so called democrats who govern today".[92] "Opposition of principles"[93] against contemporary democracy and against the course of West German politics binds

Neonazism together. A second unifying theme concerns the view of the past and has been called a "Denial of the Holocaust". In leaflets, book publications, pseudo-scientific tracts, in <u>Auschwitz</u> congresses and banner headlines in the papers and newsletters, the Nazi machinery of mass murder and the number of victims are constantly put into question. Some claim, concentration camps were erected by the Allies to discredit the Germans, some claim that there were camps but no death camps, some claim nobody was murdered, others admit to some hundred thousand dying of diseases. In short, the glorification of the past goes hand in hand with a whitewash of its darkest aspect. The <u>Deutsche Nationalzeitung</u> even increased its sales figures once it combined a regular Hitler feature or similar with "Denial of the Holocaust" reports. In 1981, the outright "Denial of the Holocaust" was ruled illegal by a German court as diffamation of the dead.

<u>Towards Terrorism from the Right</u>
In 1981, twenty-two Neonazi groups with less than one hundred members each operated in the Federal Republic. The Ministry of the Interior reported the existence of 1,800 Neonazis, 800 of these were known as members of groups, 600 seemed to operate alone, the remainder gave financial support to groups and their publications.[94] It has been known for some time that protagonists of the extreme right such as Gerhard Frey, the editor of the <u>Deutsche Nationalzeitung</u> channeled funds to Neonazi groups. Police investigations and house to house searches in 1981 revealed a sizeable circle of donors who often contributed large sums.[95] The question of financial support for Neonazism in West Germany cannot be answered fully from the information which has so far become available. The organizational structure does not indicate that Neonazism attracts much funding or had developed a costly style of operation. It seems divided into mini-groups with as many mini leaders, each aiming to speak for the whole camp. There is plentiful evidence of squabbles between groups. Michael Kühnen for example, a former Bundeswehr soldier turned Neonazi, who also entered his group as a party in the Hamburg land elections on an anti-<u>Gastarbeiter</u>, pro-Nazi ticket, has been an outspoken critic of some of his leader colleagues. Citing the leader of the German Citizens' Initiative, Roeder, he said:

Opposition from the Right

> We have to get away from this - not from the
> leader principle but from the leader cult as
> far as individuals are concerned. We have
> experienced this with Roeder. As a matter of
> principle, I do not usually criticize comrades
> from the so called Nazi scene - but when I see
> a poster at the Reichstag saying 'Our Reich -
> Our Right - Our Roeder', in this superlative,
> then I feel sick. I would never allow something
> like this to be done with me.[96]

Infighting and bickering in the Neonazi camp should not obscure the tendencies to cooperate. Activities above the local level such as celebrating the anniversary of the foundation of the German Reich or commemorating the 1953 uprising on the Day of German Unity - always draw on more than one group; even adversaries like Kühnen and Roeder will join forces, as they did for instance in protests against nuclear power plants. Cooperation on an international scale has grown considerably in the late seventies. Groups from Belgium France, Britain, Italy, Denmark and Austria keep regular contacts with German Neonazis. The most significant outside connection, the American NSDAP-AO, Nationalsocialist Workers Party Abroad, has supplied funds, propaganda materials, leaflets and periodicals. Many of the swastika stickers used in antisemitic campaigns came from this US source, although that type of material is also produced in West Germany and in other countries.[97] In 1981, the Office for the Protection of the Constitution counted twelve established periodical publications with a regular distribution of 19,340 copies.[98] Most Neonazi publications appear irregularly and their number and circulation are difficult to estimate. It has also been estimated that about 200 of the known Neonazis are really actively involved; in a population of over sixty million, a minute problem.

Since the mid-seventies, right extremism has, however, displayed a tendency towards the use of violence and terrorist means of political action. Numbers alone and the network of contacts and the circulation of publications do not give an adequate picture of the political significance of Neonazism in West German society today. It has to be seen as an opposition from the right with a preponderance towards terrorism and violence. In 1971, the protest against <u>Ostpolitik</u> brought a record number of punishable offences for that period. With political

stabilization after the Basic Treaty with East
Germany, offences from the right were less common.
In any case, most were daubings, poster campaigns,
demonstrations, slanderous publications. If violence was used, arson and assault were most widespread. The picture has changed since then. From
136 in 1974, the number of punishable offences increased to 1,643 in 1980.[99] In the early seventies,
20% involved the use of violence, now more than half
do. Assault and arson are still common, but have
been overtaken by bankraids, the use of explosives,
bombings, raids on arms depots, hordings, and, of
course, the use of arms. The political mood of
Neonazism now incorporates the use of violence and
of arms as a regular, accepted means of opposition.
"If I could be sure of getting rid of my suppressors, I would take up a weapon right away, even
against a German politician".[100] "Whoever serves
the democratic holders of power does not deserve
life".[101]

In 1979, the Regional Court in Celle classified
the <u>Aktionsfront Nationaler Sozialisten</u> as a
terrorist group. For the first time a group of the
right was deemed terrorist and the endorsement of
violence was equated to that from the left. Since
then, the terrorist dimension has become more
apparent still. In 1980, a bomb was planted at the
Munich beer festival, killing thirteen people and
injuring over two hundred. The assassin was a former member of a paramilitary Neonazi group which had
been banned only weeks earlier. The bombing was
timed to coincide with the last stages of the 1980
Bundestag elections. It may have been an attempt to
rekindle public fears of terrorism and swing the
electoral commitment towards the right. In first
statements by the Munich police, the killings were
blamed on the left. When the identity of the
terrorist was revealed, investigations could not
find any accomplices and the crime was treated as
the deed of a madman.[102] The political motives
behind other attacks from the right are less
complex. In Hamburg, two people were killed when a
bomb exploded in a hostel for Vietnamese refugees;
in Bremen, Turkish business premises and community
institutions were damaged. Neonazism had singled
out foreigners, those seeking asylum and those working in the Federal Republic, as targets in addition
to their established targets, Jews and Communists.
Some justify hostilities by referring to a segregation of species and biological nationalism.[103]

Opposition from the Right

Others cite economic and social resentments:

> Today, it is like this: a capitalist gang deals in people, one really cannot call it by any other name, a capitalist gang shoves millions of people into Germany and destroys the places of work for our young Germans. German places of work belong to German young people. The foreign workers should be sent back to their own countries.[104]

The fear and tension created by the anti-foreigner campaign among West Germany's foreign inhabitants hit the headlines prior to the elections in Hamburg in the summer of 1982 when a young Turkish woman set fire to herself to protest against the hostilities she and her compatriots had to suffer. The Neonazis who competed in these elections made hatred against foreigners a keynote of their campaign.[105]

To articulate discontent with contemporary society and politics by blaming scapegoats and by singling out and even personalizing enemies to the nation, to the state or whatever the case may be, has been common practice of political ideology from the right. Neonazism with its personal attacks against specific groups fits into this tradition. The vague nature of Neonazi ideologies even invites personalization of the alleged enemy in order to have a concrete target for action and direct opposition.

Neonazism and Society in Perspective
Some have argued that terrorism from the right is little more than an attempt to emulate the left.[106] Although there may have been some cross fertilization, imitation alone does not seem a thorough enough explanation. A government sponsored survey of 35 court cases of right extremists found some other motives which mobilized Neonazis to commit terrorist acts.[107] The researchers argued that concepts of the right, in particular clear cut notions about who is friend and who is foe, appeal to those who have "no confidence in our forms of political life". Most biographical accounts refer to young offenders searching for a group or party where they could feel at home and among friends. Before turning Neonazi, a number had tried the CDU and the NPD which they left again, feeling "isolated, neglected,

frustrated". The motivating factor in Neonazi commitment seems to be a desire to firmly belong to a group. Political parties could not provide the guidance and the secure environment which had been expected. All conventional involvement was therefore written off as futile. This also generated a sense that political violence was needed to shake up an inflexible and misguided political system. "Violence then becomes a means to force the message onto the unteachable enemies and to find some sort of way out of a political cul-de-sac". The findings of this survey cannot be called representative since the sample was very small. They point, however, in an interesting direction: They suggest that young people turn to Neonazism often after they attempted to participate elsewhere and were frustrated in their particular wishes for social and political integration.

The implication is, that political parties are not always able to respond to the needs of those who join and wish to find a political platform in them and through them. Those whose disappointment leads to Neonazism seem to look for clear-cut recipes for political action in contemporary society, and they look from a vantage point on the political right. The readiness to use violence as a means of articulating frustration with established politics and of voicing opposition to the course of West German politics follow from the political model which served to supply the answers to the question of political action and the future of Germany: the ideas, the language, the practices of Nationalsocialism including its glorification of violence and its use of intimidation.

Neonazism, it seems holds two promises: a set of readymade answers, stereotypes from the repertoire of Nationalsocialism and earlier nationalism which can be reiterated verbatim or with some timely modification. Neonazism also incorporates an aggressive gesture against West German society and indeed against all democratic societies. It underwrites anti-democratic forms of government and of everyday political behaviour to go with it. The recourse to the set pieces of the past seems to be linked to lower class and educational status. Neonazis themselves like to claim that they attract supporters from all walks of life.[108] This corresponds to the ideology of the <u>Volksgemeinschaft</u>, the people's community without class divisions which Nationalsocialism propagated - in its propaganda,

Opposition from the Right

Table 8.5: Neonazi Offenders by Occupation and by Age

Occupation	%	
Pupils, students, trainees	26	
Skilled workers, artisans	20	} 34
Unskilled workers	14	
White collar employees	14	} 27
Self-employed	13	
Unemployed	5	
Others, n.a.	4	
Total	100	

Age	Neonazis %		Offenders overall %	
14-17 years	17	} 40	16	} 30
18-20 "	23		14	
21-30 "	30	} 42		
31-40 "	12			
41-50 "	8		70	
51 and over	10			
Total	100 (1643)		100 (1334 330)	

Source: Betrifft 1980 p. 48; Kriminalstatistik für 1980, Innere Sicherheit 70, 1981 p. 597.

not in its economic and social policies. More reliable information about the social background of Neonazis comes from statistics on offenders. Table 8.5 uses data about Neonazis who were charged, though not always tried or convicted, in 1980. It confirms the observations made earlier in relation to support for the NPD: right extremism today is no longer a middle class phenomenon. The data on occupational background in Table 8.5 group artisans and skilled workers together; this prevents a clear distinction along class lines. Nevertheless, Table 8.5 indicates that roughly one third of offenders from the extreme right in 1980 were people with working class or related occupations. Middle class occupations, white collar employees and self-employed, were less frequent among offenders. Of course, a proportion of the pupils, students and trainees would also have to be counted as middle class. The class position of this group seems less interesting than the fact that they are young. In

1980, 39% of all Neonazi offences were carried out by people between fourteen and twenty years of age. By comparison, one third of offenders in all categories of crime belonged to this age group. Of the Neonazi offenders 23% were between 18 and 20 years of age, yet only 14% of all offences were committed by members of this age band. Neonazis in conflict with the law tend to be young, younger than average. Nearly 70% were under thirty. Four in five were forty or younger.

As a reflection on the social composition of Neonazi groups, these data allow some tentative conclusions. Neonazism in the seventies and eighties has been able to attract young people. It is by no means the dying creed of the old incorrigibles. The occupational structure seems weighted towards the lower status groups. The correlation between high educational levels and right extremism which applied when Nationalsocialism rose to power does no longer apply. Today, the lower educational groups are more prominent among the extreme right. This is in line with our findings on the political orientations among the young.[109] Disenchantment and principle opposition among the young tend to be articulated in a right-wing direction among those with lower educational attainment. The data on Neonazi offenders point in the same direction. Neonazism has gained strength and a new velocity in the late seventies as a protest movement of young workers, artisans, apprentices whose rejection of contemporary society and whose insecurity about their own future are articulated in the language, the ideas, the activism and more recently the defiance of democratic conduct and legal strictures of a Nationalsocialist mould.

FOOTNOTES

1. George Mosse, The Crisis of German Ideology - Intellectual Origins of the Third Reich, The Universal Library N.Y. 1964; also Ernst Nolte, The Three Faces of Fascism, Weidenfels & Nicholson 1965 esp. part IV. pp. 275-428.
2. Ossip K. Flechtheim, "Extremismus und Radikalismus" in Aus Politik und Zeitgeschichte B6, 1976 pp. 22-30. Iring Fetscher, "Rechtes und rechtsradikales Denken in der Bundesrepublik" in Fetscher (ed.) Rechtsextremismus, Frankfurt 1964 pp. 11-31 esp. p. 13.
3. e.g. Reinhard Kühnl, Die von F.J. Strauss repräsentierten Kräfte und ihr Verhältnis zum

Faschismus, Köln (Pahl Rugenstein) 1972. A similar line is taken by Blätter für deutsche und internationale Politik.

4. Abraham Ashkenazi, Modern German Nationalism, Wiley 1976 concludes with a comparative analysis of two right extremist periodicals and the CSU weekly Bayernkurier and finds striking similarities of topics with differences in the wording and weighting within each paper.

5. e.g. Hans Ulrich Wehler, Das deutsche Kaiserreich, Göttingen (Vandenhoeck & Ruprecht), 1973.

6. Betrifft Verfassungsschutz 1980 ed. Bundesministerium des Inneren, Bonn 1981.

7. See Jürgen Weber (ed.) Auf dem Wege zur Bundesrepublik 1945-1949, München (Bayrische Landeszentrale für politische Bildung) 1978 esp. chs. 1 and 2.

8. e.g. Adalbert Rückerl (ed.) NS Vernichtungslager im Spiegel deutscher Strafprozesse, München (dtv) 1977; Michael Ratz (ed.) Die Justiz und die Nazis. Zur Strafverfolgung von Nazismus und Neonazismus seit 1945, Frankfurt/Main (Röderberg) 1979; this volume also includes excerpts from official documents (1942-1979) relating to the issue. Also Tom Bower, Blind Eye to Murder. Britain, America and the Purging of Nazi Germany. A Pledge Betrayed, Deutsch 1981.

9. 1952: SRP, 1962: Bund für Gotterkenntnis (Mathilde Ludendorff) 1980: Wehrsportgruppe Hoffmann 1981: Volkssozialistische Bewegung. For the fifties and early sixties see Tauber, Beyond Eagle and Swastika I, Middletown 1967, for the seventies and eighties Betrifft and Innere Sicherheit.

10. Kurt Sontheimer, "Antidemokratisches Denken in der Bundesrepublik" in Immanuel Geiss and Volker Ulrich (eds.) 15 Millionen beleidigte Deutsche oder Woher kommt die CDU? Reinbek (Rowohlt) 1970 p. 106.

11. e.g. Ivor Montague, Germany's New Nazis, Panther 1967; T.H. Tetens, The New Germany and the Old Nazis, Secker & Warburg 1962.

12. White Paper of the Government of the Federal Republic of Germany: The Antisemitic and Nazi Incidents from 25 December 1959 until 29 January 1960, Bonn 1960 p. 41.

13. Ibid. p. 43.
14. Ibid. p. 42.
15. Ibid. pp. 18 ff.
16. Ibid. p. 16. The overall distribution was: in training 50%, workers 41%, clerical staff 8%,

civil servants in "subordinate positions" 1%. The report stresses these civil servants acted under the influence of alcohol.

17. Otto Büsch and Peter Furth, Rechtsradikalismus im Nachkriegsdeutschland. Studien über die Sozialistische Reichspartei, Berlin (Colloquium) 1957. Also Ossip K. Flechtheim, Dokumente zur parteipolitischen Entwicklung seit 1945, Bd. II, Berlin (Dokumenten Verlag) 1963 p. 13 and pp. 489-493.

18. See Heinz Brüdigam, Der Schoss ist fruchtbar noch ... Neonazistische, militaristische, nationalistische Literatur und Publizistik in der Bundesrepublik Deutschland, Frankfurt/Main (Röderberg) 1965. Also recently Peter Dudek/Hans Gerd Jaschke, Die Deutsche Nationalzeitung, Inhalte, Geschichte, Aktionen, München (PDI) 1981.

19. Ibid. p. 55.

20. Deutsche Nationalzeitung (DNZ) 20, 11.10.1974 p. 10. The publishing houses in question are in particular Lehmann, Seewald, Orion Heimreiter, Blick und Bild, Druffel, Schütz, Grabert, Stocker, Heyme, Kindler.

21. Dieter Kuhn, Luftkrieg als Abenteuer, Frankfurt/Main (Fischer) 1978 pp. 47-70; Gerhard Schneider, "Geschichte durch die Hintertür" in Aus Politik und Zeitgeschichte B6, 1978 p. 5.

22. "Nationaldemokratische Partei Deutschlands gegründet", in Reichsruf 13, 4.12.1964 p. 1.

23. A detailed account and evaluation in Kurt P. Tauber, ibid. vol 1.

24. Manfred Rowold, Im Schatten der Macht, Düsseldorf (Droste) 1974 p. 210.

25. Betrifft 1969/1970 p. 15.

26. Hermann Meyn, Die Deutsche Partei. Entwicklung und Problematik einer national-konservativen Partei, Düsseldorf (Droste) 1965 p. 74.

27. For a detailed account see Rowold ibid. p. 212 and Manfred Jenke, Die Nationale Rechte, Parteien, Politiker, Publizisten, Berlin (Colloquium) 1967 p. 117.

28. The political background of NPD leaders of the first hour is discussed in Ashkenazi ibid. p. 108, also Reinhard Kühnl et. al., Die NPD. Struktur, Ideologie und Funktion, Frankfurt/Main (Suhrkamp) 1969; Peter Brügge "Rechts ab zum Vaterland" Spiegel Serie nos. 17-20, 1967.

29. In 1980, six of these were in Bavaria.

30. Betrifft 1967 p. 28; Der Spiegel 48, 1976 p. 84; "Bund stundet NPD die Schulden" Tagesspiegel

24.12.1977.
    31. <u>Betrifft</u> 1971 p. 23.
    32. John Weiss, <u>The Fascist Tradition</u>. Radical Right-Extremism in Modern Europe, Harper Row N.Y. 1967 p. 6.
    33. Rowold ibid. p. 217.
    34. "Erfahrungen der Beobachtung und Abwehr rechtsradikaler und antisemitischer Tendenzen im Jahre 1965. Bericht des Bundesministeriums des Inneren zum Rechtsradikalismus" in <u>Aus Politik und Zeitgeschichte</u> B 11, 1966 p. 12.
    35. Membership figures which the NPD circulated in 1968 gave 40,000 members. This has not been confirmed by independent sources; it could be a deliberate exaggeration. More likely is that the party did not adjust figures for membership losses.
    36. Lowell Dittmer "The German NPD" in <u>Comparative Politics</u> vol.2 no.1, October 1969 p. 81.
    37. See <u>Betrifft</u> 1980.
    38. e.g. Alwin Meyer and Karl Klaus Rabe,"'Ohne dass ich sagen würde ich bin der neue Führer'-Gespräch mit einem jungen Nationalsozialisten" in Kursbuch Jugend No. 54, December 1978. Also Rabe (Ed.) <u>Rechtsextreme Jugendliche</u> Gespräche mit Verführten, Dortmund (Lamuv) 1980.
    39. In <u>Stimmen der hessischen NPD</u> no. 1, 1976 p. 13.
    40. "Für eine gerechte Ordnung. Ordnung - Gerechtigkeit - Solidarität: Leitsätze der NPD (Neue Rechte) zur Bundestagswahl 1972" in <u>Deutsche Nachrichten</u> Sonderausgabe 26. Oktober 1972 p. 8.
    41. See John D. Nagle, <u>The National Democratic Party</u>. Right Radicalism in the Federal Republic of Germany, Univ. of California Press 1970 ch. V, pp. 124 ff. Also: Steven Warnecke, "The future of Right Extremism" in: Comparative Politics vol. 1 no. 4, July 1970 pp. 629 ff, and in M. Kolinsky/W.E. Paterson (eds.) <u>Social and Political Movements in Western Europe</u>, Croom Helm 1976.
    42. Klaus Liepelt, "Anhänger einer neuen Rechtspartei" in: <u>Politische Vierteljahresschrift</u> June 1967 pp. 237-271. Also Dieter Thielen, "Wähler und Wählerreservoir der NPD" in <u>Blätter für deutsche und internationale Politik</u> vol. 12 no. 6, 1967 pp. 5 ff.
    43. Nagle ibid. pp. 136-138.
    44. Erwin K. Scheuch, "Politischer Extremismus in der Bundesrepublik" in: Richard Löwenthal and Hans Peter Schwarz, <u>Die Zweite Republik</u>, Stuttgart (Seewald) 1974 p. 455.

45. Betrifft 1971 p. 39.
46. Lutz Niethammer, Angepasster Faschismus. Politische Praxis der NPD, Frankfurt/Main (Fischer) 1969 p. 204.
47. A detailed analysis of the realignment of votes in Werner Kaltefleiter, Zwischen Konsens und Krise. Eine Analyse der Bundestagswahl 1972, ed. Konrad Adenauer Stiftung, Bonn (Eichholz) 1973.
48. This argument has been favoured by the extreme right itself to explain the discrepancy between manifest support and assumed potential, e.g. DNZ 48, 26.11.1976: "The NPD does not fail because there are no potential voters. It fails because the roughly 20% potential voters of the Right have a psychological blockage over the 5% clause and prefer to vote for one of the established parties".
49. A good summary of the various studies in Ashkenazi ibid. p. 55 ff.
50. Reinhard Kühnl, Rechtsextremismus in der Bundesrepublik. Paper delivered at the Liverpool Conference of the ASGP, 1974 (manuscript) pp. 8-9.
51. 5 Millionen Deutsche: 'Wir wollen wieder einen Führer haben ...' Die Sinus Studie über rechtsextremistische Einstellungen bei den Deutschen, Reinbek (Rowohlt) 1981.
51a. see Spiegel 48, 1977 p. 144: Spiegel Umfrage in Frankreich über Deutschland und die Deutschen. The data for Germany are taken from an Allensbach survey of 1977.
52. Martin Mussgnug, Rede auf dem Parteitag der NPD vom 14.11.1976 Stuttgart 1977 (manuscript) p. 8.
53. Innere Sicherheit 52, 1980 p. 26.
54. Harald Jung and Eckart Spoo, Das Rechtskartell der Reaktion in der Bundesrepublik Deutschland, München (Hanser) 1972 pp. 123-124.
55. Wolfgang Krutz, "Die Hilfstruppen des F.J. Strauss von der Deutschen Union bis zur Aktion Widerstand" in Blätter für deutsche und internationale Politik vol. 2 no. 11, 1971 pp. 1157-1171.
56. Studien für Zeitfragen, ed. Reinhard Opitz, no. II/III, 1971, p. 8. Opitz, a former member of the NPD, published detailed inside information on the extreme right in this newsletter.
57. In German: "Brandt an die Wand - Widerstand" and "Rotfront verrecke - Widerstand"; this is a direct quote of a Nazi slogan.
58. Studien für Zeitfragen I, 1971 p. 5. Background analysis and further detailed information ibid. nos. XI and XII, 1970.
59. Studien für Zeitfragen I, 19

60. Heinz Werner Höffgen and Martin Sattler, Rechtsextremismus in der Bundesrepublik Deutschland. Die 'alte' und die 'neue' Rechte und Neonazismus, Hamburg (Landeszentrale für politische Bildung) 1978 pp. 26-27.
61. Günther Deckert, "Überlegungen zur Lage der Partei", Weinheim/Bergstrasse, Jahreswechsel 1976/77 (manuscript) pp. 1-2; Also Nation Europa no. 12, 1976.
62. Innere Sicherheit 52, 1980 p. 26.
63. Innere Sicherheit 54, 1980 p. 15.
64. See Rechtsradikale Jugendorganisationen. Beiträge und Dokumentation, ed. Pressedienst demokratische Initiative PDI Sonderheft 8, München 1978 pp. 33-60 ; PDI newsletter May 1978 Initiative für ein Hannover ohne braun: Beispiel antifaschistischer Aktivitäten, München 1978; Henryk H. Broder (ed.), Deutschland erwacht. Braunbuch über die neuen Nazi Aktionen und Provokationen, ed. JUSO Landesverband Düsseldorf (Lamuv) 1978.
65. Innere Sicherheit 54, 1980 p. 15.
66. Innere Sicherheit 52, 1980 p. 26.
67. Hans Schneler, "Last des Vorurteils: Die Hälfte aller Bundesbürger ausländerfeindlich" in Die Zeit 17, 1982 p. 5.
68. Innere Sicherheit 53, 1980 p. 4; also Betrifft 1980 p. 3.
69. Innere Sicherheit 64, 1982 p.1.
70. Tagesspiegel 14.12.1977 quoting the French general Binoche.
71. Euroforum 4, 1979 p. 14.
72. Report. ed. The Embassy of the Federal Republic of Germany, January 1981 p. 10.
73. Andrew Wilson and Ludi Boeken, "Germany's New Nazis come into the open" in Observer 26.2.1978.
74. Rudolf Stefen (ed.) Gesamtverzeichnis indizierter Medien, Baden/Baden (Nomos) 1979 pp. 118-119.
75. Der Spiegel 50, 1977 pp. 214-220 "Mal was Nettes aus der Nazi Zeit".
76. The Musikarchiv, Berlin holds a comprehensive collection of these records.
77. Buchvertrieb GmbH Homberg, Liste 28, Juli 1978 p. 12.
78. Malte Ludin, "Nazi Lügen verbreiten" in Blickpunkt no. 265, ed. Senatsstelle für politische Bildung Berlin, 9.2.1978 p. 21. Also ibid. p. 39 ff "Wohin schwappt die Hiterwelle". The repercussions of the Hitler-wave in schools discusses Peter Dudek (ed.) Hakenkreuz und Judenwitz.

Opposition from the Right

Antifaschistische Jugendarbeit in der Schule, Bensheim (Pädagogik Extra Buchverlag) 1980.

79. e.g. Günther Deschner, Reinhard Heydrich, Bechtle 1977; Leonard Mosley, Göring, Lübbe 1977; Wulf Schwarzwäller, Rudolf Hess, Molden 1977; Viktor Reimann, Dr. Josef Goebbels, Molden 1975; Joachim Fest, Das Gesicht der Dritten Reiches, Piper 1978; John Toland, Adolf Hitler, Lübbe 1977; Joseph Goebbels, Tagebücher 1945, Hoffmann & Campe 1977; David Irving's Hitler's War falls in the same category. Popular magazines, especially Quick and Stern published innumerable stories about the private and inside-story life of Nazi greats. In January 1983 (no. 2) Stern for instance began to publish the childhood diaries of Himmler's daughter which show Himmler as a loving father and family man, ignoring his part in the SS and the Nazi programmes of mass murder. The abortive scoop of Stern Magazine to publish "Hitler Diaries" in 1983 fits into the same mould.

80. See Joachim Fest and Christian Herrendörfer, Hitler, eine Karriere. Bildband zum grossen Dokumentarfilm, Frankfurt/Berlin (Ullstein) 1977. Critical discussion in Jörg Berlin et. al., Was verschweigt Fest. Analysen und Dokumente zum Hitler Film, Köln (Pahl Rugenstein) 1978.

81. "Adolf Hitler - Superstar?" in Der Beobachter no. 1, 1977 p. 22. Der Beobachter was an attempt to launch a periodical from the right which would reach a wide readership. It was never published on a regular basis.

82. John Frazer "War Nostalgia, German Style" in New Statesman 8.7.1977 p. 43.

83. Aktenzeichen 141 JS 49/78. See Karl Heinz Jansen "Das Geschäft mit Hitler" in Die Zeit 19.5.1978.

84. Motorbuch Verlag, Stuttgart. Other military publishers are: Druffel, Munin, Plesse, Schild.

85. Advertising blurb, Motorbuch Verlag.

86. Interview on BBC Radio 4, 22.7.1977.

87. From Lippische Rundschau, quoted in Holocaust. Impulse, Reaktionen, Konsequenzen. Schriftenreihe des Didaktischen Zentrum, Frankfurt/Main 1980/81 p. 136.

88. Günter Bartsch, Revolution von rechts? Freiburg (Herder) 1975.

89. "Antwort auf die parlamentarische Anfrage vom 25.11.1981 im Bundestag" in Innere Sicherheit 61, 1981 p. 23.

90. Rabe, Rechtsextreme Jugendliche, Bornheim (Merten) 1980 p. 181 quoting from Wille und Weg, a sharply racist and antisemitic paper whose publication in Germany has been forbidden and which is now produced in Denmark and illegally brought into the country.
91. Ernst Roeder, Der Wind schlägt um. Das Blatt der deutschen Bürgerinitiative e.V. no. 1, October 1977 p. 1.
92. Kühnen in Rabe ibid. p. 48.
93. Innere Sicherheit 59, 1981 p. 7 quoting from a government sponsored assessment of Neonazism in the eighties.
94. Innere Sicherheit 60, 1981 p. 23.
95. Ibid. also Betrifft 1980 p. 23 reported that Roeder, the leader of the Deutsche Bürgerinitiative and former lawyer, had a bank balance of DM 84,000 (approx. 20,000 pound sterling) when he fled the country to avoid imprisonment.
96. Rabe, Rechtsextreme Jugendliche ibid. p. 176.
97. Innere Sicherheit 56, 1981 p. 45; Jörg Berlin et. al.,"Neofaschismus in der Bundesrepublik" in Blätter für deutsche und internationale Politik 5, 1978.
98. Betrifft 1981 p. 19.
99. All data Betrifft 1971-1980.
100. Deutsche Bürgerinitiative e.V.: Brief 62, n.d. p. 2.
101. Eckart, Wille und Weg, quoted in Rabe ibid. p. 181.
102. "Bombers' aim was a mass kill" in The Sunday Times, 28.9.1980 p. 6.
103. e.g. the spokesman of Kampfbund deutscher Soldaten (KDS) in an interview, Rabe ibid. p. 130.
104. Ibid. p. 98.
105. The Times, 3.6.1982
106. This argument in Kurt Sontheimer, "Gefahr von links-Gefahr von rechts" in Sontheimer et. al. (eds.) Überdruss an der Demokratie, München (Piper) 1968 pp. 34-38.
107. Detailed report in Innere Sicherheit 59, 1981 pp. 6-7.
108. Kühnen in Rabe ibid. p. 172.
109. See above chapter 6.

SUGGESTED READING

Abraham Ashkenazi, Modern German Nationalism, Wiley 1976

Opposition from the Right

Dieter Bossmann (ed.), Was ich über Adolf Hitler
   gehört habe. Folgen eines Tabus, Frankfurt
   (Fischer) 1977
Henryk H. Broder (ed.), Deutschland erwacht.
   Braunbuch über die neuen Nazi Aktionen und
   Provokationen, Düsseldorf (Juso-LV, Lamuv
   Verlag) 1978
Peter Dudek/Hans-Gerd Jaschke, Revolte von rechts.
   Anatomie einer neuen Jugendpresse, Frankfurt
   (Campus) 1981
Hans Josef Horchem, Extremisten in einer
   selbstbewussten Demokratie, Freiburg (Herder)
   1975
Heinz Werner Höffgen/Martin Sattler,
   Rechtsextremismus in der Bundesrepublik.
   Die 'alte' und die 'neue' Rechte und
   Neonazismus, Hamburg (Landeszentrale für
   politische Bildung) 1978
Reinhard Kühnl et. al., Die NPD. Struktur,
   Ideologie, Funktion, Frankfurt (Suhrkamp) 1969
John D. Nagle, The National Democratic Party.
   Right Radicalism in the Federal Republic of
   Germany, Univ. California Press 1970
Lutz Niethammer, Angepasster Faschismus. Politische
   Praxis der NPD, Frankfurt (Fischer) 1969
Alfons Silbermann, Sind wir Antisemiten? Ausmass und
   Wirkung eines sozialen Vorurteils in der
   Bundesrepublik, Köln (Wissenschaft und Politik)
   1982
Sinus-Studie: "Wir sollten wieder einen Führer
   haben ..." Die Sinus Studie über
   rechtsextremistische Einstellungen bei den
   Deutschen, Reinbek (Rowohlt) 1981
Kurt P. Tauber, Beyond Eagle and Swastika, (2 vols),
   Middletown 1967

Chapter Nine

THE GREEN PARTY: A NEW FACTOR IN THE WEST GERMAN
POLITICAL LANDSCAPE

In the Federal Republic, the sixteen or so smaller political parties which tend to compete in elections remain virtually unnoticed. The media focus on the big three who shared Bundestag representation since the early sixties and who also came to dominate the land parliaments.[1] Electoral statistics elaborate on the big three, and the varied remainder appears in a summary column of Sonstige.[2] This at least was true until the advent of the Green Party.

Small parties of whatever political orientation do not fit into the trend towards concentration or centrality of the party system, which has been diagnosed as a precondition of democratic stability. A possible and even desirable demise of the smallest of the three, the Free Democratic Party seemed never far away. The onset of a two party system, with the possibility to alternate the roles of government and opposition, appeared likely and a promise of democratic stability now and in the future.[3]

The tranquility of power sharing among the big three was only briefly disturbed when the right extremist NPD entered seven land parliaments between 1966 and 1968. In retrospect, the apprehension about the NPD successes and a possible upsurge of Neonazism into parliamentary politics may seem exaggerated: the party system was soon back in the stable pattern of the big three. Once the recession, the first after the economic miracle, was halted and unemployment reduced, the right-wing vote began to disintegrate. In 1972, the CDU/CSU had incorporated all but a tiny fraction of NPD support. The right-extremist element in the party landscape has since played a shadowy existence below the 0.5% mark, a political non-entity, relegated to the column of Sonstige, others, in election profiles.

The Green Party

A NEWCOMER WITH A POLITICAL FUTURE?

A decade or so later, the established calm of the party landscape has again been broken by a volatile newcomer with the ability to win votes: the Green Party. This new colour in West German politics embraces in its overall aims concerns for environmental protection in a world which is seen as endangered by untethered technology and designs for social change, for remodelled political institutions and new priorities of economic life. Table 9.1 illustrates that the new contestant for votes and parliamentary seats has done better from the outset than any 'other' party in the seventies and eighties. The Greens have been able to win votes and seats on all levels. By March 1983, they had about 1,000 representatives in local and district assemblies.[4] Greens had entered six land parliaments with a total of 47 delegates. After failing to jump the 5% hurdle for the Bundestag at their first attempt in 1980, the elections in March 1983 brought 5.6% of the votes and 27 seats. Together with the one representative from Berlin, a parliamentary party of 28 has become the voice of ecology in politics in West Germany.

Has the centrality of the West Germany party system, has the power sharing among the big three really been reversed by the advances of the Greens? In some ways, the political constellations and the economic constraints at the threshold of the eighties resemble those of the late sixties with their temporary diversification of the party system and their protest vote. Fifteen years or so later, again unemployment is high, nearing 2.5 million with forecasts of further increases.[5] Again, the roles of government and opposition have been reversed just after the electoral successes of the new party. Then, the SPD/FDP coalition pushed the CDU/CSU into opposition; the opposition camp subsequently proved able to incorporate the smaller party on the right. In September 1982, the SPD/FDP coalition finally fell apart and was replaced by a CDU/CSU and FDP alignment. Could this mean that the SPD might absorb the Greens and make them disappear from the political landscape - at least as far as sizeable election results are concerned? Or are the Greens about to consolidate their position as an opposition party in parliaments and in West German politics? These are some of the questions we want to examine in this chapter.

The Green Party

Table 9.1: The Green Party in Elections, 1978-1983

Election	Date	%	Seats
Hamburg +	4.6.1978	4.5	-
Lower Saxony +	4.6.1978	3.9	-
Hesse +	8.10.1978	2.0	-
Bavaria	8.10.1978	1.8	-
Rhineland-Palatine	18.3.1979	-	-
Berlin (W)	18.3.1979	3.7	-
Schleswig-Holstein	29.4.1979	2.4	-
European Elections	10.6.1979	3.2	-
Bremen	7.10.1979	5.1	4
Baden-Württemberg	16.3.1980	5.3	6
Northrhine-Westfalia	4.5.1980	3.0	-
Saarland	11.5.1980	2.9	-
Federal Elections	5.10.1980	1.5	-
Berlin (W)	10.5.1981	7.2	9
Lower Saxony	16.5.1982	6.5	11
Hamburg	6.6.1982	7.7	9
Hesse	26.9.1982	8.0	9
Bavaria	10.10.1982	4.6	-
Hamburg	20.12.1982	6.9	8
Federal Elections	6.3.1983	5.6	27 (+1 for Berlin)
Rhineland Palatine	6.3.1983	4.5	-
Schleswig Holstein	13.3.1983	3.6	-
Bremen	25.9.1983	5.3	4
Hesse	25.9.1983	5.9	7
+ all green lists and parties are put together			

Sources: Statistische Berichte for the various elections; a good analysis for the early years in Z Parl 1, 1979.

There are other changes in the overall political situation which need to be considered. The advent of the Greens as a parliamentary party has altered the political balance. In several lander, the Greens replaced the Free Democrats as third party: the FDP either won fewer votes and seats or it stumbled altogether over the 5% hurdle. Thus it was voted out of parliament in Hamburg, in Northrhine-Westfalia, in Hesse, in Bavaria, and for a term in Lower Saxony. In Berlin, it became the smallest party. In two lander, the demise of the FDP produced a temporary political stalemate. In Hamburg and in Hesse, the CDU was returned as the largest party, but without governing majority.

The Green Party

With the SPD the second largest block, the Green Party held the balance of power and found itself in the role of kingmaker or coalition partner.[6] For a party of a conventional format, such an opportunity to take on responsibilities would have been welcome. The Green Party, as we shall discuss below, does not regard itself as a conventional party and had not accepted the role of potential coalition partner in the established political frameworks.[7] In Hamburg and Hesse, the possibilities of tacit cooperation with the SPD were explored for a time, albeit half-heartedly. The Greens demanded full acceptance of their election programme as a precondition for co-operation. They also made communication difficult by sending different people everytime talks with the SPD were held. This policy of pseudo-cooperation did little to dispel doubts among the SPD whether the Greens could be regarded as a reliable partner in the day-to-day matters of regional politics. In Hamburg, the stalemate eventually led to new elections which returned an SPD government.[8] In Hesse, the Greens renounced their cooperation and their agreement to an interim budget on the eve of the Federal Elections, leaving a minority government which also headed towards out-of-term elections. The non-cooperation of the Greens in Hesse seems to have been timed to demonstrate to the potential supporters that this newcomer party was not just another coalition partner but could be relied upon to translate political critique into consistent political practice.[9]

The detachment from political responsibility which was at the core of the abortive talks in Hamburg and in Hesse, is a significant departure from established West German politics. It may resemble the abuse of political muscle by small parties in the Weimar Republic who frequently used their parliamentary votes to obstruct and even to topple a government or individual ministers without being prepared to take a share of power or carry government responsibilities. The possible impact of the Greens is, of course, curtailed by the barriers, which have been incorporated into the Basic Law. It is no longer possible to vote individual ministers out of office. To bring a government down, a constructive vote of no-confidence is required, i.e. only when parliament elects a new head of government can the government of the day be voted out of office. Despite these important limitations to the impact of opposition, the possibility of hung parliaments where the Greens can make or break a majority, gives the party unparalleled scope for political influence. It cannot make much use of it. The Greens' concept of parliamentary work has yet to emerge, their commitment to parliamentary work is still ambivalent. Even with delegates at the various levels of parliamentary- and assembly work, it is doubtful that the Greens can focus their parliamentary role towards responsible party government. So far, there is no agreed party view regarding parliaments and coalitions. In 1982, some Green spokesmen pleaded for cooperation with the SPD. Others, equally authorized Green spokesmen ruled out any cooperation, compromise, coalition.[10] The party seems unsure to what extent it could or should involve itself in politics through parliament. "Sometimes I am afraid that the Greens suddenly get 13 percent and become a party with political power. We should rather remain at 6 or 7 percent, and not compromise our principle demands. This is better than providing ministers".[11]

The difficulty with parliamentary commitment and even government responsibility rests in the self-assigned task to keep in close contact with supporters, the <u>Basis</u>. The so called Theory-of-the-two-Legs has frequently been used to explain the shifting balance between the party as a group in parliament and the party as a mouthpiece for the grass roots.

> With one leg, we stand firmly in the citizens' initiative movement and participate there actively in discussions and in actions. With the other leg, we want to be the yeast in the dough of the established parties, bring new incentives for thought into parliaments and be the parliamentary voice for the political ideas and wishes of the citizens' initiatives.[12]

The Greens may stand with equal weight on these two legs or their weight may be less evenly distributed. The Berlin Greens who operate under the name <u>Alternative Liste</u>, talk of a <u>Standbein</u>, the weight-bearing leg which is firmly implanted in the citizens' groups, the <u>Basis</u>, Green supporters and followers, the grass-roots. The other leg, the <u>Spielbein</u>, the non-weight-bearing leg is the parliamentary one: contributions to parliament and in parliament are seen as additional, even accidental pursuits. Some even question that the <u>Spielbein</u> should be used at all and advocate a "policy of empty chairs".[13] Getting elected and not taking up the seats should highlight the alleged deficiencies of the West German parliamentary system and of parliamentary practice as it has evolved. Parliament and parliamentary practice have, of course, been avidly criticized from various political positions in the course of German history.[14] From the right, they have been castigated as violating the natural order or things and the spirit of German national unity. From the left, parliament has been labelled as a body unsuited to bring about the fundamental changes envisaged by the ideology, a body of compromise and cooperation. At best, parliament may administer the status quo. Changes and progress can be realized only outside parliament, with extra-parliamentary activities and movements.

The Green critique of parliament oscillates between the anti-parliamentary positions of the right and the left. Parliaments are viewed with caution since delegates act as representatives, are bound to established procedures of debate and compromise and, above all, seem to have no meaningful links with the people who elected them.

Anti-parliamentary reservations are centred on the demand that delegates should at all times and in all political contexts be mouthpieces of their supporters and be accountable to them, i.e. introduce elements of direct democracy into a representative system found wanting.[15] The parliamentary focus of the Greens aims at creating or restoring close links between party and people, between parliamentary representatives and their voters. In this kind of anti-parliamentary parliamentarism, the emphasis of political work is on the grass roots. For the Greens in the eighties, the pressures are twofold: to become an opposition in parliament which could not and would not be absorbed and superseded by the SPD opposition; and also to become the focal point as party organization and as a party in elections for the various extra-parliamentary groups and movements despite parliamentary involvement.

ECOLOGY AND THE GREENS

The political ambivalence of the Greens can be traced to the origins of the party and more generally to the origins of ecology in West Germany as a politically significant issue.

Environmentalism and ecological issues are not altogether novel themes. Associations for the protection of nature, the preservation of forests, grasslands, open spaces among the sprawl of conurbations made their appearance in the wake of industrialization and the growth of big cities. This traditional concern with nature, ecology, environment was all but eclipsed from public awareness by the emergence of a more volatile environmentalism in the early seventies. Environmental issues soared to a position of priority or near-priority. In 1974, for instance, 41% of the electorate listed environmental protection as a very important topic. In 1979, 90% did so.[16] Economic stability, the usual front runner in the Federal Republic, had retained its place at the top of the list with environmentalism in second place. Among young people, it became the most important issue, even ahead of unemployment.[17]

The newly intensified concern with the environment generated a new form of organization, the action group or citizens' initiative. Rather than relying on the established parties to take care of these issues alongside other social and political matters, these groups tended to focus on one, localized problem and campaign to solve it: either by lobbying the administration or by utilizing the courts to avert administrative decisions which were deemed undesirable. These citizens initiatives have proved to be an attractive form of participation. While only 4% of West Germans belong to political parties and a maximum of 15% state they might join a party at some point, active membership in citizens' initiatives has already outstripped that in parties with potential membership as high as 60% of the West German adult population.[18]

Research on citizens' groups in the seventies pointed towards a relatively narrow spectrum of social support. Most of the members were middle class with grammar school- or university education. They were often members of the professions, in particular lawyers.[19] The mechanism already observed for party membership and for holding party offices seems again in evidence: the better-educated with a middle-class occupational status - or prospects of obtaining such status after their education or training - constitute the majority of active citizens. Lower class- or status groups are hardly involved in action groups or parties.

Among the many action groups, environmentalism generated the largest and the best organized sector.[20] In the wake of the oil crisis, the search for alternative energy led to an expansion of nuclear power production and plant construction. From then on, protests against the uses of nuclear energy became the most vociferous aspect of environmentalism. The determination to mount an effective battle against the nuclear programme and to bring the small and isolated groups together, generated a pressure group, the <u>Bundesverband Bürgerinitiativen Umweltschutz</u> BBU. The BBU developed into a major coordinating body. In 1977, it comprised some 900 affiliated groups and an estimated 200,000 individual members.[21]

The suggestion that the action group approach of challenging administrative decisions and of mounting court cases could be intensified if the movement had a parliamentary arm arose from within the BBU in 1977. The idea to create an ecology party was, however, not accepted unanimously.[22] Some felt that the strength of a pressure group and of the citizens' initiative movement as a whole lay in the fact that members and supporters of different political parties cooperated on issues and concerns relevant to all. The breadth and the political neutrality would be sacrificed if a party political label were to be adopted. An ecology party would weaken, if not destroy the citizens' movement. Moreover, citizens' initiatives had gained a reputation of being particularly effective in environmental protection, more so than other institutions or parties.[23] Eventually, the Green Party and the lists which preceded it were founded without official support from the citizens' initiative movement.

For the Greens, the outcome of this debate was of considerable importance. The most cohesive and organized sector of the citizens' initiatives did not endorse it. Although there was and has been some support - for example in the 1980 elections when the BBU chairman recommended to vote Green - the party cannot be considered the political wing of a broader social movement. The connections which exist with the citizens' initiatives and which figure so prominently in the Two-Leg-Theory are strictly local and regional. Various Green lists and parties have been aligned with groups in their area. These group are more diffuse than the organized ecology movement in the BBU. Hamburg is a good example for the diversity of support and group affiliations. Here, the Greens have always relied on a great number of action groups with a great number of different purposes.[24] There were environmental groups to purify the River Elbe, there were groups for women's rights, for homosexuals' equality, for the rehabilitation of criminals, to name just a few. The groups affiliated to the Greens belong to two clearly different types: the citizens' initiative whose purpose it is to influence administrative decisions with legal means, through the accumulation of scientific evidence or even through court cases; the other types are action oriented interest groups or factions who articulate their different views without attempting to persuade planning authorities and such like towards specific changes or moderations of their policies. The common denominator of these groups who call themselves Alternative Culture or Szene lies in defying the social and legal conventions on which citizens' initiatives have tended to base their impact. For the origins of the Green Party it is important that the so called citizens' initiatives or grass root groups on which the party hinges its place in society, are more diverse and politically incongruous than the ecology sector of the citizens initiative movement or the organized ecology sector in West Germany overall.[25]

The diversity of the citizens' groups contributes towards the diversity of regional Green parties. It also means that the Greens have not emerged as the political arm of a larger social movement. They are affiliated, parallel to it; not an integral part. The diversity of the action group sectors from groups for alternative culture to lobbies for environmental protection, has made it impossible for the Greens to derive political guidance from them. The diversity of this sector itself pushed the party towards a diversity of goals and an affiliation in many different directions. This makes it all the more difficult to establish a clear political profile. The Greens seem to be under pressure to prove themselves and recommend themselves constantly as the true voice of every single one of these diverse and single-minded groups. The ambiguity towards parliamentary commitment, which we mentioned earlier, is to some extent rooted in this unsteady and diverse grass root support, a support which only reluctantly subscribes to the party. Party organization itself is a problem for the Greens which overshadows its political work. Above all, the unsettled political origins of the Greens still characterize and unsettle the party.

The Green Party

Political Origins
Green lists appeared in 1977 in communal elections in Schleswig Holstein. Since 1978, they have been a regular element of elections in the lander, in the European elections, on a district and local level. The European elections provided an incentive to group the lists together into some sort of party. It was called Sonstige Politische Vereinigung. The 1980 elections gave a further push towards unifications. The party which has called itself The Greens since it was officially founded in 1980, has been helped on its way by the stricture of the West German party legislation and the timing of the elections. It was also helped on its way by the determination of some of its founding fathers to capture the diffuse environmental concerns in a political party and transpose it into votes. Other founders seemed more interested in expanding environmentalism into a level for political, socialist change. In other words, the ambiguities which have tailored the hesitant parliamentary role of the Greens, the ambiguities emanating from the multifaceted grass roots and action groups, were also apparent in the origins of the party and its founding process. In January and in March 1980, the nascent party held two founding congresses, the first one at Karlsruhe to define an organizational framework, the second one at Saarbrücken to formulate a party programme. During the land elections 1978-1980, several Green lists had competed against each other. Some were predominantly concerned with nature preservation and the protection of the environment, the so called green Greens. The red Greens amalgamated remnants of Socialism with environmentalism, the brown Greens took the threat to the environment and to nature as a threat to survival, to racial and national preservation.[26] To note this variety of Green standpoints is more important than to analyse whether these lists were really concerned with ecology and nothing else, whether they propagated Socialism thinly camouflaged as ecology, or whether the ecology umbrella disguised right-wing, even Neonazi tendencies. In our context it matters that all these strands contributed to the Green Party and that different political profiles prevailed in different regions and party segments. In Hesse for example the dominant influence on the Greens came from the defunct KPD, a Communist or better Maoist splinter group which dated back to the decay of the

Student Movement into left-wing radicalisms. At their first attempt at elections in 1978, these red Greens, remained noticeably unsuccessful.[27] But at the founding congresses the old hands at party organization, Cohn-Bendit, Dutschke, Semler were most effective in manipulating the agenda and of pushing some of their key demands into prominent place in the party programme, in particular the demand to dismember large enterprises and create small workers' cooperatives instead. Neonazi connections with the Greens have also been apparent. Kurt Oeser found that a number of Green lists, notably in Lower Saxony and Baden-Württemberg, involved Neonazis in their election campaigns.[28] These splintered radicals from the right, however, seem to have performed little more than messenger services. The "eco fascists" made little impact on the Greens. More lasting was the influence of a right-wing brand of environmentalism which condemned capitalism and unbridled technology as a threat to life, to race and national culture. The Aktionsgemeinschaft Unabhängiger Deutscher AUD, a right wing splinter party with some support in the South, the South West and in Hamburg, had taken up ecology themes under the heading of Lebensschutz, protection of life.[29] This anticapitalism with environmental trimmings has frequently been mistaken as a left-wing position. The gist of the anti-system approach does indeed sound similar: "Within the formal framework of a party, the AUD wants to mobilize the above party citizens' movement which is searching for new shores in its struggle against the tripartite state-party of capitalism in Bonn".[30] The AUD chairman since the fifties, August Haussleiter, became one of the founder members of the Greens and amalgamated his party with the Greens. Haussleiter was nearly successful in his bid for a party chairmanship. When his right-wing past was discovered, he had to resign. He continues as the party leader of the Greens in Bavaria and he edits the only membership paper, Die Grünen.[31]

The most ardent founder of the Greens, Herbert Gruhl, was driven out during the founding process. Gruhl had made his name as a member of parliament for the CDU and as tireless critic of the cultural repercussions of economic policies. After he left the CDU, he became involved in nature protection and gained fame as the author of a bestseller about impending environmental self-destruction of mankind, Ein Planet wird geplündert.[32] In 1978, he tried to pool the growing feelings about ecology and founded a party, the Grüne Aktion Zukunft. This had no visible connection with the citizens' initiative movement or the diverse groups affiliated with regional green lists. Gruhl's party was a conventional organization under the ecology trademark. It had an organization with just over one thousand members, a network of offices and a programme, the Green Manifesto which Gruhl saw as the platform for any ecology party. He seemed to have thought it an easy task to place himself at the head of the various Green lists and groupings and spearhead a mass-party. At the founding congresses, however, he suffered a series of setbacks: a Green party whose prime task it was to warn of ecological disasters rather than innovate politics and change society, was not acceptable to the majority of delegates. It had also found little support when Gruhl's party competed on its own.[34] The plan to create a formalized party structure conflicted with the determination of the majority of delegates to develop a new type of party, a party which should avoid all the assumed pitfalls of traditional party organizations and incorporate the Basis, the grass root members and supporters. Gruhl abandoned the Greens in 1981 and founded his own ecology party, the Ökologisch Demokratische Partei which has about 1,200 members and has remained an insignificant splinter group. Other conservative ecologists also left the Greens at this juncture.[35] In short, during the founding process, the green Greens, the conservative ecologists were sufficiently alienated to withdraw their backing of the new party.

The founding congresses and the party programme had claimed to bridge the cleavages among the founders by incorporating as many strands of ecological politics as seemed feasible. This proved a difficult task. At the congresses, about one thousand delegates from Green lists, local branches, action groups, and indeed anybody who was interested in the new party came together. In addition, over two hundred so called "autonomous delegates" turned up on the day and demanded equal rights, true to the principle of open government, Basisdemokratie.[36] Most of the first meeting in Karlsruhe was spent fighting over organizational control and items for discussion. Although the media tended to focus on the disorderly procedures, which contrasted sharply with the routine of ordinary party congresses, the arguments centred on some important issues. There was, first, the question of organizational identity. This meant that dual membership in the Greens and in other organizations should not be permissible. The intention was clear; to commit founding members to this party and break the influence of all the other groups and factions which had sent delegates to the congress. For delegates and Green party founders who came from other groups, the dual loyalty was a means by which to bring their political orientation as forcefully as possible into the new party. They did not want to relinquish this. After heated debates, a compromise was reached which has since been implemented: decisions about dual memberships should rest with regional parties. Controversies about the party programme were even more instructive about the diversities within the Greens.[37] There was, above all, the question of ecology. Since the unifying theme of the many political factions who had come together was the "green" theme, one might have expected the programme to open with it and to be slanted towards it. Protection of the environment, however, was relegated to section four. An introduction states the general principles as ecological, non-violent, grass root democratic. The first major section tackles the economy, followed by a passage on foreign- and peace policies which calls for world peace and assistance for the Third World. Only then does the programme turn to ecology, without in fact stating anything new. The programme opens on a theme of the left, demands for a profound economic and social reorientation; ecology takes second place as a facet of socialism. The most controversial section of the programme, however, deals with the commitment of the Greens to the interests of affiliated action groups: anti-abortionists, homosexuals, womens' groups, foreigners' leagues.[38] The endorsement of abortion was the most contested issue. The Schleswig-Holstein Green list refused to join a party who mistook the protection of the environment as a right to annihilate life.[39] Baden-Württemberg produced a programme of its own.[40] Bremen was reluctant to accept the common programme. A number of Green branches and groups disbanded in protest against the stand on abortion.[41] The left wing drift of the programme was only partly confirmed by the choice of leaders. None of the founder leaders had already a definite political profile, be it to the left or to the right.[42] The party, however, had established itself from the outset on the left of the political spectrum. The left-wing profile has been confirmed in the 1983 economic programme, published at the eve of the federal elections.

Destruction of the environment and the notion of a full-scale economic crisis as a crisis of society and capitalism go hand in hand:

> During the last decades, a life-threatening crisis has developed in all areas: environment, nature, economic and social contexts of life are increasingly in danger of complete destruction. Through the economic crisis in the last couple of years, the rise of unemployment in Western industrial nations as well as in the Federal Republic has reached frightening proportions. More and more people are pushed to the fringes of our society through unemployment and the dismantling of the welfare state.[43]

Against the backcloth of a pseudo-Marxist theory of crisis and pauperization, the Greens demanded a 35 hour working week, a redistribution of available work, a flexible approach to working hours, i.e. demands which had originated from the trade unions. In fact, the trade union position constituted the core of the section Sofortmassnahmen, Short Term Measures while the broader sweep of fundamental changes in society through a revolution in the approach to economic matters fills the bulk of the 1983 programme. As an attempt to elaborate on the left profile and as an attempt to break into an electorate close to the trade unions, the economic programme is an important step. It also reflects the difficulties of a leftist party, to remain detached from the trade unions and to nevertheless gain a firm social basis. Tangible links with the trade unions are virtually non-existent and union members have not been attracted to the Greens, despite the lipservice to their demands. The party has, moreover, been unable to draw the camp of potential supporters into the organization. Citizens' groups as a movement have remained aloof. The extra-parliamentary activities such as anti-nuclear protests remained outside the Greens and did not bring members into the party. Despite the catch-all gesture towards the left, towards dissenters, minorities, protesters, the Greens remain precariously poised on the margin of this volatile and diverse camp.

THE "ANTI-PARTY PARTY"

About one thing, organizers, protagonists, members and followers of West Germany's ecology party seem to be agreed: they do not wish to create a political party. The official name, the Greens omits the term "party". From within, the notion "Anti Party Party" has been suggested. A definition attempted in Berlin illuminates the problem:

> A party is a party. A party has an executive. A party has a line. A party has to define its boundaries vis-a-vis other parties. The <u>Alternative Liste</u> is no party. It has no executive. It has no line. It is completely different from other parties.[44]

Behind the rhetoric of anti-partism, matters are more straightforward. According to the conditions laid down in the party legislation, the Greens are a political party with a programme an executive and a party organization whose function it is to enter candidates for elections. We had observed earlier that the time schedule of creating a party from the regional and local Green lists was closely geared to elections and their legal requirements regarding party organization. By the summer of 1980, the Greens had a network of regional offices in all lander, albeit under different names. The parties in Hesse, Hamburg and Berlin continued to call themselves Alternative Lists or Green/Alternative Lists, although they were affiliated as land organizations to the headquarters of the Greens in Bonn. They also send delegates for their region, according to membership figures, to the party congresses. The Bonn headquarters was staffed by six full-timers and some part-time helpers in 1980.[45] By mid March 1983, a Telex machine had been installed and the number of part-time workers increased. The party had also moved into larger premises from the cramped two-room accommodation it had rented from landlord Gruhl before. By comparison with the other Bundestag parties, the visible Green establishment, offices, archives, equipment, staff are rudimentary.

The rudimentary character of the party organization is in itself a programmatic statement. One might assume that a new party lacks funds to equip and furbish offices, to employ staff, to establish an apparatus. In fact, the relative success of the Greens in elections ensured that it received regular

reimbursements of campaign costs. For the 1983
elections it can expect DM 8.5 million compared
with an estimated DM 700,000 actual campaign
costs.[46] The non-established appearance of the
party and its thin body of functionaries are to
show that this is not an established party but fundamentally
different. The Greens devised a number
of special regulations to underpin their segregation
from the run-of-the-mill party in West Germany.
It has three leaders of equal status and with
identical responsibilities who head the party's
eleven strong executive. The usual term of office
is two years with the possibility of re-election
into the same position no more than once. Anually,
half the executive posts are up for election. Both
provisions are to ensure rotation of office holders
and also prevent any one leader to dominate the
party and its public voice. During the first two
years, however, Petra Kelly, who was elected leader
in 1980, became the main focus of the media and
seemed to determine the image of the Greens in
society. She has since resigned her position to
stand as a candidate for parliament.[47] The separation
of party offices from political offices is a
further device to halt an accumulation of influence
by a small group of people. There are other, more
controversial conditions: all office holders, not
just those within the party, are required to rotate,
i.e. to vacate their positions and allow the next
person on the party list to take over after two
years of service. Bearing in mind that new members
of assemblies and parliaments have to accumulate
experience of procedures and practices before they
can make full use of the political scope of such an
institution, the principle of rotation seems to be
counterproductive. If applied, it would blunt the
parliamentary Greens. Predictably, it has been
challenged, even abandoned in some regions.[48] It
surprisingly re-emerged as a key theme after the
March 1983 elections and the entry of the Greens
into the Bundestag. Even before the new parliamentary
party had met, a special conference of the
coordinating body between executive and regions,
the <u>Bundeshauptausschuss</u>, met in Bonn and announced
that the novices would "rotate". In practical
terms this would mean that the elected 27 and the
27 next on the land lists would move to Bonn to
constitute the <u>Fraktion</u>. For the first two years,
the first group would sit in parliament, while the
others worked as assistants. Then, roles would be

reversed. An outcry of the prospective MPs who had
not been consulted brought an amendment. Rotation
only has to occur if the delegate is not re-elected
by the constituency party after two years. The
designated assistants faced the problem that employers may grant leave to take up seats in parliament,
they do not grant leave for the novel task of
second-in-line support. The hustle about rotation
was not the only imposition attempted by the
executive after the March elections. Remuneration
emerged in a similar way as a focal point of controversy. While political office should not generate
power it should - in the eyes of the Greens - also
not generate wealth. The <u>Alternative Liste</u> Berlin
was the first to proclaim that the average wage
level for skilled workers, about 1,900 Deutschmark
per month, would be good enough for a Green member
of parliament.[49] Gradually, the principle became
semi-official policy. In Hesse and Hamburg, the
wages rule was applied. Salary surpluses were to be
paid into an Eco-Fund administered by the party.
This could be used to assist groups who applied to
the Greens for help. In Baden-Württemberg, individual delegates keep all of their salary, but have
their own ways of redistributing some of it.
Constituency parties, specific groups, individuals
are among the beneficiaries. A unified line has not
emerged, and the principle of redistribution has
been questioned. For the Bundestag delegates, the
Eco-Fund model has been adopted - allegedly to
plough back some public money into the ecology action group sector. De facto, the financial control
of the party treasurer should give the party some
political control over the scope of the <u>Fraktion</u> and
its interrelation with the party. In view of the
fact that the principles of rotation and salary redistribution had never been unanimously accepted nor
applied in the Greens, the topicality of these
issues after the March 1983 elections points to
tensions between parliamentary party and the Bonn
based Green executive. The enforcement of these
rules made it more difficult for the <u>Fraktion</u> to
settle into its parliamentary role and accept it
without ambiguities. Moreover, the parliamentary
wing seems financially dependent on the party. This
is the important aspect. As a parliamentary body,
the <u>Fraktion</u> is also entitled to thirty or more full-
time paid administrative staff. As an organizational entity, the <u>Fraktion</u> has thus outpaced the party
in Bonn. The strictures on pay and terms of office

were to claw back some control over the parliamentary wing. They were also intended to obstruct the parliamentary sector by stressing the commitment to the Basis, the non-parliamentary sector within and outside the Greens. Organizationally, the Bundeshauptausschuss is charged with the communication between Bonn and the regions and between the parliamentary and the action group dimensions of the Greens. It meets every six weeks in Bonn, and MPs are required to travel to their constituencies at least once a fortnight. The real reason for all these regulations lies in the flimsiness of the Greens as an organization, in particular as a membership party.

Party work has to be unpaid, voluntary. In practical terms this means that only those who can find time for several hours of party activity in addition to their occupations can afford to hold posts. Consequently, the party has been run by teachers, university lecturers, students, pensioners. The social composition of the Bundestag delegation mirrors the narrow social focus of the party. In 1983 there were seven teachers, three professors, three journalists, plus a lawyer, a vet, a nurse, a retired general, two works' councillors, one "real" worker and a so called peace worker who was an unemployed sociologist. Prior to their nominations, most had held unpaid party posts. In a further sense, the party has remained narrow. Even after several years of election successes, after three years as a fully fledged party, the Greens had few members, just 25,000 in March 1983.[50] Compared with the membership in citizens' initiatives, compared with the three million or so who signed the Krefeld Appeal against cruise missiles, compared with the potential support for environmental groups, compared also with the scope of extra-parliamentary activity in West Germany since the seventies, the Green Party has been an organizational failure. Yet, the Greens have also been ambivalent towards the concept of party membership as they have been ambivalent towards forms of organization and institutional structures. On the one hand, membership alone is taken into account in determining the number of delegates a land organization may send to party congresses. These calculations are based on a monthly contribution of DM 2 per member to the Bonn office. On the other hand, party boundaries are kept deliberately open. In Hamburg, some 200 groups mounted the election campaign in 1978, groups which were not even

affiliated in a formal sense to the Greens. In
Bremen, the Greens had only 35 members when they won
four seats in the Senate. During the campaign, they
relied on helpers and spontaneous support. For
Baden-Württemberg, the Greens stress the roots of
the party in the initiatives and a responsibility
to be their voice. In the day-to-day running of the
party, these vague boundaries mean that anybody can
come along and join in. But this emphatic informality has not resulted in eager participation and involvement of the rank-and-file members in party
affairs. In Hesse, for instance, 80 of 2,500 members at the time attended a land congress to formulate the 1982 election platform.[51] Ten of these,
were members of the executive. In Baden-Württemberg,
members have been detached and apathetic.[52] In
Berlin, Green members of Senate feared to be cut-off
from the grass roots, similar complaints have come
from all regions.

    The passive core in the Green may be similar to
the passive core in all parties. In the light of
the political tasks allocated to members, passivity
deals a harder blow to the Greens than to its rivals.
The Party Statutes grant members open access to all
party functions, there should be no closed doors.
The Greens in Bad Homburg literally left the doors
to their chambers open to signal a welcome to everybody.[53] The difficulties start with the contributions expected from members: preparing the political
positions of the party, assisting elected representatives, sifting documents, shaping parliamentary
arguments. The shoestring operation which does not
permit paid, permanent helpers, forces Green representatives to rely on membership participation.
Such participation is not readily forthcoming. As
one disillusioned Green leader put it: "They come
to criticise, not to help".[54] The following impressions from Berlin seem to be typical for the problems
of practical party work and political representation
in the Greens:

> The delegates and assistants of the parliamentary party Alternative Liste ... are under
> stress, feel overloaded and abandoned by the
> grass-roots and by the 'scene'. Few take part
> in meetings to prepare the next session of
> parliament. Hardly anybody can be bothered to
> join in the discussions or to make suggestions
> ... The performance of the Greens in parliament
> that same afternoon confirms the first impress-

ion. They appear adjusted to the routine of professional parliamentarians, they do not break the pre-defined framework of rigidity, boredom, lifelessness. No self-confidence, no feeling of joy surrounds them, just uncertainty and timidity.[55]

The realization of Basisdemokratie rests on the ability of the party to mobilize its membership permanently. Members should be prepared to contribute in and through the party regardless of holding office or enjoying a specific status.[56] This does not work in practice. The reverse principle is more effective. The Greens have adopted a so called imperative mandate, an obligation for political - and party representatives to report to members regularly and to accept members' guidance for their work.[57] The practicalities of the consultation process often mean extensive sessions, discussions, misgivings. In Baden-Württemberg, members attacked the parliamentary spokesman for failing to involve them in every step when he negotiated parliamentary status. In the same region, the land delegates have started to plough part of their salaries into financing parliamentary assistants since they cannot get sufficient support from the Basis.[58]

Despite pledges to the contrary, the Greens are moving towards a more formalized established party structure. The relative passivity of the members, their limited involvement in political tasks force the Greens towards the very professionalization of politics they proclaimed to have overcome through the principle of Basisdemokratie. As in other parties, groups of functionaries and full-time party staff determine the main thrust of political practice. Moreover, the ambivalence towards parliamentary work, in particular towards the Bundestag, led to the party executive scheming to remain in charge and control the Fraktion, at least financially. As the most established segment of the Greens, the Fraktion itself begins to call the tune and dominate the projections of Green politics in the press and in society at large. The notion of Basisdemokratie has deteriorated to a smokescreen which is used to hide various designs for political control. The stress on Basisdemokratie also reflects the weakness of manifest support for the Greens. Without constantly assuring the latent, detached supporters that the Greens continue to be relevant for them, the party seems to be in danger of slipping to the fringes: by-passed by the mainstream politics and also by-passed by those forces which generated the citizens' movement, the political significance of environmental issues and the Greens themselves.

WHO SUPPORTS THE GREEN PARTY?

Support for the Green party is closely linked to agreement or disagreement with the political system in West Germany, and with the place of political parties in it. The broad acceptance of the political institutions and of the three major parties has been a significant aspect of the consolidation of democratic government in West Germany. Although Almond and Verba and also Edinger observed that West Germans in the fifties and sixties tended to endorse the rules and regulations of democracy rather than its spirit, a consensus with the democratic system emerged.[59] Over the years, the deficit of pride in democracy and in democratic values has been remedied somewhat.[60] Opinion polls have repeatedly shown a broad consensus to exist. In 1981, three out of four West Germans declared themselves completely satisfied with their political institutions. The remaining quarter were more sceptical.[61] Discontent was pronounced among those who also stated that they were supporters of the Greens. 63% were not satisfied with their political environment. Greens were also particularly negative about the role of politicians and their relevance for ordinary people. Yet, this detachment from the political framework and from the people who hold positions in it went hand in hand with political interest. Far from being detached and apathetic, Green supporters were detached and keen on politics, just not the politics of mainstream German society. In March 1982, West Germans over eighteen were asked whether they had an interest in politics and public affairs. 28% of the general public but 67% of Green supporters were interested or very interested.[62] A similar result emerged from a survey of young people under 25 which was conducted in April 1980 under the auspices of the ZDF television station: interest in politics lay above average but so did disappointment with political parties and negative views about the political system in general.[63] An Allensbach survey of August 1982 concluded: "In politics, Green supporters are anything but drop-outs. Here, they commit themselves fully. It seems the established parties are faced with the problem that young people desert them and turn to the Greens".[64]

The step from disaffection with mainstream political priorities to the Greens is, as we had seen for membership figures, somewhat tentative. Few of the potential supporters translate their political views into organizational integration. The 1981 Youth Survey compiled by the German Shell company, found that one in five West Germans under the age of 25 claimed to be Green supporters. Just six percent stated that they were members of the Greens or of alternative groupings with similar concerns.[65] Bearing in mind that 6.4 million West Germans are at present aged twenty five or under, Green support could be around one million. Membership figures are about 2% of this potential.

The Greens have been more effective in winning voters among the dissatisfied, politically interested young. They have three main footholds in the electorate: young voters, educated voters and voters who have been mobilized for environmental- or anti-nuclear issues. There is a well documented correlation between age and voting Green. The first electoral returns for Green lists indicated already that about two thirds of the Green voters were under 25. In the land elections between 1978 and the summer of 1982, the Green Party won between 8.5% and 24.3% of the electorate aged 18-24 (Table 9.2). Everywhere, the Greens had overtaken the FDP as a choice for the young. The FDP achieved its best results in Bremen with 10.3% of the electorate under 25. There, the Greens won 14.9%. In Hamburg, Berlin, Lower Saxony they secured over 20% of these voters. The Green challenge tended to hit the SPD hardest because the SPD managed to secure the largest share of the young vote during the seventies. In regions where the Greens gained twenty percent or more, among the young voters, the SPD fared worse than average among that group. Where the Green vote among that group remained under 20%, the younger than average voter still preferred the SPD. In the Saar region, 8.5% of the 18-24 year olds voted Green in 1980, the party gained 3% overall. The SPD secured 51.4% of the young vote and 46.4% overall. In Berlin, in contrast, the Alternative List managed 24.3% among the youngest voters and 7.5% overall. The SPD obtained 36.4% among the young and 38.8% overall. The electoral threat from the Greens seems most directly poised against the SPD and specifically against the youngest sector of SPD voters. In

Table 9.2: Voting in Land Elections: All Voters and Young Voters (18-24) in Comparison

Land	CDU/CSU All %	CDU/CSU Young %	SPD All %	SPD Young %	FDP All %	FDP Young %	Greens All %	Greens Young %	Others All %	Others Young %
Baden-Württemberg 1980	53.4	40.2	32.9	36.2	8.2	6.9	5.1	15.7	0.5	0.5
Bavaria 1978	58.3	54.2	32.5	34.3	6.0	5.4	–	–	3.2	5.6
Berlin 1981	47.1	32.2	38.8	36.4	5.7	5.6	7.5	24.3	0.9	1.5
Bremen 1979	32.0	16.9	49.7	50.5	10.8	10.3	5.0	14.9	2.5	7.4
Hamburg 1978	37.9	21.6	51.1	48.6	4.7	6.8	4.8*	20.6*	1.5	2.5
Hesse 1978	45.4	35.6	45.0	50.0	6.7	6.7	–	–	3.0	7.7
Lower Saxony 1982	50.8	40.8	36.9	33.3	5.6	5.2	6.3	20.3	0.3	0.4
Northrine-Westfalia 1980	41.8	30.6	49.9	53.5	5.0	5.1	2.8	10.1	0.3	0.5
Rhineland-Palatine 1979	50.1	42.7	42.6	49.5	6.1	6.4	–	–	1.2	1.4
Saar 1980	42.9	34.5	46.4	51.4	6.7	4.7	3.0	8.5	1.0	0.9
Schleswig-Holstein 1979	47.5	32.0	42.4	50.7	5.7	7.1	–	–	4.4	10.2

* Results for Green and Coloured Lists added together

Source: Z Parl 3, 1982 p. 413 based on data of the Repräsentative Wahlstatistiken der Statistischen Landesämter.

the 1983 elections, the Greens based their success
on two main groups: the first voters and voters in
the middle age range who had previously voted SPD
and had now turned to the Greens.[66] Young people,
whether Green voters or not, tend to be open towards
the new party. A pre-election survey in Lower
Saxony in 1982 revealed that 74% of the 18-25s wanted the Greens to enter the land parliament. So did
48% of the age group 25-30, 43% of those between 30
and 40, and so on, on a sliding scale to just 17% of
the over sixties in favour of Green representation.[67] Supporters of the Green Party tend to be
young, opponents older. Of the youngest voters,
aged 18 to 20, 42% declared that they would definitely or most likely vote Green in March 1980. Of
those aged 27 to 30, just 15% might have done so.
First and young voters constitute the highest voters'
reservoir of the Greens.[68]

The occupational composition of the Green
electorate and of the party membership is less well
documented. The party does not keep records or if
it does, it does not allow access to these records.
Information about the social composition has to be
pieced together from various observations. The
Greens have been called a teachers' party due to the
large number of teachers who are active in it. We
noted earlier that relatively many teachers are
among the Green delegates in parliaments. An Emnid
survey suggested in October 1978 that the Green
Party attracted support from civil servants and from
the self-employed. At that time, about one third of
the self-employed in the Federal Republic stated
that they endorsed the Green Party. Then, the conservative brand of ecology seemed to constitute the
core of the new venture. This has since changed and
it is unlikely that an affinity of the self-employed
with the leftist Greens could now be detected. Table
9.3 shows a detachment from the Greens by white
collar employees by skilled and unskilled workers
and in particular by trade union members. Although
the data on social composition are patchy, the
Greens emerge as definitely not a workers' party.[69]
If anything, the social profile points towards a
middle class composition. This is confirmed by one
factor which is clearly discernible in a decision
for the Greens: education. Green voters, supporters, members tend to be well educated. 30% of West
Germans with university education or <u>Abitur</u> supported the Greens, a further 31% were positively
inclined towards them in 1978 (Table 9.3). The

Table 9.3: Attitudes Towards the Greens by Social Characteristics

Among every one hundred people in every social category were	Opponents	Undecided	Sympathisers	Supporters	Proportion of sample (All)
Sex					
Female	19.5	33.1	26.6	20.7	53.0
Male	29.8	26.6	23.5	20.1	47.0
Occupation					
Self-employed	20.6	27.0	22.2	30.2	13.4
Employees	26.7	25.8	27.9	19.7	34.9
Civil servants	24.2	33.7	26.3	15.8	10.1
Workers	24.0	35.5	21.5	19.0	12.8
Skilled workers	24.5	31.5	25.3	18.7	28.9
Education					
Hauptschule without apprenticeship	26.1	35.8	19.4	18.8	16.8
Hauptschule with apprenticeship	23.3	32.6	25.4	18.7	57.2
O-Level (Mittlere Reife)	27.6	23.3	27.0	22.1	16.6
A-Level/university (Abitur)	22.6	16.1	31.2	30.1	9.6
Denomination					
Protestant	24.2	32.1	26.3	17.4	50.4
Catholic	23.6	28.0	25.2	23.2	45.5
Others	22.5	27.5	20.0	30.0	4.1
Trade union membership					
Yes	33.5	29.3	18.6	18.6	17.3
No	22.4	29.9	26.5	21.2	82.7
Percentage of attitudes towards the Greens in the sample	24.6	29.8	25.0	20.6	100.00

Source: Scharping/Hofmann-Göttig ibid. p. 402; based on Emnid survey of October 1978. N=1007

numerical values may have to be treated with some
caution. University education tends to produce, in
any case, more liberal attitudes in West Germany
today. The higher educated tend to be principally
more in favour of political diversity, of equal
chances for all, including new parties. Manifest
support among the better educated groups is certainly less than the survey data indicated. But
electoral analyses confirmed that the Green Party
tends to perform above average in areas where the
educational level of the inhabitants is high. In
the constituency of Brunswick University, for instance, the Greens won over 40% in 1978.[70] In
university towns like Marburg, Freiburg, Bielefeld,
Giessen, returns for the Greens have been above
average, around 10%.

The Greens are not just a party for university
students and critical intellectuals. In mobilizing
the Green support and in actually winning sufficient
votes to gain seats, environmental issues have been
of considerable importance. Where environmental
groups had already made a local impact, Greens tended to do well in elections. Moerfelden, for example,
a small town near Frankfurt and the community most
affected by a planned expansion of Frankfurt airport,
the famous <u>Startbahn West</u>, generated considerable
citizens' protest against the project. It returned
the Greens with 25.7% in the 1981 local elections.
Nearby Gross-Gerau recorded similar results.[71] In
the constituency around Gorleben, the prospective
site for a nuclear dump and the scene of many protests, the Greens did very well since 1978. The
same holds true for Wyhl, where farmers of the
Kaiserstuhl region objected to the nuclear plant and
voted above average for the Greens in the 1980 land
elections.[72] Hamburg Eimsbuettel, a prosperous sub-
urb, returned the Greens with 9% in the June 1982
land elections. A local action group to clean
the Elbe and the demands of the Greens in this area
were virtually identical: "The Elbe is a shipping
way, but it is foremost a sewage canal for any kind
of rubbish one can imagine. In the Hamburg area,
60% of all untreated waste is still pumped directly
into the Elbe".[73] Voting Green endorsed key points
of the suburbian action group. The same thing
happened in March 1983: in constituencies with on-
going environmental concerns and in urban areas with
a high concentration of university students, the
Greens scored above average.[74]

On the tide of environmental protests, the

Greens managed to break into small towns, rural areas and win a more diverse group of older voters: indeed, they won about one third of their electorate in this way. Who would have thought that the Bavarian hamlet of Neufahrn near Freising would have 9.8% Green voters? They voted in the wake of protests against a second Munich airport. The small town of Niederaichbach near Landshut, also in Bavaria, gave 11.6% to the Greens in the 1978 land elections. The plans to construct an atomic power station in the immediate vicinity had boosted support for the Greens even in a CSU stronghold.[75] In short, the ability of the Greens to attract an environmental protest vote of people who do not normally subscribe to the party is an important facet of its election results. Rather than appealing only to the slim sector of the educated young who do not identify with one of the established parties, the Greens have the potential to win a broader social spectrum. These voters seem to be mobilized against local power structures, not in a definite and deliberate decision for the Greens. There are some indications, however, that this broader electoral potential may be lost through the escalation of anti-nuclear protests into violent clashes with the police. Brokdorf is a good example. In 1978, 17.8% in the constituency voted Green. In the 1980 federal elections, after Brokdorf had become the scene of numerous clashes, the Green vote remained below average, at 1.3%.[76] Results in 1983 were similar. Other localities, Gorleben for instance or Kalkar, have been less affected and the Greens continue to win an environmental and locally based vote. Yet the danger of alienating this vote must not be overlooked.

Citizens' groups can carry the Greens into small towns and into rural areas, beyond the large conurbations and the university towns; the volatility of protests, however, can endanger this dimension of Green support. It is, at best, fragile and tentative. The backbone of the Green vote, the young votes, seem equally shaky and uncertain. It has been observed for small and dissenting parties that much of their backing tends to come from the young. This backing is likely to weaken with young voters turning to the mainstream parties when the integration into careers, professions, society has become more definite.[77] The Greens, as we saw, relies on the young vote and, as it seems, on a transient vote. There are researchers, however, who

The Green Party

regard the Green vote as anything but transient and claim that it is a solid and considered political choice: not protest or non-conformism of the young but New Politics. Let us examine the case.

Protest Vote or New Politics?
A protest vote tends to rest on a dismissal of the established parties and their answers to the political and social issues of the day. In this sense, Green voters are protest voters. They do not believe that the major parties could contribute to the improvements and changes they advocate. They also dismiss traditional left-right divisions and the boundaries of ideologies as ill-suited to the needs of the future. Green voters tend to place themselves above the left-wing spectrum in a centre position.[78] Not left, not right but up front, as a Green slogan would have it. From the vantage point of the general population, the Greens seem difficult to classify. The electorate as a whole tend to place them in the centre.[79] Seen from the CDU or the CSU position, they look decidedly left wing.[80] In the 1980 elections with its polarization of Chancellor candidates, Green votes went to Schmidt and the SPD.[81] There is a different line of argument altogether to determine the place of the Green electorate. It has been stated that a new set of priorities and values has emerged among the young in line with postmaterialism in advanced industrial societies, and that the Greens articulate those new values.[82] A series of surveys in 1981 and 1982 attempted to clarify the political priorities of Green supporters and contrast them with commonly held views. Two important observations can be based on these data: the first, Green voters hold views on certain issues which are clearly different from majority views in West Germany. The second, the Green electorate in itself is more cohesive than the electorates of other political parties.[83] To give some examples: The Nato twin track decision has become a dividing line between those who believe in military deterrent and West Integration and those who favour disarmament, neutrality, peace. Of the Green electorate, 52% were avidly opposed to the Nato decision. Only the CDU electorate was equally certain with 53% in favour. Of the Greens, 82% thought neutrality was the best solution for West Germany. Among the other parties, the FDP had the clearest position with 75% of its supporters in

favour of the Western Alliance. Similarly, confidence in the United States was low among Greens with 51% distrustful. For the other parties, the issue was unsettled; 14% of the CDU and FDP electorates declared they trusted the USA. The Peace Movement proved another dividing line. Of the Greens, 70% intended to join or had already done so. Views among the established parties were diverse. The CDU/CSU seemed most coherent with 40% against the Peace Movement. In short, the attitudes of the Green electorate or those who declared that they voted Green, are unified among themselves and distinct from the population overall. This does not just apply to current affairs. While the primacy of economic prosperity and of technological progress is widely accepted, Greens plead for zero growth and emphasize the dangers which would come from applied technology. Two in three Green supporters were convinced that so called technological progress was bound to threaten life and environment.[84] Protests against the utilization of atomic energy - 85% of the Greens oppose it - can be traced back to this controversial evaluation of economic growth and of technology for the future well-being of society. This postmaterialism entered the political arena as a cluster of attitudes and priorities, as New Politics. Here, the priorities of economic growth, of armaments, or power politics are challenged in favour of the elusive 'quality of life'. In practical terms, this translates into opposition to atomic power, support for the Peace Movement, concern about the environment, in short all those issues where the Green electorate showed such clear cohesion. The Green Party may be seen as a mouthpiece of postmaterialism, as a lever of New Politics.

Postmaterialism and New Politics in West Germany go beyond the Green Party. A recent survey among middle level party functionaries of the CDU/CSU, the SPD and the FDP showed that the New Politics had also penetrated these parties, above all the SPD.[85] One of the issues used to test the New Politics was environmental protection (Table 9.4). Here, 75% of the SPD functionaries stressed that greater efforts were needed; 55% did so for the FDP, 31% for the CDU and 25% for the CSU. An interesting suggestion contained in these findings, is that political camps today are divided along new ideological demarcation lines: while the CDU and the CSU mobilize traditionalists, the SPD attracts those with new leanings. The FDP hovers somewhere in be-

Table 9.4: Environmental Issues in Established Parties

"Greater efforts have to be made to protect our environment"

Agreement	SPD %	FDP %	CDU %	CSU %
Strong agreement	72	55	31	25
Agreement	27	41	65	67
Don't know	1	2	3	4
Disagreement	1	2	1	5
Strong disagreement	0	0	0	1

Source: Schmitt ibid. 522.

tween the two camps. A similar grouping emerged in the 1981 Youth Survey.

Political manifestations of postmaterialism were articulated in the Greens; SPD followers held an interim position with some postmaterialists and some traditional views; CDU, CSU and FDP catered for the traditionalists among the young.[86]

With New Politics stretching beyond the radius of Green support into the other parties, which factors would determine whether postmaterialism crystallizes as a drive for change within the established framework or as a drive for change through the anti-system gesture of the Greens? Buerklin has pursued this question in recent research and suggested that there was no difference of substance between Green postmaterialists and those who voted for or belonged to the SPD. The lever to swing postmaterialists towards the Greens was, he found, "a low level of integration into existing social and political networks".[87] Among those who opted for the Greens, the "threshold of departure was rather low". Such integration may be defined as social status, as occupational or professional advancement. Here, the transition of the young into a career might transfer the Green support of the students, trainees etc. into support for the mainstream parties, in particular of the SPD.

The concepts of social integration and of a threshold of departure may be somewhat vague, but they link up well with our earlier observations about the critical detachment of Green supporters from political institutions. They also link up with the observations about the age structure of the

Green support. Those 20% of the youngest electorate who do not vote for one of the big parties, may have a low degree of integration, socially and politically, the element Buerklin singled out as the element which makes New Politics into Green Politics.

The dependence of the Green support on a low degree of integration also suggests that in some respects the Green vote is a protest vote. With a consolidation of career patterns and social integration, it could gravitate from the Greens to an established party. The New Politics are possibly transient in a further respect. As a product of affluence, the postmaterialism on which New Politics rests, may not survive the altered economic circumstances. Unemployment and economic stagnation if not recession could halt the emergence of new values and restore traditional patterns of social thought and action. At least among the young generation who grew up in the seventies and early eighties and who will reach voting age in the latter half of the decade, new values and postmaterialism may no longer be evident. The future of the Greens as a voters' party seems to be under pressure from two sides. The process of change in views and values away from postmaterialism and the likely absorption of young voters into mainstream parties in adulthood. The answer of the Green Party to plot its own survival has to lie in the political profile it shaped in practical politics, in parliaments and assemblies. A political consolidation on that level would free the party from the pressures emanating from the social and economic circumstances and the party political constellation of the eighties in West Germany.

THE GREEN PARTY IN ASSEMBLIES AND PARLIAMENTS

With the SPD in opposition and perhaps more conciliatory towards its postmaterialists, the political survival of the Green Party seems uncertain. The easy juxtaposition to the governing party, which aided the founding process, is no longer possible. On the left-right spectrum, the Greens were close to the SPD even when the SPD was in government. Against an SPD opposition they have to defend their separate identity by developing, within the opposition camp, a separate and visible profile. This would mean to translate the Green aims and principles into

parliamentary practice and political proposals.
　　The contributions of Green delegates are perhaps the best pointer to the profile the party has achieved or seems able to achieve through parliamentary representation. To date, the strongest impression is diversity. In the district of Kreuzberg in Berlin, for instance, the Greens have become the voice of squatters who protest about demolition or rennovation of older properties which would make them too expensive for established tenants. In defence of these aims, even the use of violence is condoned:

> For many, the use of violence is the most effective and most radical counter-language (Gegensprache) which will also be noted by the other side. Stones can be arguments if those in power refuse to improve the inadequacies for which they are criticized. Only after window panes were broken...did a discussion about housing even commence.[88]

Elsewhere, the position of the Greens has been more conventional, even conservative on the surface. In Bremen, the parliamentary group argued in favour of private schools to meet the needs of religious sects and other minorities.[89] In Baden-Württemberg, the Greens objected to regional schools and pleaded in the land parliament for the re-introduction of village schools to provide a more balanced environment. This demand has last been voiced by the CDU in the fifties. Across the board, Greens advocate decentralization. The replacement of industrial concerns by workers' cooperatives and small workshops had already been a point in the party programme. In land parliaments the abolition of unemployment benefits was proposed to reduce the dependence of the individual on the state. In the Bundestag, the Greens emerged as spokesmen for small farmers against the pressures of European agricultural policies and rationalization.[90] Other issues echoed left-wing inclinations. In June 1983, the Greens in the Bundestag forced a debate on the situation of the steel industry, partly, it was proposed, to collect information on the official government position, partly to gain maximum publicity for their demands to redistribute labour, change working hours and break up large enterprises. A notion of nationalization also crept into the debate, not state control but control by the people, a variation of the cooperatives' and workshop model mentioned earlier.

In Baden-Württemberg, the first parliamentary initiative of the Greens aimed at basing local government on "direct democracy", on plebiscite. In fact, the party had not attempted to find out whether such a proposal was likely to be welcomed at local government level or by the citizens who were to benefit from it. When the land government put the matter to mayors and local assemblies, no support was forthcoming.[91] In other words, the seemingly constructive proposal of the Greens was only rooted in the party's own priorities. Politically, it remained abstract, unworkabable. The same can be said for a series of armament debates on the land level.[92] A great deal of time and effort was invested to force the land parliament of Baden-Württemberg to debate the stationing of cruise missiles. The land parliament, of course, has no jurisdiction in matters of defence. It only has the right to ask the government of the region to bring a matter to the attention of the Bundesrat. With the Green's initiative on armament, even this did not happen, the effort was ill-prepared and wrongly angled. Again, the aim appears to have been gaining publicity for Green policy priorities, not achieving anything within parliament. By using parliament as a platform for key issues, the party can impress upon its potential supporters that it acts as the champion of their views. Because the focal point of parliamentary work seems to be to the outside, towards the tentative supporters, regional parties have remained diverse. These diversities have also entered the Bundestag Greens. The common aim seems to be to articulate all kinds of points, even contradictory ones, as doggedly and as spectacularly as possible. The aim is not to devise a formula for workable change through parliament. An effective means for this approach, an effective means of ensuring media coverage and showing supporters that the Greens are not just ordinary parliamentarians, has been the political happening. Be it the horse-and-cart entry of the Greens in the Bundestag, alongside 'the chauffeur driven Mercedes cars of the more established; be it the wearing of gas-masks to debate nuclear energy;[93] be it the walk-outs and protests about conventions and procedures in the Bremen Senate;[94] the Greens have made ample use of political happenings and have been rewarded with ample public attention for it. They have shown

ridicule if not disdain for some aspects of
parliamentary life, in particular the rituals and
conventions; they may also have alerted the public
to believe there could be too much ritual and form-
ality in West German parliamentary work. Overall,
Green opposition to date has been largely propagan-
dist, declamatory. An analysis of contributions in
land parliaments revealed recently that speeches
were usually general criticisms without any attempts
to forge them into suggestions, practical proposals
which could be implemented. Despite the priorities
of <u>Basisdemokratie</u> and decentralization, the political scope of Green parliamentary work is confusing-
ly wide, oscillating between conservatism and un-
dogmatic socialism. This does hardly add up to a
political profile. The abstract generality of Green
parliamentary contributions may be caused by the
reluctance of the rank-and-file to knuckle down and
help with preparations and documentation of arguments. In the Bundestag, where full-time assistance
has been available, the same weaknesses of political
projection continue. In the debate following the
German equivalent of the Queen's Speech, the
<u>Regierungserklärung</u> by the Kohl government, the
Greens proceeded to elaborate on all aspects of
their politics, at times referring to government
plans, often without such reference. No reforms,
programmes, parliamentary tasks were formulated
which the government should undertake and for which
the Greens would provide the data basis or had already done so. Some speeches, in particular on
technology and the economy were riddled with data;
but these were not forged into proposals for
policies. The format of parliamentary work in the
land parliaments has also penetrated the first steps
of the Greens in the Bundestag: abstract, declamatory politics, aimed more at the uncertain following outside than at the level of workable parliamentary measures. A touch of <u>Spielbein</u> theory is
still apparent in the Bundestag: the Greens have
remained basically extra-parliamentary in character
and approach. They have, of course, refrained from
adopting the policy of "empty chairs". A convincing
parliamentary profile has yet to emerge together
with a modification of the extra-parliamentary
leanings of the party and of its potential followers
and voters.

THE GREEN PARTY AND THE PEACE MOVEMENT

The place of extra-parliamentary activities in opposition politics has been underpinned by the affiliation of the Greens to the so called Peace Movement. On the surface, this affiliation was straightforward enough. Why should not a party which opposes civilian uses of nuclear power also oppose military uses? This at least is the position adopted in the Peace Programme of the Green Party.[96] Petra Kelly tried for some time to obtain control of the amorphous amalgamation of Communists, survivors of Nazi persecution, churchmen, trade unionists, various party politicians, writers, academics and Greens.[97] This proved impossible. Nor is it clear whether a movement has in fact been created in the name and for the aims of peace. To date, the so called "Krefeld Appeal" against cruise missiles and the Bonn demonstration for peace are the two mass events which seem to indicate that a movement with social breadth and political potential had emerged. Do the two million or so signatories and the 300,000 demonstrators point at a new political and social factor in West Germany? Has the coordinated week of peace actions with sit-ins at military bases, with a human chain of protest and mass rallies simultaneously staged in a number of cities, including Bonn - did the events of October 1983 and the policy of 'hot autumn' consolidate the new and diverse movement?

The spark which kindled the movement i.e. rendered peace into a political slogan against specific forms of armament and military policy, was the so called <u>Doppelbeschluss</u>, the Nato decision to station cruise and other nuclear missiles in Europe if disarmament talks should fail.[98] Various Communist factions, organizations of Nazi survivors, peace societies, the long-standing and luckless Peace Union as well as a number of anti-nuclear groups, the Greens, anti-militarists came to regard this decision as a turning point between a world threatened by nuclear destruction and one enveloped in peace and blessed with international harmony. There has been considerable argument over the Communist involvement in shaping the so called Peace Movement and in wording the Krefeld Appeal.[99] It was first published in September 1980, about one year after the Nato decision, a delay which may cast some doubt on the spontaneous impact. The appeal itself made the decision into the symbol for the

arms race which it has since become. This was
helped by the wide circulation of the document
through political groups and parties, through the
churches and the so called alternative press. The
appeal itself created a camp for peace which had in
this fashion not existed before. The large number
of signatures generated a feeling that something
big and powerful had been unleashed. The most
notorious convert to the peace theme was the former
general of the Bundeswehr, Bastian, since March
1983 one of the Greens in the Bundestag.[100] While
masses seemed to flock in support of peace and a
groundswell of two or three million gave political
reality to the peace theme, the established parties
largely ignored the new developments.[101] West
Germans were not unduly alarmed about the dangers
of nuclear weapons, at least not in international
comparison.[102] The twin themes of peace and nuclear
dangers tended to concern the youngest age groups
most (Table 9.5). The peace issue is a factor in
West German society but not a dominant one. During
the 1983 election campaign, 37% of West Germans
rated peace as the most important political topic,
some 60-70% were more concerned about economic
stability and living standards. For the Greens,
however, the peace issue is central.

The nuclear theme corresponds to the campaigns
against the uses of nuclear energy for civilian
purposes. The followers of the Peace Movement tend
to come from the same segment of society as the
Green supporters.[103] The theme of peace has also
remained sufficiently global to accommodate a range
of ideologies and aims: some see the Americans as
aggressors, some maintain the Soviets strive for
peace, some insist that both sides need to disarm
completely or at least reduce their stocks of
nuclear missiles.[104] The range of peace ideologies
feeds into a large number of small groups, initiatives etc. In February 1982, about 300 different
groups, some well established like the BBU, the
Peace Union, most of them informal ad-hoc creations
met in Dortmund to consider future directions and
activities under the auspices of what became known
as the Peace Movement.[105] The conference decided
against mass rallies and favoured regional and local
activities. More importantly, it could not agree on
the important point who should be the convenor and
thus the national leadership group of the movement.
This issue remained unresolved, despite the umb-
rella-theme of peace. Communists, ecology- and

Table 9.5: Does the Stationing of US Cruise Missiles Increase the Security or the Danger?

	Age				
	18-19 %	20-29 %	30-49 %	40-64 %	65+ %
Danger increases	48	38	30	21	17
Security increases	34	31	42	52	46
No answer no influence	18	31	28	27	37

Source: Der Spiegel 10, 1982 p. 97.

other segments of the disjointed movements remained organizationally and politically apart. In 1983, Jo Leinen from the citizens' initiatives BBU and Lother Vack from the Deutsche Friedensgesellschaft, German Peace Association, a group which dates back to the fifties and has been accused of Communist leanings, emerged as joint coordinators of Peace Movement activities. Overall, about twenty-five groups were active under the peace heading.[106]

On one level, the Peace Movement aided the Greens. It created a political climate in which issues of nuclear power and nuclear weapons gained wide publicity and the Greens could emerge as the only party which addressed itself to these issues. The ascent of the Greens into the Bundestag has to be seen in this light. The mere existence of the Peace Movement challenged the Greens to accommodate the aims of peace, even spearhead the movement. The party papers reflect this trend: issues of peace displaced concerns with ecology, reports about regional or local activities of the party or its accomplishments in parliaments and assemblies. By displacing the organizational themes, the Peace Movement hampered the process of party political consolidation of the Greens. The political pitch of the peace theme makes it also more difficult for the Greens to develop a parliamentary role. The Peace Movement has to date been extra-parliamentary and its topics have no place on the local and regional levels where Greens could operate politically since 1978. In the Bundestag, defence issues can be debated; yet the cross-pressures of an opposition of principle and the need to appear as the parliamentary voice of a non-parliamentary force, push the Greens towards show-case politics and a facade of fighting for radical alternatives. The interpenetration of Peace Movement and Greens is likely to

weaken the parliamentary commitment of the Greens
and to strengthen the inclination towards an extra-
parliamentary position. The drain on the grass-
roots is of equal importance. The initiatives and
small groups in and around the Peace Movement offer
that type of immediate, small scale involvement
which corresponds to the political interests of the
young and their desire to have an immediate feed-
back of their participation. The role of the Basis
in the Greens, to become the backbone of party work
and parliamentary preparations had already, as we
had seen, been difficult to achieve. Apathy and a
predominantly critical approach to the party were
the main obstacles. With the affiliated outlet of
peace initiatives, potential young supporters of the
Greens have found a less onerous way of showing
their opposition. Between the cross-pressures of an
extra-parliamentary Peace Movement and the parliamentary potential of an SPD opposition, the Greens
seem precariously poised. The peace theme was the
all-important above-regional lever to attract voters
across the Federal Republic, a lever which had been
missing in 1980. At the same time, the peace-theme
is likely to weaken the Greens as a membership
organization based on membership participation.

FOOTNOTES

1. Ursula Kaack, "Nicht-etablierte Parteien und Bundestagswahl" in Heino Kaack and Reinhold Roth (eds.) Parteien Jahrbuch 1976. Dokumentation und Analyse der Entwicklung des Parteiensystems der Bundesrepublik Deutschland im Bundestagswahljahr 1976. Meisenheim (Hain) 1979, p. 507.
2. Suzanne Schüttemeyer, "Ergebnisse der Landtagswahlen in den Bundesländern 1946-1979" in Z Parl 2, 1980 p. 250-255.
3. Werner Kaltefleiter, "Wandlungen des deutschen Parteiensystems" in Aus Politik und Zeitgeschichte. B 14, 1975 pp. 3-10. Also Gordon Smith in: Döring/Smith, Party Government and Political Culture in West Germany, Macmillan 1982.
4. Jörg R. Mettke, "Auf beiden Flügeln in die Höhe. Grüne, Bunte und Alternative zwischen Parlament und Strasse" in Mettke (ed.) Die Grünen. Regierungspartner von morgen? Spiegelbuch, Rowohlt 1982 p. 9. Since the Hamburg elections of December 1982, there are 47 delegates altogether.
5. See the report on unemployment prospects in

Das Parlament, 15.10.1982 p. 2.
   6. e.g. FR 1.10.1982 "Sie lehnen Neuwahlen und Koalitionsverhandlungen ab"; FR 9.10.1982 "Hessens Grüne strecken ihre Fühler zu Landtagsparteien aus"; FR 27.10.1982 "Gratwanderung der Grünen zwischen Parlamentsarbeit und Basisdemokratie"; FR 1.11.1982 "Die Zwickmühle der alternativen Wahlbewegung"; Spiegel 36, 1982 p. 26 "SPD/GAL: Unter Druck; The Sunday Times, 3.10.1982 p. 17 "Germany: into the Unknown. Will Petra be the kingmaker"?
   7. See Joseph Huber, "Wo das Grün unklar wird" Vorwärts 16.9.1982 p. 24.
   8. Held on December 20th, 1982 SPD: 51.3% (64 seats), CDU: 38.9% (48 seats), Greens (GAL): 6.9% (8 seats), FDP: 2.5% (- seats).
   9. Die Grünen im Landtag. Landtagsinfo Nr. 2 Wiesbaden n.d. (March 1983); also FAZ 25.1.83; dpa 2.3.83.
   10. See FR 5.11.82, Petra Kelly in preparation of the meeting of Green delegates at Hagen on November 12-14, 1982. Also: FR 23.10.82 (Kretschmann) and FR 1.11.82 (Burgmann).
   11. Jörg Mettke/Hans Dieter Degler, "Wir müssen die Etablierten entblössen wo wir können. Spiegel Gespräch mit der Bundesvorsitzenden der Grünen, Petra Kelly" in Mettke, ibid. p. 32.
   12. Wolf Dieter Hasenclever, "Die Grünen im Landtag von Baden-Württemberg" in Mettke, ibid. p. 104.
   13. Martin Jänicke, "Parlamentarische Entwarnungseffekte. Zur Ortsbestimmung der Alternativbewegung" in Mettke, ibid. p. 75.
   14. Good summary and discussion in Hartmut Wasser, Parlamentarismuskritik vom Kaiserreich zur Bundesrepublik. Analyse und Dokumentation. Series Problemata. Stuttgart (Fromman/Holzboog),1974 pp. 114-123.
   15. Detlef Murphy, "Grüne und Bunte: Theorie und Praxis 'alternativer Parteien'" in Joachim Raschke (ed.) Bürger und Parteien. Ansichten und Analysen einer schwierigen Beziehung. Opladen (Westdeutscher Verlag) 1982 pp. 333 ff.
   16. Hilde Simek, Environmental Protection in the Federal Republic of Germany. Internationes Sonderdienst 3, 1979 Bonn 1979 p. 1. Also: Infas surveys quoted in Martin and Sylvia Greiffenhagen, Ein schwieriges Vaterland. München (List) 1979 p. 405.
   17. Die Einstellungen der jungen Generation zu

Arbeitswelt und Wirtschaftsordnung. Studie im Auftrag des Jugendwerkes der Deutschen Shell. Hamburg 1980 pp. 23-25. Also: Hans Joachim Fietkau, "Vom Umweltbewusstsein zur Umweltpartei" in Z Parl 2, 1979 p. 158.

18. Bernd Guggenberger, Bürgerinitiativen in der Parteiendemokratie. Von der Ökologiebewegung zur Umweltpartei. Stuttgart (Kohlhammer) 1980 pp. 26-27 points out the uncertainties about the exact size of citizens' initiatives and numbers of members organized.

19. Sonderheft Bürgerinitiativen, Z Parl 1, 1978.

20. Walter Andritzky, "Erstmals wissenschaftlich untersucht: Bürgerinitiativen" in Bild der Wissenschaft 2, 1978 p. 30.

21. Michael Pollak, "Ambiguity as the Source of Political Efficacy: the Contradictions of the German Anti-Nuclear Movement" in Charles R. Foster (ed.), Comparative Public Policy and Citizens' Participation: Energy, Education, Health and Urban Issues in the US and Germany, Pergamon Press 1980 pp. 73 ff.

22. For a summary of the main arguments see the interview with Roland Vogt, then chairman of the BBU in Langer Marsch. Zeitung für eine neue Linke No. 13 Dec. 1977 p. 10-11.

23. The question: "Where will an effective contribution to environmental problems most likely come from during the next five years?" was answered as follows:

1. citizens' initiatives 48%
2. industry 38%
3. the Federal Government 31%
4. consumers 25%
5. an ecology party 21%
6. the courts 14%
7. the political parties 8%
8. the trade unions 2%

Source: Wissenschaftszentrum Berlin (ed.) Die Einstellung der Berliner Bevölkerung zu Umweltfragen und zur Umweltpolitik, Berlin 1978 p. 9. Also in Guggenberger, ibid. p. 28.

24. Rolf Lange, "Die Wahl zur Hamburger Bürgerschaft am 4. Juni 1978: ein Ende des Dreiparteiensystems in Sicht?" in Z Parl 1, 1979 p. 5-16.

25. Der Spiegel 33, 1977 p. 54 reported that Gruhl, one of the founders of the Greens, was also chairman of the Bund für Natur-und Umweltschutz.

This has some 35,000 members; the Naturfreunde, the largest association of this kind has well over 100,000 members. Both have emphasized environmental issues, but neither associated itself in any way with the ecology party or with the anti-nuclear movement in the seventies and eighties.

26. See Eva Kolinsky, "The Green Party in West German Politics" in *Journal of Area Studies* no. 3, Spring 1981 pp. 14-19.

27. Horst-Dieter Rönsch, Die hessische Landtagswahl vom 8.10.1978 - Beginn eines neuen Trends? in *Z Parl* 1, 1979 pp. 34-49.

28. Kurt Oeser, "Politische Strömungen in der Ökologiebewegung" in *Aus Politik und Zeitgeschichte* B 43, 1979 pp. 13-19.

29. Richard Stöss, *Vom Nationalismus zum Umweltschutz. Die Deutsche Gemeinschaft/Aktion Unabhängiger Deutscher im Parteiensystem der Bundesrepublik.* Opladen (Westdeutscher Verlag) 1980.

30. *Deutsche Gemeinschaft* No. 5, 3.1.1976, p. 6.

31. e.g. Jens Fischer,"Vom Brauen zum Grünen", *Vorwärts* 17.4.1980; Herbert Riehl-Heyse,"August: Haussleiter - Viele Fahnen getragen", *SZ* 3.4.1980 Michael Schwelien,"Die Fünfte Partei des 75-jährigen. Eine Welle, die jeden umschmeisst", *Stuttgarter Zeitung* 15.4.1980; also: *Der Spiegel* 27, 1980 pp. 85-87.

32. Herbert Gruhl, *Ein Planet wird geplündert. Die Schreckensbilanz unserer Politik,* Frankfurt (Fischer) 1978.

33. See: Wolfram Bickerich, "Schön ist es hier und richtig grün" in Der Spiegel 34, 1978 pp. 29 ff.

34. See Wolfgang Jüttner/Klaus Wettig, "Die niedersächsische Landtagswahl am 4. Juni 1978: Wem schadeten die Grünen? wem die Nichtwähler?" in *Z Parl* 1, 1979 pp. 17-33.

35. *Der Spiegel* 27, 1980 pp. 83-84; *SZ* 1980 pp.1-2. A good summary of the various groups who were involved in the fouding processes from the left and right in: Rolf Meyer/Gunter Handlögten, "Die Grünen vor der Wahl" in *Aus Politik und Zeitgeschichte* B 36 1980 pp. 3-21.

36. e.g. reports in *Vorwärts* 17.1.1980 p. 8; *Generalanzeiger* 24.3.1980; *FR* 24.3.1980; *FR* 6.4.1980; *Tageszeitung* 24.3.1980.

37. *Die Grünen. Das Bundesprogramm*, Bonn 1980.

38. Ibid. p. 30-39.

39. *Tageszeitung* 18.4.1980; also *Stuttgarter*

Zeitung 22.7.1980.
  40. Die Grünen Baden-Württemberg. Das Programm. Stuttgart n.d. (1980).
  41. e.g. SZ 3/4.4.1980; FR 9.4.1980.
  42. e.g. Der Spiegel 13, 1980 pp. 19 ff.
  43. Sinnvoll arbeiten - solidarisch leben. Gegen Arbeitslosigkeit und Sozialabbau, Stuttgart (Sindelfingen) 1983 p. 3.
  44. Ernst Hoplitschek, "Partei, Avantgarde, Heimat -oder was? Die 'Alternative Liste für Demokratie und Umweltschutz' in West Berlin" in Mettke, ibid. p. 82.
  45. Lucas Beckmann in a letter to the author on September 4, 1980. Land organizations at that time had also some paid help, mostly part-time.
  46. Interview with Eberhard Walde, one of the two business managers at the Bonn office, 15.3.1983. Also interview with Gustine Johannsen, a member from Hamburg in the Bundeshauptausschuss, 14.3.1983.
  47. FAZ 15.11.1982. The Hamburg leader Reiner Tampert and Wilhelm Knade from Mühlheim/Ruhr replaced Kelly and Burgmann. Rudolf Bahro, the GDR expellee was voted into the wider executive.
  48. Felix Ungemach,"'Grüne' wollen nun Profis sein" in Vorwärts 11.2.1982 p. 8.
  49. Der Spiegel 20, 1982 p. 97.
  50. Petra Kelly, Rechenschaftsbericht, in Die Grünen 9.1.1982 p. 4, also Walde - interview.
  51. FR 16.8.1982.
  52. Wolf-Dieter Hasenclever, MdL, "Die Grünen und die Parlamente", in Z Parl 3, 1982 p. 417-422. Also: Hasenclever, "Die Grünen und die Bürger - ein neues Selbstverständnis als politische Partei?" in Raschke, ibid. pp. 309-322.
  53. Mettke ibid. p. 21.
  54. Werner Harenberg, "Sicherer Platz links von der SPD? Die Wähler der Grünen in der Demoskopie" in Mettke, ibid. p. 46.
  55. Tageszeitung 22.7.1981.
  56. Murphy ibid. p. 329.
  57. See Der Spiegel 14, 1982 p. 86.
  58. Der Spiegel 16, 1980 p. 57.
  59. Gabriel Almond and Sydney Verba, The Civic Culture, Boston Little Brown 1965, p. 64;
  60. David Conradt "Changing German Political Culture" in Almond and Verba, The Civic Culture Revisited, Little Brown and Co. 1980 pp. 212-272.
  61. Harenberg ibid. p. 46.
  62. Ibid. p. 38.
  63. Jugend Heute. ZDF programme and surveys,

April 1980, see chapter 6.
    64. Handelsblatt 31.8.1982.
    65. Jugend '81. Lebensentwürfe, Alltagskulturen, Zukunftsbilder, Leverkusen, (Leske) 1982 p. 674.
    66. K-J. Beyer (Bundesgeschäftsstelle der FDP) Die Bundestagswahl 1983.
    67. Harenberg ibid. p. 37.
    68. In detail: 42% of the 18-20 age group
                    38: of the 21-30 age group
                    28% of the 24-26 age group
                    15% of the 27-30 age group,
see Der Spiegel 13, 1980 p. 30.
    69. A survey conducted in March 1980 also showed that the priorities of Green supporters were different from those of average young people. Most of these were concerned about unemployment, inflation, job security. For the Green supporters, environmental protection was the most pressing issue; unemployment for example troubled only one in three. See Z Parl 3, 1982 p. 403.
    70. Z Parl 1, 1979 p. 30.
    71. Die Ergebnisse der Kommunalwahlen, FAZ 24.3.1981.
    72. Geoffrey Pridham, "Ecologists in Politics: The West German Case" in Parliamentary Affairs XXXI, no. 4, Autumn 1978; and Abteilung Planung und Grundsatz: Wissenschaftlicher Dienst der Friedrich Naumann Stiftung (ed.) Die Landtagswahl in Baden Württemberg am 16.3.1980, Bonn, 17.3.1980 pp. 9-10.
    73. Viola Roggenkamp "Die Elbe gehört uns allen" in Die Zeit 18.6.1982 p. 33. Also: Peter Rühmkorf, Die Hamburger Strafzettelwahl, ibid.
    74. Details in FAZ 8.3.1983; special issue Süddeutsche Zeitung 8.3.1983.
    75. See Heinz Höfl, "Okologie in Lederhosen. Grünsein in Bayern" in Mettke ibid. p. 59.
    76. "Sind die Erstwähler der Grünen ihre Stammwähler" in FAZ 14.10.1980.
    77. Ferdinand F. Müller, "Wahlverhalten der Jungwähler. Gefährlich für die Parlamentsparteien?" in Z Parl 2, 1980 pp. 256-263. Also F.F. Müller, "Die Jungwähler, die Grünen und die Bundestagswahl 1980" in Die Neue Gesellschaft no. 4, 1980.
    78. Klaus G. Troitzsch, "Grenzen der Stabilität des etablierten Parteiensystems" in Kaack/Roth (eds.) Handbuch der deutschen Parteien I, Opladen (Leske) 1980 p. 256.
    79. William P. Bürklin, "Die Grünen und die

'Neue Politik'. Abschied vom Dreiparteiensystem?" in PVS no. 4, Dec. 1981, p. 367.

80. Der Spiegel 12.11.1979: "Grüne über Grüne: keine Linken". According to survey data published here, 41% of CDU/CSU voters saw the Greens as left wing, 46% saw them as centre; of the SPD voters, about one third saw the Greens on the left, so did 28% of the FDP voters. 53% and 54% respectively believed the Greens were in the centre. The remainder gave no answer or were undecided.

81. So already in the March 1980 Emnid Survey, Der Spiegel 13, 1980. p. 31.

82. Baker/Dalton/Hildebrandt, Germany Transformed: Political Culture and New Politics, Harvard University Press 1981, p. 151.

83. Data collected in: Harenberg, ibid.

84. See Bürklin ibid. pp. 362-365.

85. Hermann Schmitt, Oskar Niedermeyer, Kurt Menke, "Etablierte und Grüne. Zur Verankerung der ökologischen Bewegung in den Parteiorganisationen von SPD, CDU und CSU" in Z Parl 4, 1981, p. 520.

86. Jugend '81, ibid. p. 680 ff.

87. Bürklin ibid. p. 367.

88. A first analysis of the parliamentary role of the Greens has been conducted and based on contributions in the Landtage: Rudolf Scharping and Joachim Hofmann-Göttig, "'Alternative' Politik in den Landesparlamenten? Ideologiekritische Inhaltsanalyse von 300 Redebeiträgen 'grüner' Parlamentarier" in Z Parl 3, 1982 pp. 391-415. Also Scharping/Hofmann-Göttig, "Nur Protest oder auch politische Ziele? Grüne Praxis in den Landesparlamenten" in Das Parlament 27, 10.6.1982 p. 6.

89. Scharping/Hofmann-Göttig, Z Parl ibid.

90. Das Parlament 25, 1983 p. 8 and pp. 12/13.

91. In detail: Stuttgarter Zeitung 23.9.1980 and Süddeutsche Zeitung 16.8.1980.

92. Documentation in Die Grünen im Landtag Nr. 6, Die Grünen Stuttgart n.d. (1982).

93. e.g. FR 25.6.1981, "Die Grünen und die CDU im offenen Schlagabtausch".

94. "Nach der Wahl", in Bremer Blatt no. 4, Nov. 1979 p. 1.

95. See Scharping/Hofmann-Göttig, ibid.

96. Friedensmanifest der Grünen. ed. Bundesvorstand der Grünen, verantwortlich i.s.d.P. Lucas Beckmann, Bonn n.d. (1981).

97. Wilfried von Bredow, "Zusammensetzung und Ziele der Friedensbewegung in der Bundesrepublik Deutschland" in Aus Politik und Zeitgeschichte

B 24, 1982 pp. 3-13.

98. Ernst-Otto Czempiel, "Nachrüstung und Systemwandel. Ein Beitrag zur Diskussion um den Doppelbeschluss der NATO" in Aus Politik und Zeitgeschichte B 5, 1982 p. 22-46.

99. The petition is neutrally worded. "Krefeld Appeal to the Federal Government: I join the Krefeld Appeal to the Federal Government to withdraw its agreement to stationing Pershing II missiles and Cruise missiles in Central Europe." The text is headed by two slogans: "Atomic death threatens us all" and "No nuclear missiles in Europe". It is also backed by a number of prominent signatories, among them Gert Bastian, the retired Bundeswehr general, Martin Niemöller, the church leader, and Petra Kelly, the leader of the Greens. Der Spiegel 36, 1981 pp 26/27 reported about a counter appeal launched by a group Bürger für Frieden und Freiheit who stated that they were ashamed of the Krefeld Appeal. Nothing has been heard about its success or failure.

100. Aufmarsch gegen die Rüstung: Die neue Friedensbewegung" in Der Spiegel 1981, pp. 24-29; Der Spiegel 15, 1982 pp. 98 ff, also Innere Sicherheit 60, 1981 p. 3; Der Arbeitgeber 34 no. 10, 1982 pp. 562-563.

101. Dieter Lattmann, "The SPD at the Crossroads. The Peace Movement in the Federal Republic of Germany". Paper delivered at the Goethe Institute, London 16.9.1981 (manuscript); see also the debate at the SPD party congress in Munich, 1982.

102. The question posed in the international survey was: "Peace movements have emerged in Western Europe. How do you personally feel about them?"

	West Germany %	France %	UK %	Netherlands %
In full agreement with the aims	23 }59	22 }50	23 }52	46 }79
In general agreement with the aims	36	28	29	33
Not really in agreement	22 }38	13 }34	15 }39	9 }17
Definitely not in agreement	16	21	24	8
Don't know	3	16	9	4

Source: Le Nouvelle Observateur, 21.11.1981 p. 33

103. Günther Schmid, "Zur Soziologie der Friedensbewegung und des Jugendprotestes" in Aus Politik und Zeitgeschichte B 24, 1982 pp. 15 ff.

104. Der Spiegel 49, 1981 pp. 94-106: "Jeder vierte Pazifist gegen die Friedensbewegung".
105. Vorwärts 11.2.1981, p. 8. A leaflet advertised the meeting: "Der Atomtod bedroht uns alle! Keine Atomraketen für Europa. Zweites Forum der Krefelder Initiative" 21.11.1981 in Dortmund, Responsible: Krefelder Initiative, Köln 1981. See also the series of articles by W.L. Webb in The Guardian 12.10.1981; 13.10.1981; 14.10.1981; 15.10.1981.
106. Innere Sicherheit 66, 1983 pp. 1-4.

SUGGESTED READING

Baker/Dalton/Hildebrand, Germany Transformed: Political Culture and New Politics Harvard Univ. Press 1981

Wilhelm P. Bürklin "Die Grünen und die 'Neue Politik'" in Politische Vierteljahresschrift 22 no. 4, Dec. 1981

Bernd Guggenberger, Bürgerinitiativen in der Parteiendemokratie. Von der Ökologiebewegung zur Umweltpartei, Stuttgart (Kohlhammer) 1980

Herbert Gruhl, Ein Planet wird geplündert. Die Schreckensbilanz unserer Politik, Frankfurt (Fischer) 1978

Eva Kolinsky, "The Green Party in West German Politics" in Journal of Area Studies 3, Spring 1981

Jörg R. Mettke (ed.), Die Grünen - Regierungspartner von morgen? Hamburg (Spiegelbuch-Rowohlt) 1982

Detlef Murphy et. al., Protest. Grüne, Bunte und Steuerrebellen. Ursachen und Perspektiven Reinbek (Rowohlt) 1979

Dorothy Nelkin/Michael Pollak, "Political Parties and the Nuclear Energy Debate in France and Germany" in Comparative Politics 12 no. 2, Jan. 1980

J.F. Pilat, Ecological Politics. The Rise of the Green Movement, Washington Papers Vol. 77 Sage 1980

Geoffrey Pridham, "Ecologists in Politics: the West German Case" in Parliamentary Affairs XXXI No. 4 Autumn 1978

Joachim Raschke (ed.), Bürger und Parteien. Ansichten und Analysen einer Beziehung Opladen (Westdeutscher Verlag) 1982

Richard Stöss, Vom Nationalismus zum Umweltschutz. Die Deutsche Gemeinschaft/Aktion Unabhängiger Deutscher im Parteiensystem der Bundesrepublik,

The Green Party

Opladen (Westdeutscher Verlag) 1980

CONCLUSION

PARTIES, OPPOSITION, AND SOCIETY - STRUCTURES AND TRENDS

With the change of government in 1982 from an SPD led coalition to one led by the CDU/CSU, the Federal Republic has entered its third major stage of political development. The first twenty years were dominated by the aims and aspirations of the CDU/CSU. Foundations of post-war politics were created such as the social market economy and the association with the Western powers and NATO. The next thirteen years saw the SPD in the senior government role, again generating important political realities such as Ostpolitik, an expansion of the welfare state, a consolidation of co-determination. The new CDU/CSU led government which was confirmed in office in the March 1983 elections, seems set to reduce the role of the state, to boost private enterprise, to reinforce the market economy structures against an increasingly modifying and mediating influence of the state, and to dismantle aspects of the welfare state in education and the general field of social services. The commitment to the Western alliance and Ostpolitik both are to be continued.
    Dividing post-war politics into these three phases may well be justified in terms of major policy orientations. Matters, however, are more complex. Since 1949, nearly all governments have been coalition governments, with the FDP the junior partner of both larger parties. Although the FDP changed its political focus from a right-liberal to a left-liberal and again to a right-liberal position, it also provided an element of continuity in the government changes, and more importantly, it forced governments to practice compromise and modify party political goals. The need to compromise was even more apparent when CDU/CSU and SPD entered

into the Grand Coalition in the sixties.
At that time, a great number of changes to the Basic Law passed the Bundestag, the governing coalition generated a political consensus across party lines. Consensus politics may be called the core to the West German practice of parliamentary government. The formula of coalition governments presupposes party consensus. When consensus can no longer be secured, as for instance between SPD and FDP from 1980 to 1982 on matters of economic policy and strategies to combat unemployment, a political reorientation is called for. In Hesse, where a minority government failed to secure a working consensus in the <u>Landtag</u>, new elections in September 1983 were meant to solve the problem: although they returned the SPD with more seats than before, a majority has not been found, nor was a working consensus or coalition agreement between SPD and one of the other parties, CDU, FDP and Greens established. Hesse may be seen as a test case for the principle of party consensus without formal coalition commitments.
In the West German political system, other mechanisms underpin the principle of consensus politics. The working practice of parliaments incorporates all parties into the decision making processes through proportional representation in parliamentary committees and aims at a consensus formula as basis for legislation. Even parliamentary opposition is thus not fully removed from the work of government, or able to detach itself from government priorities by highlighting alternative policies. Opposition in West Germany is integrated opposition, part of the governing process and at the same time the voice of political criticism, alternative policies and calls for change. Other institutions also serve to remove government policies from the party political grid. Economic policies for instance tend to be based on the recommendations of the Wise Men, a group of economists from a number of academic institutions, research institutes and with varying political affiliations, who present an analysis of the state of the economy, its likely development, and the consequences for wage levels, pricing levels, profits. With government economic policies guided by such an expertise, it is to a large extent consensus based.
The party system itself and the major political parties can also be discussed under the perspective of consensus politics. The strictures of the Basic

Law stipulate a consensus of parties with the democratic political framework in West Germany. The emergence of Volksparteien has only been possible because cleavages between party ideologies have decreased if not disappeared. Indeed, the self-awareness of those parties which have been represented in the Bundestag since 1949 as semi-official organs of the state gives them sufficient common ground to mellow controversial political goals. The issue of party finance can highlight both the united front of the so called established parties in defence of their vital role in politics, and the differences which remain in the practical question of party alliances with socio-economic interest sectors. The first decade of post-war politics was dominated by alliances between parties and organized interests to secure party funding, until the Constitutional Court raised the objection that chances in politics may be unequal and favour those who become spokesmen of the wealthiest segments of society. The following phase of state funding for those parties who were represented in parliaments showed the consensus of all parties about their importance as organs of the state and their joint determination to restrain other parties from entering the political arena on competitive terms. Party funding has since been modified to allow for some public accountability and a combined system of private and public funding for all but the most marginal political parties. Yet, the common stance of the established three has survived the changes and surfaced again in the recent discussion on modifications to the law on party finance. Despite this unison, we saw that significant differences can be detected in the position of parties in society: the Christian Democratic parties and the Free Democrats are clearly aligned to industrial and business interests which provide a sizeable share of their party budgets in particular in election years. The SPD has been closer to the trade union sector and remained closer to that sector despite the transition towards a Volkspartei. Financially, however, the party is less well provided for than its major competitors, and the scale of political self-projection adopted by West German parties together with the extravagances of election campaigning have brought the SPD into considerable debts without obvious sources of additional income, except the long standing search for better access to public funds or donations.

Party funding suggests that the principle of

Volkspartei, of the German format of the catch-all party with an overall consensus between parties, has become reality only to some extent. Under the surface of similar political programmes, of a broad appeal to all social groups, differences between parties have remained. Our analysis of the social support mobilized by political parties in West Germany showed two important and conflicting developments. Taking electorates, West German political parties have moved a little closer together than at the start of the post-war period. They have, however, remained different with the SPD mobilizing a more working-class electorate, the CDU/CSU a middle to upper range, and the FDP a slim middle class wedge. The social differentiation of the electorates corresponds to the public awareness about parties. The SPD is still associated with the lower status groups, CDU/CSU and FDP with the higher status groups. The seventies saw some important changes which have modified the electoral allegiances. Since the fifties, denomination had declined as a factor influencing political preferences. This process culminated in 1972 when the SPD won more catholic voters than ever before. Since then, catholicism has reemerged as a determining factor in political choices, and CDU/CSU have been able to win voters from all status groups with denomination guiding politics. While the middle class image of the Christian Democratic parties and the FDP prevailed, denomination reemerged in their favour. In other words, since the mid-seventies, these parties were able to mobilize voters on both grounds, middle class aspirations or self-awareness and also denomination as a means of political and social identification. This process was temporarily disrupted by the Anti-Strauss elections in 1980, but re-emerged as the determining trend of politics in the 1983 elections. CDU gains occurred in catholic regions and among those working class or white collar voters whose income and social status had come to border a middle class level and who feared in the face of recession and unemployment social demotion. Class and social divisions, although blurred by comparison with Weimar, still shape the electoral map of West Germany. The changes in the occupational structure of West Germany overall, the decline of the traditional working class jobs, the expansion of the new middle class in the service industries and in administration, have brought the electorates of all parties closer together, they compete to a large extent for the same electoral support. Yet, social identifications of parties have survived these changes, and the electorates of the major parties still show traces of the old working class-middle class divisions.

Within the parties, these traces have all but vanished. None of the political parties has a membership whose social composition bears similarity to the social fabric or society as a whole. In all parties, the white collar sector and the civil service have emerged as the core of party memberships; women and workers are poorly represented, even in the SPD. On the functionary and leadership levels, the dissimilarities between parties and society increased, with the better educated and the civil servants dominating political representation in and through the parties. The Verbeamtung of parliaments, the large proportion of civil servants who have been elected as members of parliament reflect the social imbalances in the political parties. The scanty representation of women in West German parliaments also commences within the parties. Party organization and party membership determine the recruitment of political elites, the representatives in assemblies and parliaments and to a large extent the selection of front bench spokesmen for governments and for oppositions. Parties are at the heart of the process which gives society a voice in politics. Bearing in mind the magnitude of this task, West German parties are small. Altogether, they organize some two million people, about 4% of the population. During the seventies, party membership nearly doubled. The numerical expansion did not significantly alter or widen the social spectrum of party memberships. Rather, it has contracted still further towards the civil service sector. In terms of membership and in their social composition, West German political parties cannot be called Volksparteien.

The membership developments during the seventies affected the three established parties in different ways. CDU and CSU experienced a dramatic numerical membership expansion; their social position in society, their roots in the middle strata remained unaltered. Adjustments in the party concerned administrative cohesion and a strengthening of central control. The FDP suffered throughout the decade from the after-effects of switching coalition partners. It also proved ill equipped to keep many of the new members it could attract. The party was beset by instability and disruptive membership fluctuations, not just by the trauma of failing at the 5% hurdle. An FDP sponsored study recommended the party should intensify grass root work, it should build up well structured medium sized branches and place more emphasis on the local and communal levels of politics. None of these pieces of advice have yet been heeded. The party is still geared to winning votes and snatching a place in government. The tedious dimensions of grass root politics and organization are overshadowed if not obliterated by the hankering for power. The 1982 coalition scoop will not settle the disarray of the FDP. For the SPD, the challenge of the eighties lies in a similar direction for quite different reasons. Compared with the CDU, the SPD experienced moderate membership gains. Most of these new members came from the educated middle class and from the professions; they significantly altered the social composition of the SPD. One might say, internally the SPD caught up with the transformation of social and political aims which was finalized in Godesberg. The established procedures of party organization and of membership participation were ill-suited to the motivation and expectations of the newcomers. The new ways of these members and their drive to become party functionaries on the other hand alienated older members with different ideas about the place and reality of the SPD in German society. There seems to be a danger in the SPD of apathy and indifference among many members. Running the party has become a matter for the determined few. Within the SPD this means that the traditional working class element no longer joins and that those who are still in the party have less and less say in its organization and in political representation. The inability of West German political parties to attract members among the ordinary people, the lower educated, the social rank-and-file makes the parties socially lopsided. It also means that these groups do not receive an adequate voice in political parties and through them in political affairs.

Young people have come to be regarded as a problem group in West German politics. Most are loyal to system and parties insofar as electoral support is concerned. Yet, signs are mounting that young people have begun to turn away. Memberhsip recruitment into established parties, which used to be lively in the early seventies, has become a mere trickle. Votes of the young have been increasingly withheld or cast for the party which did not appear to be a party in the traditional sense, the Greens. The SPD had been most successful in attracting the young; it is bound to be the party to suffer most from the reversal of political mood. It will be the party most directly challenged to counteract an exodus of the young from established party politics.

Our discussion on youth and politics (chapter 6) rendered a number of observations which can illuminate the stalemate between young people and mainstream parties. Young people tended to be sceptical about the even-handed approach of parties; they suspected politicans may just feather their own nests. There was despondency about joining a party: the themes and the organization which seemed to characterize parties did not correspond to political hopes and expectations. With all this scepticism, two apparently conflicting aspects also emerged: young people were overall satisfied with the political system and its institutions; and young people had a keen interest in politics and wanted to participate in a way that they could see the results of their efforts and commitments. Here, of course, rests a challenge for the political parties to rethink their organizational structures and their channels for participation sufficiently to allow that diffuse interest to flow into the parties and contribute within them on a local and community level. In SPD and CDU, a handful of efforts have been made to generate a new relationship between community, including the young people, and party. But while the priorities of party political activity in society remain with pulling in votes, other levels of party work receive little attention and the distance between West Germany's young and her political parties may well remain. The distance has been greatest to young people with higher education who tend to be most outspoken and uncompromising in their critical condemnation of parties as a feasible framework for political activity and for participation in democracy.

During the seventies, several strands of opposition from the left, from the right and from an ecology and anti-nuclear position tried to make headway in society by advocating new policies, new values, new priorities, in particular new inroads for personal involvement and meaningful participation. On the left, the Student Movement had experimented with new forms of protest which seemed to hold the promise that everybody could influence events and perpetrate changes in society, politics, university life. A combination of a utopian belief in an imminent revolution and social isolation, radicalized the movement in two diverse directions: into left-wing terrorism which tried to coerce society into that elusive revolutionary change and into various Communist orthodoxies which each tried to prescribe a party line and scope for individual commitment from above. Both provided political homesteads largely for left-wing academics and some old-time Communists. On the right, the NPD of the sixties became a political platform for former Nazis, for DRP functionaries, similar in fact to the petrified Communist Party. Political stagnation and electoral disintegration unleashed a radicalization on the right with terrorist tendencies. Contrary to the left, however, the core of Neonazi groups consists of working class and lower middle class people, most of them under thirty. Mass following for Neonazism is unlikely now and in the near future. Yet, Neonazism seems to be the only political grouping to win active support among the less privileged in society: this reflects the inability of the established parties to relate to these strata; it also reflects the fact that the left mobilizes mainly in academic circles today; the right wing inclination of the lower educated provides a ready reservoir for the messages from the right. Since they are so poorly integrated into the mainstream parties, a broadening of the slim Neonazi sector of today cannot be ruled out.

  The Green Party has been the most volatile in recent years. It managed to win a number of parliamentary seats and raise its voice as a political opposition. It draws its support, voters and members, from the same slim segment of young academics, teachers, professionals which has become so important in West German parties and opposition. The Green Party is inclined towards an opposition of principle. It hovers between parliamentary and anti-parliamentary attitudes; it toys with advocating violence to shake the system into change and maybe get rid of nuclear power; it castigates state schools, large enterprises, any centralization. It has amused and alarmed other parties by questioning hierarchies, by insisting on leadership rotation, by asking its members to be constantly involved in the policy making of the party and in day-to-day political work. On paper, open government, open participation, free involvement seem to be on offer, a format which could prove attractive to those young people who wish to participate but who object to the organizational inflexibility of the large parties. The young constitute the strongest sector of support for the Green Party. The process of professionalization however seems well under way. After entering the Bundestag, policy pronouncements and party initiatives came increasingly from the Fraktion, the small parliamentary group, not the party organization. The concept of involving members, of Basisdemokratie all but failed in view of members' passivity. Many supporters drifted into other social movements, in particular into the Peace Movement. In order to hold on to their sceptical and volatile following, the Greens have to prove themselves as the spearhead of extra-parliamentary action, not as an effective and innovative parliamentary opposition.

The political aims and ideologies of the left, of the right and to a considerable extent of the Greens are held together by a common core of principle criticism of political democracy and the fabric of society in Germany. All these opposition movements fight the system in differently coloured packages. This anti-system slant of opposition seems ill-suited to answer the specific discontent we detected with parties and politics: discontent does on the whole not challenge the system. Most people, young and old, declare themselves well satisfied. Discontent relates to a lower level of opposition, the possibilities to contribute, to get involved, to pursue one's aims and intentions. This discontent has not been met by the opposition movements. Instead they all compete for the few who are more deeply dissatisfied: this also accounts for the overlap between left-wing opposition and high academic and educational attainment. The anti-system slant on the right appeals to the opposite social spectrum.

If West German opposition movements of the seventies and eighties are still stuck in the gesture of fundamental rejection so familiar from German history, and if they have been unable to relate to the concrete levels of discontent which has emerged during the seventies, the political parties likewise showed their limitations. Opposition from their vantage point was hostility against the status quo of democracy - they could not accept it as stimulating conflict in society which may enhance and develop democracy. The parties also remained inflexible in the face of the challenge, expecting consensus with their place in politics rather than creating it. Internally, reforms of organizational practices and procedures are not seriously pursued although there are some voices who call for a revitalization of local branches and their links into the communities. Since mainstream politics in the parties are happening, as ever, at a higher level, the drives for party renewal from below do not carry much promise to succeed. The tendency of the parties to dismiss critics of the status quo and above all to dismiss any opposition against their established priorities and practices as ill-informed and destructive does not generate a climate of political re-orientation.

There is a chance that new politics, new issues, may unleash a new political climate and again win the political commitment of young people and educated critics. As <u>Ostpolitik</u> and the promise of more democracy at the threshold of the seventies have shown, the political mood can unleash a considerable mobilizing force. West Germany's critical youths who are not reached by the opposition of principle, since most do not in principle oppose "the system", could well be integrated into political parties, become a constituent element of their place in society. This process may have commenced with the SPD in opposition and its new-found political flexibility. With the people across the educational divide, matters seem much more difficult. For them, only voting remains, perhaps underpinned by a right-wing drift in political attitudes. The political parties do not seem to have and do not appear to develop a place for them, win them as members and close the educational rift which runs through parties, opposition and society in West Germany today. The task of being a voice for the whole of society and a political home for all groups and segments has still to be attempted by all parties - those who have been called "established" and those who see themselves as opposition to remedy the course of society and politics in West Germany.

INDEX

Adenauer, Konrad, 22, 122, 123, 126, 179, 256
Aktion Widerstand 269
Aktionsfront Nationaler Sozialisten 279
Aktionsgemeinschaft Unabhängiger Deutscher 302
'Alternative' Culture 180-181, 300
Alternative Liste (see also Green Party) 296, 306, 308, 310
Antisemitism (see also Racism) 254, 256-257, 277

Baader, Andreas 237, 238
Basic Law 2, 4, 22, 28, 33, 215, 254, 272, 295, 340-341
Bastion, Gert 327
Baum, Gerhart 116, 170
Bavarian People's Party (BVP) 18
Berg, Fritz 22
Berufsverbot see Radikalenerlass
Block der Heimatvertriebenen und Entrechteten (BHE) 260
Böll, Heinrich 177, 236, 239
Börner, Holger 73, 74, 85
Brandt, Willy 93-94, 170, 179,184,238,240,267,276

Buback, Friedrich 237
Bundestag (see also under parties)
- and interest groups 28, 29, 33, 37, 38-39, 40-44
attitudes towards - 3
occupational structure of - 45-47
organization of - 6-9
Bundesrat 8-9, 324
Bundesverband Bürgerinitiativen Umweltschutz (BBU) 299, 327
Bundeswehr 208

Centre Party (Zentrum) 18, 21
Christian Democratic Union (CDU) 5, 6, 18, 58-69, 75, 122-164, 216, 267
- associations 36, 128-129, 132-133
- electorate 5-6, 10, 18, 22, 60-67, 292, 294
- finance 24-26, 33, 341-342
- membership 76, 132-156
- membership participation 142-146,156
- in coalition 82, 123, 207, 218, 293, 339

349

INDEX

- in opposition 132ff, 242
- office holders 149-154
- parliamentary party 145, 147, 150-151, 155
- party organization 122-129, 147-148, 155-158
- programmes 126-127
- social composition 134-140, 149-153
- youth section (JU) 132, 133, 152, 153, 156-157

Christian Democrats (CDU/CSU) <u>122-164</u>
- and environmentalism 320-322
- and terrorism 242-243
- and trade unions 42-43
- interest affiliation 22-38
- party finance 24-26, 33
- social support 10, 22, 76

Christian Social Union (CSU) 18, 54-55, <u>129-132</u>
- election results 131
- electorate 61, 65-66, 67-68
- membership 130
- party organization 129-132

Citizens Initiatives (<u>see also</u> Bundesverband Bürgerinitiativen Unweltschutz) 115, 234, 298, 299, 318, 331
Cohn-Bendit, Daniel 302
Communism in West Germany 205-209
Communist Groups 232-233, 301
Communist Party (KPD; <u>see also</u> German Communist Party) 4, 17, 206-207, 232
Consensus in Politics 339-342
Concentration Camps 17, 20, 271, 277

Deckert, Günther 269-270
Denazification 2, 18
Deutsche Friedensunion (DFU) 206-207, 327
Deutsche Nationalzeitung 277
Deutsche Partei (DP) 259, 260
Deutsche Reichspartei (DRP) 257, 259-261
Dissent (<u>see also</u> Opposition) 183, 188-195
Dregger, Alfred 36

350

INDEX

Drenkmann, Gunther 237
Dutschke, Rudi 231, 302

Easter Marches 208, 224
Economic Council 19
Economy and Politics 3,
    168, 172-173, 182,
    205, 266-267, 292,
    298, 339, 340
Education and Politics
    45-46, 166, 168,
    173-178, 183-184,
    189-195, 196, 197,
    298, 316, 339
Educational Reforms
    227 ff.
Electorate 4, 5, 10,
    55-69, 166, 222-223,
    258, 262, 265, 292,
    293-294, 339-345
    by denomination 60-63
    by social class 57-59,
        59-60, 64-65, 167,
        342-343
    women 60, 65-66
    youth 55, 56, 66-69,
        171, 172 (see also
        parties)
Electoral System 4-5, 25,
    40
Electoral Turnout 3-4,
    54, 55
Emergency Legislation 36,
    207, 209
Enabling Act 1
Environmental Protection

(see also Citizens'
    Initiatives) 297-298,
    299, 300, 320, 321
Ensslin, Gudrun 237,
    238
Erhard, Ludwig 122-123
Ertl, Josef 102

Federal Constitutional
    Court 4, 22, 23, 28,
    33, 37, 38, 46, 106,
    227, 254, 341
Federal Elections (see
    electorate; also
    parties) 5, 294, 295
Federal President 37
Federation of German
    Industry 22, 35-36
Free Democratic Party
    (FDP) 5, 18, 75,
    101-121, 134, 292
    - electorate 10,
        59-60, 61-63, 119,
        294, 313-314
    - finance 30-32,
        341-342
    - in coalition 106,
        113, 116, 117, 184,
        293, 339, 340
    - interest affiliat-
        ion 23, 42-44
    - membership 10-11,
        55, 101-111,
        112-113
    - office holders 112,
        116-117

351

INDEX

- organization 101-105, 115
- programmes 113

Gastarbeiter 254, 270, 277, 279-280
Geissler, Heiner 157-158
Genscher, Hans-Dietrich 116
German Communist Party (DKP; see also Communist Party) 11-12, 209-226, 268
 - and protest movements 224-226
 - finance 30, 220
 - organization 212-213, 220-222
 - origins 209-211
 - social composition 224-226
German Democratic Republic (GDR) 20, 30, 219-220
German Party see Deutsche Partei
German Peace Union see Deutsche Friedensunion
German Reichsparty see Deutsche Reichspartei
Gesamtdeutsche Partei 260
Gollwitzer, Helmut 236,237
Grand Coalition (see also CDU and SPD) 36, 123, 207, 208, 340
Green Party (Die Grünen) 4, 11-12, 29, 94, 233, 292-338, 346-348
 - and environmentalism 301, 302-303, 318
 - and 'New Politics' 319-322
 - and parliament 296, 297, 322-325, 328
 - and peace 326-329
 - and the left 301-302, 319, 335
 - and the right 302, 319
 - electorate 68-69, 313-314, 319-322
 - election results 5, 293, 294, 317-318, 319
 - origins 297-305
 - party organization 306-312
 - programmes 304-305
 - supporters (Basis) 296, 297, 310-311, 316, 325

Hallstein Doctrine 184
Hauff, Volker 90, 170
Haussleiter, August 302
Heinemann, Gustav 210
Hitler Wave 272-275

Imperial Germany 1, 13, 38, 167, 195, 254

352

INDEX

Jungdemokraten see Free
  Democratic Party
Junge Nationaldemokraten
  (JN) see National
  Democratic Party
Junge Pioniere (see also
  German Communist
  Party) 222
Junge Sozialdemokraten
  (JUSO) see Young
  Socialists
Junge Union (JU; see also
  Christian Democratic
  Union) 132, 133, 152,
  153, 156-157

Kajoten 180
Kelly, Petra 307, 326
Kenneqy, John F. 179
Kiep, Walther Leisler
  35, 36, 128
Kiesinger, Kurt Georg 123
Komm Youth Centre 171,
  172
Kommune I (see also
  Student Movement) 236
Krefeld Appeal 309, 326,
  237, 336
Kohl, Helmut 157
Koschnik, Hans 73, 74, 85
Kühnen, Michael 277

Lambsdorff, Count Otto von
  116
Leber, Georg 45
Loderer, Eugen 216

Lorenz, Peter 237

Mahler, Horst 238
Mann, Thomas 186
Marcuse, Herbert 235
Marxism (see also
  Communism; Student
  Movement) 205, 207
Marxist Student Associa-
  tion Spartakus 221,
  224
Mediating Panel 9
Meinhof, Ulrike 237, 238
Mies, Herbert 214
Mobilized Society 19-20
Movement Second of June
  (see also Terrorism)
  238
Mussgnug, Martin 268

National Democratic
  Party (NPD) 11, 28-32
  257-271
  - electorate 261-262,
    264-266, 268, 292
  - finance 28-32, 262
  - membership 262-263,
    265-267, 269
  - origins 259-261
  - party organization
    261, 268
  - radicalization
    268-271 (see also
    Neonazism)
  - youth sector (JN)
    269-271

353

INDEX

Nationalism (see also
  Neonazism) 253-254,
  255
Nationalsocialism 13,
  17-18, 19-20, 169,195
  - impact today 253,
    254, 255, 271, 275,
    281
Nato (and twin track
  decision) 92, 94, 208,
  319, 320, 326, 339
Nau, Alfred 35
Neonazism 11, 253-255,
  271-283, 346
  - ideology 275-277
  - membership 262
  - offenders 256-257,
    279, 282-283
  - use of violence
    277-280, 282
Nuclear Plants 171, 172,
  233, 299, 318

Opposition 4, 5-10,
  11-12, 28, 166-167,
  168, 171, 188-194,
  346-348
  and the Greens
    296-325, 346-348
  and the left 204-242,
    346-347
  and the right 253-283,
    346-347
Ökologisch Demokratische
  Partei (ÖDP) 303
Ostpolitik 23, 184, 185,

253, 267, 268-269,
278, 339, 348

Parliament (see
  Bundestag)
Parliamentary Council
  19, 22
Party Finance 22-38,
  340, 342
  - and party legisla-
    tion 4, 28-32, 33
  - from 1949-1958,
    23-26
  - from 1958-1966,
    26-28
  - from 1967-1983,
    33-38
  types of - 25, 27-28,
    30-35, 36, 37
Party memberships (see
  also parties) 20, 21,
  54-55, 167, 344-346
Party System 3, 4, 6,
  180-182, 292-293,
  341-344
Peace Movement 92, 93,
  191, 224, 233, 320,
  326-329, 336
People's Party see
  Volkspartei
Political Culture 3, 8,
  55-56, 168-169,
  180-182, 183-184,
  268, 313, 319-322,
  327-328, 336
Ponto, Jürgen 327

INDEX

Postmaterialism (see also Green Party; Political Culture) 188-189, 203, 320
Presidential Decree 1

Racism (see also Antisemitism, Neonazism) 253-254, 275, 279-280
Radikalenerlass (Radicals Decree) 240, 242, 243
Raspe, Jan Carl 237
Red Army 19
Red Army Faction 236, 237, 238, 239 (see also Terrorism)
Refugees 19-20
Reimann, Max 211
Right Extremism (see also Nationaldemocratic Party, Neonazism) 18, 254, 255, 258, 268
Ring Christlich Demokratischer Studenten (RCDS) 194
Roeder, Ernst 278
Roth Wolfgang 90

Schleyer, Hanns Martin 237
Schmid, Carlo 256
Schmidt, Helmut 80, 90, 92, 93, 95, 179, 271, 319
Schumacher, Kurt 17
Semler, Wolfgang 303
Social Democratic Party (SPD) 5, 6, 7, 9, 17-18, 58-69, 73-100, 206, 216, 267, 329-339
- and trade unions 36, 41-42, 216-217
- associations 36, 57, 88-91
- electorate 5-6, 10, 58-69, 73-75, 313-315
- finance 23-38
- in coalition 9, 123-124, 184, 239, 242, 293, 339, 340
- in opposition 7, 92-95, 322, 329, 339
- membership 10, 20-22, 55, 75-80, 83-87
- membership participation 74, 83-84, 98, 144
- organization 74, 80-83, 85-87
- office holders 77-78, 80, 81-83, 84-87
- parliamentary party 41-42, 81
- programmes 6, 95, 206-207
- youth section (JUSO) 57, 88-91, 99 see also Young Socialists
Social Democratic Uni-

355

INDEX

versity Association (SHB) 90, 224, 228
Socialist German Student Association (SDS) 90, 207, 208, 228, 230, 233
Socialist Office 209, 210-211
Socialist Reichsparty (SRP) 4, 257-258
Socialist Unity Party (SED) 17, 211, 227
Sonstige Politische Vereinigung (see also Green Party) 301
Sozialistische Deutsche Arbeiterjugend (SDAJ see also German Communist Party) 221-222, 224, 225
Spontis 180, 225
Springer Press 231
Squatters (Hausbesetzer) 171, 195, 225-226
Stadtindianer 180
Startbahn West 171, 172, 317
Strauss, Franz Josef 57, 132, 342
Student Movement 169, 195-196, 227, <u>228-232</u>, 236-239, 345
Surveillance 241-242

Terrorism 236-238, 239-243, 276, 277-278, 346
Thielen, Fritz 260
Trade Union Federation (DGB) 10, 29, 39, 41-44, 95, 207, 209, 216-219, 232
Travolta, John 179
Tunix 180-181

Universities (see also Education) 227, 228, 229
Unemployment 34, 173, 175, 181, 196, 293, 298

Verheugen, Günter 105
Vermittlungsausschuss see Mediating Panel
Violence, Use of 172, 195, 226, 233-239, 278-283, 323
Vogel, Hans-Jochen 87, 91
Volkspartei (see also parties) 5-6, 7, 9-10, 18, 20, 22, 39, 44, 57, 74, 134, 264, 340-343
Voters' Initiatives 56

Wehner, Herbert 277
Weimar Republic 1, 2, 3, 4, 13, 18, 24, 75, 169, 195, 206, 207, 255, 295, 342
Western Allies 2, 18, 257, 276